Migrant Letters

The migrant letter, whether written by family members, lovers, friends, or others, is a document that continues to attract the attention of scholars and general readers alike. What is it about migrant letters that fascinates us? Is it nostalgia for a distant, yet desired past? Is it the consequence of the eclipse of letter writing in an age of digital communication technologies? Or is it about the parallels between transnational experiences in previous mass migrations and in the current globalized world, and the centrality of interpersonal relations, mobility, and communication, then and now?

Influenced by methodologies from diverse disciplines, the study of migrant letters has developed in myriad directions. Scholars have examined migrant letters through such lenses as identity and self-making, family relations, gender, and emotions. This book contributes to this discussion by exploring the connections between the practice of letter writing and the emotional, economic, familial, and gendered experiences of men and women separated by migration. It combines theoretical and empirical discussions which illuminate a variety of historical experiences of migrants who built transnational lives as they moved across Europe, Africa, Latin America, and the United States.

The chapters in this book were originally published as a special issue of *The History of the Family*.

Marcelo J. Borges is Professor of History at Dickinson College, PA, USA, where he teaches Latin American history and migration history. He has published on migration, labor, and migrant letters. He is the author of *Chains of Gold: Portuguese Migration to Argentina in Transatlantic Perspective*.

Sonia Cancian is Assistant Professor of History at the College of Humanities and Social Sciences at Zayed University, Dubai, UAE. She has published on migration, gender, family, emotions, and migrant letters. She is the author of *Families, Lovers, and their Letters: Italian Postwar Migration to Canada*.

Migrant Letters

Emotional Language, Mobile Identities, and
Writing Practices in Historical Perspective

Edited by
Marcelo J. Borges and Sonia Cancian

Routledge
Taylor & Francis Group

LONDON AND NEW YORK

First published 2018 by Routledge

2 Park Square, Milton Park, Abingdon, Oxfordshire OX14 4RN
52 Vanderbilt Avenue, New York, NY 10017

Routledge is an imprint of the Taylor & Francis Group, an informa business

First issued in paperback 2020

Introduction, Chapters 1–5, 7–8 © 2018 Taylor & Francis
Chapter 6 © 2018 Liz Stanley. Originally published as Open Access.

British Library Cataloguing in Publication Data
A catalogue record for this book is available from the British Library

ISBN13: 978-1-138-56019-2 (hbk)
ISBN13: 978-0-367-59311-7 (pbk)

Typeset in Myriad Pro
by diacriTech, Chennai

Publisher's Note
The publisher accepts responsibility for any inconsistencies that may have
arisen during the conversion of this book from journal articles to book chapters,
namely the possible inclusion of journal terminology.

Disclaimer
Every effort has been made to contact copyright holders for their permission to
reprint material in this book. The publishers would be grateful to hear from any
copyright holder who is not here acknowledged and will undertake to rectify
any errors or omissions in future editions of this book.

Contents

CONTENTS

Citation Information

The chapters in this book were originally published in *The History of the Family*, volume 21, issue 3 (August 2016). When citing this material, please use the original page numbering for each article, as follows:

Introduction
Reconsidering the migrant letter: from the experience of migrants to the language of migrants
Marcelo J. Borges and Sonia Cancian
The History of the Family, volume 21, issue 3 (August 2016) pp. 281–290

Chapter 1
Moving backward and moving on: nostalgia, significant others, and social reintegration in nineteenth-century British immigrant personal correspondence
David A. Gerber
The History of the Family, volume 21, issue 3 (August 2016) pp. 291–314

Chapter 2
'I never could forget my darling mother': the language of recollection in a corpus of female Irish emigrant correspondence
Emma Moreton
The History of the Family, volume 21, issue 3 (August 2016) pp. 315–336

Chapter 3
Adjusting and fulfilling masculine roles: the epistolary persona in Dutch transatlantic letters
Babs Boter and Suzanne M. Sinke
The History of the Family, volume 21, issue 3 (August 2016) pp. 337–349

Chapter 4
'If it is not too expensive, then you can send me sugar': money matters among migrants and their families
Sonia Cancian and Simone A. Wegge
The History of the Family, volume 21, issue 3 (August 2016) pp. 350–367

For any permission-related enquiries please visit:
http://www.tandfonline.com/page/help/permissions

Notes on Contributors

Marcelo J. Borges is Professor of History at Dickinson College, PA, USA, where he teaches Latin American history and migration history. He has published on migration, labor, and migrant letters. He is the author of *Chains of Gold: Portuguese Migration to Argentina in Transatlantic Perspective*.

Babs Boter is a Lecturer in Literature and Society at the Vrije Universiteit Amsterdam, the Netherlands. Her research looks at the construction of national and cultural identities in twentieth-century travellers' accounts of North America and other continents.

Sonia Cancian is Assistant Professor of History at the College of Humanities and Social Sciences at Zayed University, Dubai, UAE. She has published on migration, gender, family, emotions, and migrant letters. She is the author of *Families, Lovers, and their Letters: Italian Postwar Migration to Canada*.

David A. Gerber is Professor Emeritus in the Department of History at the University of Buffalo, NY, USA. He is the author of *American Immigration: A Very Short History* (2011), and the editor of *Ethnic Historians and the Mainstream: Shaping America's Immigration Story* (with Alan Kraut, 2013).

Romeo Guzmán is Assistant Professor in the Department of History at Fresno State University, CA, USA. His work focuses on twentieth-century Mexico, Mexican migration, Chicano/a studies, and oral history.

Laura Martínez Martín is a postdoctoral researcher in the Centre of Linguistics at the University of Lisbon, Portugal. Her research investigates digital archiving of ordinary peoples' writing in Portugal and Spain.

Emma Moreton is a Senior Lecturer in Corpus Linguistics and Stylistics in the School of Humanities at Coventry University, UK. Her research focuses on how historical documents such as letters, diaries, and first-person narratives can help us to understand the lives and experiences of ordinary people.

Suzanne M. Sinke is Associate Chair of Graduate Studies in the Department of History at Florida State University, FL, USA. A specialist in migration and gender studies in the United States, she is the author of *Dutch Immigrant Women in the United States, 1880–1920* (2002).

NOTES ON CONTRIBUTORS

Liz Stanley is Professor of Sociology at the University of Edinburgh, UK. She is the author of *The Racialising Process: Whites Writing Whiteness in Letters, South Africa 1770s–1970s* (2017), and *The Archive Project: Archival Research in the Social Sciences* (with Moore, Salter and Tamboukou, 2016).

Simone A. Wegge is Associate Professor in the Political Science, Economics, and Philosophy Department at the College of Staten Island, City University of New York, NY, USA. Her research focuses primarily on improving our understanding of historical migration processes.

Reconsidering the migrant letter: from the experience of migrants to the language of migrants

Marcelo J. Borges 🆔 and Sonia Cancian

ABSTRACT

Following a century of scholarly attention, the migrant letter, whether written by family members, lovers, friends, or others, is a document that continues to attract the attention of scholars and general readers. Over time, the study of migrant letters has developed in myriad directions. It has adopted methodologies ranging from the publication of complete collections and excerpts to the close analytical and computational readings of letters and their authors examined through the lens of gender, identity, family, and emotions. Regardless of the methodology, the history of migrant letters remains tied to the history of the family. This introduction presents an overview of the historiographical evolution of the study of migrant letters from the early twentieth-century onwards. It highlights the ways in which this Special Issue contributes to the discussion by exploring the connection between the practice of letter writing and the emotional, transnational, economic, and familial experiences of individuals separated by migration.

In 1916, American sociologist William I. Thomas and his Polish colleague Florian Znaniecki began a collaboration which resulted in one of the most influential works of the twentieth century on individual and family experiences amid rapid social and cultural changes brought on by the expansion of capitalism, urbanization, and migration (Zaretsky, 1984). *The Polish Peasant in Europe and America* (Thomas & Znaniecki, 1918, 1919–1920, 1927) was also a major methodological turning point in its extensive use of first-person accounts and life documents, most notably a large collection of letters from Polish migrants and their families. A century later, the migrant letter, whether written by family members, lovers, friends, or others is a document that continues to attract the attention of scholars and other readers. With migration occupying a central role in the twenty-first century and digital communication technologies morphing our world as we once knew it, the practice of letter-writing and the letters themselves have become fragments of the past for many. Yet, when we think of the migrant letter today, the image of a mother reading aloud to her family the letter received from her migrant son or daughter continues to resonate among us. What exactly is it about this form of writing that perplexes, fascinates, and continues to elude us? Is it nostalgia thrusting us to a distant, yet desired past? Is it the consequence of the letter's eclipse resulting from the prevalence of digital communication technologies? Or is it about the centrality of family, mobility, and communication, then and now, in the face of change and continuity?

The work on migrant letters pioneered by Thomas and Znaniecki had initially few followers among migration historians. In the United States, George Stephenson's and Theodore Blegen's studies of letters of Scandinavian migrants (for example, Blegen, 1931; Stephenson, 1929) started a new tradition of inquiry which led the way to social historians' interest in letters as a way to incorporate migrants' own perspectives in the study of migration.[1] Since then, letters have been at the center of scholars' preoccupation with mobility. Over time, scholars' questions, approaches, and methodologies have varied considerably. Thomas and Znaniecki used migrant letters (which they called 'peasant letters') to show the impact of modernization on traditional societies and the resulting breakdown in family solidarity and organization. Early historians interested in the 'America letter,' like Theodore Blegen, George Stephenson, and Marcus Hansen saw the immigrant letter as the ideal source for research on migration. They viewed the migrant letter as a catalyst of mass migration (Gerber, 2006, p. 41). Scholarly interest shifted to the migrant letter as a privileged source to learn about the experiences of migration, motives of emigration, places of settlement, migrants' daily lives and socio-economic adaptation. Beginning in the 1950s, edited collections of migrant letters began to appear in their original language and in English translation (Blegen, 1955; Conway, 1961). These volumes and numerous others that followed provided qualitative first-hand testimonies of migrants' efforts in adjusting to social and economic shifts in a variety of contexts (for example, Baily & Ramella, 1988; Barton, 1975; Blasco Martínez & Rubalcaba Pérez, 2003; D'Agostin & Grossutti, 1997; Erickson, 1972; Fitzpatrick, 1994; Franzina, 1979; Kula, Assorodobraj-Kula, & Kula, 1986 [1973]; Miller, Schrier, Boling, & Doyle, 2003; Soutelo Vázquez, 2001). With the emergence of the New Social History, historians began to see as well 'the analytical potential of many of the usual deletions [from complete collections] … discussed as trivial, such as, health, family gossip, friendship, personal inquiries, and so on' (Gerber, 2006, p. 55). In most of these cases, if not all, the perspective that was featured belonged to the migrants. All too often, and for practical limitations especially, many of the collections underscored one side of the correspondence, that is the migrants' (for example, Kamphoefner, Helbich, & Sommer, 1991), leaving it to the researcher to provide commentary based on the content in the letters. Since the 1990s, scholars have also begun to pay special attention to the language of the letters as well as their place in the context of broader epistolary practices (for example, Fitzpatrick, 1994, 2006; Franzina, 1981, 1987; Gibelli, 1989; Lyons, 2013; Miller, 1985; Moreton, 2012; Vargas, 2006). Several works also considered the meaning and functionality of migrant letters as vehicles for nurturing and (re)negotiating family relations and personal networks altered by migration, for cultivating new ideas of self and others, and for expressing emotions in contexts of migration (for example, Cancian, 2010, 2012a, 2016; Da Orden, 2010; DeHaan, 2001, 2010; Errington, 2008; Gerber, 2006; Gibelli, 1989, 2002; Liu, 2005; Murray, 2004; Sinke, 2002). These approaches were in part influenced by developments in other disciplines and fields like critical theory, literary analysis, social psychology, feminist anthropology, gender studies, literacy studies, linguistics, and more recently, the history of emotions.

Most of the original discussion of migrant letters took place in the context of immigration in North America and the North Atlantic world, but over time a broader community of international scholars began to look at the place of migrant correspondence in other countries of immigration and emigration. Conferences and initiatives of international collaboration have resulted in diversified theoretical and methodological approaches. They have also facilitated a dialogue among different scholarly traditions (for example, Elliot, Gerber, & Sinke, 2006).[2] There are, however, still some parallel developments in the study of migrant letters across borders. For example, scholars in Europe have paid more attention to migrant letters in the context of 'popular' or 'working-class' writings and traditions of 'popular literacy' than those in the United States (for example see Barton & Hall, 2000; Castillo Gómez, 2002; Lyons 2012, 2013). On the other hand, studies of migration and mobility within European imperial spaces and the writing practices of individuals and families of the middling and upper sectors who moved in these spaces have developed in parallel (but not necessarily in dialogue) with studies of migrant letters (Pearsall, 2008; Rothschild, 2011).[3] There is, therefore, plenty of room for comparisons and collaborations by scholars at the international level, in a way that is closer to the experience of migrants themselves who traversed national boundaries and were exposed to multiple cultural influences. The study of letter-writing by migrants and their families in different historical, geographic, and cultural contexts, and through multiple disciplinary lenses will result in a fuller understanding of its meaning, purpose, and characteristic features – what is unique, what changes across groups and contexts, what are the differences and commonalities with broader letter-writing practices at home and abroad.

Questions of representativeness have also been raised in the field of migrant letters. The number of letters available for research and the overall number of letters that were written and those that were not exchanged between individuals and families have perplexed researchers (Erickson, 1972; Fitzpatrick, 1994; Helbich & Kamphoefner, 2006; Richards, 2006). These questions have compelled historians Helbich and Kamphoefner (2006) to ask 'how similar or different the socioeconomic and demographic profile of these individuals was, compared to those who did write … what sort of letters survived and surfaced, what may distinguish them from those that did not, and which part of the chain composed by writer, recipient, preservers, and finally donor may have been most essential' (p. 30). In other words, how representative were the conclusions culled from the available letters if researchers did not have access to all the letters composed, delivered, and preserved over time? As valid as this caveat may be, historical records are always partial and fragmentary, and in this regard letters written by migrants are no different from other sources. Expanding the types of repositories and voices represented by letters is one way to strive for as large and diverse a population as possible. This is particularly important for letters from the barely literate, semi-literate, or even illiterate (who wrote with other people's assistance), which constituted the majority of migrants during the period of mass transoceanic migrations in the nineteenth and early twentieth centuries. As scholars of working-class writings remind us, separation caused by migration was one of the biggest pushes for millions of people to start writing for the first time, whatever their capacity (Gibelli, 2002; Lyons, 2013). Access to a variety of letters from diverse populations also creates interesting possibilities to shed light on the ways in which cultural practices, worldviews, expectations, and strategies varied according to class and cultural backgrounds, and how these factors may have shaped letter-writing among migrants.

Briefly, the study of migrant letters has developed in myriad directions adopting methodologies ranging from the publication of complete collections to the publication of large excerpts of letters as illustrations of historical events and experiences to close readings of letters, and interdisciplinary and multidisciplinary approaches with a focus on gender, identity, family, and emotions in content analysis, and more recently, computational analysis.

Regardless of the methodology, the history of migrant letters remains tied to the history of the family. From Thomas and Znaniecki on, scholars have underscored the value of migrant letters in historical illustrations, descriptions, and the re/telling of migration experiences on behalf of individuals, families, and communities.

Since then, other questions and approaches have been pushing the boundaries of inquiry in the field. One of the questions, 'Can migrant letters speak for themselves?' asks to what extent the presentation of a letter collection provides a reading into the experiences of migrants and their significant others? The work of Fitzpatrick (1994), Gerber (1997), and Miller, Schrier, Boiling, and Doyle (2003) ushered in closer readings of migrant letters leading to a more in-depth understanding of migrants' 'constructions of experience' (Fitzpatrick, 1994, p. 5). This line of inquiry has been expanded and enriched during the last two decades with the work of other scholars interested in the possibilities of content analysis (qualitative and quantitative) to explore migrants' constructions of identity, language, and emotions (for example, Cancian, 2010, 2012a; Da Orden, 2010; DeHaan, 2001, 2010; Elliot et al., 2006; Gerber, 2006; Moreton, 2012; Sinke, 2002).

Similar to other narrative sources, emotions, affect, and intimacy are integral to migrant letters. Within the context of family and migration, Loretta Baldassar and Donna Gabaccia recently noted that 'families are increasingly understood as sites of disagreement and contest, particularly along gendered and generational lines as well as of bonds of emotion that, along with economic concerns, often provide the affective drivers for migration' (Baldassar & Gabaccia, 2011, p. 3). What kinds of emotions and emotional energies (Altman, 1982) can be mined from migrant letters? Recent works (Cancian, 2010, 2012a, 2012b; Errington, 2008; Gerber, 2006) have contributed to underscoring the importance of emotions, affect, and intimacy in migrant correspondence.[4] In doing so, they have begun to explore more closely the state of mind and state of heart of the letter-writers on both sides of the migration process, making evident the interior complexities of leaving one's family and being left behind.

Equally important has been an emphasis on transnationality that has emerged among scholars in the late twentieth century. Defined as 'a way of life that connects family, work, and consciousness in more than one national territory,' transnationalism, historian Donna Gabaccia notes, was viewed 'as a normal dimension of life for many, perhaps even most, working-class families in Italy [and other countries of emigration] in the nineteenth and twentieth centuries. Family discipline, economic security, reproduction, inheritance, romance and dreams transcended national boundaries and bridged continents' (Gabaccia, 2000, p. 11). In this light, the letters of migrants and the letters of their significant others who remained behind are crucial. Increasingly, beginning with the works of Liu (2005), Gerber (2006), and Cancian (2010), for instance, the links, continuities, and negotiating efforts illustrated in letter collections between migrant letter-writers and their family members back home became important sources for analysis. Transnational links between families continue to serve as an important conduit of inquiry for current scholarship.

Building on this rich trajectory, the articles in this Special Issue offer new insights from case studies and methodological and theoretical discussions that reflect the current state of historical analysis of migrant letters and contribute to setting the agenda for further historical inquiry. Contributors use a variety of approaches and engage in multidisciplinary dialogue to illuminate the practice of letter-writing, its multiple meanings and functions, and its connection with the experiences and identities of individuals and families separated by migration.

David Gerber's article uses letter-writing to identify the process of 'immigrant self-making'; in particular, the uses of migrants' memory of their past lives and the relationships they left behind as they built new lives in the places of settlement. Using insights from literary analysis and social psychology, the article explores migrants' use of nostalgia in migrant letters as a strategy of personal adaptation that bridged the former selves and new selves in-the-making, as a 'mechanism of reconciliation' with their new lives. Musing about their previous lives could act as a 'bridge' or a 'barrier.' Nostalgia could operate as a means to facilitate change or, in less successful or functional cases, it could lead to brooding sentiments of inadequacy. Gerber analyzes these different processes of memory work and identity-making in the letter collections of three individual British migrants to the United States in the nineteenth century.

The contribution of Emma Moreton also looks at migrants' memory work as a way to bring together the country they left behind and their new lives as immigrants. Her study adds a different methodological and theoretical approach to the discussion; it uses content analysis techniques from corpus linguistics to examine the letters of Julia Lough, an English migrant woman living in the United States during the late nineteenth and early twentieth centuries which are part of a larger collection of family correspondence. While Gerber's article looks at nostalgia as a state of being 'temporarily and unexpectedly overcome by memories,' which in some cases could be a primer for more conscious memory work such as recollection, Moreton's analysis complements the discussion by concentrating on the ways migrants constructed the language of recollection. Moreton identifies verbal strategies used by Julia Lough in order to emphasize past experiences with family who remained at home, thus strengthening emotional bonds and connections to shared meaningful places. This migrant used the language of recollection to connect with family members back home while positioning herself in her new environment and identity without losing a sense of attachment to home. Letter-writing was equally important for the emotional ties of families separated by migration and for migrants' identities. Moreton's analysis shows how it provided Julia Lough with a vehicle to keep emotional ties with the family left behind and facilitated her process of self-fashioning as an immigrant.

The letters analyzed in the first two articles facilitated epistolary conversations between female and male migrants and a variety of interlocutors back home – parents, siblings, cousins, uncles and aunts. In which ways did different recipients contribute to shaping different narrative strategies? Babs Boter and Suzanne Sinke consider this question in their article which analyzes the impact of epistolary audiences and perceptions of expected gender and family roles in migrants' letter-writing practices. The authors compare the letter-writing of two Dutch men who migrated to Canada and the United States in the early twentieth century; one wrote mostly to his parents, the other to the wife he left behind and with whom he was hoping to reunite abroad. In their letters back home, they presented 'epistolary personae' that made use of varied ideas of their roles as men, and of their place within and responsibility toward their family. The comparison of the letters of these two men illustrates a 'successful' and a 'failed' case in migrants' use of letter-writing to cultivate emotional and material connections with loved ones left behind, and to fulfill expectations as men and responsible family and community members. This discussion shows, as the authors put it, that 'audience mattered,' as did gendered understandings of self and family obligations.

Other contributions in this Special Issue expand the discussion of family expectations and obligations expressed and (re)negotiated through letter-writing to other migrant groups, and add different analytical approaches. The article by Sonia Cancian and Simone Wegge focuses more specifically on material support and economic matters discussed through the language of emotions in letters exchanged by migrants from Europe and their families during the first half of the twentieth century, now digitally available as part of the University of Minnesota's Digitizing Immigrant Letters Project. The authors explore the many ways in which economic and financial concerns appeared in letters sent both by migrants and by family members in their places of origin. Economic concerns discussed in these letters included the use of migrants' remittances, details of domestic economics and market prices for essential goods, management of family property, and the hardships of relatives who stayed behind. Money matters were often discussed from the point of view of emotions, using language of affect and emphasizing family ties and expectations. The discussion on migrant letters examined from the viewpoint of socioeconomic conditions brings to light the shifting importance that economic matters occupied in transnational family relations and their letters. Perhaps unsurprisingly, economic matters appeared more frequently in letters whose authors exhibited greater economic need.

For its part Marcelo Borges' article looks at migration, gender roles, and family expectations through the lens of married couples living apart as a result of labor migration from Portugal in the late nineteenth century and the first three decades of the twentieth century. Focusing on personal letters sent from husbands, and sometimes fathers, working abroad which were put to use as 'call letters' to facilitate family reunification, the article explores narrative strategies and language usage which contributed to presenting migration as a family strategy. Letters conveyed messages of marital duty and family obligations, as well as ideas of migration as a common life project. Married men built epistolary personae clearly anchored in ideas of responsibility, gender roles, and marital duty, and they expected reciprocity from their wives. These ideas were communicated through a language of affect that contained both emotional and material components. These letters also showed the effect migration could exert on customary gender and marital roles, and were used as a vehicle to maintain emotional bonds and to negotiate the impact of distance and time of separation on marital and family relations.

As the last articles illustrate, both economic and emotional matters figured prominently in the letters of many migrants, and they were closely connected with migrants' self-making through family correspondence. The project of migration was usually associated with perceived opportunities for well-being and security based on economic betterment. It was common for migrants to continue playing a significant economic role for their families in their places of origin, even when projects of temporary migration turned into long-term or permanent resettlement. As the article by Liz Stanley argues, however, the interplay of emotional and material considerations in migrant letter-writing and their connection with identity have not been fully examined in migrant letters scholarship. Stanley brings to the discussion of migrant letters a different type of migrant experience and analytical approach. Part of what Stanley calls the 'middling sort,' the Forbes family was active in a number of economic activities in both Scotland and South Africa's settler society during the second half of the nineteenth century and the early twentieth century. The Forbes' transnational lives produced voluminous writing in the form of letters and other personal and business documents. Using Michel de Certeau's concept of 'scriptural economy' Stanley analyzes the letter-writing practices of this family within the framework of migrant letters historiography, emphasizing shared characteristics with epistolary practices in general and, at the same time, identifying some distinctive features in the context of migrant correspondence – namely, a preoccupation with 'exteriority' and shared economic interests over personal matters or affect, and a focus on the present more than on the past.

Stanley's study of the Forbes' case contributes to the general discussion of the characteristics and function of letter-writing among families separated by migration and living in transnational situations by considering other contexts and cultural and socioeconomic backgrounds. Could some of these differences be attributed to the social dynamics created by settler migration (as opposed to labor migration which characterized most moves from Europe to the Americas)? Looking at the full range of cases included in this Special Issue allows us to consider some commonalities between settler migrants and labor migrants, which open new avenues for exploration of the multiple ways in which economic interests, family obligations, and considerations about the present and the future influenced epistolary narratives and identity-making among migrant letter-writers and their families together with memories of experiences and relations located in the past.

Laura Martínez's analysis of the letter-writing (and reading) among Spanish migrants from the region of Asturias who settled in the Americas from the mid-nineteenth century to the 1930s and their families provides a revealing complement to the discussion of migrant epistolarity. Like Stanley in the previous article, Martínez places migrant letters within larger epistolary practices, but the lens here is set on the writing practices of the popular classes, to which the majority of transatlantic labor migrants belonged. Martínez's analysis considers letter-writing in contexts of migration as an activity that transcended the individual to involve the family in letter production, circulation, and reception. To illustrate this dynamic, the author focuses on examples of delegated and multiple writing, and also on practices of collective reading and circulation beyond the original recipient, common in this corpus of migrant letters. The author identifies these practices through analysis of letter content as well as through traces that 'writing with other hands' left on the letters themselves. These practices of collective writing and reading were not necessarily the result of low levels of literacy, but more importantly they were the product of the 'familiar and cooperative' nature of migration itself among Asturian migrants.

Finally, the article by Romeo Guzmán examines many of the topics outlined above but it zeroes in on the epistolary exchanges of one family of Mexican migrants in the United States, providing a rare opportunity of analyzing the perspective and voices of multiple individuals on both sides of the migratory experience. In doing so, it captures the multiple uses of letter-writing as family members adapted to living transnational lives amid rapidly changing political and economic circumstances – the Mexican Revolution, the Great Depression and its anti-Mexican backlash in the United States, and World War II. The family also experienced several lengths of absence and separation, including multiple migrations and returns. The correspondence exchanged by the Venegas family between Jalisco and California involved many family members who participated in the process of writing and reception. Letter-writing replicated gender and family roles, and it provided a space to reinforce emotional bonds and nurture processes of identity-making. At the same time, it provided opportunities to discuss common interests and to weigh options for the future. Guzmán conceptualizes correspondence as a vehicle for sustaining a transnational experience and a form of 'cultural citizenship' that bridged the places of origin and settlement.

The preceding notes identify some of the key contributions of the articles included in this Special Issue and suggest a number of ways in which they dialogue with each other, contribute to current debates, and indicate emerging questions and perspectives for future inquiry. There are, of course, other possible readings and connections. We invite the readers to explore and discover them.

Notes

1. References to scholarship about migrant letters in this Introduction are not exhaustive but illustrative of some key works, approaches, and trends. For a recent, comprehensive list of works on migrant letters, see chapter two in Sanfilippo (2015).
2. Noteworthy and promising are also several initiatives and platforms for international collaboration, such as Digitising Experiences of Migration: The development of interconnected letters collection, organized by Emma Moreton and Hilary Nesi, at Coventry University, UK (http://lettersofmigration.blogspot.com), and the Digitizing Immigrant Letters Project at the University of Minnesota (https://www.lib.umn.edu/ihrca/dil).
3. See also the Whites Writing Whiteness project, co-directed by Liz Stanley and Sue Wise (http://www.whiteswritingwhiteness.ed.ac.uk).
4. See also the Digitizing Immigrant Letters Project (https://www.lib.umn.edu/ihrca/dil).

Disclosure statement

No potential conflict of interest was reported by the authors.

ORCID

Marcelo J. Borges (iD) http://orcid.org/0000-0002-0741-5220

References

Altman, J. (1982). *Epistolarity: Approaches to a form*. Columbus, OH: Ohio University Press.

Baily, S., & Ramella, F. (1988). *One family, two worlds: An Italian family's correspondence across the Atlantic, 1901–1922*. New Brunswick, NJ: Rutgers University Press.

Baldassar, L., & Gabaccia, D. (Eds.). (2011). *Intimacy and Italian migration: Gender and domestic lives in a mobile world*. New York, NY: Fordham University Press.

Barton, H. A. (1975). *Letters from the promised land: Swedes in America, 1840–1914*. Minneapolis, MN: University of Minnesota Press.

Barton, D., & Hall, N. (Eds.). (2000). *Letter writing as a social practice*. Amsterdam: John Benjamins.

Blasco Martínez, R., & Rubalcaba Pérez, C. (Eds.). (2003). *"Para hablarte a tan larga distancia…": Correspondencia de una familia montañesa a ambos lados del Atlántico (1855–1883)* ["To talk with you at such great distance…": The correspondence of a Montañesa family at both sides of the Atlantic (1855–1883)]. Santander: Estudio.

Blegen, T. (1931). Early "America letters". In T. Blegen (Ed.), *Norwegian migration to America, 1825–1860* (pp. 196–213). Northfield, MN: Norwegian America History Association.

Blegen, T. (Ed.). (1955). *Land of their choice: The immigrants write home*. Minneapolis, MN: University of Minnesota Press.

Cancian, S. (2010). *Families, lovers, and their letters: Italian postwar migration to Canada*. Winnipeg: University of Manitoba Press.

Cancian, S. (2012a). The language of gender in lovers' correspondence, 1946–1949. *Gender and History, 24*, 755–765.

Cancian, S. (2012b). "My dearest love…": Love, longing, and desire in international migration. In M. Messer, R. Schroeder, & R. Wodak (Eds.), *Migrations: Interdisciplinary perspectives* (pp. 175–186). Vienna: Springer-Verlag Wien.

Cancian, S. (2016). From Montreal and Venice with love: Migrant letters and romantic intimacy in Italian migration to Postwar Canada. In M. Epp & F. Iacovetta (Eds.), *Sisters or strangers? Immigrant, ethnic, and racialized women in Canadian history* (2nd ed., pp. 191–203). Toronto: University of Toronto Press.

Castillo Gómez, A. (2002). *La conquista del alfabeto: Escritura y clases populares* [The conquest of the alphabet: Writing and popular classes]. Gijón: Ediciones Trea.

Conway, A. (Ed.). (1961). *The Welsh in America: Letters from the immigrants*. Minneapolis, MN: University of Minnesota Press.

D'Agostin, A., & Grossutti, J. (1997). *Ti ho spedito lire cento: Le stagione di Luigi Piccoli, emigrante friulano: Lettere ai famigliari (1905–1915)* [I sent you a hundred lire: The seasons of Luigi Piccoli, Friulian emigrant: Letters to family (1905–1915)]. Pordenone: Edizione Biblioteca dell'Immagine.

Da Orden, M. L. (2010). *Una familia y un océano de por medio: La emigración gallega a la Argentina: Una historia a través de la memoria epistolar* [A family and an ocean in between: Galician emigration to Argentina: A history through epistolary memory]. Barcelona: Anthropos.

DeHaan, K. (2001). "Wooden shoes and mantle clocks": Letter writing as rhetorical forum for the transforming immigrant identity. In L. Gray-Rosendale & S. Gruber (Eds.), *Alternative rhetorics: Challenges to the rhetorical tradition* (pp. 53–72). Albany, NY: SUNY Press.

DeHaan, K. (2010). Negotiating the transnational moment: Immigrant letters as performance of a diasporic identity. *National Identities, 12*, 107–131.

Elliot, B., Gerber, D., & Sinke, S. (Eds.). (2006). *Letters across borders: The epistolary practices of international migrants*. New York, NY: Palgrave Mcmillan & Carleton Centre for the History of Migration.

Erickson, C. (1972). *Invisible immigrants: The adaptation of English and Scottish immigrants in nineteenth-century America*. Coral Gables, FL: University of Miami Press.

Errington, J. (2008). Webs of affection and obligation: Glimpse into families and nineteenth century transatlantic communities. *Journal of the Canadian Historical Association, 19*, 1–26.

Fitzpatrick, D. (Ed.). (1994). *Oceans of consolation: Personal accounts of Irish migration to Australia*. Ithaca, NY: Cornell University Press.

Fitzpatrick, D. (2006). Irish emigration and the art of letter-writing. In B. Elliot, D. Gerber, & S. Sinke (Eds.), *Letters across Borders* (pp. 97–106). New York, NY: Palgrave Mcmillan & Carleton Centre for the History of Migration.

Franzina, E. (1979). *Merica! Merica!: Emigrazione e colonizzazione nelle lettere dei contadini veneti in America Latina, 1876–1902* [Merica! Merica!: Emigration and colonization in the letters of Venetian peasants in Latin America, 1876–1902]. Milan: Feltrinelli.

Franzina, E. (1981). Frammenti di cultura contadina nelle lettere degli emigranti [Fragments of peasant culture in the letters of emigrants]. *Movimento Operaio e Socialista, 4*, 49–76.

Franzina, E. (1987). L'epistolografia popolare e i suoi usi [Popular epistolarity and its uses]. *Materiali di Lavoro, 1–2*, 21–76.

Gabaccia, D. (2000). *Italy's many diasporas*. London: UCL Press.

Gerber, D. (1997). The immigrant letter between positivism and populism: The uses of immigrant personal correspondence in twentieth-century American scholarship. *Journal of American Ethnic History, 16*, 3–34.

Gerber, D. (2006). *Authors of their lives: The personal correspondence of British immigrants to North America in the nineteenth century*. New York, NY: New York University Press.

Gibelli, A. (1989). "Fatemi unpo sapere…": Scrittura e fotografia nella corrispondenza degli emigrati liguri ["Let me know a little . . .": Writing and photography in the correspondence of Ligurian emigrants"]. In Fondazione Regionale Cristoforo Colombo & Centro Ligure di Storia Sociale (Eds.), *La via delle Americhe: L'emigrazione ligure tra evento e racconto: Catalogo della mostra, settembre-dicembre 1989* [The way to the Americas: Ligurian emigration between even and story: Exhibit catalogue, September-December 1989] (pp. 87–94). Genova: Sagep.

Gibelli, A. (2002). Emigrantes y soldados: La escritura popular como práctica de masas en los siglos XIX y XX [Emigrants and soldiers: Popular writing as a practice of the masses in the nineteenth and twentieth centuries]. In A. Castillo Gómez (Ed.), *La conquista del alfabeto: Escritura y clases populares* [The conquest of the alphabet: Writing and popular classes] (pp. 189–223). Gijón: Ediciones Trea.

Helbich, W., & Kamphoefner, W. (2006). How representative are emigrant letters? An exploration of the German case. In B. Elliot, D. Gerber, & S. Sinke (Eds.), *Letters across Borders* (pp. 29–55). New York, NY: Palgrave Mcmillan & Carleton Centre for the History of Migration.

Kamphoefner, W., Helbich, W., & Sommer, U. (Eds.) (1991). *News from the land of freedom: German immigrants write home* (S. Vogel, Trans.). Ithaca, NY: Cornell University Press.

Kula, W., Assorodobraj-Kula, N., & Kula, M. (1986). *Writing home: Immigrants in Brazil and the United States, 1890–1891*. (Wtulich, J., Ed. and Trans.). Boulder, CO: East European Monographs. (Original work published 1973).

Liu, H. (2005). *Transnational history of a Chinese family: Immigrant letters, family business, and reverse migration*. New Brunswick, NJ: Rutgers University Press.

Lyons, M. (2012). New directions in the history of written culture. *Culture & History Digital Journal, 1*(2), e007. doi:10.3989/chdj.2012.007

Lyons, M. (2013). *The writing culture of ordinary people in Europe, c. 1860–1920*. Cambridge: Cambridge University Press.

Miller, K. (1985). *Emigrants and exiles: Ireland and the Irish exodus to North America*. New York, NY: Oxford University Press.

Miller, K., Schrier, A., Boling, B., & Doyle, D. (2003). *Irish immigrants in the land of Canaan: Letters and memoirs from colonial and revolutionary America, 1675–1815*. New York, NY: Oxford University Press.

Moreton, E. (2012). Profiling the female emigrant: A method of linguistic inquiry for examining correspondence collections. *Gender & History, 24*, 617–646.

Murray, E. (2004). *Devenir irlandés: Narrativas íntimas de la emigración irlandesa a la Argentina (1844–1912)* [Becoming Irish: Intimate narratives of Irish emigration to Argentina (1844–1912)]. Buenos Aires: Eudeba.

Pearsall, S. (2008). *Atlantic families*. New York, NY: Oxford University Press.

Richards, E. (2006). The limits of the Australian emigrant letter. In B. Elliot, D. Gerber, & S. Sinke (Eds.), *Letters across Borders* (pp. 56–74). New York, NY: Palgrave Mcmillan & Carleton Centre for the History of Migration.

Rothschild, E. (2011). *The inner lives of empire: An eighteenth century history*. Princeton, NJ: Princeton University Press.

Sanfilippo, M. (2015). *Nuovi problemi di storia delle migrazioni italiane* [New historical issues in Italian migration movements]. Viterbo: Edizioni Sette Città.

Sinke, S. (2002). *Dutch immigrant women in the United States, 1880–1920*. Urbana, IL: University of Illinois Press.

Soutelo Vázquez, R. (Ed.). (2001). *De América para a casa: Correspondencia familiar de emigrantes galegos no Brasil, Venezuela e Uruguai (1916–1969)* [From America to home: Family correspondence of Galician emigrants in Brazil, Venezuela, and Uruguay (1916–1969)]. Santiago de Compostela: Consello da Cultura Galega.

Stephenson, G. (1929). When America was the land of Canaan. *Minnesota History, 10*, 237–260.

Thomas, W. I., & Znaniecki, F. (1918, 1919–1920). *The Polish peasant in Europe and America* (Vols. 1–2; 3–5). Chicago, IL: University of Chicago Press; Boston: Badger.

Thomas, W. I., & F. Znaniecki. (1927). *The Polish peasant in Europe and America* (Rev. ed.) (Vols. 1–2). New York, NY: Alfred A. Knopf.

Vargas, M. (2006). Epistolary communication between migrant workers and their families. In B. Elliot, D. Gerber, & S. Sinke (Eds.), *Letters across Borders* (pp. 124–138). New York, NY: Palgrave Mcmillan & Carleton Centre for the History of Migration.

Zaretsky, E. (1984). Editor's introduction. In W. Thomas & F. Znaniecki (Ed. & abr.), *The Polish Peasant in Europe and America* (pp. 1–53). Urbana, IL: University of Illinois Press.

Moving backward and moving on: nostalgia, significant others, and social reintegration in nineteenth-century British immigrant personal correspondence

David A. Gerber

ABSTRACT

Nostalgia among immigrants frequently has been conceived of as a brooding and obsessive homesickness that leads to depression, lassitude, and neurotic misery among those who have left their original home and resettled elsewhere. Recent social psychological, literary and philosophical work, however, has sought a reformulation of nostalgia that instead emphasizes the positive uses to which memory, even painful memory, may be put in the effort to confront the challenges to personal identities of such massive changes in the lives of an individual as immigration. Through exploration of the letters to family members of three British immigrants to North America in the nineteenth century, this essay seeks to demonstrate how symbolic representations of the personal past inscribed creatively in letter-writing may function, or alternatively fail to function, to provide associations that bridge the gaps between past and present. The past may serve up mental images of pleasant circumstances involving people, places and events that serve as metaphoric building blocks by which the mind may ultimately place the individual in new circumstances, now made more familiar by virtue of their comparability to the past. Or, the tendency toward nostalgic memory may simply be overtaken by immersion in new circumstances that work in time to lead individuals realistically to draw pleasure from the past, while understanding its declining day-to-day relevance.

1. Introduction

In this essay I extend the work I have done on the psychology of immigrant epistolarity by delving further into letter-writing as part of the project of immigrant self-making (Gerber, 2006). Through analyzing the personal correspondence of immigrants to understand their engagement with their personal pasts, especially their relationships to family, both nuclear and extended, I seek to understand the ways in which the past may serve as a bridge or alternatively a barrier to fashioning a transformed self capable of living productively under circumstances of resettlement in a new land. At the heart of the inquiry is understanding *nostalgia*, an emotion that has been sharply contested among those who have studied it over the course of centuries. Appearing for analysts over time as a disease, a flight of fantasy into the past, a balm against the wounds created by change, or an asset in building the present and the future on the foundations of the past, the experience of nostalgia emerges and re-emerges as a problem or a resource. Here, it appears in both guises, and we will seek to understand ways in which it functions so differently from one individual to another, and how it becomes inscribed in the immigrant's own letter-writing and through letter-writing in the immigrant's emerging self.

In my work in the past, I have emphasized letter-writing as an aspect of the individual immigrant's need for continuity amidst the radical change in circumstances prompted by emigration and resettlement.[1] This insight has been based on a model of personal identity that holds that personal identities are premised on the necessary understanding that we are the same people that we have been in the past, and that, just as we must spatially integrate ourselves so that our bodies and minds form one entity, our existential security depends on this temporal integration. The organization of such signposts as abiding personal relationships with significant others – family, kin, and friends – is a crucial element in the quest for this continuity. Personal identities are interpersonal and intersubjective, and they are distributed, with various facets of ourselves going out to those with whom we form relationships, and the more significant and abiding the relationships, the more essential they are to identity. We cannot advance whatever plans we have for ourselves in the social world, and hence integrate ourselves socially, without achieving these primary and largely semi-conscious forms of integration (Bruner, 1990, 1997; Grinberg & Grinberg, 1989; Habermas, 1979.)

This is a special project for voluntary immigrants, such as the approximately 35 million Europeans who came to the United States between 1820 and 1920. So much about the lives of immigrants is changed by their resettlement in a new place, where culture and societal organization are different, and where the differences challenge them daily. They are people, risking rootlessness and disconnection from their sources of personal continuity – family relationships and friendships and the home places and material objects left behind – who experience massive and frequently deeply unsettling changes at every level of their lives (Handlin, 1973).[2] Yet they are in a psychological bind to the extent that they themselves have voluntarily embraced leaving their homes in the hopes of self-improvement. Of course, poverty and lack of opportunity do not create a perfect context for free choice, but we should remember that not everyone left Europe during that century; many chose strategies closer to home, and thus less disruptive, for confronting the economic difficulties imposed by modernizing economies. Immigrants, thus, must address the unintended, often negative consequences of their own, positively conceived actions. To that extent, in pursuit of a societal integration that encompasses fulfilling their own aspirations for opportunity and security, immigration demands personal growth and enlarged, but realistic perspectives on the world as well as on oneself. Of necessity, it demands a changing self that nonetheless must still reach back into a tenuously held past, for much of its personal identity. Immigrants face an especially challenging version of the paradox that each of us faces daily: they must stay the same and grow simultaneously. They must balance off the losses that may come with change, losses in familiar, primary face-to-face relationships, familiar places, and familiar objects, with the gains they seek from new possibilities. They must move backward and forward simultaneously.

Of course, immigrants do not exist in a social vacuum. They do not face such challenges as solitary individuals, each of them daily reinventing themselves *de novo* and alone. They are assisted greatly in meeting these challenges by the social networks within which long-distance immigration is organized, and by the ethnic communities in lands of resettlement which provide familiar social and cultural opportunities that cushion and facilitate the various practical and daily challenges they face in resettlement. Together, they can construct a familiar community, create new relationships and new homes, and possess new objects. Historians and social scientists know a great deal about these networks that organize migration flows and about the organization and multiple functions of ethnic groups (Bodnar, 1985; Faist, 2000; Hoerder, 2002). But the work of maintaining continuity amidst demands for change did not only go on at the level of organized social structures. Of necessity, it also went on in the minds of individual men and women who were always and at some level, like all of us, alone with their thoughts.

1.2. Reading immigrant letters: finding the mental life of immigrants

Immigrant personal correspondence gives us windows into the consciousness of individual immigrants confronting these fundamental questions, when we choose to read their letters with that goal in mind. If immigrants could not maintain face-to-face relationships with family, kin, and friends, they could write letters. The nineteenth-century expansion of modern, bureaucratically organized postal services across the Atlantic guaranteed increasing efficiency, speed, and security for personal as well as commercial correspondence. Immigrants from Europe to North America could maintain their valued relationships through the international mails, which millions of them, taking advantage of the proliferation of literacy skills throughout Europe in the eighteenth and nineteenth centuries, chose to do over the course of many decades (Gerber, 2006, pp. 73–91, 140–161).

In their letters were embedded relationships made vulnerable by long-distance, often lifetime separation. Decoding these relationships from the text is difficult, because in the large majority of cases, historians have access to only the letters sent to Europe, not the ones received in the New World. We must struggle to reconstruct the two-way conversation that constitutes personal correspondence, and find the implicit voice of the other party in the letter of his or her immigrant correspondent. We must also, of necessity, imagine another absence: an absence of truth and relatedly, the problem of what is not shared and explicitly addressed in letters, whether it is lied about or omitted because it involves what writers do not wish to share with their correspondents (Gerber, 2005).

Another and more frequently explored way of reading these letters involves less of this sort of interpretive struggle with the text. Historians interrogate personal correspondence to discover documentation of what they think they already know, or at least intuit, from other sources, such as newspapers, state records, or the sacramental records of religious organizations. To that end, we may go to immigrant letters to seek *information*. We want to know about purposeful behavior, and ask questions about the acquisition of skills, jobs, higher wages, and places of residence, about the formation of the domestic or household economy and in that connection family and gender roles, about the organization of ethnic institutions, and about voting and political alignments, and we seek to build a convincing enough, because sizeable, body of evidence in behalf of our generalizations.

But to the extent it is difficult to infer consciousness from behavior, tracking behavior through letters does not necessarily guide us, if our desire is to understand the mental lives of immigrants, and especially to ask questions about the challenges to personal identities that long-distance migrations created. I seek instead to use what immigrants write to significant others to interrogate consciousness itself, and to that end I conceptualize immigrant experience at a variety of psychological levels, utilizing psychological concepts. I document daily life in the service of understanding the mental lives of individuals, especially the choices they see before them and make or fail to make in the service of the immigration project on which they have embarked. Since my analysis is textual as much as contextual, it lies at the juncture of the intersection of history, literary studies, social and individual psychology, and philosophy, a place I recognize that most historians do not usually visit, or, in fact, desire to visit. Most historians are resistant to trust, let alone make explicit, intuitions about the mental life of their subjects, and to build upon those intuitions with theories and concepts from other disciplines – especially those disciplines like literature and philosophy that are not empirical, and which use the word 'theory' to mean abstract, conceptual thinking not anchored in the messy work of reading one letter after another until one has enough confidence in one's impressions to draw conclusions. But disciplines especially sensitive to language and to textual qualities present us with the strongest assistance we can ask for in finding the writer embedded in the prose of the letter. In the case of *nostalgia*, there is, in fact, little evidence that immigration historians have consulted the relevant literatures from other disciplines cited in this essay. Treatments of nostalgia in immigrant letters, as we shall shortly see, are often sensitive and searching, but the authors do not problematize the concept in the attempt to derive a more critical analysis of its implications.

2. Memory: nostalgia, recollection, homesickness

In the service of understanding immigrant self-making, I want to ask questions of letters about the processes by which immigrants held on to relationships and to memories of people, places and objects from the past, while growing, or failing to grow, to meet the demands of their new circumstances in the present. My approach here involves the concept of *nostalgia* understood not exclusively as a pathological attachment to the past, or, as it is conceived colloquially today, as a romanticization of the past, but also, as in contemporary social psychological literature, an adaptive mental strategy for negotiating continuity and change. Though the lines between these concepts can never be perfectly drawn, for analytical purposes at the onset it is necessary to distinguish *nostalgia* from both *recollection* and *homesickness*. By *recollection*, I mean a conscious and intentional effort to reconstruct the past. Recollection is systematic memory work. *Nostalgia*, in contrast, in my usage is more or less a spasm of memory. It may well, as in the work of Marcel Proust, have sensory prompts, such as an odor, a taste, sound, or the atmosphere felt in a room. It is often experienced most powerfully as sudden and involuntary, but it may also be, as it were, conjured up in the hope of entering a mood that provokes memory. It leads one to be temporarily and unexpectedly overcome by memories, usually pleasant ones, but not always, because nostalgia can involve ambiguous memories, such as of a sharp rebuke by a stern but loving parent or of rough treatment in childhood at the hands of admired older siblings. Nostalgic memory is experienced, often powerfully, as a flood of feeling that diverts us temporarily from the present and immerses us in the past. Nostalgia can provide a framework and an inspiration for recollection, but at the point at which individuals consciously and more or less systematically make time to work at memory they leave nostalgia behind for a more disciplined mental activity. *Homesickness*, too, is experienced in emotional terms, but while nostalgia may be pleasant, homesickness is a painful and obsessive longing for a place, in connection with both its material characteristics and social and interpersonal associations. In a chronic form, as opposed to as a passing mood, homesickness wears at the mind, and erodes resistance to depression, lassitude, and neurotic misery. Nostalgia and homesickness (whether short-term or chronic) are very common among immigrants, and they may be experienced simultaneously, but as I intend to argue nostalgia may provide a strategy for untying bothersome psychological knots, and the most significant knot it may seek to overcome is homesickness itself (Colley, 1998, p. 3; Davis, 1979; Fisher, 1989; Grinberg & Grinberg, 1989; Naqvi, 2007; Rosen, 1975; Starobinski, 1966).[3]

3. Three case studies

After a review of the relationships between self, memory, and nostalgia as they have been established, in general and in regard to immigrants, in contemporary academic literatures, I will develop as case studies three immigrant letter-writers, Mary Ann Archbald, Mary Cumming, and Joseph Hartley (English, Irish Protestant, and Scottish respectively), each of whom has appeared in the past in my writing about immigrant letters and letter-writers. The letters of each of the three had in common, to varying degrees, manifestations of both painful homesickness and spasms of nostalgia, in the form of daydreams, nocturnal dreams, and sudden, involuntary reveries. Moreover, to varying degrees and lengths of time, all three shared a conscious resistance to giving themselves over completely to their new circumstances in the United States. The fact that in the case of both Hartley and Archbald they might have had ample reason to be bitter against their native lands for having to seek a livelihood abroad did not lessen these tendencies, and indeed might well have increased them by adding to an abiding sense of loss. Nor did the fact that Cumming was leaving her Irish home to start a new married life with the man she loved. All three expressed the hope in their letters to family members that they might return to their original home, though none of the three accomplished that hope. Archbald reluctantly grew accepting of her life in the United States, which promised a better life for her three children, and provided the Archbald family with a secure and abundant life, but did not fulfill her cultural aspirations. Both Hartley and Cumming died too young for us to judge whether they would have eventually been able completely to reconcile themselves to their American circumstances, though Hartley was certainly on his way to doing so on the basis of the material security he was achieving. All three used their letters to family to record episodes of nostalgia and to organize and formulate conscious recollection of the past, memory work about their former physical home and of those, especially family members, they left behind there. But they also spoke about the qualities and ordinary activities that characterized their new lives. Letters were not simply reflections of these mental processes, but instead constitutive of them. Letter-writing formed each immigrant's identity in consequence of creative and self-probing engagement on the page in dialogue with significant others. In composing their thoughts and sharing them with those they trusted to receive them and to evaluate them generously, immigrants composed their identities. Unfortunately, we rarely know for certain how their correspondents replied. Did they reinforce nostalgia and homesickness by recollecting the past in ways that perhaps unintentionally stimulated one or the other? Did they question or explicitly criticize nostalgic memory? We know only that out of their experiences and ruminations, including their letter-writing, Hartley and Archbald largely succeeded in the struggle to make peace with their new and immediate circumstances and the changed selves they had become. Overcome by nostalgia and by obsessive recollection inspired by nostalgia, Cumming did not, and grew more miserably homesick and less reconciled to her new life.

3.1. Nostalgia in history and theory

How has nostalgia been analyzed in works on the immigrant letter in the past? All too often, the answer is that it has not been. Though nostalgia is frequently referenced in analytical treatments, including the introductions to the many collections of immigrant letters, it is mostly unproblematized to the point at which it is not even an index category. It is instead a noun or an adjective marking or describing a condition too ordinary to require explanation. Its meaning is left to common, colloquial understandings. Fortunately, however, there are historians who respond to its frequent appearance or to discourse about it in other historians' work by recognizing and analyzing it. These efforts may be grouped into at least five categories:

(1) For some analysts, nostalgia is a malady-like *encumbrance* that may be briefly indulged, but must ultimately be overcome for successful adaptation to take place. It may be paired with loneliness, and contrasted with hope or optimism (Cancian, 2010, pp. 56, 98, 101, 117, 127, 150; Serra, 2009). Illara Serra, who writes on the letters of Italian immigrants to the United States, for example, sees nostalgia as an old laggard self that appears in correspondence in opposition to a newly emerging self that displays an 'undying American confidence' (Serra, 2009, pp. 140–141).

(2) Nostalgia may be seen as *situational*. Speaking for the 'preponderant mentality of the majority of Europeans who entered the United States', Orm Øverland finds a contrast between their daily lives and their letters. The Norwegian immigrants whose letters and life writings he has studied intensely for many years were 'forward looking' people who fashioned 'successful' American lives. But the very act of writing to significant others whom they might never see again and the circumstances of composition in solitary settings at the end of a long, tiring work day produced lapses into sentimentality. The writers were, in effect, not really themselves in their nostalgic expressions (Øverland, 2000, pp. 26–27, 2005, pp. 9–10).

(3) Nostalgia may be seen as *negligible* in letters, though it is acknowledged that it did exist as a sort of self-indulgent feeling of loss ('*pathos*') felt and expressed in other areas of life. Arnold Barton, who has long been engaged in editing and analyzing Swedish immigrant letters, agrees with Øverland that nostalgia was not integral to the immigrants' characters, which instead manifested 'hardiness, adaptability, cocky self-assurance, and dogged cheerfulness' in letters home to family and friends, but he goes further than Øverland in denying its frequency. While he does concede that immigrants might not have been honest in their letters about failure or disappointments for fear of discouraging people to follow them to America or of admitting that their own choices were ill-advised, he concludes, 'Pathos is remarkably absent in the "America letters"'. Nostalgia instead appeared in the organization of the ethnic community, where it formed the emotional basis for the organization of churches, lodges, and the ethnic press, and the appearance of neo-traditionalist

family rituals expressed in recipes, meals, and the celebration of holidays (Barton, 1979, pp. 159–161, 1983, pp. 133–134).

(4) Nostalgia may be seen as a mechanism for a type of *vernacular comparative social analysis*. Commenting on the appearance of ruminations about the past in the letters of rural English immigrants to Upper Canada (Ontario) in the 1830s they anthologized in an imposing collection, Wendy Cameron, Sheila Haines, and Mary McDougall Maude find nostalgia to be a more or less consciously mobilized mental resource for making judgments about what was better or worse in their homeland and in Canada. Its hold on the emotions is less the point for these authors than the type of accounting device it provides (Cameron, Haines, & McDougall Maude, 2000, pp. xli–xlii).

(5) Nostalgia may be formulated as *compensatory*, as in David Fitzpatrick's analysis of its evocation in his elaborately edited collection of and commentary upon Irish Australian letters. In a close inspection of immigrant language, particularly in the relevant case of the usage of the word *home* in letters, he finds none of the anguished and brooding evocations of the past, the *pathos*, present in Kerby Miller's contro-versial claim (Miller, 1985) that Irish migration was experienced as forced exile, not as voluntary movement in the service of self-improvement. For Fitzpatrick, instead nostalgia formed an 'affectionate affirmation' of family, village and the Old Country itself, and *home*, by which they always referenced Ireland and not Australia, served the letter-writers as a 'symbol of comfort, stability, and usually affection'. Nonetheless, he allows that in providing this symbol, *home* was 'an important source of solace for those facing the taxing and insecure life of the emigrant' (Fitzpatrick, 1994, pp. 609, 617, 626–627).

Whether seeing nostalgia as pervasive or uncommon and situational, benign and com-pensatory or an encumbrance, or practical and utilitarian or emotional, these understandings share some common and plausible but unconnected elements that point the way toward the need for a type of unified field theory of nostalgia in the consciousness of immigrants. Each of the authors suggests to one extent or another that individuals must reconcile past and present, and in the process undertake some conscious or semi-conscious course of self-examination that poses the issue of the relevance of the past to the present and to making the future. But they do not explicitly develop the idea of a *process* in which the past may evolve into an asset or a hindrance. Øverland may come closest with his evocation of a common event in immigrant life (writing letters at the close of the day) and the emotions writing letters to distant significant others may evoke. But to the extent this formulation poses the suggestion, as do Barton's and to some extent Fitzgerald's views, that the nostalgic self is somehow not the real or complete self, it poses a metaphysical paradox: *How can we ever be anything but ourselves, no matter how contradictory certain manifestations of ourselves may appear?* That paradox poses a challenge: can we create a model of self-making that is large enough to accommodate a wide, varied and evolving engagement with the past?

In an important analysis of the uses of nostalgia in the forming of immigrant mentalities, the literary scholar Andreea Deciu Ritivoi, herself a Romanian immigrant to the United States, explicitly specifies a model of self that provides a credible framework for a process of trans-formation of the individual consciousness. She offers the outlines of unified field theory of nostalgia that can reconcile some of these contrasting positions. Ritivoi does not explicitly deal with immigrant personal letters but instead looks at fiction and life writings, but probes continually in the service of seeking change and continuity in immigrant self-making at the questions which some of us seek to answer about the psychology of immigrant letter-writers (Ritivoi, 2002). Can we really 'start afresh' in a new place, or do memories of people, places, and events in the past that accompany us continually assert themselves, propelling us back in time, and threatening to divert us from our practical purposes in migrating? If we can indeed start afresh in a new country, is it reasonable to continue to assume that we really do belong someplace? Is *home* a culturally conventionalized, much romanticized notion, or an artifact of something deep within us that begs for the assurance and security of rootedness and belonging? What, in fact, is this *fresh start*, and what role do ongoing negotiations over individual personal identity have in making it possible or impossible? Are our identities dependent on our ability to grow and change, or on a stable and continuous understanding of self, or are both different sides of the same coin?

To answer these questions, Ritivoi begins by noting two conceptions of *self* that have been identified out of Latin usage by the philosopher Paul Ricoeur in his work *Oneself as Another* (Ricoeur, 1992). Ricoeur seeks to understand how we could simultaneously be the self we have been and yet change as life requires us to do. The *other* here is the *who* we change to become while remaining an individual self. Ricoeur distinguishes between two senses of self: *idem* (lit., *the same*), a strong self that is unchanging in its nature, and *ipse* (lit., *self*, as in *himself; herself; itself*), a mutable or changing self without claims to permanence. The former is the self claimed by those who might hold that there is an unchanging core, an *arch-self*, to each of us that can be identified, for example, by the assignment of a trait or a feature (i.e., for example, out-going or inner-directed; ruminative or intuitive; bold or timid, etc.) that is, in effect, what is the *given* in us and always accompanies us in identifying the self who we are. This is the self we might claim for ourselves or others for us, if asked to provide a quick summary of our dominant trait. Or, it may perhaps be the character we would like to claim for ourselves or have others attribute to us. It skates over manifestations of episodic contradictory behavior, such as moments of impulsiveness in an otherwise cautious individual. Such exceptions are every bit as much who we are as our dominant self, but to the extent we believe in the latter, or others believe it about us, the *idem* may become something to value, an ideal. Or, perhaps it may be something that we wish to overcome. The *ipse*, in contrast, is the selves, plural and mutable, that are constructed in a variety of social and cultural contexts. It is well known in postmodern constructions of the individual. It is less a recognition of these seemingly contradictory manifestations of ourselves than of the fact that we are destined to play different, contingent roles in different settings, whether public and private or institutional and informal, according to different expectations and codes of behavior.

While Ricoeur sees these two selves as opposites involved in a contestation to claim the self, for Ritivoi they are, in fact, complementary parts of a dialectical process of growth. In her analysis of immigrant adjustments to the challenges of resettlement recorded in a variety of fictional texts and autobiographies, she seeks to find the balance individuals attain between 'survival', which involves the maintenance of an 'already-existing identity configuration' and change prompted by new circumstances, or, as she puts it in summary, the balance between 'self-reinforcement and self-repudiation' (Ritivoi, 2002, pp. 45–48). Of course, changing with new circumstances is not necessarily literally self-repudiation, but, as immigrants frequently can attest, learning that old habits are dysfunctional may at any given time, even in the most ordinary and fleeting of social circumstances, be experienced as a strong rebuke and embarrassment to oneself.

In the service of establishing a dialectical relationship between the two selves that form the immigrant's changing self-understanding, Ritivoi sees the significance of *nostalgia* as often, though not inevitably, a mechanism of reconciliation. As she explains, 'Nostalgia encourages the immigrant to see the contingent nature of personal identity as a conclusion, rather than a premise, and the search for developing a sense of one's self as a constantly renewed and renewable process.' Nostalgia thus serves immigrants to shape 'the dialectics between the search for continuity and the threat of discontinuity [and] to cover the gap between the then and the now' (Ritivoi, 2002, pp. 30, 170). It is at this point in her analysis, we may join her efforts to our own in seeking to understand the way identities and selves are constituted in personal letters between immigrants and the significant others. Letters often explicitly contain memory of the shared past in one form or another. Of course, implicitly, the act of personal correspondence is itself reclaiming the past through renewing a valued relationship.

The applicability of a concept of *nostalgia* to the immigrant letter may seem like an unnecessary and irrelevant encumbrance, if we conceive of nostalgia exclusively as a romanticization of or a pathological obsession with the past or a situational phenomenon. Certainly for most of its surprisingly long conceptual history, nostalgia was regarded as more or less an illness. It entered literature in 1688, in the University of Basel dissertation of the medical student Johannes Hofer, who brought together, from the Greek, *nostos* (i.e., *return to the native land, or homecoming*) and *algea* (i.e., *pain, suffering* or *grief*) to form an illness that had been observed among members of military organizations stationed far from their homes for long periods of time. Their obsessive dwelling on images of home, Hofer argued, caused an imprinting on their minds of indelible, haunting images that dragged them further and further into despair. In the eighteenth and nineteenth centuries, a number of European analysts delved further into the phenomenon from medical and military points of view. They found soldiers suffering from nostalgia to reject the customs, languages, and foods of the places in which they were stationed, to become despondent, and to manifest such physical symptoms as sleeplessness, physical weakness, declining sensory powers, poor digestion, loss of appetite, and heart palpitations. Unit morale could be deeply affected by this state of mind shared among men in close proximity, and to that extent nostalgia seemed contagious (Hofer, 1688, 1934).[4] In her research on nostalgia and recollection the literary scholar Ann Colley found that in some military installations, soldiers might be subject to discipline for 'singing or whistling tunes that would remind them of home' (Colley, 1998, p. 3) Often, when conventional medical therapies like bleeding failed, the only cure seemed to be sending the ailing man home. During the American Civil War, psychological difficulties found in soldiers, and after the war, among disabled veterans, were commonly ascribed to nostalgia or to a lasting trauma caused initially by nostalgia that had somehow become chronic (Dean, 1997, pp. 1, 26, 116, 128–130). Into the 1950s, even as the concept became increasingly popularly admitted into usage as an idealization of the past, nostalgia also continued to be looked at clinically in the medical and psychological literature not as an emotion like love or fear, but instead as a malady akin to depression (Lowenthal, 1985, pp. 3–13).

In transforming our conception of nostalgia away from these popular, colloquial and medicalized understandings, we are assisted by work beginning in the 1970s of psychologists, sociologists, social psychologists, and literature scholars (Boym, 2001, 2007; Chase & Shaw,

1989; Davis, 1979; Fisher, 1989; Routledge, Sedikides, Wildschut, & Juhl, 2013; Routledge, Wildschut, Sedikides, Juhl, & Arndt, 2012; Routledge et al., 2011; Vess, Arndt, Routledge, Sedikides, & Wildschut, 2012). From the efforts of these analysts, it is possible to abstract an understanding of nostalgia as a non-pathological consciousness of the past offering a type of mediation forming a bridge between past and present and between the immutable self of *idem* and the mutable self of *ipse*.

3.2. Restorative and reflective nostalgia

Given Ritivoi's direction and new views of the functional utility of nostalgia, critical now for our use of *nostalgia* is distinguishing, as the comparative literature scholar Svetlana Boym has done in her examination of the works of literary exiles, between two types – *restorative* and *reflective* – of its manifestations. Out of nostalgia, we may emphasize *nostos*, the return, and come to seek a restoration of lost worlds, usually conceived as veritable Edens, and see anything that blocks that restorative outcome as oppression to be met by resistance, whether psychological or physical, and a source in some of unbearable grief or suffering. This is a vision of the past common to romantic cultural nationalists in modern history, but it is also the common fate of many individuals who, amidst the dislocations of modernity, recapitulate the suffering of those early modern soldiers identified by Hofer, and cannot ever reconcile themselves to their changed circumstances. Here, restoration does not represent a positive step toward wholeness or toward health, as if we had taken a restorative tonic, but instead the opposite: it serves to create a widening gap between past and present that can only prove dysfunctional to the individual in new and greatly changed circumstances. In contrast, what Boym calls *reflective* nostalgia, representing *algea*, may lead us to brood about the past being lost, hence not restorable and inexorably slipping away. We may become melancholic, but also, in direct proportion to a sense of loss, resigned to the necessity of finding a new plane on which to exist (Boym, 2001, 2007; Ritivoi, 2002, p. 32). In this way, immigrants may employ reflective nostalgic memory to reconcile past and present, when it is recognized that not only is the lived past dead and irretrievable except to memory, but that it may somehow also be the basis of building a new future. Memory may function through symbolic representations of the past to provide associations that bridge the gap between past and present. Such symbolic representations as *home, village, orchard, family supper table*, or *Christmas dinner*, common nostalgic references in European immigrant letters, might have challenged immigrant letter-writers to form a new present and future, to build upon rather than simply brood about the loss of the past (Ritivoi, 2002, p. 32). They might accept more easily a new home, village, orchard, family supper table, or Christmas celebration by virtue of compartmentalizing the past as a bygone stage of life, yet building from its imaginative and emotional foundations.

In letters we may see these transformations taking place, and through examining the processes of their writing, we may see immigrants adjusting to new circumstances, while transforming their identities. They do not erase who they were, but rather grow on the foundation of who they have been. Or, we may see them failing to change. I will take the three case studies from the letters I have analyzed in the past to provide examples in two cases of what I regard as examples of proactive, reflective nostalgic memory that leads to change and growth, and a third of a restorative, less functional nostalgia that produced stasis and melancholia. In each example, nostalgia becomes explicitly a part of the composition of the immigrant's personal letter, and inspires the development of a trope or explicit comparisons between the past and present that bring to life in prose the immigrant's mental activity in developing a process for confronting change. The letter functions as a heart-to-heart conversation with a trusted correspondent who is a sounding board for assisting in this process. These immigrants are conscious of being confronted with the question of change, and writing serves what today we would call, to be sure anachronistically in the nineteenth-century context, *therapeutic* purposes for them, whether they accept the need to change or resist it. Whether willing the memory of a nostalgic episode or semi-consciously conjuring up one while writing, the more they write in this vein, I contend, the more they probably help fix themselves in one posture or another. What these modes of writing may explain, in contrast, about literate immigrants who choose not to write personal letters, or those who do write such letters but engage in no explicit reminiscence opens yet another chapter in the analysis of immigrant personal correspondence, but one that cannot be addressed here.

Similarly, the writers' identities do not exist in a sociological void. They intersect with race, religion, ethnicity, age, gender, level of education, and social class, which assist in providing the complex, ramifying totality that is the individual. Intersectionality is suggested here in comparing the three case studies. This seems especially the case with regard to gender, for it is plausible to speculate that the relative powerlessness of women in the form especially of the extent to which immigration decisions might be exclusively controlled by men left women like Mary Cumming and Mary Ann Archbald particularly vulnerable to alienation and regret. But some of the existing research on gender and nostalgia actually disagrees dramatically on the validity of such speculation, as a significant debate between Charles Zwingmann and Fred Davis makes clear. Zwingmann, who studied nostalgia among contemporary immigrants in the 1970s, for example advanced the plausible hypothesis that women did indeed suffer nostalgia more than men. Men, he argued, pick up their trades and professions and lose themselves quickly in their public role as breadwinners and its usual routines, while women experience isolation at home and lose the web of relationships to other women they knew in their homelands (Zwingmann, 1973, p. 29). Davis argued the exact opposite: women have suffered less, because the familiar circumstances of marriage, home, children, and kin remain the same in both old and new worlds, while men, such as the surgeon who cannot obtain a medical license in a new land and thus is working as a parking lot attendant, experience greater discontinuities in status and roles (Davis, 1979, pp. 54–55). As we shall shortly see, neither of these neat propositions speaks to the complex states of mind of Cumming, Hartley, and Archbald, all of whom seem to suggest the necessity of a move toward more elaborate theorization of gender in the context of nostalgia that is not possible here. Intersectionality and nostalgia must remain on the agenda of further explorations of identity and consciousness of a personal past.

4. Mary Craig Cumming

For the sake of contrast to those manifesting reflective nostalgia, we begin with the example of Mary Craig Cumming (1790–1815), whose brooding, self-identified homesickness and restorative nostalgia weighed heavily on her mind, and became a regular feature of her personal letters to her principal correspondent and best friend, her older sister Margaret. In 1811 Mary Craig, the daughter of an Ulster clergyman, married William Cumming, a prosperous Irish-born tobacco, flour and cotton merchant employed by a wealthy cousin at

Petersburg, Virginia. They met when William was in Ireland for some months visiting his parents. She was 20 years old; William seems to have been somewhat older. Mary Cumming had never before left her home, Strawberry Hill near Lisburn in Ulster, before accompanying her husband to Virginia. It seems that she had an understanding with Cumming that they would eventually return to Ireland permanently. The couple was to reside in Virginia for no more time than William imagined it would take to be able to settle his business affairs there on favorable terms, and transfer his interests to Ireland. Though Mary anticipated a timely return to Ireland, this did not occur because the War of 1812 interfered with travel back to Britain and disrupted the tobacco trade.[5] While we must take William at his word, the settling of his business affairs, including taking enough money out of them to set him up for life as a wealthy merchant and member of the Irish rural gentry, was a complex matter, and it is not clear how easily it might have been accomplished. The war aside, therefore, it would not have been a surprise, if Mary had had to stay longer in Virginia than she planned.

She had every reason to be disappointed, however, and perhaps to lapse into a melancholic state of mind, even as she knew the war would eventually end, and travel and business across the Atlantic would be restored. Of course, other immigrants encountered similar frustrations, from many different types of circumstances, in realizing their initial plans to return to their homelands, and often ended up giving up on those plans after a period of calculating the gains and losses of staying where they had resettled. Mary's nostalgic longing, on the other hand, seems over-determined. Whatever there was ultimately in Mary Cumming's character and temperament that made it impossible for her to become reconciled cannot be determined easily, if at all. We certainly are not in a confident position to apply the categories that come out of latter-day psychoanalytic or clinical psychological theories of personality development to understand her.

What is clear is that from the very beginning of her leave-taking from Ireland she began to develop a nagging longing for the people and places that she would soon identify in a letter as 'maladie du pays', i.e., homesickness.[6] It becomes manifest in her first letters to Margaret, even before she arrives in America, when she is crossing the Irish Sea and then briefly resident in England, awaiting passage across the ocean. She relates reliving the agony of her departure, and experiences the emotions of leave-taking. She hastened to tell her sister on two occasions that each time she ended a letter to her, she experienced a painful spasm of the memory of those final moments in Ireland. 'Do you know', she wrote, 'it is like a second parting with you for me to quit writing?' Thereafter, the letters, through newly composed images wrought by nostalgia or through the memory of recently experienced nostalgic thoughts, are frequently the site for sharing episodes of nostalgia and relating homesickness.[7] At first her evaluations of the prospects of her new life were positive. But, after a several months in Petersburg, where from the beginning of her residence she had a large and well-appointed house, servants (actually, to Mary's discomfort, African American slaves), and a garden, and neighbors she found congenial (including a number of Irish-born and Irish American residents), opportunities for a rich social life including election to the Board of Trustees of the elite Female Orphan Asylum, and enjoyed the affections of a doting husband in a companionate marriage, she recorded a series of intrusive, involuntary associations with her home in Ireland. They were caused, for example, by the rain beating against the window pane, and they prompted nostalgic daydreaming. She found opportunities frequently to compare Ireland and Virginia to the detriment of the latter. To some extent, she became isolated by the war, because she favored the British side, and had to avoid conversations with her patriotic American neighbors, but she also isolated herself to the extent American ways, including Irish American ways, seemed inferior to her. She refused to attend the large annual St Patrick's Day ball, put on by the town's Irish Americans, because Irish folk dances were slighted in favor of American dances.[8]

Mary herself would invent a trope for her nostalgic daydreams of Ireland and her family and for the imagined scenes that would attend her reunion with her loved ones. She referred to them in her letters as 'castlebuilding', a striking image of defensive security and self-enclosure for her spontaneous nostalgic reveries or those conjured-up nostalgic ruminations composed in her letters to Margaret. Castlebuilding appears to have been an old habit of mind, perhaps in her girlhood providing a rich fantasy life of romantic possibilities. Now, Mary's *castles* functioned to fuse past and present to the extent that she mobilized restorative images of her Irish home and family from the past to provide the backdrop for her return to Ireland. She wrote her sister in 1814 that though thus far disappointed in her plan to return to Ireland, '… I still continue to have the same fondness for castlebuilding which I formerly had[;] indeed it is the source of great amusement to me in planning my return to my beloved home once more.' A few months later, she used the same metaphor for her hopes again, and spoke of how often she was consumed by this fusion of nostalgia and projection forward in time. 'I will not be satisfied till we are all once more under the same roof,' she wrote Margaret. 'Many is the castle I build. I hope they will not all prove without foundation.'[9]

This stream of consciousness daydreaming, which might well have been a sort of *idem* accompanying her to the New World, could be pleasant, but it was also the cause of anxiety for her. Just as her nostalgic daydreams might sometimes bring her 'great amusement', these fantasies could also cause her insomnia, she wrote on another occasion, as her mind raced forward in time to all that needed to be done in preparation for her removal from Virginia and relocation at Strawberry Hill, which was an imagined materialization of the castle Mary built in her nostalgic reveries. Of the prospect of a return home to Ireland, she wrote, 'I think of it during the day, and at night it almost prevents me from sleeping.'[10]

There seems little doubt that she brooded a great deal about leaving Virginia and about reunion. Even before the war was over, when fighting still raged on American soil, Mary daydreamed of the moments of saying farewell to now familiar American places and people around her in Petersburg.[11] In addition to stoking her anxiety about the length of her American residence, though she claimed to be sustained by her Christian faith, her daydreams probably reinforced the sadness that attended the death of her first-born and shortly thereafter, a miscarriage late in her second pregnancy. Sadly, one of the castles she had built, before the death of her first-born, was a vision of being at Strawberry Hill standing beside her father who has her baby daughter in his arms. 'I live', she had written Margaret in 1812 on the occasion of experiencing this restorative image in her mind, 'in the sweet hope of one day having [this] realized.'[12]

Mary would not live to return home to her family. In one of her frequently made comparisons to the detriment of North America, the relative health of Ireland, she was incontestably correct. The city of Petersburg was long identified as an unhealthy place, with an especially high infant mortality rate, where fevers raged in the poorly drained environs of the Appomattox River, which bordered the town.[13] Weakened by the effects of her two pregnancies and the heroic medical therapies of bleeding, blistering, and salivating used to treat the fevers from which she suffered, Mary Cumming died in 1815 shortly after the war ended. Toward the end, she wrote as a Christian that the reunion she had frequently anticipated in her castlebuilding reveries would now occur in the life beyond.[14]

Again, we cannot know why Mary Cumming was unable to transform her longing for the past into engagement with the present and planning for future. Nor should we leave as our judgment of her that she was simply weak, immature, and neurotic, and hence, not equal to the circumstances she willingly entered. A diagnosis of those we barely know, dead for nearly two centuries, is hardly a credible practice. What is clear is that she was not capable of transforming her restorative nostalgic brooding into positive reflective energies to propel her forward into a new life.

5. Joseph Hartley

Mary Cumming thus stands in sharp contrast to Joseph Hartley (1838–1876), an English stonecutter resettled in Lockport in northwestern New York State, who, though he also had a tragically shortened life, accomplished that transformation effectively, thanks in significant part to his capacity for reflective nostalgia. In correspondence with family members in England between his emigration in 1858 and his death from a lung disease common to quarry workers and stonecutters,[15] Joseph alone and eventually in letters written by his wife Rebecca that were the couple's collaborative production, blended together the imagery of past and present. In so doing, he used nostalgia as a vehicle for embedding himself in a new identity that helped him to negotiate a new way of living.[16] Joseph Hartley was no older and probably no more experienced in the world beyond his village than Mary Cumming when he left his home at Brighouse in Yorkshire in 1858, and he, too, probably had never traveled beyond the village in which he was born. Like Mary, he emigrated in the context of family. She had her husband, and Hartley emigrated with cousins as well as friends. Like Mary, Joseph resettled in a cultural environment in which he was partly surrounded by people who were familiar, if not necessarily through personal relations then through common regional and national origins. Stonecutters from the Brighouse area had been engaged in transnational labor circuits between Yorkshire and New York State quarries for almost three decades when Hartley arrived, and the towns, such as Lockport, involved in the stone industry area had a resident English ethnic population, with its own social networks and Methodist churches (Gerber, 2009, pp. 14–16, 22).

While gendered options for self-determination doubtless presented Hartley with greater opportunities to control his fate, in numerous ways Hartley and Cumming had much contextually and situationally that made their histories similar. This included, too, the expectation that immigration was not a permanent situation. In Hartley's case there was no definite plan to return, but he kept that option open in his mind for some time, and fluctuated between giving it consideration and backing away from it in the belief that he could not live as well in England as he could in the United States. He would only return to England, he said, if he could set himself up permanently in a situation in which he would not have to depend on his wages to support himself. Meanwhile, he fused the vision he had of the future, which was built on the quarrymen's experience and work culture in England, with American opportunities, and, accepting what he believed to be manageable debt, was able to buy a house and the land adjacent to it for use as a small farm, and enjoyed a good life on his own terms in the short time that he had before he died. Joseph, Rebecca, and their four children were integrated into the English ethnic culture in the area. They attended a

Wesleyan Methodist church alongside other English residents, with whom they socialized (Gerber, 2009, pp. 22–25).

Realistic and pragmatic habits of mind, Hartley's *idem*, facilitated his transition. In early letters home to siblings, cousins, uncles, and aunts, he wrote of his difficulties resettling in America, in which he experienced spasms of nostalgia and brooding homesickness. These early years taught him a lesson he would not forget. He had come to America to take advantage of its promises of freedom and opportunity. But he learned from these early bouts of unemployment and poverty that America was a free country in so far as, he explained in 1859, 'when you have no munny you can goe with out'. In other words, you were free to starve. Hartley did not forget this lesson, and much of his life in America was spent protecting himself against a reversal of fortune caused by the fluctuations in the general economy and the dangers and cycles of the industry in which he was employed. But in the midst of his early difficulties, he was still able to say that it was possible that, on balance, life in America, while not perfect, might offer him better prospects than life in the quarries of Yorkshire. His bitter insights into the life of American workmen did not stop him from planning deliberately for his future, while immersing himself in an ethnic way of life that embodied what he could reconstruct of the world of his past, and thus dealing proactively with his nostalgia and homesickness. The same habits of mind were apparent in an 1861 letter to a cousin, in which he explained the decision to get married, a decision that also placed him in the position to accept the fact that his resettlement might well be permanent, even if the question remained not completely settled in his mind throughout the rest of his life. His employer, who was lacking currency in the midst of the late 1850s economic recession, could not pay him wages, but asked him if he would accept land instead. Hartley explained matter-of-factly, 'I tought I woad And put A hous on it then get Marred and [settle] down.' He continued, 'I think I can keep A wife ass chep as pai board.'[17]

But it was the variety of ways in which he cultivated simultaneously his *ipse*, and creatively fused his homesickness and nostalgia with the ongoing negotiation of his new American life that must claim our attention here. Hartley understood it was necessary for him to change if he was to fulfill his evolving aspirations to improve himself. The letters record his awareness of what he referred to in various letters as 'home sickness' and being 'home sick' among immigrant workmen, and early in his resettlement described experiencing it himself.[18] He longed for the familiar occasions and landscapes of his English home and for his English kin. But he understood the dangers in that type of nostalgia, both for himself and for immigrants in general. In the immigrants around him, he recognized homesickness, brooding obsessively over the past, as counter-productive to making a new life; it served, he said, to make them feel listless and lazy, and thus deepened their inability to help themselves.[19]

Of course, Hartley would not have thought of one of the methods, a combination of comparison and analogy expressed in personal correspondence, by which he combated such restorative nostalgia in himself, as *therapeutic*. He was probably only semi-consciously aware that he was involved in a process of self-guided adjustment when he confronted his need to come to terms with being away from Brighouse on symbolic occasions, such as holidays, which formed significant points in marking his distance from the past. His own letters and the collaborative letters he later wrote with Rebecca record a complex process of analogizing past and present, and employing the pleasant memories of the former to enhance the making and sustaining of new traditions. They created a way of bridging the gap between past and present in a way that was impossible for Mary Cumming to do, and personal correspondence with his kinfolk was a key element in developing the imaginative capacity to do so.

This process for dealing with the past was present in one of his earliest letters, shortly after arriving in the United States. Hartley was feeling nostalgic. In response to an inquiry relayed to him in a family letter, in which a local woman had asked his family members if Joseph had already forgotten her, he wrote his aunt and cousin, '... I shall never forget Brighous ... nor none of them that live there.'[20] But shortly thereafter, in the same letter, he indirectly made reference to a mental process by which he was already developing a dual time frame for analogizing past and present. Rushbearing (or, *Rushbiren/Ruchbiren*, as he referred to it) is a folk festival still celebrated in Lancashire and Yorkshire, and was apparently a much-anticipated part of the calendar at Brighouse when Hartley was growing up there (Littleborough Events & Associations, 2013). Its origins date from the tenth century, when Pope Gregory decreed that rushes should be brought to churches on their individual saint's days to cover the cold floor and serve as insulation. A procession of the faithful bearing rushes to church, in the specially decorated carts transporting some of them there, was attended apparently with behavior raucous enough that later in the nineteenth century the holiday was intermittently banned for giving rise to 'drunkenness and lewd behavior'. At Brighouse and some other towns in the region, Rushbearing was celebrated in early July, prompting Joseph to write, 'I should like to now what kind of Rushbiren you have had and wether it rain or not[.] we had our Ruchbiren on the 4 of July.'[21] Whether or not Hartley exclusively celebrated either Rushbearing (raucous or religious) or the American Fourth of July, or along with other Yorkshire workingmen and their families created some fusion of the two, we cannot know. But he must have been conscious from the Americans enthusiastically celebrating their national holiday around him that old and new traditions were threading their way through his mind, and that the pleasure he took in the English tradition could help elevate his mood for the American one.

Christmas and the inception of the New Year served similar purposes. When he was newly arrived in the United States and living a very spare existence boarding with other immigrant workingmen, he lamented ironically 'that all the Christmas we had' was watching a local mill burn down.[22] Hartley enjoyed a good-natured celebration and genial company, so he must have felt this deprivation deeply. Even in his first difficult years in America, he sought opportunities to socialize. He journeyed to nearby Niagara Falls to watch, with thousands of others, the French tightrope walker Blondin traverse the chasm just below the falls. The next year, during the 1860 presidential election campaign, with no apparent interest in the election's issues and unable to vote because he had not declared the intention to become a naturalized citizen, he nonetheless participated in the local Republican Party Wide Awake's nightly, torchlight parades. Pleased to be given an 'oil Cloth sute' to wear for the occasion, he declared, 'i tell you we have grate fun.'[23] Hartley's choices functioned variously to further his tentative American civic integration.

Once he and Rebecca set up their own household and began to have children, he was determined to celebrate holidays in a style equal to what the occasion had meant to him in England. He wished his kin holiday greetings in January 1868, noting they had entertained friends for New Year with roast beef and plum pudding, and also killed one of their pigs, as they would do annually, for their table. He continued, 'Now we wish you all a happy new year and plenty of money and plenty of beer and a good fat pig[.] we have pig and beer.'[24] Later that year, anticipating Christmas, the couple imagined, in daydreaming fashion, a holiday reunion with their English family: '... nothing would give us moor [pleasure] than to take a peep at you all this Christmas and have a good sing with you ...'[25] 'What a joy it wold be', they wrote in 1870, 'and pleashure it wold give us if we could all meet at one table on Christmas day.'[26] This was Joseph's memory work, nostalgic reveries in which he embedded the present and future in a fondly remembered past. Meanwhile, he and Rebecca experienced multiple tables at which they ate their roast beef and Yorkshire pudding or their pork roast and drank their beer. They organized the same festivities, inviting English neighbors and kinfolk around them in Western New York to celebrate with them, while again imaginatively projecting simultaneously themselves across the ocean, as they said in another letter in 1870, to 'take a peepe at you all this Christmas'.[27] Though he would die within the decade, Hartley's capacity for reflective nostalgia, which provided a means to reconcile past and present, had propelled him in the last years of his life into greater peace with his new circumstances in the United States.

6. Mary Ann Archbald

Another example of reflective nostalgia embedded in the practice of letter-writing may be found in the letters of Mary Ann Wodrow Archbald (1762–1840). She was married with four children when she very reluctantly agreed with the plan that her husband, James, put before her about emigrating. The deterioration of their economic prospects as independent farmers and wool raisers on Little Cumbrae Island in western Scotland's Firth of Clyde left them no choice but to take what was left of their assets and resettle in the United States. Victims of the familiar processes of modernization of the countryside that saw the death of an old, comfortable if modest and mostly stable way of life, she and James were especially concerned about the prospects for the lives of the children, whose downward mobility seemed assured, if the couple stayed in Scotland. Emigration meant leaving behind her aged mother and her dearest and lifelong friend, a cousin Margaret Wodrow, with whom she had grown up, and often lived in the same house. The women were, in fact, more sisters than cousins. Mary Ann's own nuclear family was disrupted by ill-health and, according to family oral tradition, the alcoholism of her father. Her father had been a Presbyterian minister, for whom residence on Little Cumbrae was a type of forced retirement and retreat organized, or insisted upon, by the Church of Scotland, in which a number of the Archbald men had long served, some famously, in the clergy. (The family contained men in distant generations who heroically resisted suppression of the Church of Scotland, and one Archbald who was the pioneer historian of the church.) Margaret's supportive mother and father, who was also a Church of Scotland minister, were resident on the mainland of western Scotland in a preacher's manse, a second home that Mary Ann would remember as, during her girlhood, a place of peace and stability in the midst of the difficulties of her own birth family. Yet she never lost affection for what she called 'the little isle', the wild, windswept place with a commanding view of the firth on which her family suffered a kind of exile, and from which she would be exiled by impersonal economic forces. The island would be nostalgically imagined as an 'abode of peace, of comfort, and friendly intercourse'. Indeed the *little isle*, a usage frequently appearing in her letters, was a central symbol summarizing her bouts of nostalgia and homesickness and the recollections of the past. It functioned in her imagination in a way that *castles* did in Mary Cumming's (Gerber, 1998, 2006, pp. 281–308).[28]

Archbald and Cumming have in common their lesser power, as women involved in marriages to men endowed with the power to make decisions for their spouses. In her letters to Margaret Wodrow from the central New York farm with a commanding view of the valley of the Mohawk River on which the Archbald family settled, she expressed many of the same sharp spasms of regretful, restorative nostalgic feelings as Mary Cumming had about leaving her friend and her family and the tranquil, lovely setting in which she had lived, and vowed someday to return to resume her old life. She, too, in fact, found her ties to her homeland and the prospects of re-emigration, or at least a return visit, disrupted early in her life in America by the War of 1812, and experienced that separation as acutely painful. That *someday* would never occur. Archbald never visited Scotland again, and she died on the farm in central New York State that she and James created (Gerber, 2006, pp. 284–285, 293–294).

Her remarkable correspondence with Margaret Wodrow, however, went on over three decades to the end of her life. It was a forum for her to rehearse the disappointments of her life, the principal one of which was being forced by circumstances about which she remained bitter to leave her home, and to engage in recollections of the childhood the two women had shared. Mary Ann took great pride in the national prestige and intellectual heritage of the Archbald family, and was herself not only educated (largely self-taught and informally tutored), but extensively intellectually self-cultivated through reading and diary writing. She complained especially bitterly about her, to her mind, coarse German and genially thoughtless American neighbors, whose interests ranged no further than farming and moneymaking, and about the middling cultural standards and self-congratulatory patriotism of Americans in general. She complained frequently enough about both her emigration and the circumstances of her American life, that she admitted to Margaret that the letter she was writing, like others in the past, was 'of the croaking order', a continual and unbalanced complaint (Gerber, 2006, pp. 302–303).[29]

In contrast to Hartley's immersion in the English ethnic group in Lockport and Cumming's somewhat distant but at times fond relation to the local Irish, she did not seek Scottish company as relief from dealing with her neighbors. She preferred to idealize the Scots from a distance, and did not require an ethnic community to sustain her nostalgic memories. She held the mirror of a superior Scotland of her nostalgic imagination up to America as often as she could – so often, in fact, that she invited resistance from Margaret, who seems to have sought from time to time to remind her that the Scots were, after all, ordinary human beings. In doing so, Wodrow may well have helped her friend question her own nostalgic memories. In 1821 and again in 1822, she reported scandals that wracked western Scotland, the first involving a corrupt lawyer and then, second, some sexual transgression. Mary Ann, who was deeply disturbed by both scandals, was forced on the occasion of hearing of the second scandal to admit that her bitterness about their emigration aside,

> Amidst all my care and regrets about my native land still I could indulge in the fond dream of its being superior to every other country upon earth and when I meet here with instances of avarice and chicanery I say with James, 'it is just like the Yankees – how different the people at home.' I did not think these same people at home perfect whilst I was among them but absence was like death[;] their faults were buried or softened and their good qualities only remembered. (Gerber, 2006, pp. 306–307)

[30] This telling exchange offers the possibility that one antidote for restorative nostalgia was the frank criticism of those with whom one corresponded, a possibility that is not suggested in either the Cumming or the Hartley letters.

All the while, the Archbalds succeeded in farm-making, insured a better future for their children, and became members of the local community. A devout, if understated, Christian she regularly attended a local church, in whose graveyard she and James are buried. In her way, she integrated herself into the life around her. Her deep skepticism about the society in which she lived did not stop her from taking part in efforts to improve it. She wrote letters to the local newspaper in behalf of the participation of women in local affairs, and she petitioned Governor Dewitt Clinton in behalf of some Irish canal laborers she believed, correctly as it turned out, to have been falsely accused of a crime. She took great pride in the American accomplishments of a son who was a self-taught engineer. She recognized that her children's lives were destined to be spent in the United States. Like Hartley's rather comic entrance into the 1860 presidential election campaign, Mary Ann Archbald's more serious civic activities served further to integrate her somewhat into a society from which she might have been inclined to isolate herself (Gerber, 2006, pp. 303–307).[31]

In light of her lifelong engagement with language, we would expect that Archbald's letters to Margaret Wodrow were not simply well composed and literate, but often inventive in their use of imagery and figurative writing. She was an ambitious letter-writer, who aspired not only to report, but to create an epistolary commune of souls that united the two women in what they most desired, an intimate conversation. At no time was this more obvious than in an annual New Year's Eve letter she wrote to Margaret for approximately 10 years. Usually composed after the family had returned to their farm from a party in their neighborhood, or had ended their own celebration, the letter was part of a ritual that Archbald consciously and explicitly understood to be conjuring up a nostalgic mood in which to relive the past. This strategy for imagining the past complemented other sorts of nostalgic reveries during the same years – nocturnal dreams and daydreams that were less voluntary, also deeply impressed Archbald. In 1817, she wrote Margaret, that, after a storm, the sound of water running in the small creek behind her farmhouse suddenly had reminded her of the surf at the beach at Little Cumbrae, and in 1822, while briefly quite ill, she recorded a dream in another letter to her cousin, in which she was in Scotland searching for her friend.[32]

The New Year's Eve act of invention was quite ritualized. Her planning the composition of the letter began in her mind before midnight, and then not long after midnight, by candlelight at a desk in the farmhouse's central room where Margaret's portrait hung facing her as she wrote, with upstate New York's arctic winter and fields of snow just beyond the door, Archbald began a long letter. She sometimes then worked on it for days, or even months to the extent it was difficult for her to post her letters in the midst of the isolation that winter imposed before the coming of the railroad. What mattered was that it was begun at the New Year, so that she could begin the letter by conjuring up nostalgic memory and warm feelings of the many New Year's celebrations she could remember spending with her cousin at her uncle's manse on the mainland. While the letter was not all romantic or brooding nostalgia, and contained news, gossip, and the usual complaints about her circumstances, its initial section invoked a feeling of the past. As she explained at the beginning of her 1824 letter, 'Once more I am permitted to end the year with you and fain would I for a little while lose the present in the past.' The mood was further deepened as she pictured in her mind herself and her cousin, uncle and aunt, and others anticipating the New Year long ago when she was a girl: '… the happy group seated around the parlor table in the Manse and waiting till 12 would strike …'. After a decade, this epistolary ritual suddenly and apparently without explanation ended, though correspondence between the two women continued (Gerber, 2006, pp. 298–301).[33] Perhaps by that time, Archbald's need for nostalgic reveries had declined, and she had become reconciled to her new circumstances.

The function for Archbald of the nostalgic occasion of this annual letter seems clear. It served to assist her in the transition between the *idem* that she had been and the *ipse* she needed to become. On the one hand, there was the girl who had lived in the romantic setting of a windswept island and possessed the cultural ambitions to improve her mind, but whose story was nonetheless ultimately that of a variety of losses. On the other hand, there was the woman she was of necessity, a farmwife and mother in a faraway place she did not much like, but represented nonetheless what she reluctantly had to admit was best for her family. Like Joseph Hartley, only more so because of her high degree of literacy, in her letter-writing she achieved a healing union of the two selves that helped reconcile her to the future.

7. Conclusion

Consciousness of the past and of the experience of change, as individual immigrant subjects knew and used their own existential categories to understand it, has not been a major priority on the agenda of the social history of immigration. The legacy of the once hegemonic New Social History of the late decades of the twentieth century has been to conceive of immigrants as tightly bound by *group* solidarities and as endlessly resilient, gaining strength from the force of their ambitions for self-improvement and from the families, ethnicities and communities they formed in the lands in which they came to resettle. Later, this positive vision of empowerment would be adjusted and extended by the diasporic imagination, which has understood the immigrant's resources as not simply national, but international and transnational such that group, community, and family might become empowered on a global stage.

Such immigration history has added enormously to our knowledge of why immigration projects quite often succeed in material and group social terms, but it never has been able systematically to address the deeper psychological recesses of the stories of individuals caught up in the same processes of change. It ceded little to the possibility that its positivity glossed over the otherwise widely and anecdotally reported difficulties that individuals in the historical past had accepting such large changes as leaving their homes and families, even when they opted to do so. To this extent, in contrast to filmmakers and novelists who have often captured the complexities of immigrant mentalities, historians have not possessed a realistic psychology of immigration and resettlement, for in their work individuals get lost amidst the presumed triumph of the mass.

If we aspire to write a history of lived experience, however, we must adjust our analytical framework. In this effort, the concept of nostalgia, which possesses its own meandering intellectual history, proves a significant resource for examining the individual at this juncture of memory, self and identity, and relationships with significant others. Reading the letters of immigrants, with an eye to interrogating their efforts at self-making in the service of reconciling past and present, provides an occasion for knowing the immigrants at the intimate level at which they sought to know themselves.

Notes

1. In this essay, I cite my own work in discussing the history of personal correspondence and the theorization of that history. When citing specific letters and letter-series analyzed in my published work, however, I make reference to the original letters in their published or archived forms, and not to my published analysis of them.

2. To cite Handlin's *The Uprooted* after the critical pounding it has taken over the course of the last 50 years is to risk not being taken seriously by one's peers. For all of its errors and overstatements and such failures of perspective as deeply emotionally wrought but uncritical extrapolations from personal history, it nonetheless has a point – the inner difficulties faced by individual immigrants in electing to leave their homelands amidst the pressures of modernizing economies and cultural modernity – that has always needed understanding, and has for too long been off the agenda of historical studies. *The Uprooted* is a resource that needs rediscovery in the service of a more rounded social history of immigration.

3. My definitions of *homesickness* and *nostalgia* differ significantly from the most recent and comprehensive *historical treatment* of the subject done by an Americanist; see Matt (2011). Matt devotes significant space to international migrants, but I believe errs on casting too wide a conceptual net for homesickness in their case, conceiving of a number of complex phenomena, such as ethnic neighborhoods or re-emigration, as homesickness (Matt, 2011, pp. 141–175, 238–247). She also errs, I believe, in conceiving of homesickness and nostalgia as apart from one another to the extent the latter is conceived as a mental state that represents a successful and progressive resolution of homesickness (Matt, 2011, p. 171).

4. For discussions of the history of nostalgia and research on nostalgia in the more distant past, see Naqvi (2007), Rosen (1975), Starobinski (1966); one of the earliest medical observations of nostalgia in English (of a Welsh soldier stationed in the north of England and suffering far from his home) is Hamilton (1787).

5. There is published edition of Mary Craig Cumming's letters home to her Irish family (Irvine, 1982). This collection is based on the archives collection (T1475/2) at the Public Record Office of Northern Ireland (PRONI), at Belfast, Northern Ireland. There are a total of 20 letters (1811–1815) in the collection, some to her father and to her brother, but the great majority to her sister, and they are faithfully edited and included in the published collection. We cannot, of course, know whether these are the only letters Mary wrote to her family in Ireland. In this essay, I cite the archived originals, as the true and unedited documents. For Mary's family history and biography prior to emigration, see Irvine (1982, pp. 5–7).

6. Mary Cumming to Margaret, 31 March 1812, T1475/2, PRONI.

7. Mary Cumming to Margaret, 30 August 1811, 22 September 1811, T1475/2, PRONI.

8. Mary Cumming to Margaret, 24 February 1812, 24 April 1812, 26 May 1812, 24 June 1812, 17 November 1812, 9 March 1814, 4 June 1814 and Mary Cumming to Father, 6 December 1811, T1475/2, PRONI. On her decision not to attend the ball, Mary Cumming to Margaret, 10 March 1813, T1475/2, PRONI.

9. Mary Cumming to Margaret, 9 March 1814, 4 June 1814, T1475/2, PRONI. It is a bitter irony that Mary might well have returned to Ireland only to find that after her years in Virginia, both Ireland and she herself had changed, and that the place there she so desperately coveted no longer existed. She might even have come to lament the loss of her American life. Both responses, a type of dual alienation, and in an acute form *placelessness*, were a not uncommon experiences among re-emigrants (Matt, 2011, pp. 170–175).

10. Mary Cumming to Margaret, 9 March 1814, 4 June 1814, T1475/2, PRONI.

11. Mary Cumming to Margaret, 4 June 1814, T1475/2, PRONI.

12. Mary Cumming to Margaret, 26 May 1812, PRONI.

13. On Petersburg in the years Mary Cumming resided there see Scott and Wyatt (1998, pp. 24, 41); Lebstock (1984, pp. 4, 160).

14. Mary Cumming to Margaret, 14 October 1814, 17 November 1814, 9 February 1815, T1475/2, PRONI. Mary's last letter, written in 1815, was sent from Baltimore, where she had gone to seek medical care, as her condition deteriorated. William was not with her, and hence her last

letter was sent to him; Mary Cumming to William, 24 March 1815, T1475/2, PRONI. She urged William, 'Go to our native land, there you will find peace. Talk to my beloved friends of me. Tell them we will meet in a better world. If I can I will hover round and bless you wherever you go.' Perhaps then Mary also saw herself still returning, as a spirit, to Ireland.

15. For transcriptions of the original Hartley letters, see Drake (1964, pp. 222–264), numbering 27 letters ([1858–1876?]; two written by Rebecca Hartley after Joseph's death). Endnote references to individual Hartley letters and the page numbers in parenthesis following the letter references are to Drake's (1964) edition. I have written about Hartley in the context of these letters and of the meanings he attached to his resettlement in the United States (Gerber, 2009, pp. 7–33). In this essay, I cite this published work in discussing Hartley, unless quoting directly from or referring explicitly to his letters.

   There is an ambiguity about the identity of those addressed in these letters that reflects on who the significant others were that Hartley sought to stay connected with through correspondence. In the early years, they are sent to 'aunt' and 'cousin', but whether these are always same people is not clear. When the more comfortably literate Rebecca Hartley takes over the chore of writing from her husband, the letters are now addressed to 'brothers and sisters' or some variation on that formulation. Because tone and theme in the letters do not change, I believe these to be the same people that Hartley was writing at the start of the correspondence, and that Hartley did not, in fact, for some unknown reason, correspond with his own nuclear family. Rebecca Hartley felt more comfortable addressing his family in the fond and familiar 'brothers and sisters' than the more distant 'cousins'.

16. Hartley did not like writing letters, most probably because he struggled with his limited technical skills. In January, 1868, he gave up the struggle, and henceforth his wife Rebecca wrote letters to his English family. These letters were signed with some variation on 'Rebecca and Joseph', replacing the previous 'Joseph Hartley'. Internal evidence indicates that these letters were collaborative in their authorship. Rebecca frequently wrote in the voice of Joseph, who appears to have been in the room while she wrote. The likelihood that the letters were collaborative is, of course, increased by the fact that they were written to Joseph's family and kin, whom Rebecca had never met and would need his help addressing (Gerber, 2009, pp. 11–12).

17. Joseph Hartley to Hant and Cussen, 15 April 1859 (p. 230); Joseph Hartley to Cusen, 27 August 1861 (p. 235).

18. Joseph Hartley to Hant and Cousen, 3 May 1860 (p. 232). In this, Hartley mocked contemporary commentators, whose gendered explanations of homesickness among British immigrants supposed that it was largely a female malady. As Matt suggests, it is possible that expressions of resentment of immigration decisions made by husbands and fathers in their behalf seemed to these commentators to be symptoms of longing for home rather than a plausible complaint about unequal power relations between men and women (Matt, 2011, pp. 55–56).

19. Joseph Hartley to Sisters, 18 June 1866 (p. 239); Joseph Hartley to Brothers and Sisters, 5 January 1868 (p. 240).

20. Joseph Hartley to Hant and Cusen, 12 September 1858 (p. 227).

21. Joseph Hartley to Hant and Cousen, 29 December 1858 (pp. 227–228).

22. Joseph Hartley to Hant and Cousen, 29 December 1858 (p. 229).

23. Joseph Hartley to Hont and Cusen, 21 October 1860 (p. 234).

24. Joseph Hartley to Brothers and Sister, 5 January 1868 (p. 241).

25. Unsigned [probably Joseph and Rebecca Hartley] to Sister and Brother, 12 December [1868] (p. 246).

26. Rebecca and Joseph to Sisters and Brothers, 12 December [1870] (p. 248).

27. Rebecca and Joseph to Sisters and Brothers, [December] 1870 (p. 250).

28. The originals of the Archbald letters are in the History of Women Collection (HoWC), Smith College, Northampton, Massachusetts. There are 46 letters written over 33 years (1807–1840) in the Archbald correspondence. We have no way of knowing whether this is the sum-total of the correspondence, though it seems doubtful there were not more letters than have been preserved. For the characterization of the Little Cumbrae, see, Mary Ann Archbald to Mr McFarlane, January 1817 (HoWC).

29. Mary Ann Wodrow Archbald to Margaret Wodrow, 7 May 1830 (HoWC).

30. Mary Ann Wodrow Archbald to Margaret Wodrow, 10 August 1822 (HoWC).
31. Mary Ann Wodrow Archbald to editor, *Montgomery Republican*, 1818 (or 1820); and Mary Ann Archbald to Governor Dewitt Clinton, October, 1821 (HoWC).
32. Mary Ann Wodrow Archbald to Margaret Wodrow, 1817, and 13 January 1822.
33. Mary Ann Wodrow Archbald to Margaret Wodrow, 31 December 1824 (HoWC).

Disclosure statement

No potential conflict of interest was reported by the author.

References

Barton, H. A. (1979). Editor's corner: Two versions of the immigrant experience. *Swedish-American Historical Quarterly, 30*, 159–161.

Barton, H. A. (1983). Swedish Americans and the Old Country, Kungliga Humanistika Vetenkaps-Sanfundet I Uppsala, Arbok, 1981–1982, 133–134. Uppsala.

Bodnar, J. (1985). *The transplanted: A history of immigrants in urban America*. Bloomington, IN: Indiana University Press.

Boym, S. (2001). *The future of nostalgia*. New York, NY: Basic Books.

Boym, S. (2007). Nostalgia and its discontents. Retrieved from http://www.iasc-culture.org/2007_10/9.2cBoympdf

Bruner, J. (1990). *Acts of meaning*. Cambridge: Harvard University Press.

Bruner, J. (1997). A narrative model of self-construction. *Annals of the New York Academy of Sciences, 818*, 145–161.

Cameron, W., Haines, S., & McDougall Maude, M. (Eds.). (2000). *English immigrant voices: Labourers' letters from upper Canada in the 1830s*. Montreal and Kingston: McGill- Queen's University Press.

Cancian, S. (2010). *Families, lovers, and their letters: Italian postwar migration to Canada*. Winnipeg: University of Manitoba Press.

Chase, M. & Shaw, C. (1989). The dimensions of nostalgia. In C. Shaw & M. Chase (Eds.), *The Imagined Past* (pp. 1–17). Manchester, NH: Manchester University Press.

Colley, A. (1998). *Nostalgia and recollection in victorian culture*. New York, NY: St. Martin's Press.

Davis, F. (1979). *Yearning for yesterday: Sociology of nostalgia*. London: Free Press.

Dean, E. (1997). *Shook over hell: Post-traumatic stress disorder, Vietnam, and the civil war*. Cambridge: Harvard University Press.

Drake, M. (1964). 'We are yankees now': Joseph Hartley's transplanting from brighouse wood yorkshire, old england to lockport, new york, told by himself and his wife in letters home. *New York History, 45*, 222–264.

Faist, T. (2000), *The volume and dynamics of international migration and transnational social spaces*. Oxford: Oxford University Press.

Fisher, S. (1989). *Homesickness, cognition, and health*. Hillsdale: Erlbaum.

Fitzpatrick, D. (1994). *Oceans of consolation: Personal accounts of irish migration to Australia*. Ithaca: Cornell University Press.

Gerber, D. (1998). Ethnic identification and the project of individual identity: The life of mary archbald (1768-1840) of little cumbrae Island, Scotland and Auriesville, New York. *Immigrants and Minorities, 17*, 1–22.

Gerber, D. (2005). Acts of deceiving and withholding in immigrant letters: Personal identity and self-presentation in personal correspondence. *Journal of Social History, 39*, 315–330.

Gerber, D. (2006). *Authors of their lives: The personal correspondence of british immigrants to North America in the nineteenth century*. New York, NY: New York University Press.

Gerber, D. (2009). "Yankees now?": Joseph and Rebecca Hartley's circuitous path to american identity – a case study in the use of immigrant letters as social documentation. *Journal of American Ethnic History, 28*, 7–33.

Grinberg, L. and R.Grinberg (1989). *Psychoanalytic perspectives on migration and exile*. (N.Festinger, Trans.). New Haven, CT: Yale University Press.

Habermas, J. (1979). *Communication and the evolution of society*. (T.McCarthy, Trans.) Boston, MA: Beacon Press.

Hamilton. R. (1787). History of a remarkable case of nostalgia affecting a native of wales and occurring in britain. *Medical Commentaries for the Year 1786 [Edinburgh]*, *1*, 343–348.

Handlin, O. (1973). *The uprooted: The epic story of the great migrations that made the american people* (2nd ed.). Boston, MA: Little, Brown, and Company.

Hoerder, D. (2002). *Cultures in contact*. Durham: Duke University Press.

Hofer, J. (1688). *Medical dissertation on nostalgia* (Unpublished doctoral dissertation). University of Basel, Switzerland.

Hofer, J. (1934). Texts and documents: Medical dissertation on nostalgia by Johannes Hofer, 1688. (C. K. Anspach, Trans.). *Bulletin of the Institute of the History of Medicine*, *2*, 376–391.

Irvine, J. (Ed.). (1982). *Mary cumming's letters home to lisburn from America*, 1811–1815.Coleraine, North Ireland: Impact-Amergin.

Lebstock, S. (1984). *The free women of petersburg: Status and culture in a southern town, 1784–1860*. New York, NY: Norton.

Littleborough Events and Associations (2013). Rushbearing festival. Retrieved from www.rochdaleonline. co.uk/sites/littleborough-events-and-associations-forum/rushbearing-festival

Lowenthal, D. (1985). *The past is another country*. Cambridge: Cambridge University Press.

Matt, S. J. (2011). *Homesickness: An American history*. New York, NY: Oxford University Press.

Miller, K. (1985). *Emigrants and Exiles: Ireland and the Irish Exodus to North America*. New York: Oxford University Press.

Naqvi, N. (2007). *The nostalgic spirit: A genealogy of the 'critique of nostalgia'* (Working Paper No. 23). University of Messina, Italy: Centro Interuniversitario per le Richerche sulla Sociologica del Dritto della Instituzioni Giuridiche.

Øverland, O. (2000). *Immigrant minds, American identities: Making the United States home, 1870–1930*. Urbana: University of Illinois Press.

Øverland, O. (2005). Visions of home: Exiles and immigrants. In Peter I. Rose (Ed.), *The Dispossessed: An Anatomy of Exile* (p. 2005). Amherst: University of Massachusetts Press.

Ricoeur, P. (1992). *Oneself as another*. (K.Blamey, Trans.). Chicago, IL: University of Chicago Press.

Ritivoi, A. D. (2002). *Yesterday's self: Nostalgia and the Immigrant identity*. Lanham: Rowan and Littlefield, Publishers.

Rosen, G. (1975). Nostalgia: A "forgotten" psychological disorder. *Clio Medica*, *10*, 28–51.

Routledge, C., Sedikides, C., Wildschut, T., & Juhl, J. (2013). Finding meaning in one's past: Nostalgia as an existential resource. In K. D. Markham, T. Proulx, & M. J. Lindberg (Eds.), *The psychology of meaning* (pp. 297–316). Washington, DC: American Psychological Association.

Routledge, C., Wildschut, T., Sedikides, C., Juhl, J., & Arndt, J. (2012). The power of the past: Nostalgia as a meaning-making resource. *Memory*, *20*, 452–460.

Routledge, C., Arndt, J., Wildschut, T., Sedikides, C., Hart, C. M., Juhl, J., ... Schlotz, W. (2011). The past makes the present meaningful: Nostalgia as an existential resource. *Journal of Personality and Social Psychology*, *101*, 638–652.

Scott, J. G. & Wyatt, E. A., III (1998). *Petersburg's story*. Petersburg, VA: Dietz Press.

Serra, I. (2009). *The imagined immigrant: Images of the Italian emigration to the United States*. Cranbury: Associated University Presses.

Starobinski, J. (1966). *The Idea of Nostalgia*. (W.S. Kemp, Trans.). *Diogenes*, *14*, 81–103.

Vess, M., Arndt, J., Routledge, C., Sedikides, C., & Wildschut, T. (2012). Nostalgia as a resource for the self. *Self and Identity*, *11*, 273–284.

Zwingmann, C. (1973). The nostalgic phenomenon and its exploitation. In C. Zwingmann & M. Pfister-Ammende (Eds.), *Uprooting and After*, 19–50. New York, NY: Springer-Verlag.

'I never could forget my darling mother': the language of recollection in a corpus of female Irish emigrant correspondence

Emma Moreton ⓘD

ABSTRACT

The post-famine period from the 1850s to the 1920s was a time that saw a significant increase in female migration from Ireland to North America. A small glimpse into the lives of these women – their preoccupations, feelings, perceptions and beliefs – can be found in the letters they wrote home to their families. This article uses a mixed methods approach to analyse the letters of one female Irish emigrant called Julia Lough. First, a close, qualitative reading of the letters is carried out to identify topics and themes within the discourse. Computational methods are then used to examine the language of one of those topics - 'Recollections' - to see what linguistic patterns emerge. The essay concludes by discussing how memories of events, people and places contribute to a sense of closeness and attachment between author and recipient.

1. Introduction

The post-famine period from the 1850s to the 1920s was a time that saw a significant increase in female migration from Ireland to North America. Economic changes in Ireland, including declining wage-earning capabilities due to the de-industrialisation of the Irish countryside, as well as changes in inheritance practices from partible to impartible inheritance systems, led to changes in marriage trends. In short, women married 'less frequently and at later ages than in the pre-famine past', thus contributing to 'a massive post-famine emigration by young, unmarried women' (Miller, 2008, p. 302). Between 1852 and 1921 the median age for female Irish emigrants was 21.2 and after 1880 young women constituted the majority of the departing Irish (Miller, 1985, p. 392). A small glimpse into the lives of these young women – their preoccupations, experiences, perceptions and beliefs – can be found in the letters they wrote home to their families in Ireland.

This article uses a mixed methods approach to a calendar of female Irish emigrant corre-spondence – the Lough family letters[1] – extracted from a larger collection of Irish emigrant correspondence collated by Professor Kerby Miller in the 1970s.[2] It combines traditional

35

historical sciences methods with digital humanities, using corpus[3] and computational tools (including *Sketch Engine*[4] and *Wmatrix*[5]) to mine the texts for particular attributes, discussed further in section 4. In so doing, it offers new insights into the study of the female emigrant letter, whilst at the same time proposing a method of content analysis that could be applied across letter collections. This article locates itself at the nexus of migration history, gender and emotions.

2. The Lough letters

The Lough family letters are from Professor Miller's personal archive of Irish emigrant correspondence, housed at the University of Missouri. Significantly, these letters are drawn from a much larger body of Irish emigrant correspondence collected by Miller. Miller himself has explored this wider corpus in several pioneering works on Irish emigration (see, for instance, *Emigrants and Exiles: Ireland and the Irish Exodus to North America* (Miller, 1985) and *Irish Immigrants in the Land of Canaan: Letters and Memoirs from Colonial and Revolutionary America, 1675–1815* (Miller, 2003) and his archive of over 5000 letters has been referred to by many scholars including Emmons (1990), Koos (2001), Bruce (2006), Corrigan (1992) and Noonan (2011). But the Lough family correspondence, which is a small but significant part of Miller's collection, has attracted less attention.[6]

In most cases, the Lough collection contains a photocopy of each original manuscript (Figure 1) together with a typed transcription (Figure 2). In 2011, Emma Moreton, Coventry University produced digital transcriptions of the letters (Figure 3). The digital transcriptions retain the original spellings, grammar, punctuation and line breaks.

What follows is some brief background information, gathered by Miller, relating to the Lough sisters.[7] The five Lough sisters – Elizabeth, Alice, Annie, Julia and Mary – came from a Roman Catholic family in Meelick, in what was then called Queen's County (now County Laois), Ireland. The five sisters were daughters of Elizabeth McDonald Lough and James Lough who lived on a smallholding consisting of two fields; one of the fields, according to family legend, was sold to pay for the sisters' passages. The Lough family was not of the lowest class as both parents and daughters were able to write. Apart from Mary – the youngest sibling – all the Lough sisters emigrated to America between 1870 and 1884. The sisters who emigrated

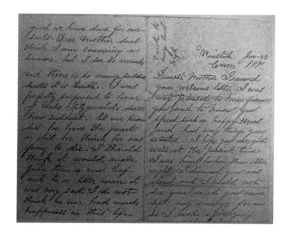

Figure 1. Photocopy of original manuscript (*Julia Lough Collection*, 25 January 1891).

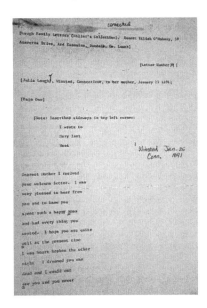

Figure 2. Miller's typed transcription (*Julia Lough Collection*, 25 January 1891).

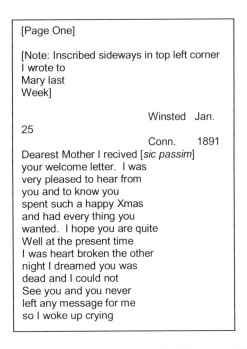

Figure 3. Moreton's digital transcription (*Julia Lough Collection*, 25 January 1891).

were, in Miller's words, four 'very dutiful, hard-working, and pious Irish female immigrants'; the sisters remained close both geographically and emotionally throughout their lives.[8]

In his 2008 study, *Ireland and Irish America: Culture, Class, and Transatlantic Migration*, Miller (2008, p. 307) argues that 'Irish emigration was based on *family* – not individual – decisions: choices by Irish parents as to which of their children to send or allow to go abroad first; and choices by Irish Americans as to which of their siblings, cousins, or other relatives to encourage and assist to emigrate and join them'. Indeed, this familial dynamic is clearly evident in the migration story of the Lough sisters. Elizabeth Lough (sometimes referred to as Liz or Lizzie) was the first sister to emigrate in 1870. She initially lived with her aunt and uncle from her mother's side – George and Anne Burke – who preceded Elizabeth to America and may have contributed to her passage. In turn, it is likely that Elizabeth contributed to the migration costs of her younger sisters. Elizabeth lived in Winsted, Litchfield County, Connecticut, where she worked mainly as a seamstress. She married Dan Walsh, who worked on a passenger train, and had five children (Tom, Alice, John William, Catherine Elizabeth and James). Dan Walsh appears to have died on 20 November 1896; Elizabeth died several years later on 28 July 1923.

Alice Lough (sometimes referred to as Alisha or Alicia) emigrated in the 1870s. Alice appears to have married before she emigrated – Miller has a copy of her marriage certificate dated 27 May 1875. In America, her husband, Edward Elliott, was an employee in a shop or factory that made coffins. Alice and her husband lived in Winsted between 1870 and 1880 before moving to Hampden County, Massachusetts in 1881 with several of their eventual seven children (Mary Elizabeth (born 14 August 1876), Edward, James (a railroad conductor, who died on 8 April 1918), William (who served in World War I), John, Alice and Phillip). Alice died on 23 September 1922.

Annie (sometimes referred to as Nan) Lough was the third sister to emigrate, in 1878; she lived in Winsted all her life where she appears to have worked as a servant for a while. Annie married John McMahon on 9 June 1886 – a labourer or factory worker – however, she bore no children. Annie died in Winsted in 1935; her husband died on 18 September 1936.

And finally, Julia Lough emigrated in September 1884 at the age of 13. After arriving in America, Julia lived in Winsted with her sister Elizabeth and her brother-in-law Dan Walsh between 1884 and 1894. In approximately 1895 she moved to Litchfield County, Connecticut, where she remained until at least 1927, the point when her letters stop. Julia was some-what of a success story, working as a seamstress to begin with, then from the age of 19 as an apprentice dressmaker, before becoming a professional dressmaker and opening up her own shop on Main Street, where she employed several members of staff. On 21 June 1897, at the age of 25, Julia married a well-respected, Irish-born railroad engineer, Thomas McCarthy, with whom she had six children (although only one, Elise, is named in her letters). Julia died in Torrington, Litchfield County on 22 February 1959; her husband died shortly after on 8 April 1959.

Mary Lough remained in Ireland with her mother and father, helping to run the family home. She married John Fitzpatrick and had four daughters. Her siblings, it seems, viewed Mary as 'the lucky one', being allowed to remain in Ireland with her parents. In a letter dated March 1893, Julia writes: 'See what a different life yours and mine has been I am sure you are happy in having such a good husband and Now your own children and having Mother there always but then I think you were always the best to Mother and it is only fair you Should receive the reward [sic passim]' (Julia Lough Collection, 21 March 1893).[9] Besides Mary, there may have been one other Lough sister who stayed in Ireland, whose married name was Hickey. However, this is unconfirmed.

There are 99 letters in the Lough collection. This article will focus on 35 of those letters, namely, the correspondence of Julia Lough (see Table 1 for an overview of the Julia Lough Collection). Table 1 shows that 23 of the 35 letters are addressed to Julia's mother, while 12

Table 1. The Julia Lough Collection.

	Reference	From: town	From: country	Recipient	To: town	To: country	No. of words	Day	Month	Year
1	LOUGH_005	Queens-town	Ireland	Mother	Meelick	Ireland	40	27	September	1884
2	LOUGH_062	-	Ireland / England	Mother	Meelick	Ireland	98			1884
3	LOUGH_006	Winsted	America	Sister	Meelick	Ireland	519	20	December	1884
4	LOUGH_079	Winsted	America	Mother	Meelick	Ireland	190			1884–1894
5	LOUGH_008	Winsted	America	Mother	Meelick	Ireland	342		December	1888
6	LOUGH_009	Winsted	America	Mother	Meelick	Ireland	444	3	November	1889
7	LOUGH_010	Winsted	America	Mother	Meelick	Ireland	436	2	December	1889
8	LOUGH_089	Winsted	America	Mother	Meelick	Ireland	487			1889–1890
9	LOUGH_072	Winsted	America	Mother	Meelick	Ireland	259			1889–1894
10	LOUGH_013	Winsted	America	Mother	Meelick	Ireland	463	9	March	1890
11	LOUGH_015	Winsted	America	Mother	Meelick	Ireland	366	10	August	1890
12	LOUGH_017	Winsted	America	Mother	Meelick	Ireland	350		December	1890
13	LOUGH_018	Winsted	America	Sister	Meelick	Ireland	348	18	January	1891
14	LOUGH_019	Winsted	America	Mother	Meelick	Ireland	351	25	January	1891
15	LOUGH_034	Winsted	America	Mother	Meelick	Ireland	225	30	March	1891
16	LOUGH_020	Winsted	America	Mother	Meelick	Ireland	317	18	October	1891
17	LOUGH_021	Winsted	America	Mother	Meelick	Ireland	300	14	December	1891
18	LOUGH_068	Winsted	America	Mother	Meelick	Ireland	400	11	May	pre-1892
19	LOUGH_023	Winsted	America	Mother	Meelick	Ireland	396	1	September	1892
20	LOUGH_064	Winsted	America	Mother	Meelick	Ireland	321			1892–1893
21	LOUGH_105	Winsted	America	Sister	Meelick	Ireland	423	21	March	1893
22	LOUGH_070	Winsted	America	Mother	Meelick	Ireland	305		May	1893
23	LOUGH_025	Winsted	America	Mother	Meelick	Ireland	340		July	1893
24	LOUGH_075	Winsted	America	Mother	Meelick	Ireland	356	3	September	1893
25	LOUGH_029	Winsted	America	Mother	Meelick	Ireland	334	10	October	1893
26	LOUGH_026	Winsted	America	Mother	Meelick	Ireland	451		December	1893
27	LOUGH_076	Torring-ton	America	Sister	Meelick	Ireland	183	25	March	1894
28	LOUGH_085	Torring-ton	America	Sister	Meelick	Ireland	477	24	May	1893–1894
29	LOUGH_074	Torring-ton	America	Sister	Meelick	Ireland	354			1889–1894
30	LOUGH_027	Winsted	America	Sister	Meelick	Ireland	736	4	June	1894
31	LOUGH_028	Winsted	America	Sister	Meelick	Ireland	469		November	1895
32	LOUGH_086	Queens-town	Ireland	Sister	Meelick	Ireland	44	8	July	1895
33	LOUGH_031	Torring-ton	America	Sister	Meelick	Ireland	416		August	1895
34	LOUGH_102	Torring-ton	America	Sister	Meelick	Ireland	331	17	March	1919–1920
35	LOUGH_057	Torring-ton	America	Sister	Meelick	Ireland	349	9	November	1927

are addressed to Julia's sister, Mary. Most of Julia's letters (33 out of 35) date from 1884 to 1895. Two later letters were sent from Julia to Mary between 1919 and 1927. Some of the letters are not dated, but their content has allowed them to be placed within an approximate timeframe. There is a 24-year gap in Julia's writing between LOUGH_031 (number 33 in the first column) sent in 1895 and LOUGH_102 (number 34 in the first column) sent in 1919–1920. In addition to managing her business these were Julia's childbearing years, and it is quite possible that Julia may have been unable to muster a remittance during this critical period, which might explain the lack of communication. However, this is not to say that Julia did not write any letters home during this period; rather, there are no letters in Miller's collection from this time. Most of the letters dated between 1884, when Julia first emigrated, and 1894 were sent from Winsted in Connecticut. In around 1895 Julia relocates to Torrington, Connecticut. By this time, Julia's mother had died, and the six letters sent from Torrington are addressed to Mary. The average word length for Julia's letters is 349.

3. Historiography

The personal letter has been one of the main mechanisms for accessing and understanding 'history from below'.[10] While many important studies in British and European history have focused on rescuing the voices of the poor and retrieving 'working-class "ego-documents" and autobiographical writings' (Richards, 2006, p. 58) – see for instance the collection of *Essex Pauper Letters, 1731–1837* (Sokoll, 2001) written by, or on behalf of, paupers seeking support from the local poor law in the county of Essex[11] – there has been little 'sign of any convergence with recent comparable work on emigrant letters' despite the fact that migrant correspondence frequently does reach into comparable layers of society (Richards, 2006, p. 59).[12] At the same time, however, the emigrant letter is different from the pauper letter in that 'it was rarely the plea of "the powerless to the powerful". Emigrants were likely to have been much more literate than paupers (though some were both paupers and emigrants)' (Richards, 2006, p. 61).[13] Additionally, while pauper letters may reveal something about social hierarchies of the time, the emigrant letter offers insights into family power paradigms and intergenerational sensibilities (knowing one's place within the notional familial hierarchy and knowing how to write a certain way to different family members).

For some scholars, the emigrant letter provides 'the unmediated voice … the voice of pure experience' (Elliott, Gerber, & Sinke, 2006, p. 7). O'Farrell, for example, examining Ulster emigrants to Australia, maintains that correspondence provides 'an intimate insight into what the migrant actually thought and felt, expressed without constraint, and with the honesty and candour appropriate to close family situations' (O'Farrell, 1984, p. 3, cited in Fitzpatrick, 1994, p. 25). However, as Elliott et al. (2006) point out, this is not entirely true as writers were almost certainly influenced by the language of church or politics and 'most probably they learned to write letters by reading the letters of others' (p. 7).[14] Nevertheless, whilst recognising influencing factors such as the context of situation (the circumstances in which the letter was produced) or broader still the context of culture (the societal pressure for the author to perform in a particular way – by writing the letter in the first place and by respecting a particular culture of letter writing when doing so), nineteenth-century migrant correspondence, or more specifically the language contained therein, provides the best evidence available for understanding experiences of migration. Examining the language of personal correspondence reveals something about how the letter writer construed events and perceived the world, as well as providing insight into how family relationships were reinforced and reconfigured over distance and time.[15]

Previous research that examines topics and themes within the discourse of Irish migrant correspondence typically involves a close reading of the letters in question. Two of the most notable studies are Miller's (1985) book *Emigrants and Exiles* and Fitzpatrick's (1994) book *Oceans of Consolation*. Miller (1985) examines Irish migration to North America from 1607 to 1921. He argues that although most Irish who crossed the Atlantic were 'voluntary emigrants who went abroad in search of better economic and social opportunities – that is, for the same reasons motivating emigrants from other parts of Europe' (p. 6) they often viewed themselves as involuntary exiles, 'compelled to leave home by forces beyond individual control, particularly by British and landlord oppression' (p. 556). To explore this incongruity, Miller (1985) analyses 5000 emigrant letters and memoirs (as well as poems, songs and folklore), looking at how references to homesickness and separation, as well as references to the homeland and the New World, contributed to the theme of emigration as exile. Miller's argument is that 'Irish-American homesickness, alienation, and nationalism were rooted ultimately in a traditional Irish Catholic worldview which predisposed Irish emigrants to perceive or at least justify themselves not as voluntary, ambitious emigrants but as involuntary, nonresponsible "exiles"' (p. 556).[16] Fitzpatrick, using a much smaller dataset and focusing on a much shorter time span, explores nineteenth-century Irish migration to Australia. Unlike Miller, Fitzpatrick publishes his letters in full (111 letters of which 55 were sent to Australia and 56 to Ireland, between 1843 and 1906) and then analyses those letters for topics and themes so as to lay bare 'at least one reading of the … letter[s]' (Fitzpatrick, 1994, p. 26). Fitzpatrick observes themes such as 'home', 'loneliness', and 'nostalgia' – features of emigrant correspondence that are also noted by Miller; however, he 'reports no comparable use of the ['exile' trope] among the Irish migrants in Australia' (Elliott et al., 2006, p. 11).[17]

More recent research in the, now burgeoning, field of the history of emotions demonstrates how the meaning and use of terms such as 'homesickness' and 'nostalgia' have changed since their introduction into the English language in the seventeenth and eighteenth centuries.[18] Matt (2011) points out that 'while generations of scholars long assumed that emotions were "tangential" to the fruitful study of the past, historians of the emotions argue that they are central to historical narratives, for their shifting meanings reveal much about the social attitudes and outlooks that were prevalent in earlier eras' (p. 9). Central to the growing interdisciplinary interest in emotions is the idea that 'human feelings are influenced by cultural and social life' which 'serves as the basis of modern historical explorations' (Matt & Stearns, 2014, p. 41 citing Lucien Febvre). For many historians, the study of language is key to understanding emotions history since 'feelings cannot exist completely independently of language … [b]y choosing to identify and name one's feelings in one way rather than another, individuals define their emotions in the process of expressing them' (Matt & Stearns, 2014, p. 43). Whilst I would certainly agree with the notion that language both reflects and constructs reality (see note 15), identifying emotions in ego-documents such as personal letters can be challenging, even more so when dealing with hundreds, sometimes thousands, of texts, as the labels that have been assigned to particular emotions – 'homesickness', 'nostalgia', or 'regret', for instance – are rarely used by the authors themselves. Julia, for example, often refers to weather and the changing seasons when expressing feelings of homesickness: 'The leaves are falling very fast today looks like winter makes me lonesome' (*Julia Lough Collection*, n.d. 1889–1894); a search for the word 'home/homesick/homesickness' in her correspondence, however, would yield no results. This raises the question of how emotions are verbally expressed by individual letter writers; and, from a methodological perspective, in searching emigrant letter collections for emotional content, what in the language should we be searching for?

Another issue in examining topics, themes and emotions in personal correspondence is the question of whether to go big (examine lots of letter collections) or go small (focus on one letter series). As Richards (2010) points out, 'emigrant letters speak for the individual letter-writer but, in sufficient numbers, they also create a collective account of the world into which they were relocated, uprooted or otherwise' (pp. 3–4). Some studies use emigrant letters as a way into understanding the collective – 'historians commonly extrapolate informally and unconsciously from individual testimony towards a view of "the spirit of the age", or the common "mentalities", or "ways of thinking" of the times'; other studies are more interested in 'the dense specificity of personal experience' which 'is always unique, because each of us has a slightly or very different personal history, modifying every new experience we have' (Richards, 2010, pp. 3–4 citing Lodge, 2002, pp. 10–11).

While studies that prioritise the collective might be accused of assigning the migrant to an anonymous mass, thereby silencing the various individual voices of the letter writers, studies that prioritise the individual might be accused of not doing anything more than offering a biography and life story; as Richards (2010, p. 13) puts it, 'returning [migrant correspondence] to the micro-historical form' simultaneously 'denies that emigrants' letters can be made the basis of any kind of historical sociology'.[19] Richards (2010, p. 13) goes on to say that this approach (which focuses on the psyche of the individual writer) 'is an austere and severely constraining formulation which restricts the source too much, and empties out the baby with the bath water'.

However, arguably, the overarching question is not so much about whether to focus on the individual or the collective (since both approaches offer valuable new insights), it is more to do with how to reconcile the individual with the general; the fragments with the whole (Lyons, 2010, p. 14). In other words, how can the voices of individual migrants be understood within their broader historical context, thereby giving 'a human dimension to significant historical issues'? (Lyons, 2010, p. 18). Indeed, as argued by Guldi and Armitage (2014, p. 113), '… questions about how to preserve subaltern voices through the integration of micro-archives … form a new and vitally important frontier of scholarship'. Furthermore, as pointed out by O'Sullivan (2003, p. 131), 'no one academic discipline is going to tell us everything we want to know about the Irish [or other] Diaspora. The study of migration, emigration, immigration, population movements, flight, scattering, networks, transnational communities, diaspora – this study demands an interdisciplinary approach'.[20]

The solution to these issues, I want to argue, lies in the digital humanities (which includes corpus and computational methods of analysis such as those described in this article). A multi- and inter-disciplinary field of study, the digital humanities brings together scholars from across the disciplines to look at ways of harnessing the power of new technologies in humanities research. Once letters are digitised and annotated in a formalised and consistent way it is possible to interconnect micro-archives, allowing the user to constantly move between the individual and the whole, comparing individual letters against letter collections to notice uniqueness and difference, as well as patterns and trends, within the data. As summarised by Guldi and Armitage (2014, p. 119), 'micro-history and macro-history – short-term analysis and the long-term overview – should work together to produce a more intense, sensitive, and ethical synthesis of data'. The digital humanities also offers exciting possibilities for the study of emotions history. In this article I propose one possible method for analysing topics, themes and emotions within digitised emigrant letter collections. This involves identifying and extracting all instances of a particular topic within a letter series before using corpus methods to analyse the language to see if any linguistic patterns can be identified. Through this process a local grammar of the various topics, themes and emotions begins to emerge which can be compared against other datasets, taking into consideration

Table 2. Topics in the Julia Lough Collection in alphabetical order.

Topic	Tag
Daily Life	\<dailyLife>\</dailyLife>
Deaths	\<deaths>\</deaths>
Education	\<education>\</education>
Enclosures	\<enclosures>\</enclosures>
Family/Friends	\<familyFriends>\</familyFriends>
Future Letters	\<futureLett>\</futureLett>
Greeting	\<greet>\</greet>
Health/Illness	\<healthIll>\</healthIll>
Homesickness/Separation	\<homeSeparation>\</homeSeparation>
Identity	\<identity>\</identity>
Ireland/America	\<IrelandAmerica>\</IrelandAmerica/>
Migration	\<migration>\</migration>
News Event	\<newsEvent>\</newsEvent>
Previous Letters	\<previousLett>\</previousLett>
Recollections	\<recollections>\</recollections>
Religion	\<religion>\</religion>
Remittance	\<remittance>\</remittance>
Reunion	\<reunion>\</reunion>
Salutation	\<salutation>\</salutation>
Sign Off	\<signOff>\</signOff>
Transportation	\<transportation>\</transportation>
Weather	\<weather>\</weather>
Work	\<work>\</work>
Writing Process	\<writingProcess>\</writingProcess>

Table 3. Topics organised by function and/or frequency.

Column A (Topics which help to structure the letter content)	**Column B** (Topics with a frequency of 10 or less)	**Column C** (Topics with a frequency of more than 10)
Previous Letters (49)	News Event (10)	Ireland / America (66)
Future Letters (41)	Reunion (10)	Family / Friends (58)
Greeting (35)	Deaths (9)	Religion (48)
Salutation (35)	Daily Life (8)	Recollections (31)
Sign Off (33)	Writing Process (8)	Homesickness / Separation (28)
Weather and Seasons (31)	Identity (6)	Health / Illness (24)
	Education (2)	Work (23)
	Migration (1)	Enclosures (17)
	Transportation (1)	Remittance (16)

sociobiographic variables such as class, sex and cultural background. These local grammars potentially offer new insights into the migrant experience which may compliment existing research that focuses more on the social conventions that guided and facilitated emotional expression in the first place.[21]

4. Methodology

I began by reading Julia's letters – identifying sequences in the discourse that appear to be lexically related – to see what broad topics emerged. Twenty-four distinct topic categories were identified, listed alphabetically in the 'Topic' column of Table 2, below.[22]

The next stage was to annotate each letter for topics. The 'Tag' column in Table 2 shows the tags (in angle brackets) that were used to mark where a topic begins and where it ends. Thus, for the topic 'News Event' (used to describe any reference to local, national or international news), the opening tag \<newsEvent> was used to show where the topic begins and the closing tag (with forward slash) </newsEvent> was used to show where the topic ends, as follows:

> **<newsEvent>**I suppose you must have heard of the hard times is all over the country and all the shops and factories shut down We have read about some in New York Starving it seems to be a scarsety of money and all the banks have nearly all failed or closed I hope there will be some change for the better soon**</newsEvent>** (*Julia Lough Collection*, 3 September 1893)

In cases where the discourse could be interpreted in more than one way, two or more tags were assigned. This meant that a section could be said to be 'about' just one topic, or it could be said to be 'about' a number of topics. In the example above, where the text is annotated with the tags <newsEvent></newsEvent>, an alternative interpretation might be the topic 'Ireland / America' (used to describe any reference to life in Ireland or America – although it is worth noting that the words 'Ireland' and/or 'America' rarely appear in Julia's letters, instead she uses person and place deixis[23] such as 'we', 'here' and 'this country' when referring to America, and 'you', 'there' and 'over there' when referring to Ireland). In cases where a section of the discourse could be interpreted in more than one way the annotation would be as follows:

> **<newsEvent><IrelandAmerica>**I suppose you must have heard of the hard times is all over the country and all the shops and factories shut down We have read about some in New York Starving it seems to be a scarsety of money and all the banks have nearly all failed or closed I hope there will be some change for the better soon**</IrelandAmerica></newsEvent>** (*Julia Lough Collection*, 3 September 1893)

Additionally, it is possible for a topic (or several topics) to be embedded within a main topic. In the example below, for instance, Julia enquires about her sister's children and as such this section could be said to be about 'Family / Friends'. Within this section Julia makes specific reference to the importance of schooling, so the tag for the topic 'Education' (used to describe any mention of learning) has been embedded within 'Family / Friends', as follows:

> **<familyFriends>**Well Mary Dear I had no idea you had so many children I knew Lizzie was about the same age as Katherine Walsh let me know all about them and who they look like **<education>**above all things keep they to school regular and as long as you can. There is nothing like a good education. No matter where they roam it is every thing now**</education></familyFriends>** (*Julia Lough Collection*, n.d. 1889–1894)

Once all 35 letters had been annotated for topics it was possible to do two things: (1) count the number of times a topic occurs within Julia's letters; (2) write a simple program to automatically extract all instances of a particular topic to look more closely at the language.

To get a better sense of the topics – what they are and how often they occur – Table 3 organises the topics into three columns, with the raw frequencies shown in brackets.

The Column A topics have been separated out because of their function. These tend to be highly routine and/or genre-related formulaic and structural features that occur in all correspondence[24] (that is, features which help to organise the letter content – the salutation, the greeting, references to previous and future letters, the sign off, and so on). The topics 'Future Letters' and 'Previous Letters', for instance, are a significant part of Julia's correspondence (and emigrant correspondence more generally), often taking up large sections of the discourse, and potentially providing useful insights into letter writing networks and the flow of correspondence over time. Additionally, the 'Greeting', 'Salutation' and 'Sign Off' (which typically include the use of vocatives and honorifics), although very conventional and formulaic in nature, can reveal something about the educational background of the letter writer as well as the relationship between author and recipient. Finally, 'Weather and Seasons' (occurring in 23 out of 35 letters) also appears to be a structural feature of Julia's correspondence, helping to organise the discourse by signalling a change of topic.

Column B shows the topics that occur 10 times or less across the 35 letters. Some of these topics ('Daily Life', 'Identity' and 'Migration', for instance), although not very frequent, seem to be more personal and reflexive in nature, showing moments of greatest authenticity, directness, expressiveness and personal identity.

Finally, Column C lists the remaining – higher frequency – topics. As one might expect, the topics 'Family / Friends' and 'Ireland / America' score high in Julia's letters. 'Remittance' (any reference to money sent from America to Ireland) is a particular feature of emigrant correspondence that is certainly worth further exploration as the strategies employed by letter writers to justify and/or explain the remittance (the amount of money being sent, what it should be used for, or why money has not been sent) potentially offer another layer of insight into the personal relationships embodied within the correspondence.

There is some overlap between some of the topics listed in Table 3. 'Homesickness / Separation', 'Recollections' and 'Reunion', for instance, are certainly linked, thematically. However, there were noticeable differences between these topics which justified them having categories of their own. Whilst the topic 'Recollections' refers to instances in which Julia remembers specific events from the past ('This time a year ago she was near been called away. She used to dread the winter so much' (*Julia Lough Collection*, n.d. November, 1895)), 'Homesickness / Separation' refers to those instances where Julia expresses feelings of nostalgia and loneliness as well as anxieties and fears about family and home ('I was heart broken the other night I dreamed you was dead and I could not See you and you never left any message for me so I woke up crying and I was so frightened till I realized it was only a dream' (*Julia Lough Collection*, 25 January 1891)). The topic 'Reunion', on the other hand, refers to those instances where Julia states her hope, desire or intention to, one day, return to Ireland to be reunited with her family. These tend to be short, freestanding statements, helping to reassure the recipient (Julia's mother or sister) that they are missed ('when you see me again I hope we will spent a happy time together yet perhaps sooner than you thing [*sic passim*] I know you would grow young again' (*Julia Lough Collection*, n.d. December 1888)).

Because it is possible for a section of the letter to be 'about' more than one topic, the next stage of the study involved looking at how often each topic was in primary position (i.e. where it was the main focus of a particular section of the letter) or secondary position (i.e. where it was an alternative interpretation of a particular section, or it was a topic embedded within another, primary, topic). It should be noted that nearly all of the topics can be in primary or secondary position. However, from reading the letters, there appeared to be patterns: some topics seemed to dominate a particular letter/s whereas others seemed to be a background theme carried across all correspondence. Table 4 details the number of times a topic was primary (column A), or secondary, tertiary, etc. (columns B to I). The figures in Table 4 represent the number of occurrences of a particular topic. Focusing on 'Family / Friends', for example, we can see that this topic was in primary position (column A) 48 times, it was in secondary position (column B) 3 times, tertiary position (column C) 5 times, and so on.) Topics that most frequently occur in primary position are shown in bold; those that most frequently occur in secondary (or other) position (columns B to I) are highlighted in italics; and topics that occur in primary and secondary position roughly the same number of times (within + or −2) are shown in grey. Looking at Table 3 and Table 4 together, some

Table 4. Primary versus non-primary topics.

Topic	Primary	Secondary or other position							
	A	B	C	D	E	F	G	H	I
Family / Friends	48	3	5	1	1	0	0	0	0
Salutation	35	0	0	0	0	0	0	0	0
Previous Letters	34	12	1	0	1	1	0	0	0
Greeting	33	1	0	0	0	1	0	0	0
Sign Off	33	0	0	0	0	0	0	0	0
Future Letters	27	6	6	1	0	0	0	1	0
Weather	21	6	3	0	0	0	1	0	0
Recollections	16	2	6	3	3	0	1	0	0
Religion	*14*	*18*	*7*	*5*	*2*	*1*	*1*	*0*	*0*
Homesickness / Separation	13	9	5	0	0	0	1	0	0
Remittance	12	3	1	0	0	0	0	0	0
Health / Illness	*10*	*5*	*6*	*1*	*1*	*0*	*1*	*0*	*0*
News Event	9	0	1	0	0	0	0	0	0
Enclosure	8	4	3	2	0	0	0	0	0
Reunion	8	0	0	2	0	0	0	0	0
Ireland / America	*7*	*41*	*9*	*4*	*3*	*1*	*0*	*0*	*1*
Writing Process	6	2	0	0	0	0	0	0	0
Work	*5*	*6*	*5*	*3*	*1*	*2*	*1*	*0*	*0*
Death	4	4	1	0	0	0	0	0	0
Daily Life	4	4	0	0	0	0	0	0	0
Transportation	1	0	0	0	0	0	0	0	0
Education	*0*	*2*	*0*	*0*	*0*	*0*	*0*	*0*	*0*
Identity	*1*	*1*	*2*	*2*	*0*	*0*	*0*	*0*	*0*
Migration	*0*	*0*	*0*	*1*	*0*	*0*	*0*	*0*	*0*

observations can be made. Structural features (those topics that are listed in Column A of Table 3) are typically primary, helping to organise the flow of discourse. Topics which occur 10 times or less (Column B of Table 3) also tend to be primary; these topics are rare, but when they do occur they are given prominence in the letters. Finally, the topics listed in Column C of Table 3 are secondary, tertiary, or other (i.e. they are not the main focus of the letter); these topics (often implicit references repeated across Julia's correspondence) seem to contribute to underlying themes within the discourse. For example, the topic 'Ireland / America' is almost always in secondary position (59 out of 66 occurrences). Although it is quite rare for Julia to speak directly about life in America (which might alienate the recipient), the reader gets a sense of her feelings, experiences and perceptions from the comments that are made in the context of other topics, such as 'Weather' or 'Work', as follows:

> **\<weather>\<irelandAmerica>We** have had such cold rainy weather till now There is nothing planted here yet that I can see The trees are coming to bud and sweet May is **here** again\</irelandAmerica>\</weather> (*Julia Lough Collection*, n.d. May 1893)

> **\<work>**I am sure you work hard but Lizze will soon be able to help you work that seen good **\<irelandAmerica>We** all work hard **here\</irelandAmerica>\</work>** (*Julia Lough Collection*, n.d. 1889–1894)

The study so far has involved a personal reading of Julia Lough's correspondence to identify topics and themes. The (digitised) letters were then annotated, allowing me to count the number of times each topic occurred within Julia's letters, noticing when a topic was the main focus of a particular section of the letter and when it was more of a passing comment – an aside, or background information – embedded within another, primary, topic. The next stage involved extracting all instances of a particular topic to see if any patterns in the language emerged, which might, in turn, reveal something about Julia's experiences and relationships. In this article I shall concentrate on one topic – 'Recollections'. Indeed,

Table 5. Ten most frequent 2-grams occurring 10 times or more within the topic 'Recollections' in the Julia Lough Collection.

N-gram	Pattern	Freq.	Examples
1	*Personal Pronoun + Verb (Present Tense)*	30	I remember (7) / I hope (6) / I suppose (5) / I know (2) / you see (2) / I dont (1) / I think (1) / me know (1) / you do (1) / you hate (1) / you know (1) / you look (1) / you make (1)
2	*Determiner + Singular Noun*	23	every thing (3) / the family (2) / a look (1) / a picture (1) / a prosession (1) / a shilling (1) / a year (1) / all winter (1) / an try (1) / any way (1) / every night (1) / that yard (1) / the fall (1) / the last (1) / the rest (1) / the side (1) / the size (1) / the winter (1) / this time (2)
3	*Personal Pronoun + (Present Tense) Verb*	22	she used (3) / we used (3) / you used (3) / I used (2) / I did (2) / he used (1) / I looked (1) / I noticed (1) / I saw (1) / it recalled (1) / it used (1) / you got (1) / you reminded (1) / I felt (1)
4	*Preposition + Personal Pronoun*	21	of them (2) / of you (2) / to me (2) / to you (2) / with me (1) / about me (1) / about us (1) / as it (1) / as you (1) / for me (1) / for us (1) / if I (1) / if it (1) / if she (1) / in I (1) / like me (1) / to we (1)
5	*Infinitive 'To' + Verb (Base Form)*	19	to get (3) / to go (2) / to mass (2) / to buy (1) / to do (1) / to dread (1) / to give (1) / to hear (1) / to pray (1) / to promise (1) / to say (1) / to see (1) / to think (1) / to try (1) / to write (1)
6	*Personal Pronoun + Adverb*	19	I never (2) / I often (2) / she always (2) / I always (1) / me not (1) / she often (1) / them well (1) / they still (1) / us all (1) / us here (1) / you either (1) / you good (1) / you often (1) / you so (1) / you still (1) / you yet (1)
7	*Adjective + Singular Noun*	17	back view (1) / common sense (1) / convent garden (1) / different life (1) / fine time (1) / good picture (1) / good time (1) / great change (1) / hearty cry (1) / last evening (1) / last time (1) / last year (1) / little trunk (1) / other night (1) / poor picture (1) / precious baby (1) / red ribbon (1)
8	*Verb (Present Tense) + Personal Pronoun*	15	suppose you (4) / hope you (3) / do they (1) / hope she (1) / know I (1) / know you (1) / remember them (1) / remember you (1) / see you (1) / suppose he (1)
9	*Adverb + Adjective*	14	as bad (2) / very thankful (2) / almost past (1) / as good (1) / just right (1) / not able (1) / only last (1) / so good (1) / so many (1) / so much (1) / very happy (1) / very poor (1)
10	*Determiner + Adjective*	14	a great (4) / the same (3) / a good (2) / a different (1) / that precious (1) / the back (1) / the last (1) / the other (1)

memories and nostalgia are features of Irish emigrant letters observed by both Miller and Fitzpatrick, so a closer look at the language of recollections may provide new insights into how these sentiments are discursively constructed.

5. Findings

Having extracted all occurrences of 'Recollections', the corpus tool *Sketch Engine* was used to observe patterns in the language. Within the 'Word List' option in *Sketch Engine*, all Parts of Speech (POS) tags with an n-gram value of two, which occur 10 or more times in the *Julia Lough Collection* were extracted. N-grams are defined as X number of words which appear consecutively Y number of times; the analyst can set the parameters. Table 5 gives the 10 most frequent POS 2-grams for 'Recollections'. What follows is a summary of some of the main observations.

5.1. Remembering

N-gram 1 shows a relatively high frequency of the pattern *Personal Pronoun + (Present Tense) Verb* in Julia's letters, as in 'I remember', 'I hope', 'I suppose', etc. 'I/she/you remember' is the most frequent combination (see concordance lines (1) to (8), below). In six of these occurrences, Julia is the subject of the clause – the participant who is remembering. Julia remembers physical objects: for instance, 'those beads' (3); actions and events: 'how long you used to pray' (5); and experiences and feelings: 'how delighted I was' (4). The act of remembering is evident across most of the letters and serves to authenticate Julia's attachment to the homeland. Recalling specific details about people, places and events creates a bridge between the two worlds enabling author and recipient to be united through their past, shared experiences.

Turning now to n-gram 3 – *Personal Pronoun + (Past Tense) Verb*, as in 'I used to', 'I looked', 'I noticed', etc. – 13 out of the 22 occurrences contain the verb 'used (to)'. Julia is the subject of just two of those structures: 'how delighted I used to be' (4) and 'I used to long for one of them goosebirrys [*sic passim*]' (12). In the remaining 11 occurrences, Julia recalls the actions, routines and habits of others: her father (4), her family (5), (6), her sister (5), (6), (9), (13), and her mother (10), (11). In these occurrences, Julia reassures the recipient of the letter (her mother or sister) that they – and family in Ireland – are remembered, whilst at the same time demonstrating that she 'knows' and understands their likes, dislikes, traits, fears and routines. In these occurrences a sense of 'knowing' is textually performed through the language of recollection. By talking about shared experiences and by demonstrating that she remembers all details about home, Julia seeks to reinforce bonds with loved ones in Ireland.

(1) Liz is very thankful to you <u>She often</u> talks about home and **remembers** every thing that happened there (*Julia Lough Collection*, 3 November 1889)

(2) write so and dont forget that where ever I am **I remember** you yet (*Julia Lough Collection*, 1 September 1892)

(3) supposing you are not able to go to mass all winter I am sure you make those beads of yours rattle in fine time every night. **I remember** them well the size of them (*Julia Lough Collection*, n.d. December 1893)

(4) **I remember** how delighted I used to be when he used to give me a shilling at xmas I hope Dear Father is praying for us all in Heaven. (*Julia Lough Collection*, n.d. December 1893)

(5) I have thought of Mother very much all through May **I remember** the prayers **we used to** say during May let me know do you pray as much now as when I was at home. **I remember** well how long **you used to** pray <u>I never</u> could be as good as you any way Dear Sister <u>I often</u> think of those Dear old happy days. I know <u>you</u> **used to** <u>always</u> agree with me in everything an try to think every thing I did was right (*Julia Lough Collection*, 4 June 1894)

(6) <u>you</u> **used** <u>always</u> be so good to me wasent I bold but I did not have common sense then have you got that little trunk yet we used to try hard to get a look in **I remember** (*Julia Lough Collection*, n.d. 1889–1894)

(7) That is certainly the back view of Asylum. in viewing it it recalled a great many things to my mind **I remember** going there to see Father (*Julia Lough Collection*, 24 May 1893–1894)

(8) you see how little I know after so many years, **you** will **remember** us (*Julia Lough Collection*, 17 March 1919–1920)

(9)   I am sure you are not lonesome with that precious baby if she looks like me Mary will have to buy her that yard of red ribbon **she used to** promise me (*Julia Lough Collection*, 1 September 1892)

(10) This time a year ago she was near been called away. **She used to** dread the winter so much (*Julia Lough Collection*, n.d. November 1895)

(11) does your cough be as bad as **it used to** be or do you go to Mass every Sunday I hope you get along well (*Julia Lough Collection*, 30 March 1891)

(12) do <u>they still</u> have a prosession in Convent garden. how **I used to** long for one of them goosebirrys (*Julia Lough Collection*, 24 May 1893–1894)

(13) I <u>often</u> think of Mary when **she used to** go to [Toyer?] I hope she has a good time now and sleeps till nine oclock mornings (*Julia Lough Collection*, n.d. 1889–1890)

(14) Indeed I <u>never</u> could forget my darling Mother (*Julia Lough Collection*, n.d. December 1888)

5.2. Time and frequency

N-gram 6 shows a relatively high frequency of the pattern *Personal Pronoun + Adverb*, as in 'I never', 'I often', 'she always', etc. Some of these pronoun/adverb combinations can be found in the examples above (underlined in examples (1), (5), (6), (12), (13) and (14)). Here, the adverbs are used to emphasise the extent to which Julia thinks about home: 'I often think of those Dear old happy days' (5) and 'I often think of Mary' (13), for instance. In the case of example (14) – 'I never could forget my darling Mother' – Julia underscores the impossibility of her ever being able to forget. Additionally, the adverb 'always' seems to be used to emphasise the sense of 'knowing' described previously. In examples (5) and (6) Julia demonstrates that she knows and understands her sister based on past experiences, repeated over time: 'you used to always agree with me' and 'you used always be so good to me'. This demonstration of knowledge about family seems to be a strategy for reinforcing family bonds.

Another observation, looking at examples (1) to (14), is to do with the use of time deixis including seasons: 'Winter' (3), (10), months 'May' (5), and yearly events 'Xmas' (4), as well as references to the passing of time: 'after so many years' (8) and 'this time a year ago' (10). Seasons, months and yearly events appear to trigger specific memories. These deictic features place Julia at a particular point in time: writing in the present, she places herself firmly in the past to a period when she and her family were together.

5.3. Predicting

N-gram 8 shows a relatively high frequency of the pattern *Present Tense Verb + Personal Pronoun*, as in 'suppose you', 'hope you', 'know you', etc. A closer look at these n-grams in context reveals that they are typically part of what Halliday and Matthiessen (2004) describe as projection structures. Projection structures consist of two main components: the projecting clause (*I suppose*) and the projected clause (*he is married*). In these structures the primary (projecting) clause (*I suppose*) sets up the secondary (projected) clause (*he is married*) as the representation of the content of either what is thought, or what is said (Halliday & Matthiessen, 2004, p. 377).[25] Projection structures have the ability to articulate the author's expectations, desires, or beliefs on to the recipient thus contributing to the intersubjective nature of correspondence. There are, of course, interpretative limitations when working with one-directional correspondence collections, such as the Lough letters. For one, it is simply not possible to know how the recipient of the letter responded to its content. However, an analysis of projection structures will reveal something about 'the writer's [or author's] expectations about what the addressee [or recipient] may bring to the text and the kinds of response that the text will elicit from the addressee' (Thompson, 2012, p. 80).

In structures containing the verb 'suppose', Julia is always the subject of the projecting clause (*I suppose*). These structures seem to function in two ways: (1) they contribute to the interactive nature of the letters, requiring the recipient to agree, disagree, confirm or deny the statements being put forward; and (2) they help to construct an imagined world based on Julia's past knowledge of family and friends in Ireland. This imagined homeland relies, however, on things in Ireland having stayed the same since Julia's departure: 'supposing you are not able to go to mass' (15), 'I suppose you still do the same' (18) and 'I suppose you look about the same' (19). In these occurrences Julia predicts that people, places and routines have not changed in Ireland – people 'do' the same, and 'look' the same. Unfortunately, letters from Julia's mother and sister are not available, so the extent to which Julia's family in Ireland confirmed or rejected these projections is unknown.

In summary, the verb 'suppose' is very 'other' oriented. In using 'I suppose you' the author performs awareness of the recipient's world (i.e. the content of the projected clause is about the recipient's world rather than the author's) and in imagining the recipient's world the author shows how vivid that world – home – is for them.

In contrast, the verb 'hope' seems to represent powerless wishing – it is a very deferential verb. It expresses a wish for another person without assuming the right or the power to make the wish come true. In some ways it resembles praying to a greater power – the author hopes or wishes for things for other people without making any presumption that they have the right, power or authority about whether it happens, or not, as in: 'you are much smarter than when I was home but I hope you will not have so much to do anymore' (*Julia Lough Collection*, n.d. December 1888).

(15) **supposing** you are not able to go to mass all winter (*Julia Lough Collection*, n.d. December 1893)

(16) I was dreaming the other night about Dick Conroy. I suppose he is married by this time (*Julia Lough Collection*, n.d. November 1895)

(17) **I suppose** you often talk about me and what a little snit I was but you know I am eight years older now and that makes a great change we will hope for the better it was only last evening Liz and I was talking she says she always considered me different in all my ways from the rest of the family. I think every thing she says is just right – she always cared for me and treated me the best in the family (*Julia Lough Collection*, 10 October 1893)

(18) **I suppose** you still do the same with yours (*Julia Lough Collection*, 24 May 1893–1894)

(19) **I suppose** you look about the same you See what a different life yours and mine has been (*Julia Lough Collection*, 21 March 1893)

Table 6. Key semantic fields in the Recollections Corpus compared with the Letters Reference Corpus.

Semantic tag	Semantic field	Log-likelihood (LL) score	Examples
T1.1.1	Time: Past	40.12	used to, last year, last time, ago, the other night, last evening
X2.2+	Knowledgeable	18.48	remember, now, remembers, recalled
X2.1	Thought, belief	15.67	think, suppose, considered, trust, thought, felt, thinking, viewing
N6+++	Frequent	14.79	always
X2.2-	No knowledge	13.12	forget, forgotten
N6+	Frequent	12.35	often, every Sunday, again, every night
E4.1+	Happy	9.83	happy, joys, enjoy yourself, delighted
Z8	Pronouns	9.08	I, you me, she, it, that, your, we, us, yours, them, my, he, they, what, its, her, everything
A8	Seem	7.18	looked, look
A5.1+	Evaluation: Good	6.82	good, great, well, fine

5.4. Sameness and difference

N-gram 9 shows a relatively high frequency of the pattern *Adverb + Adjective*, as in 'as bad'; and n-gram 10 shows a relatively high frequency of the pattern *Determiner + Adjective*, as in 'the same'. In examples (20) and (21) Julia appears to be posing questions relating to her mother's health and whether her health is the same, or different (that is, worse). Examples (22) and (23) are part of the projection structures mentioned in the previous section. In these examples the author predicts that the recipient of the letter does the same and looks the same; however, in example (23), Julia gestures to a sense of difference. Whilst Julia predicts that things are the same in Ireland, she suggests that things are very different for her in America. And in example (24) Julia reports that she has changed, she is different. Ireland represents lack of change, while America represents progress.

(20) does your cough be **as bad as** it used to be or do you go to Mass every Sunday I hope you get along well (*Julia Lough Collection*, 30 March 1891)

(21) and if your Cough does be **as bad as** usual and are you able to get out to mass every Sunday (*Julia Lough Collection*, 25 January 1891)

(22) I suppose you still do **the same** with yours (*Julia Lough Collection*, 24 May 1893–1894)

(23) I suppose you look about **the same** you See what **a different** life yours and mine has been (*Julia Lough Collection*, 21 March 1893)

(24) but you know I am eight years older now and that makes **a great change** (*Julia Lough Collection*, 10 October 1893)

Using *Sketch Engine* to identify n-grams is one way of examining the topic 'Recollections'. Another way is to use the online corpus analysis and comparison tool *Wmatrix* to identify key semantic fields within the language. To do this, the extracts for 'Recollections' were compared against a general reference corpus. The results are summarised in Table 6 and would appear to supports the *Sketch Engine* findings. The semantic fields 'Time: Past' and 'Frequent', for example, reveal that phrases expressing time and frequency are statistically significant in the 'Recollections' corpus, when compared to a general corpus of letters. Additionally the semantic fields 'Knowledgeable', 'No knowledge' and 'Thought, belief' would support earlier observations regarding the high frequency of verbs which express memories ('remember', 'used to', etc.) and predictions ('suppose'). However, some new observations do appear to come to light from the *Wmatrix* investigation: the semantic fields 'Happy' and 'Evaluation: Good' may suggest a connection between recollections and positive emotions, as in: 'Dear Sister I often think of those Dear old happy days' (*Julia Lough Collection*, 4 June 1894) and 'I remember how delighted I used to be when he gave me a shilling at xmas' (*Julia Lough Collection*, n.d. December 1893). Recollections, it seems, evoke positive feelings.

6. Discussion and conclusion

Ultimately, the methodologies I have been outlining in this article allow us to explore the language Julia uses to talk about different topics and emotions. In the case of 'Recollections', the verbs 'remember' and 'used (to)' feature heavily in Julia's letters. Julia recalls the personal traits and physical appearances of family back in Ireland (what they used to do and what they used to look like, for instance) as well as remembering specific places, events, and experiences. This contributes to a theme of 'knowing' within Julia's letters. By recounting, in very specific detail, a person, place or event, Julia is able to connect with family back home. 'Home', as Fitzpatrick (1994, p. 494) puts it, becomes 'a spiritual rendezvous for separated kinsfolk' providing correspondents with 'common moments of imaginable communion'. Additionally, *Personal Pronoun + Adverb* combinations ('I always', 'I often') are used to emphasise how frequently Julia remembers home, while time deixis (references to months, seasons and annual celebrations, such as Christmas or St Patrick's Day) are a trigger for certain memories and, it would seem, positive emotions.

Another significant feature of the language of recollections is the high frequency of projection structures containing the verb 'suppose', which are used to construct an imagined homeland based on past, shared experience. In these structures Julia predicts that things have not changed in Ireland – the landscape, the people and places are exactly as Julia left them. In contrast, however, America represents change, difference and progress. This dualistic position is, arguably, a common feature of emigrant letters more generally where 'the greater the tensions incidental to exposure to new social systems and cultures, the greater … the desire to preserve a feeling of rootedness in a personal past' (Elliott et al., 2006, p. 2).

The idea of Ireland representing sameness most probably stems from Julia's need for 'rootedness'; it is imposed on the recipient (Julia's mother and sister) as without this common ground Julia's sense of self, in relation to her family, may be threatened.

The focus of this article has been narrow, examining just one collection of correspondence from the much larger archive of 5000 emigrant letters held by Miller. But through repeating the process I have described here, using letters by authors from a range of socio-historical, economic and cultural backgrounds, a more comprehensive local grammar of my key topics may begin to emerge, providing a fuller picture of the language and functions of emigrant correspondence and a stronger case for the various resulting readings and interpretations. Future research will involve establishing local grammars for all 24 topics and then testing to see whether those local grammars (specific words, phrases and patterns in the language) might indicate the thematisation of a particular topic in other letters. This process may, in turn, lead to the semi-automation of topic detection in emigrant correspondence, allowing much larger datasets to be analysed for topics, themes and emotional content; there is, however, a long way to go. Equally too, of course, this further research may show that the linguistic features and themes I have identified here need to be expanded or refined as other, more typical ones emerge. Nor should we forget that the discourses and topics that do not emerge may be as telling as the ones that do. Indeed, a more detailed keyword or key semantic field comparison, with a suitable reference corpus, might pinpoint some notable absences, as negative key items, for instance.

Notes

1. Among the Irish relatives the spelling later became 'Locke' – very close to the Irish pronunciation of the name – and was written Lowe on some official documents.
2. Professor Kerby Miller, Curators' Professor, Department of History, University of Missouri: http://history.missouri.edu/people/miller.html.
3. A corpus can be defined as a 'bod[y] of naturally occurring language data stored on computers' and corpus techniques of analysis as the 'computational procedures which manipulate this data in various ways … to uncover linguistic patterns which can enable us to make sense of the ways that language is used' (Baker, 2006, p. 1).
4. Kilgarriff and Kosem (2012). See also Kilgarriff, Rychly, Smrz, and Tugwell (2004).
5. Rayson (2009). See also Rayson (2008).
6. In the early 1950s, a few of the Lough letters were initially donated by Canice and Eilish O'Mahony of Dundalk, County Louth, to Arnold Schrier, then a graduate student at Northwestern University, now Professor Emeritus at the University of Cincinnati, who subsequently employed them, alongside other epistolary documents, in his 1958 book *Ireland and the Irish Emigration, 1850–1900* (Schrier, 1958). In 1977–1978 the rest of the Lough letters were donated to Miller by the O'Mahonys and by Edward Dunne and Kate Tynan of Portlaoise, County Laois. Both Miller and Schrier, who thereafter collaborated in researching Irish migration to America, made photocopies and transcriptions of these letters, and Miller returned the original manuscripts to their donors.
7. I am indebted to personal communications with Kerby Miller for the information that follows. See too Miller (2008).
8. This quotation is taken from correspondence between Miller and Mrs Edward McKenna (one of the donors).
9. This family structure (whereby the older siblings emigrated while the youngest sibling remained at home to look after the family) may reflect ultimogeniture practices in rural Ireland. See Ó Gráda (1980).
10. A term coined by the Spanish writer Miguel de Unamuno in 1985. 'It refers to the value of the humble and anonymous lives experienced by ordinary men and women in everyday contexts which form the essence of normal social interactions, as opposed to the lives of leaders and famous people that are generally accounted for in canonical histories' (Amador-Moreno, Corrigan, McCafferty, Moreton, & Waters, In press).
11. Other studies which focus on the writings of the poor include Burnett, Vincent, and Mayall (1984), Fairman (2000) and Yokoyama (2008).
12. Although emigrants came from a range of socioeconomic backgrounds the vast majority were, as Erickson (1972, p. 1), puts it, 'ordinary working people'.
13. Richards (2006, p. 61) quoting James Scott in Hitchcock, King, and Sharpe (1996, p. 6).
14. In other words, 'immigrant writers were immersed in cultures which informed their often tentative writing' (Elliott et al., 2006, p. 7).
15. As argued by Scott (1992), it is not possible to separate language and experience since language constructs identities, 'position[s] subjects and produce[s] … experiences' (p. 25). Scott's view is shared by linguists Halliday and Matthiessen (2004) and Hoey (2005). Whilst what underpins Halliday and Matthiessen's work on systemic functional grammar is the notion of choice (the lexiogrammatical possibilities that 'allow [a] speaker to represent the world in a particular way' (Hunston, 2006, p. 65)), what underpins Hoey's theory of lexical priming is the idea that individuals are primed to use language in a certain way, therefore raising questions regarding

the very notion of choice. Both theories, however, come from the standpoint that language and experience are inherently connected.

16. This worldview, Miller (1985) suggests, dates back to pre-modern times when 'Gaelic culture's secular, religious, and linguistic aspects expressed or reinforced a worldview which deemphasized and even condemned individualistic and innovative actions such as emigration' (p. 556).

17. See, also, O'Farrell (1984, 1987, 1990) for accounts on Irish migrants in Australia and New Zealand, based largely on letters and family memoirs. See also McCarthy's (2005) study, *Irish Migrants in New Zealand*, which – 'in order to facilitate comparative endeavours ...' follows the classification used by the Thematic Index of David Fitzpatrick's *Oceans of Consolation*. For a detailed account of patterns of Irish migration to other countries including Australia, New Zealand and South Africa see Akenson (1993).

18. Matt (2011) points out that 'before the seventeenth century, the word nostalgia did not exist, and before the eighteenth century the English word homesickness did not either'. Matt goes on to say that 'the invention of these terms reflected a new concern about the emotions that were becoming apparent in early modern society' (pp. 9–10).

19. Here, Richards is referring to Gerber (2006) who argues that 'emigrant letters, or indeed any type of personal correspondence, is almost always a commentary on the individual psyche of the writer ... [letters] are restricted to the way individual writers recreated their own personalities, their emotional conditioning to the experience of emigration, reformulating their relationships and reconstructing their personal identities' (Richards, 2010, p. 13 summarising Gerber, 2006).

20. See also Brettell and Hollifield (2000, p. vii).

21. See, for example, Reddy (2001) and Matt (2011).

22. Full descriptions of all 24 topics are detailed in Moreton (In press).

23. 'Deixis concerns the ways in which languages encode or grammaticalize features of the context of utterance ... and thus also concerns ways in which the interpretation of utterances depends on the analysis of that context of utterance' (Levinson, 1983, p. 54).

24. The term 'formulaic language' is used here to refer to multi-word units that closely resemble phrases found in similar generic points with similar functions in personal letters generally.

25. For a more detailed account of the use of projection structures in the Lough letters see Moreton (2015).

Disclosure statement

No potential conflict of interest was reported by the author.

ORCID

Emma Moreton (iD) http://orcid.org/0000-0003-4182-4586

References

Akenson, D. H. (1993). *The Irish diaspora: A primer*. Toronto: P. D. Meaney Co.

Amador-Moreno, C., Corrigan, K. P., McCafferty, K., Moreton, E., & Waters, C. (In press). Irish migration databases as impact tools in the education and heritage sectors. In K. Corrigan & A. Mearnes (Eds.), *Creating and Digitizing Language Corpora – Volume 3: Databases for Public Engagement*. London: Palgrave.

Baker, P. (2006). *Using corpora in discourse analysis*. London: Continuum.

Brettell, C., & Hollifield, J. F. (Eds.) (2000). *Migration Theory: Talking Across Disciplines*. New York and London: Routledge.

Bruce, S. U. (2006). *The Harp and the Eagle: Irish-American volunteers and the union army, 1861–1865*. New York, NY: New York University Press.

Burnett, J., Vincent, D., & Mayall, D. (1984). *The autobiography of the working class. An annotated, critical bibliography. vol. 1: 1790-1900*. Brighton: Harvester Press.

Corrigan, K. P. (1992). 'I gcuntas Dé múin Béarla do na leanbháin': eisimirce agus an Ghaeilge sa naoú aois déag' ['For God's sake teach the children' English: Emigration and the Irish language in the nineteenth century]. In P. O'Sullivan (Ed.), *The Irish World Wide* (pp. 143–161). Leicester: Leicester University Press.

Elliott, B. S., Gerber, D. A., & Sinke, S. (Eds.) (2006). *Letters across borders: Epistolary Practices of International Migrants*. London: Palgrave Macmillan.

Emmons, D. M. (1990). *The butte Irish*. Urbana: University of Illinois Press.

Erickson, C. (1972). *Invisible immigrants: The adaptation of english and Scottish immigrants in nineteenth-centrury America*. London: Weidenfeld & Nicolson.

Fairman, T. (2000). English pauper letters 1800-34 and the english language. In D. Barton & N. Hall (Eds.), *Letter writing as a social practice* (pp. 63–82). Amsterdam: John Benjamins.

Fitzpatrick, D. (1994). *Oceans of consolation: Personal accounts of Irish migration to Australia*. Cork: Cork University Press.

Gerber, D. A. (2006). *Authors of Their Lives: The Personal Correspondence of British Immigrants to North America in the Nineteenth Century*. New York: New York University Press.

Guldi, J., & Armitage, D. (2014). *The history manifesto*. Cambridge: Cambridge University Press.

Halliday, M. A. K. & Matthiessen, C. M. I. M. (2004). *An introduction to functional grammar*. London: Arnold.

Hitchcock, T., King, P., & Sharpe, P. (1996). *Chronicling poverty the voices and strategies of the english poor, 1640–1840*. London: Palgrave Macmillan.

Hoey, M. (2005). *Lexical priming*. Oxon: Routledge.

Hunston, S. (2006). Phraseology and system: A contribution to the debate. In S. Hunston & G. Thompson (Eds.), *System and corpus: exploring connections* (pp. 55–80). London: Equinox.

Kilgarriff, A., Rychly, P., Smrz, P., & Tugwell, D. (2004). The sketch engine. Proceedings from EURALEX (105-116), Lorient, France.

Kilgarriff, A., & Kosem, I. (2012). Corpus Tools for Lexicographers. In S. Granger & M. Paquot (Eds.), *Electronic Lexicography* (31–56). New York, NY: Oxford University Press. Retrieved from http://www.sketchengine.co.uk

Koos, G. (2001). The Irish hedge schoolmaster in the American backcountry. *New Hibernia Review, 5*, 9–26.

Levinson, S. C. (1983). *Pragmatics*. Cambridge: Cambridge University Press.

Lodge, D. (2002). *Consciousness and the novel: Connected essays*. Massachusetts: Harvard University Press.

Lyons, M. (2010). A new history from below? The writing culture of European peasants, c. 1850 – c. 1920. In A. Kuismin & M. J. Driscoll (Eds.), *White Field, Black Seeds: Nordic Literacy Practices in the Long Nineteenth Century* (Studia Fennica Litteraria) (14–29). Helsinki: Finnish Literature Society.

Matt, S. J. (2011). *Homesickness: An American history*. Oxford: Oxford University Press.

Matt, S. J., & Stearns, P. N. (2014). *Doing emotions history*. Urbana, Chicago, Springfield: University of Illinois Press.

McCarthy, A. (2005). *Irish migrants in New Zealand, 1840–1937: The desired haven*. Suffolk: The Boydell Press.

Miller, K. A. (1985). *Emigrants and exiles: Ireland and the Irish exodus to North America*. Oxford: Oxford University Press.

Miller, K. A. (2003). *Irish immigrants in the land of canaan: Letters and memoirs from colonial and revolutionary America, 1675–1815*. Oxford: Oxford University Press.

Miller, K. A. (2008). *Ireland and Irish America: Culture, class, and transatlantic migration*. Dublin: Field Day.

Miller, K. A., Doyle, D. N., & Kelleher, P. (1995). For love and liberty: Irish women, migration and domesticity in Ireland and America, 1815–1920. In P. O'Sullivan (Ed.), *The Irish World Wide* (pp. 54–61). Leicester: Leicester University Press.

Moreton, E. (2015). 'I hope you will write': The function of projection structures in a corpus of nineteenth century Irish emigrant correspondence. *Journal of Historical Pragmatics, 16*, 277–303.

Moreton, E. (In press). Letters from America: Exploring topics within a collection of Irish emigrant correspondenc'. In C. M. Bernier, J. Newman, & M. Pethers (Eds.), *A Companion to Nineteenth-Century American Letters and Letter-Writing*. Edinburgh: Edinburgh University Press.

Noonan, A. J. M. (2011). 'Oh those long months without a word from home', Migrant letters from mining frontiers. *The Boolean*, 129–135. Retrieved from http://publish.ucc.ie/boolean/

Ó Gráda, C. (1980). Primogeniture and ultimogeniture in rural Ireland. *Journal of Interdisciplinary History, 10*, 491–497.

O'Farrell, P. (1984). *Letters from Australia 1825–1929*. NSW: New South Wales University Press.

O'Farrell, P. (1987). *The Irish in Australia*. NSW: New South Wales University Press.

O'Farrell, P. (1990). *Vanished kingdoms, Irish in Australia and New Zealand, A personal excursion*. NSW: New South Wales University Press.

O'Sullivan, P. (2003). Developing Irish diaspora studies: A personal view. *New Hibernia Review, 7*, 130–148.

Rayson, P. (2008). From key words to key semantic domains. *International Journal of Corpus Linguistics, 13*, 519–549.

Rayson, P. (2009). *Wmatrix*. Lancaster University. Available from: http://ucrel.lancs.ac.uk/wmatrix/.

Reddy, W. M. (2001). *The navigation of feeling*. Cambridge: Cambridge University Press.

Richards, E. S. (2006). The limits of the Australian emigrant letter. In B. S. Elliot, D. A. Gerber, & S. M. Sinke (Eds.), *Letters across Borders: The Epistolary Practices of International Migrants* (pp. 56–74). New York, NY: Palgrave Macmillan.

Richards, E. S. (2010). Australian colonial mentalities in emigrant letters. *Australian Studies, 2*, 1–17.

Schrier, A. (1958). *Ireland and the Irish emigration, 1850-1900*. Minneapolis, MN: University of Minnesota Press.

Scott, J. W. (1992). Experience. In J. Butler & J. W. Scott (Eds.), *Feminists Theorize the Political* (pp. 22–40). New York and London: Routledge.

Sokoll, T. (2001). *Essex pauper letters, 1731–1837*. Oxford: Oxford University Press for the British Academy.

Thompson, G. (2012). Intersubjectivity in newspaper editorials. *English Text Construction. Special issue: Intersections of Intersubjectivity, 5*, 77–100.

Yokoyama, O. T. (2008). *Russian peasant letters*. Wiesbaden: Harrassowitz.

Adjusting and fulfilling masculine roles: the epistolary persona in Dutch transatlantic letters

Babs Boter and Suzanne M. Sinke

ABSTRACT
People involved in migration across borders in the past wrote letters. To write back to family and friends served to reaffirm relationships, but also to readjust those relationships. Mobile letter writers of the past nurtured an epistolary persona – sharing certain information that they expected would sustain or foster the relationship they sought, while withholding other information. Various social roles fell within this persona, in part depending on the recipients. This article explores how visions of gender shape the writing in two letter collections in Dutch from just after the turn of the twentieth century. One comes from a man who left his family to migrate to the United States and where only one (his) side of the story remains. A second collection of family letters illuminates a cross-Atlantic relationship from multiple perspectives. Both collections show how related individuals presented their roles to an epistolary audience and how they negotiated their relationships when it became impossible to fulfill what they and their families saw as appropriate behavior. Both illuminate visions of masculinity and how these tied to other familial roles.

What can letters demonstrate about change and continuity in gender relations? In an age when we re-evaluate the medium and speed of communication, it serves us well to think back to people who used the communications of their time to negotiate their closest relationships. People involved in migration across borders in the past wrote letters. To write back to family and friends served to reaffirm relationships, but also to readjust those relationships (Sinke, 2006). Individuals nurtured an epistolary persona – sharing certain information that they expected would sustain or foster the relationship they sought. Various social roles fell within this persona, in part depending on the recipients (Bosch, 2012; Nestor, 2010; Simon-Martin, 2013). For men it drew upon expected forms of masculinity. In moving from one cultural setting to another, individuals could and often did encounter differences in the form of gender identity they experienced. How much did that letter persona reflect the circumstances of their new setting? Individuals who maintained relationships across borders via letters utilized epistolary ethics, acceptable patterns of what to write (and what not to write) (Fitzpatrick, 1996; Gerber, 2000). Beyond that, they chose the elements to include:

expressions of love or piety, news of success or change, requests for money, information, contact and photos (Cancian, 2010; Gerber, 2006). Those choices helped shape an epistolary persona.

This article explores how visions of gender shape the writing in two letter collections in Dutch from just after the turn of the twentieth century. Unlike some collections, these two do not feature particularly prominent Dutch North American migrants such as those featured in the Stellingwerff (2004) or Lucas (1997) edited editions. They are more akin to those found in the Brinks (1995), Bakker (1999), or Beltman (1996) books. They owe their existence primarily to the interest of family members. If at some point in time family did not want to save the documents for lack of space or interest, those stories disappeared. Because no unified corpus of letters of migrants exists, we cannot claim them categorically as representative. As one study of letters of German migrants suggested, compared to the millions of letters sent, the ones that end up in collections are far too few to appear representative (Kamphoefner, Helbich, and Sommer, 1991, p. 28). Yet these two collections exemplify different elements of a gendered persona and how people adjusted over time. One comes from a man who left his family to migrate to the United States and where only one (his) side of the story remains. A second collection of family letters illuminates a cross-Atlantic relationship from multiple perspectives. We focus there on one man writing to different audiences during a period of both unexpected trauma and normal change. Both collections show how related individuals presented their roles to an epistolary audience and how they negotiated their relationships when it became impossible to fulfill what they and their families saw as appropriate behavior. Both illuminate visions of masculinity and how these tied to other familial roles. Physical distance creates an imperative to write in order to maintain ties, while cultural distance challenges expectations. Migration across borders tends to bring to light differences in expected gendered behavior.

Following the work of R.W. Connell, we adopt the concept of masculinities as multiple, hierarchical, and malleable projects. In other words, within a particular location at a specific time a hegemonic masculinity along with multiple subordinate masculinities may exist, along with their counterparts in femininities. These gendered visions operate as working projects for individuals, and as a basis for power relations in many cases (Connell, 2005; Connell & Messerschmidt, 2005; Schippers, 2007, pp. 85–86). A person crossing cultural borders encounters variations on known themes. For this reason researching the experiences of international migrants exposes gendered experiences and provides insights into a developing global gender order (Connell, 2005, pp. xx–xxii). Moreover, in the context of the early twentieth-century migration from the Netherlands to North America, most adult migrants could (and frequently did) utilize correspondence to maintain ties. Letters thus provide a window on these projects of gendered self-(re)formation. In this we agree that authors create masculinity in part discursively (Connell & Messerschmidt, 2005, p. 841; Talbot, 1998, p. 191). Talbot's definition is useful when we wish to explore the ways in which the (male) migrant letter writers confirm as well as challenge existing versions of hegemonic masculinity institutionalized in the patriarchal model of the early twentieth-century Dutch Protestant family in which women and children were subordinate to men, heterosexuality prevailed, and a man acted as breadwinner or economically responsible head of the household. Yet the migrants also partook of other realms of identity, also in flux. For Dutch men, whiteness typically increased their stature in a North American context, while the status as migrant might point to a lower class status, at least initially. Some of their expectations or activities could blur gendered lines and call the categories into question. Creating a persona within these at least somewhat fluid categories, and finding one's location in the power dynamics that crossed the Atlantic, were part of what took place within an epistolary world.

In correspondence, Cancian claims, letter writers find a way to search into the self, and through their use of language these writers unwittingly construct their identities (Cancian, 2012). Yet the choices may be quite conscious at times as the letter writer adjusts this epistolary identity according to their audience. This in turn can affect the writer's self-perception (DeHaan, 2010; Sheridan, 2014). Part of this identity construction is about gender. A study of language used in certain letters indicates the gender attitudes and norms of sender and possibly receiver. They hint at the ways in which the writers 'accepted, negotiated and challenged expected gender norms and ideologies' (Cancian, 2012, p. 759).

Let us meet our writers.

1. The collections

The letter writers both arrived in North America during a high point for international migration generally and Dutch migration more specifically around the turn of the century. Roughly 48,000 Dutch migrants came to the United States in the period 1901–1910 and another 32,300 in the subsequent decade (Stokvis, 1994, p. 160). Somewhere around 20,000 Dutch migrants went to Canada in the period from 1890 to 1914 (Ganzevoort, 1999a, p. 438). People moved back and forth across the US–Canadian border, which remained extremely porous in this era. Those who made their way to Canada often did so because land remained open for homesteading, and a significant number of Dutch migrants sought land (Ganzevoort, 1999b, pp. 6–7; Ganzevoort, 1988). The proportion of men coming to North America alone rose after the turn of the century, though the Dutch still included larger concentrations of families in the migration than many other nationalities. Even in cases where individuals arrived alone, most formed or reunited with families quickly (Krabbendam, 2009, pp. 147–148; Sinke, 2002). The letter writers shared the desire for family connections and reunification that characterized much of Dutch North American letter writing for this period. Within the Dutch Canadian Protestant subculture to which one of the writers belonged (Sinnema, 2005) active church participation figured as a key element of status for men. If becoming a landowner and successful farmer figured both in the Canadian and Dutch contexts, the subculture also placed great emphasis on religious roles (Bratt, 1984; Connell, 2005; Douma, 2014, ch. 4; Kroes, 1992; Swierenga, 2006). Religious leadership fell to men in this version of hegemonic masculinity, both literally in terms of preaching and serving as a deacon or an elder, but also in terms of organizing the logistics of founding a congregation, getting a church built, and calling on denominational authorities for assistance. While many collections of Dutch letters exist, most present them without substantial commentary as sources of information on migration, settlement, religion and other topics (e.g. Brinks, 1995; Stellingwerff, 2004). Examining the performative elements of writing and the negotiations of identity which take place in the context of migration holds center stage in DeHaan's study of diasporic identity in the writings of one Dutch migrant to Chicago in 1916 (DeHaan, 2010). Ganzevoort also looked briefly at gendered elements in letters (Ganzevoort, 1999b, pp. 17–18). This study builds upon these lines of inquiry.

2. A man building a future

Brieven uit het Verleden/Letters from the Past appeared with Dutch transcriptions and English translations as a manuscript book in 1981. As the transcriber noted, the letters 'show a remarkable variety of style and content' (Verbrugge, 1981, p. 3).[1] Since then, family members uncovered additional letters from the group involved in the move to Canada, which we use for the analysis here (Griffioen, n.d.). Most of the writers hailed from the province of Utrecht. Harmen van der Lee was one of these. In his first year in Canada he wrote at least 18 letters to his parents. In addition he wrote to other more distant family members, in particular the Van der Vliet family. Harmen's sister had married Jacobus van der Vliet and Harmen went to Canada with her brother-in-law Cornelis van der Vliet.

Sinke has written elsewhere about Cornelis van der Vliet and his spouse Jantje Enserink (Sinke, 1999, pp. 17–21 and Sinke, 2002, pp. 168–169). In brief, Cornelis brought Jantje to Canada right after their marriage in the Netherlands in 1909. She moved into a newly con-structed house which would serve as a home for the newlyweds and several of the men Cornelis had recruited to work there. Jantje soon fell ill and went to Minnesota, where Cornelis's sister Maria and family lived. While recovering from a miscarriage there Jantje got word of Cornelis's death. After a period of mourning she returned to the Netherlands (Sinke, 2002).

Harmen, the writer of the letters we consider first of all, came as part of the group going to Canada with Cornelis, and he provided other elements of the story. In particular, Harmen was traveling to Edmonton with Cornelis when Cornelis fell ill with appendicitis and then died of peritonitis. Harmen faced the task of informing family and friends of Cornelis's death and handling all the local arrangements.

Harmen's letters include varying self-representations not just over time in different cir-cumstances, but also to people in somewhat different positions relative to him. Harmen's first extant letter from Canada went not to his parents, but to his brother-in-law, Jacobus van der Vliet (the man married to his sister). Jacobus was Cornelis's brother. From the 'you will be surprised by this letter … because it comes from someone who has never written you, either in Holland or from Canada' (29 August 1909, Verbrugge, 1981, pp. 113–117) to a thank you for a pipe the brother-in-law had given him at departure and congratulatory wishes for an impending birthday, Harmen gives justifications why he writes. After noting that 'much has already been written', hinting that Cornelis could have sent information, he went on to provide some news: 'if it is not new, then let it be a piece of old shortbread … People sometimes say, Deventer cake only becomes delicious when it gets old' (Verbrugge, 1981, p. 115). Reading between the lines, Jacobus wanted information about life in Canada, and Cornelis did not provide much.

In the following analysis we will point out how Harmen, in his letters, seems to negotiate various components of his persona: that of him as laborer, as Dutchman, as Christian, and as a family member. Harmen did not send a letter to his parents until several months later, explaining 'I had promised Van der Vliet not to write about my work here before this was ready' (30 December 1909, Griffioen, n.d.). Waiting until he had substantial earnings to report did not appear easy for Harmen, who had a minor epic penned and ready to send. Earlier Harmen did not hesitate to tell his brother-in-law about the manual labor 'digging ditches'. He clarified it is 'making a water removal system. That sounds more dignified, but the name does not change the case' (29 August 1909, Verbrugge, 1981, p. 117). Presenting himself as a manual laborer, even if he was earning good wages, was not something Harmen (or Cornelis) apparently wanted to do. If being a good man entailed an economic role making 'good' money or starting a farm or business – and many of the family letters include an expectation that men will do this – then Harmen sought not just to attain the goal through migration, but also to report on it. Not all of the process of getting there had to be in the letter if it would disappoint the recipients. We can see in this microcosm why so many men report on how hard they had to work in North America without providing much detail. Correspondence came in fits and starts, depending in part on the degree to which the writers fulfilled expectations.

Harmen's description of Polish migrants on the boat with him from Europe offered greater detail. Harmen's party complained about having to share a cabin with these people at first, arranging to share instead with a Swede and a Belgian. Then Harmen noted the Poles ate in a separate room: 'they were not civilized enough for our people' (30 December 1909). In other ways Harmen offered less national identification: 'the love for my home country is not so high as Mie [sister Maria] thinks' (31 December 1909). In May 1910, barely a year after his arrival, he wrote he could not go back to his old life in the Netherlands: 'it is not easy if you have seen everything here' (24 May 1910). His religious identity as a believer in Christian doctrine and member of a Dutch Protestant denomination came through in many ways, from in-depth descriptions of churches and sermons, intertwining of religious language such as biblical metaphors, or simply mentioning to his parents that they should look for an article in their church paper about a minister who recently visited his group in Edmonton (27 November 1910).

Harmen often included the obligations he associated with being a friend or family member: sending birthday greetings, thank you wishes, letters, presents, answering the questions someone sent or that he assumed someone would ask. In this world of international migration much kinship work shifted to an epistolary form (Di Leonardo, 1987). Men who migrated alone regularly had to take on these tasks that might otherwise fall to women. This shift away from a pattern of hegemonic masculinity, at least at times, put men like Harmen into uncomfortable circumstances. Look, for example, at what Harmen wrote about Cornelis's funeral: 'I have done everything in my power in his sickness and funeral. If there should be something that you would have wished different, do not hold it against me. I was alone and do not speak much English' (26 April 1910, Verbrugge, 1981, p. 147). In reporting about his first letter he explained 'I discover a great mistake I made' (31 December 1909) which was putting the wrong postage on a letter, meaning someone would have to pay for it. One part of Harmen's apologies may have stemmed from regular complaints coming from home. In a letter of 29 July 1910 he reported to his mother how she kept changing her mind. First she did not want him to work for the railroad (when he left the Netherlands), but wanted him to work in farming instead. Then when he wanted to go into farming around Edmonton she was against that, hoping he would keep earning wages first. Here we find hints at the criticism he faced from home.

The circumstances of Harmen's arrival and settlement in Canada mitigated bouts of homesickness and loneliness. After the group with which he arrived finished constructing a dwelling, Harmen wrote 'I like to be with the comrades, in front of the house we built, on my camp stool' (30 December 1909). Only after Cornelis's death did Harmen describe breaking down. With no reports coming back after he sent telegrams and letters about the death, and no local Dutch contacts, Harmen went on to Edmonton to visit friends. 'When I think about these days, I go soft inside …' (6 May 1910). Harmen, however, soon presented himself bouncing back, attending church services and buying land together with a couple of others hoping to found a colony (2 July 1910; 21 August 1910). Through writing he fashioned his identity as a man who could handle the loss in stride. We might say he created this persona both for his readers and for himself (Bosch, 2012; Nestor, 2010; Simon-Martin, 2013). Harmen embraced both the economic role and the religious role that his subculture promoted and he wrote about them regularly.

Though Harmen clearly made church going an important part of his life in his letters, his texts do not reflect the degree of religious language as in those of other migrants of similar background. Reporting on death, he included how the minister presiding spoke in English, and that he understood 'God is the same everywhere … you know where power and strength can be found, in joy and sorrow.' Finally he noted 'calmly [Cornelis] entered eternal rest' (26 April 1910, Verbrugge, 1981, pp. 145–147). In comparison, Maria Verbrugge (Cornelis's sister in Minnesota) wrote much more effusively in religious text to her parents 'the Lord is a refuge in the depths of anxious sorrow. Grace alone teaches silence …' (11 May 1910, Verbrugge, 1981, p. 157). Another paragraph consisted of a biblical verse and her musings about how she must prepare herself for eternity. To what degree this was a gendered difference is not obvious, though all women correspondents in the letter collection employed religious language extensively at times, especially in reporting on emotion. Both men and women provided very detailed descriptions of last moments, hearing about death, and religious services. These had to take the place of being at the bedside or attending the funeral for the relatives across the ocean. Those grieving on the North American side also sought to share the burden – and to receive confirmation of their roles in the process of mourning. It may be in part because of this role that Harmen repeatedly stated how he hoped he did the right thing. Harmen also wrote to his brother-in-law about visiting the grave with friends. He shared a discussion with Cornelis that took place not long before the illness, a discussion that suggested Cornelis, who had spent the last few years moving from one location to another on three continents, wanted to finally settle down in one place (Verbrugge, 1981, p. 158).

Over time, as Harmen's letters indicate, he earned more money, bought farming equipment and animals, and began taking an active role in the newly fledged church. He also seemed to gain confidence. 'Things are going particularly well with my horses' (18 September 1910). Then Harmen decided he needed to borrow money to buy a farm. He turned to his father, describing his current purchases and future plans, in particular regarding land, and explaining both how much money he wanted and how to send it. 'I hope that you can help me' (22 November 1910). His letters, fast and furious, became less about answering the questions from home: 'I will leave that list of questions from my mother for a while; there is so much at the same time at the moment' (20 November 1910). The role of family financing often appeared in letters of migrants. Whereas the impression is sometimes of money coming from North America to Europe, what scholars today refer to as remittances, the financing of the younger generation in another country by their parents appears frequently in letters as well. Harmen could anticipate assistance in part because he had remained in touch since his departure. He both fostered the connection and developed an epistolary persona that his family would both recognize and reward. His persona of loyal son, hard worker, member of a Dutch immigrant community, and pious church member would earn economic as well as emotional dividends.

3. A wandering man

Migrants did not just send requests for money. Many sent more or less desperate appeals for their relatives and other loved ones to join them. The second letter collection offers this scenario (Bakker & Van der Tuin, 2015). In October 1915, 25-year-old Willem Bakker deserted his family in Groningen, a rural, northern province in the Netherlands, leaving behind his wife and children as he headed off to North America. Willem, a grocer by profession, had been married to Jantiena Velthuis since 19 April 1912, and they had two young daughters, Hillie and Frouke. Seven of the letters he penned to his wife 'Tieni' and children after he left remain. He wrote to them over two and a half years, beginning about three and a half months after his departure.[2]

In contrast to immigrant letters we have come to know thanks to edited collections such as the one by Herbert J. Brinks, this set of letters does not detail the material, financial and logistic details of life in the US (Bakker, 1999; Beltman, 1996; Brinks, 1995; Lucas, 1997 [1955]; Stellingwerff, 2004 [1975]). Instead, Willem's letters consist of an almost heartbreaking lament on his life in the US, his feelings of guilt, and his grief over his lost family. No letters from Jantiena have been left to us, although we can deduce some of their contents from Willem's writing. In his final letter, issued on 11 October 1918, he writes that he has received Tieni's last two letters, and that he has 'understood that she wished to know what his plan is'. In the same letter Willem refers to Tieni's request to him to return to the Netherlands, which he explains he is unwilling to do due to the lack of economic possibilities and social gossip, which he understands is the case. Thus, we are only able to obtain a mediated version of her words in Willem's writing. Willem may have misinterpreted or misread some details of Jantiena's letters; he may also have changed them on purpose, as his aim seemed to be to have his wife and children come over and join him to start a new life – a way to compensate for his misbehavior and the pain he caused them. We do know that despite several plans made by the couple to reunite, Jantiena ('Tieni') never emigrated to America. She finally divorced Willem in 1921 and remarried Hendrik Kol six years later, on 2 February 1927. Willem married a woman from Germany and never returned to the Netherlands.

If we assume that Willem wrote no more letters than the ones that remain, seven letters in a period of two and a half years, and the texts hint at this, then great interludes of non-communication occurred between the two spouses. Willem confirms one of the long pauses in his letter of 10 January 1917, stating he 'more than desires' a letter from his wife, as she has not written in more than eight weeks. In turn, Willem frequently rationalizes his own failure to write more often. In November 1916 he states that he finds it difficult to come up with topics to write about because all he sees is his failure to have the family come over (19 November 1916). In April 1918, he accounts for the lack of correspondence by explaining that he has been ill for six or seven months, during which he underwent a kidney operation:

> I thought it better that I do not write for what could I write after we almost had everything ready for you and the children to come over, and then write that I was ill and that it would be better for you to stay in Holland, that I could not do either. (25 April 1918)

The fact that Willem sent these letters from different addresses in Mississippi and Michigan, and in addition refers to his quarters in Memphis, implies that he had no stable domestic life in those first two years in the US. Indeed, in his first letter he literally calls himself a 'lonely wanderer on earth', who is 'Here on my own as Dutchman among Americans' (30 January

1916). In the same letter he states that he has written several letters to the Netherlands (presumably to relatives or friends) in order to hear something about Jantiena, the children, and his other relatives, but complains that he has not received any responses whatsoever. Such references to loneliness coming from a Dutch male migrant in that time period are rather rare, but seem to be the dominant theme of his correspondence (19 November 1916; 10 January 1917).

Willem's suffering from loneliness is only augmented by his feelings of guilt: 'I am feeling so lonesome, and then the burden that I am suffering from having left you and the children alone, having left without a word or sign' (27 June 1917). Willem twice suggests he has thoughts of suicide (25 April 1918, 11 October 1918). In October 1918 he reports 'my life is nothing without you and our dear children and I have to resist the urge to do something really terrible.' He also indirectly refers to his drinking, but assures Jantiena that it offers no solace (11 October 1918). Willem's emotional tone and his references to suicide and drinking may be part of his strategy to prove his emotional and physical vulnerability and lack of certainties in life, which in turn will convince his wife and children to join him. On the other hand, they may also imply a reflection of his resignation to a more 'subordinate' kind of masculinity, as opposed to the hegemonic kind as introduced above (Talbot, 1998, p. 193). The notion of 'subordinate masculinity' as theorized by Talbot includes, among other features, heavy alcohol use, unemployment, manual labor and poor housing. Paradoxically, Willem implicitly seems to continue to support the ideology of hegemonic masculinity, as is exemplified by his fantasy, expressed in several letters, of a family reunion that he would initiate and facilitate. As head of the newly organized American household he would earn enough money so that Tieni would no longer have to sell milk on the streets (i.e. 11 October 1918).

In the letters Willem repeatedly asks Tieni for a photo, an image which possibly could function as a substitute for the family he so misses. Many if not most Dutch migrants in North America requested photographs. Though they could carry around letters as tokens of family connections, photos allowed a more prominent function of display. For Willem we might add that the desire for a photograph meshed with his desire to create an ideal family in his own mind, even if the reality fell far from that standard. This echoes insights from Marianne Hirsch on the role of photographs in constructing family relationships (Hirsch, 1997). His epistolary persona of father and husband sought a visual reminder, a symbolic object that could make this role tangible on a daily basis.

4. Different roles, different voices

In comparison, the first author, Harmen van der Lee, arrived in the company of others – a chain migration – and remained part of an active Dutch migrant community: the small group with whom he crossed the ocean, a larger familial group spread over the North American plains, and an ethnic community in the making in Edmonton. If we compare Harmen and Willem, we could say that Harmen adopts an epistolary persona that functioned more in a public and civic sense, as a member of various communities of related persons. We might anticipate that he wanted his letters shared with other friends and extended family members, as was often the case for letters from North America in this period. The audience, his parents, other family members, and perhaps interested acquaintances, clearly determined part of this emphasis. Willem, in contrast, presents himself in a domestic sense, as a husband and father. Willem signs his letters by stressing his role as head of the family: 'greetings from your loving husband. Byyeee Froukje; Byyeee Hilli' (10 January 1917). A subtle variation in a later letter is telling: 'your *still* loving husband and father' (25 April 1918). In the letters he also addresses himself as 'Pa', and additionally emphasizes his role as father by stating: 'I can imagine how the children long for their Pa' (27 June 1917). The encoders of 'byyeee', 'Pa' and 'their Pa' do not just show Willem's compliant following of epistolary conventions, or an implicit expression of his psychological proximity to his wife and children. They mostly seem to emphasize his (desired) familial, masculine role (Moreton, 2012, p. 618). His epistolary persona in these letters does not reach out much beyond the bounds of his nuclear family. The focus on the familial in letters, and the extra modifiers in standard forms of closing, both fit a model more commonly associated with women among the Dutch in America and some other northwestern European groups (Dossena, 2007, p. 18; Sinke, 2002).

A second striking difference between the two sets of letters is that whereas Harmen stresses what happens to his initial group, which disbands, and the genesis of an ethnic community (Dutch people who have built houses and firms, the establishment of a religious community), Willem mostly refers to the changes within himself (24 May 1910). We do not know much about his possible adjustment to American life and culture other than that he refers to his new American identity as 'Wm Baker' in the address he sends his wife (27 June 1917). When he does refer to any adjustments, it is on a very personal level seemingly unconnected to his ethnicity or nationality: in a letter dated 27 June 1917, he spells out how the old Willem, who was lazy, a drunkard, and who had lost direction, has changed considerably. This, of course, should be taken with a grain of salt; it is part of his strategy to convince his wife to emigrate as well, and reunite with him in America. This epistolary persona envisions the ideal reunion and ignores the war in Europe and the dangers of sea crossing in that context.

Thirdly, and related to the juxtaposition of community versus family, Harmen and Willem are brokers of information, but in very distinct ways. Harmen calls for his addressees to 'tell the minister […] tell brother-in-law […] (6 May 1910), 'all the others who have not asked for me […]' (30 December 1909). He asks about the well-being of 'all the friends' and about the state of construction of a church in the Dutch village of Abcoude (21 August 1910); he informs his addressees that another migrant 'Vos has not had problems of home-sickness. He has got a harmonica […]' (29 July 1910) and promises to send a picture of Chonders' house to his aunt Annachen. 'You see, she had sent along a cup for me, and now I will send her something as well' (25 December 1910). Harmen exchanges news, objects such as pictures, and appears to be one of the many strands in a web of Dutch migration to North America. His epistolary persona links people on both sides of the Atlantic and gains status by fostering that link. In contrast, Willem focuses his writing entirely on the exchange of information between himself, Tieni, and their children. He expresses his hope that Tieni will tell their children about their 'Pa who is so far away and longs for all of them so much' (19 November 1916). He also inquires about their health, and whether they wish to reunite with 'Pa' (10 January 1917). He tells her that when he studies their little faces on the photo portrait she has sent him, he wonders what they will think of their ill-functioning father (25 April 1918). Only in two instances does Willem draw other subjects into his epistolary orbit of the nuclear Bakker family – namely his brother Harm whose parents wish for him to be able to emigrate as well, and a befriended Detroit couple that could report to Tieni of Willem's living conditions and improved habits (11 October 1918).

Willem does not make mention of any friends other than the two he has in Detroit. He presents his social life as being non-existent, merely laboring to be able to have his wife and children come over (30 January 1916; 19 November 1916). Harmen, who needs his addressees to financially support him and who wants others to follow in his footsteps, tells of the social network he has built up while continuing his overseas contacts. In one of his letters he states that his 'purpose' in life is the acquiring of a piece of land in America (6 May 1910). Harmen's encouragement to join in the emigration project to those left behind in the Netherlands includes his statement that he 'wished … that I could get more Dutch farmers to come here […]. Look at Rijneveld – that fellow has bought some land here' (27 November 1910). In another letter he inquires how 'cousin H' is doing now that he is again in Vreeland. 'What does he say about America?' (18 September 1910). Harmen also reports of the visit of the deputy of the minister, and adds: 'it exceeded his expectations and he could confidently advise people to come here' (27 November 1910).

Willem's letters, finally, appear to fit in a romantic discourse of immigration and reunion. He has envisioned his reunion with his wife and children as follows, as becomes clear from several letters: he will save money, arrange for a new home, and 'naturally' wait for Tieni at the station (10 January 1917). In the meantime, Tieni should promptly sell her stuff and come over with their children. Thus they will be able to start a new and happy life that is better than life in the Netherlands (7 December 1916; see also 10 January 1917, 27 June 1917, 25 April 1918). But all hope for such a picture book happy ending is gone when Willem becomes ill. He cannot save money: in his correspondence of 25 April 1918, he appears to resign himself to the bad luck that has befallen them: 'I cannot help that this is how things are with me and this is probably the way it should be.' Did Tieni finally give up waiting for the pre-paid tickets that never came? Did Willem finally give up his vision of reunion? In any case his epistolary persona takes on the mantle of fate that separates the nuclear family. Unable to earn a sufficient amount to reunite his family, he literally takes leave from the role of father and husband. In that sense Willem ultimately does not seem to be able to live up to the conventional gender expectations of his time. His (gendered) immigrant existence fails to confirm, perform and embody the concepts and practices that Talbot indicates make up traditional, hegemonic masculinity that involves male dominance and control (Talbot, 1998, p. 194). If he wrote again, we do not know. No other letters remain – the collection ends.

In both cases the audience mattered. Writing to a spouse as opposed to parents and extended family created different expectations. Harmen could not easily delude his family because he was linked too closely with many others. His letters show how the family found out about some of the omissions his friend Cornelis deployed. In contrast, Willem's letters lack that context. Harmen presented himself as fulfilling his role as an adult man – earning money, working to start a farm, helping to form a church. At the same time he was at least at times a good son, sending messages and doing what his parents considered right. His epistolary persona included roles as attentive relative or friend. Willem was trying to regain a role he had abandoned. He could try to continue the emotional link as husband and father at a distance, but without the economic wherewithal to support the family as a breadwinner, he would fail to fulfill the role over and over.

For scholars of migration and family, Harmen's letters and the epistolary persona he fosters fit one stereotypical model of immigration and settlement, of better economic opportunities and freedom of religious expression. Willem's epistolary persona brings out a rather different example of masculinity in migration, one we find less frequently in letter collections. In one large study of who saved immigrant letters, Wolfgang Helbich and Walter Kamphoefner noted that among their German donors it tended to be more affluent, and particularly agricultural families who stayed in place over generations who remained the repositors and later became donors of letters to their immigrant letter collection. Compared to the immigrant population statistics, the letter writers tended to also be more affluent and disproportionately men (Helbich & Kamphoefner, 2006). How many families threw away the letters of a ne'er do well, the man who could only ask for money but never made any, the father who left behind the wife and children and never managed to reunite? How many discarded letters because they were only about family matters and not 'history' as the later readers defined it? We do not know.

If 'America letters' often sounded formulaic in some parts and conversational in others in many nineteenth-century examples, the letters of Harmen and Willem demonstrate a shift in the early twentieth century (Fitzpatrick, 2006; Elspass, Langer, Scharloth, & Vandenbussche, 2007). The emotionality scholars found in erudite letters of the eighteenth century – the letters of spouses or those of men seeking spouses, for example – appear more common in these letter collections (Pearsell, 2008). Some sections of Harmen and Willem's letters may be conversational or just providing information, but others utilize language in ways that suggest training in written forms. Harmen's first letter to his parents, articulated clearly as one story, with pauses at points, shows the influence of a distinct narrative line. He demonstrated his ability to tell a story, just as he might have in person, but also to use the conventions of correspondence to convey it. The felicity with language this implied also made the expression of a range of feelings easier. Willem utilized writing conventions of his time, but in different ways. He seems to have written his letters from a more primary, emotional starting point (for lack of a better word) that seems to evoke a melodramatic and tragic discourse. The two collections, even if they are only samples, demonstrate the variety of factors that came into play when Dutch migrant men negotiated and articulated their relationships across great distances in letters, creating epistolary personae for their readers. Key factors are motivations for emigration, the migrant's local religious and ethnic community affiliations, familial bonds, gender expectations of the time, and health.

Notes

1. The authors consulted the Dutch originals and have changed wording in the translations slightly when they felt it would improve comprehension for English speakers.
2. The private collection of seven letters was kindly donated to Boter by Dr Iris van der Tuin, Utrecht University, who is the great-granddaughter of Willem Bakker. The collection also includes two photographs. Van der Tuin obtained the collection from her father, Henk van der Tuin.

Disclosure statement

No potential conflict of interest was reported by the authors.

References

Bakker, U. B. (Ed.). (1999). *Zuster, kom toch over: Belevenissen van een emigrantenfamilie uit Friesland. Brieven uit Amerika in de periode 1894-1933* [Sister, please come over]. Winsum, NL: Ulbe B. Bakker [privately printed].

Bakker, W., & Van der Tuin, H. (2015). [Personal collection of letters and photographs].

Beltman, B. W. (1996). *Dutch farmer in the Missouri valley: The life and letters of Ulbe Eringa, 1866–1950*. Urbana: University of Illinois Press.

Bosch, M. (2012). Persona en de performance van identiteit: Parallelle ontwikkelingen in de nieuwe biografische geschiedschrijving van gender en van wetenschap [Persona and the performance of identity: Parallel developments in the new biographical historiography of gender and of science]. *Tijdschrift voor Biografie, 1*, 10–21.

Bratt, J. D. (1984). *Dutch calvinism in modern America*. Grand Rapids, MI: Wm. Eerdmans.

Brinks, H. J. (Ed.). (1995). *Dutch American voices: Letters from the United States*. Ithaca: Cornell University Press.

Cancian, S. (2010). *Families, lovers, and their letters: Italian postwar migration to Canada*. Winnipeg: University of Manitoba Press.

Cancian, S. (2012). The language of gender in lovers' correspondence, 1946–1949. *Gender & History, 24*, 755–765.

Connell, R. W. (2005). *Masculinities* (2nd ed.). Berkeley: University of California Press.

Connell, R. W., & Messerschmidt, J. W. (2005). Hegemonic masculinities: Rethinking the concept. *Gender and Society, 19*, 829–859.

DeHaan, K. A. (2010). Negotiating the transnational moment: Immigrant letters as performance of a diasporic identity. *National Identities, 12*(2), 107–131.

Di Leonardo, M. (1987). The female world of cards and holidays: Women, families, and the work of kinship. *Signs, 12*, 440–453.

Dossena, M. (2007). 'As this leaves me at present' – Formulaic usage, politeness, and social proximity in nineteenth-century Scottish emigrants' letters. In S. Elspass, N. Langer, J. Scharloth, & W. Vandenbussche (Eds.), *Germanic language histories 'from below'* (pp. 1700–2000). Berlin: Walter de Gruyter.

Douma, M. J. (2014). *How Dutch Americans stayed Dutch: An historical perspective on ethnic identities*. Amsterdam: Amsterdam University Press.

Elspass, S., Langer, N., Scharloth, J., & Vandenbussche, W. (Eds.). (2007). *Germanic language histories 'from below' (1700–2000)*. Berlin: Walter de Gruyter.

Fitzpatrick, D. (1996). *Oceans of consolation: Personal accounts of Irish migration to Australia*. Melbourne: Melbourne University Publishing.

Fitzpatrick, D. (2006). Irish emigration and the art of letter-writing. In B. S. Elliott, D. A. Gerber, & S. M. Sinke (Eds.), *Letters across borders: The epistolary practices of international migrants* (pp. 97–106). New York, NY: Palgrave Macmillan.

Ganzevoort, H. (1988). *A bittersweet land: The Dutch experience in Canada, 1890–1980*. Toronto: McClelland and Stewart.

Ganzevoort, H. (1999a). Dutch. In P. R. Magocsi (Ed.), *Encyclopedia of Canada's peoples* (pp. 435–450). Toronto: University of Toronto Press.

Ganzevoort, H. (Ed.) (1999b). *The last illusion: Letters from Dutch immigrants in the 'land of opportunity'*. Calgary: University of Calgary Press.

Gerber, D. A. (2000). Epistolary ethics: Personal correspondence and the culture of emigration in the nineteenth century. *Journal of American Ethnic History, 19*, 3–23.

Gerber, D. A. (2006). *Authors of their lives: The personal correspondence of British immigrants to North America in the nineteenth century*. New York: New York University Press.

Griffioen, A. (Ed.) Letters of Harmen van der Lee. Manuscript copies.

Helbich, W., & Kamphoefner, W. D. (2006). How representative are emigrant letters? An exploration of the German case. In B. S. Elliott, D. A. Gerber, & S. M. Sinke (Eds.), *Letters across borders: The epistolary practices of international migrants* (pp. 29–55). New York, NY: Palgrave Macmillan.

Hirsch, M. (1997). *Family frames: Photography, narrative and postmemory*. Cambridge: Harvard University Press.

Kamphoefner, W. D., Helbich, W., & Sommer, U. (1991). *News from the land of freedom: German immigrants write home*. Ithaca: Cornell University Press.

Krabbendam, H. (2009). *Freedom on the Horizon: Dutch Immigration to America, 1840–1940*. Grand Rapids, MI: Eerdmans Publishing Company.

Kroes, R. (1992). *The persistence of ethnicity: Dutch calvinist pioneers in Amsterdam, Montana*. Urbana: University of Illinois Press.

Lucas, H. S. [Arr.]. (1997 [1955]). *Dutch immigrant memoirs and related writings*. Grand Rapids, MI: Wm. B. Eerdmans.

Moreton, E. (2012, November). Profiling the Female emigrant: A method of linguistic inquiry for examining correspondence collections. *Gender & History, 24*, 617–646.

Nestor, P. (2010). New opportunities for self-reflection and Self-fashioning: Women, letters and the novel in mid-victorian England. *Literature & History, 19*, 18–35.

Pearsell, S. M. S. (2008). *Atlantic families: Lives and letters in the latter eighteenth century*. New York, NY: Oxford University Press.

Sheridan, V. (2014). Letters of love and loss in a time of revolution. *The History of the Family, 19*, 260–271.

Schippers, M. (2007). Recovering the feminine other: Masculinity, femininity, and gender hegemony. *Theory and Society, 36*, 85–102.

Simon-Martin, M. (2013). Barbara Leigh Smith Bodichon's travel letters: Performative identity-formation in epistolary narratives. *Women's History Review, 22*, 225–238.

Sinke, S. M. (1999). Migration for labor, migration for love: Marriage and family formation across borders. *OAH Magazine, 14*, 17–21.

Sinke, S. M. (2002). *Dutch immigrant women in the United States, 1880–1920*. Urbana: University of Illinois Press.

Sinke, S. M. (2006). Marriage through the mail: North American Correspondence Marriage from early print to the web. In B. Elliott, D. A. Gerber, & S. M. Sinke (Eds.), *Letters across borders* (pp. 75–94). New York, NY: Palgrave Macmillan.

Sinnema, D. (Ed.). (2005). *The First Dutch settlement in Alberta: Letters from the pioneer years 1903–1914*. Calgary: University of Calgary Press.

Stellingwerff, J. (2004 [1975]). *Iowa letters: Dutch immigrants on the American frontier*. Grand Rapids, MI: Wm. B. Eerdmans.

Stokvis, P. R. D. (1994). International migration from the Netherlands, 1880–1920. In R. Hoefte & J. C. Kardux (Eds.), *Connecting cultures: The Netherlands in five centuries of transatlantic exchange* (pp. 155–169). Amsterdam: VU University Press.

Swierenga, R. P. (2006). Walls or bridges? Acculturation processes in the reformed and Christian reformed churches in North America. In G. Harinck & H. Krabbendam (Eds.), *Morsels in the melting pot: The persistence of Dutch immigrant communities in North America* (pp. 33–42). Amsterdam: Vrije Universiteit.

Talbot, M. M. (1998). *Language and gender: An introduction*. Cambridge: Polity Press.

Verbrugge, F. (Comp. & Ed.). (1981). *Brieven uit het Verleden* [Letters from the Past]. manuscript University of Minnesota.

'If it is not too expensive, then you can send me sugar': money matters among migrants and their families

Sonia Cancian and Simone A. Wegge

ABSTRACT

Discussions about money among migrants and their families have long been a financial and emotional concern. Earning money, or more money, and securing a family's present and future well-being were significant factors when men and women made the decision to immigrate abroad over the twentieth century. With postal services globally systemized, literally tons of letters crossed oceans and continents for migrants, their families, and others to remain in touch. Letters, as historians and other scholars note, provide a plethora of information and insight on the lives and experiences of migrants and non-migrants. These micro-narratives set against the backdrop of national and local macro-narratives, contribute to understanding the state of mind and the state of heart of correspondents whose reason for writing was directly linked to migration. In this paper, we examine issues that relate to money and its emotional underpinnings as conveyed by a number of migrants and their more sedentary families over the first half of the twentieth century. The letters we examine in our paper are part of the Digitizing Immigrant Letters Project collection housed at the University of Minnesota's Immigration History Research Center (archives.ihrc.umn.edu/dil/index.html). The letters, originally written in Italian, Ukrainian, Russian, Slovak, Slovenian, Croatian, and Latvian, were translated into English as part of the Digitizing Immigrant Letters Project. Here, we examine migrant family letters using an interdisciplinary, comparative approach drawn from economic theory, social history and migration history. Some of the questions we explore are: What kind of monetary issues mattered and to whom? In what ways did these issues impact migrants and their families? How did money and familial intimacy intervene with processes of migration? What are some of the prominent links between money, family and migration discussed in migrant correspondence?

1. Introduction

Economics and emotions intersect with migration and mobility in fascinating and complex ways. When we combine the notions of migration, family, and money, the word that most often

Table 1. Details on the DIL letter collections.

Family number	Family	Language used	Year of emigration	Years written	Number letters	Main author (s)	Location of author	Occupation of author	# Photos included
1	Diego Delfino	Italian	1908	1925–1926	7	Self	Ohio, USA	Medical doctor	1
2	Alexander Granovsky	Ukrainian	1913 or earlier	1913–1939	7	Brother and sister of Alexander	Berezhtsi, Ukraine	Poor farmer (collective?)	5
3	George Greben-stchikoff	Russian	1925 or earlier	1917–1931	5	Self; mother, son & brother of George	CT, USA; Kazakhstan, Russia	GG: Writer, artist	11
4	Paul & Veronica Kovac	Slovak	1917 or earlier	1917–1927	7	Self	Bridgeport, CT, USA	Soldier (US Army); laborer?	4
5	Anton Nemanich	Slovenian	Around 1882	1921–1924	5	Brother of Anton	Slovenia	Vintner (poor)	1
6	Edward Paikens	Latvian	1949	1956–1957	7	Mother of Edward, his wife, self	Lencini, Latvia	Peasant farmer on collective (Kolhoz)	3
7	Mike Vukasinovich	Croatian dialect	1920 or earlier	Pre-1936, not clear	4	Mother of Mike	Plavnice, Croatia	N/A	None

Source: Digitizing Immigrant Letters, Immigration History Research Center, University of Minnesota – Minneapolis. http://ihrc.umn.edu/research/dil/

comes to mind is remittances. For millions, letters frequently included cash remittances – a source of income that countless working-class and rural-based migrants and their families in the homeland depended on (Cohen, 2005; de Haas, 2007; Ghosh, 2006).[1] Over the nineteenth and twentieth centuries, as men and women became dissatisfied with the lack of economic opportunities in their homelands, many chose to migrate on their own or with their families, moving across their country's borders and to other lands. As individuals and families moved, the need to stay in touch with family members and others who remained behind proved vital. Before long-distance phone calls and Internet technologies became accessible to the larger populations, letter writing was essential for staying in touch. To write a letter to a family member following a lifetime of face-to-face communication required the refinement or altogether learning of writing skills. For individuals who had not learned to read or write, a scribe, that is, a family member, a teacher, or a young school child was beckoned to write a letter on behalf of the less literate correspondent. Like face-to-face interactions, reading and writing communication came with its own rules, signs, and symbols. The endeavor to maintain a relationship at a distance generated a constellation of emotions, including tensions, disappointments, misunderstandings, often combined with hope, nostalgia, and joy.

Letters are cultural artifacts that advance our understanding of the local and global experiences of voluntary and forced migration, told or retold by migrants, their loved ones (families, friends, neighbors, kin and non-kin) who remained behind in the homeland, and those who immigrated elsewhere. Historical documents of this nature written by non-professional writers provide insight regarding the personal lives and mindsets of women, men, and children. Letters are also a lens onto the intimate, emotional and rational mappings of minds. Viewed as 'a great spur to mass migration', which, in the words of one scholar, 'certainly transformed both Europe and North America, and linked their histories inseparably' (Gerber, 2006, pp. 40–41) migrant letters contribute to the powerful re/telling of the lives experienced first-hand by migrants and their families. While narratives often oscillated between overt and covert messages, in many cases, the letters also document stories about home and nostalgia, about the missing plate at the family table, news, the need to stay connected, and the need for material and emotional support in the face of temporary or permanent separation. For many migrants and their loved ones, separation compelled individuals and families to communicate on paper both rational and emotional matters occurring, as they were, at home, work, in the neighborhood, and in the larger community.

When we consider the study of migrant letters, early volumes include the work of William Thomas and Florian Znaniecki (1918–1920) (*The Polish Peasant in Europe and America*), Isaac Schapera (1941), Theodore Blegen (1955) and others.[2] Already in the 1920s a call for 'America Letters' and letters originating in Norway had been launched by Blegen during his travels between the US and his native country. From the 1950s onwards, a sequence of migrant letter collections was published (Barton, 1975; Brinks, 1995; Cameron, Haines, & Maude, 2000; Conway, 1961; Erickson, 1972; Hale, 1984; Houston & Smyth, 1990; Miller, Schrier, Boling, & Doyle, 2003; Wtulich et al., 1986). Many of these works underscore findings on social and economic adjustment and settlement, working and living conditions, motives for emigration and networks of support. In-depth analyses of migrant letters emerged in the 1990s especially with the work of Kamphoefner, Helbich & Sommer (1991) and Fitzpatrick (1994), Sinke (2002), Liu (2005), Gerber (1997, 2004, 2005, 2006), Cancian (2007, 2010, 2012), which examine dynamics associated with intimacy, education, psychology, family, gender, economics, and emotions of migrants and their loved ones. Their work calls attention to the intersections and transformations that occurred in relationships, identities, emotions, ideas, ideologies, and norms as a result of migration. We expand on this literature by adding material from economics, psychology, and sociology to underscore that those who moved usually chose to do so (were self-selected) and were often more ambitious and risk-taking than their sedentary family members. We point out how this divergence in attitude or orientation affected the communications between the two parties (Boneva & Frieze, 2001; Chiswick, 2000; Jaeger et al., 2010; Mckay, 2007; Singh, 2006; Wegge, 1998, 2008).[3]

In concert with a number of recent works, our paper contributes to the current emotional turn in history (Frevert, 2011; Matt & Stearns, 2014; Plamper, 2015; Rosenwein, 2002). We examine ways in which money matters were discussed through the language of intimacy, emotions and relations in seven collections of migrant letters. Part of a larger project, the letters we selected and analyzed have been published digitally through the Digitizing Immigrant Letters (DIL) Project at the Immigration History Research Center at the University of Minnesota.[4] Launched in 2009, the Digitizing Immigrant Letters Project serves to survey the range of emotions and intimacy in a growing body of letters written in languages other than English. Most of the letter collections featured are drawn from the Immigration History Research Center's archived collections. Written by migrants and their more sedentary friends and family members in contexts of international migration over the nineteenth and twentieth centuries, the letters underscore, among other themes, the familial and affective ties and concerns and preoccupations shared between family members belonging to diverse classes, ethnic groups, occupations, and stages in their lives.[5] The Digitizing Immigrant Letters collection is among the most ethnically diverse collection of migrant correspondence available in a digital platform, and provides digital access to letters written between 1850 and 1970 for research and teaching (Cancian & Wegge, 2014).

Money and its emotional role in families have been largely understudied especially in relation to migration movements (Singh, 2006, p. 387). Our analysis compares the letter collections of one Italian family and six Eastern and Central European families, letters exchanged between family members who had immigrated to the US and family members who had stayed behind. We compare a single theme across several immigrant groups and families. Examined closely, these letters point to the conclusion that migrants tended to be more economically ambitious than their sedentary loved ones. The willingness to travel far and wide to North America may have played a role. By contrasting and evaluating all seven collections alongside each other, we find that those who stayed in the home country and belonged to the poorer families of our group were eager to maintain ties, both for emotional reasons and in the hope of benefiting from a real or imagined newly achieved prosperity of family members in the US. Their letters emphasize economic and financial matters more than others, across time, geography and language.

By examining seven digitized collections of the Digitizing Immigrant Letters Project, first, we underscore the usefulness of a digital source – such as the DIL Project – for advancing research in the study of migration. Next, we cast our net wide to capture the economic and related emotional concerns of migrants and their families especially from a comparative viewpoint. Economics is intrinsically related to migration. Much research on international migration shows that, 'economic factors play an important role in the process: People tend to emigrate from less to more economically advanced countries' (Boneva and Frieze, 2001). There is a consensus among migration researchers that 'migration occurs between demand-pull factors that draw migrants into industrial countries, supply-push factors that push them

out of their own countries, and networks of friends and relatives already in industrial societies who serve as anchor communities for newcomers' (Boneva & Frieze, 2001, pp. 477–478;
Martin, 1993). Similarly, a summary of theories across disciplines modeling how migrants
behave shows that the field of economics emphasizes wage differentials and push and pull
factors, while the fields of sociology and history tend to underscore networks and gender
(Brettell & Hollifield, 2000, p. 19).

In our analysis, we turn to seven of the letter collections available in the DIL project,
written between 1913 and 1957, of which most of the letters were written prior to the start
of World War II. Details of the letter writers are provided in Table 1. Importantly, all of the
migrants in these seven families moved westward at some point in their lives, from various
parts of Eastern and Western Europe to the US.

We chose letters of individuals and families who discussed money matters and concerns,
the material restrictions they faced, the emotions that the dearth of economic means consistently engendered in them, and the need or not to communicate their state of heart in a letter
to a family member. In our selection of letters for this study, we focused on the economic
challenges (in terms of both money and provisions for subsistence) discussed in the light
of migration of a loved one, people who fretted about money over the short and long term,
and people who worried about their loved ones' concerns about money and related matters,
including inheritance, education, food provisions, farming costs, and life cycle events.

In this paper, we analyze correspondence exchanged between migrants and their loved
ones who remained behind as a window into understanding poverty and the emotional
underpinnings that were communicated to and from migrants in their homelands and the
United States via correspondence. As is the case for other themes, the category of poverty is
not readily accessible in an archive's catalogue of finding-aids.[6] This means that the researcher
is required to read the whole collections of letters available, and mine them for evidence of
financial and economic concerns that were voiced either explicitly or implicitly. While what
was not said in letters is arguably equally important as what was said, understood, implied,
or kept necessarily absent, because of the fragmentary nature of the letters and the dearth
of information about the authors, our reading here is based primarily on content analysis of
the letters. Close readings of the letters for this study enabled us to examine and compare
economic and material concerns through the language of affection, familial ties and expectations across space, class, ethnic groups among migrants and those who remained behind.
Of course, numerous themes and concerns outside money matters shared between migrants
and their loved ones are also imbedded in these letters. These include concerns like inheritance and testaments 'Mother didn't make a will and no will was bequeathed' (Granovsky,
May 25, 1914); education 'Your little brothers … in the convent, where they study arduously'
(Delfino, April 8, 1925); life cycle events 'Mother write me about your decision and when the
wedding will take place' (Paikens, October 7, 1957); health 'Right now we are healthy, and
how it will be later I don't know' (Grebenstchikoff, August 14, 1917); war 'In the beginning
of the war, we still lived at home …' (Granovsky, December 3, 1922); death 'You need not
die, but live as much time as God has assigned to you' (Granovsky, May 25, 1914); staying in
touch 'give us news that you are among the living, I wait impatiently' (Granovsky, November
25, 1915); and the fear, among others, of being alone 'I am all alone' (Paikens, April 14, 1957).

2. Migration and relative poverty in the early twentieth century

Many of the migrants who authored the selected letters were to some large degree economic migrants. Economic migrants are identified as migrants who moved if they could afford to, or if an outside organization or individual paid for their travel and settlement, and if they estimated that they could do economically better at their destination. They are described as 'tending, on average, to be more able, ambitious, aggressive, entrepreneurial, or otherwise favorably selected than similar individuals who choose to remain in their place of origin' (Chiswick, 2000, pp. 61, 71). Still, as Chiswick notes, these characteristics apply to some degree for all migrants, including ideological migrants or refugees, but just less 'intensely' (Chiswick, 2000, p. 71). Such differences in personalities and temperaments between migrants and their family members who stayed home often led to tensions and other dynamics, as we also discovered in our research for this paper.

Here, we examine the letters of the Delfino, Grebenstchikoff, Granovsky, Kovac, Nemanich, Paikens and Vukasinovich families. For most of the letter collections, we were able to observe especially one side of the correspondence due to limited availability of the letters. In the Delfino and Kovac series, the letter writers were migrants who had settled in the US, while in the other five series, the writers were family members who had remained in their home country in Eastern Europe or Russia, or in later periods the Soviet Union. With the exception of Edward Paikens, the migrants in these families left Eastern Europe before 1926, with five of the seven in our selection of letters written before 1922, the year the Soviet Union was formed.

Six of the seven letter collections analyzed involve migrants who left countries in pre-Soviet Eastern Europe or the Soviet Union. On average, citizens in these parts of Europe were financially worse off than those in Western and Southern Europe, not only in terms of life expectancy, but also in critical economic terms: these regions had substantially lower levels of labor productivity and per capita GDP (Berend, 2006).[7] While late Soviet society could boast a social safety net (close to zero unemployment and homelessness), most of the migrants whose letters we examine did not experience such a thing in the years before they left their homelands, as this was achieved well after the Russian revolution of 1917 (Berend, 2006, p. 185; Harrison, 2014, pp. 397–398). Researchers have described this region of the world in the nineteenth century and before 1917, in comparison to the west, as economically backward: freedom from serfdom and the right to emigrate came much later than in the west; and the general shortage of labor, high illiteracy rates, and high transportation costs (huge expanses of land), among other factors, including cultural ones, made industrialization difficult or slow in many parts.[8] An ambitious and impatient individual who wanted to earn a higher wage or build a business often needed to seek his fortune elsewhere. The revolution in 1917 brought uncertainty and at times significant political, social and economic turmoil to Russian society and many parts of Eastern Europe.

In light of the dearth of information on the levels of income of the letter writers and their families, we substitute income levels with occupation and knowledge that is made available through the letters to determine the economic well-being of the letter writers and their families. For instance, if they stressed that they were short of money or food, we can assume they suffered some form of financial hardship.

The occupations of the main authors of the letters are shown in Table 1. While Diego Delfino worked as a medical doctor and George Grebenstchikoff as a writer and artist, the other authors were mostly farmers, agricultural workers or laborers. The less well-off letter writers in this selection had fewer economic resources, a lower standard of living and experienced more episodes of crises related to the provision of basic necessities of life. More broadly, across Europe and North America, the average European in the late nineteenth and early twentieth centuries before the existence of modern welfare states had few savings or capital assets, resources they could turn to during a financial crisis. They also did not have as many ways to insure themselves against bad economic outcomes. When they could, in a financial crisis they relied on family members or meager levels of community assistance.

Many migrants moved to seek out a better existence compared to what they were experiencing in their homelands. Often this had to do with being unable to provide well enough for themselves or for their children in an economic sense. In other cases, migration had to do with the political or institutional (religious, social) conditions at home that prevented them from living a life they had envisioned for themselves. By moving to a country like the US, they hoped to improve their respective lot in life. Migration also entailed financial constraints: migrants moved if they had the financial resources to pay travel costs or if they could secure a loan from a family member or friend who could help them pay the costs of traveling.[9] The very destitute with few monetary resources were less likely to move unless they had a social network that supported them and their project via remittances or through family support, or they moved to places like Australia and Canada which offered assisted-migration programs.

3. Did migrants think differently about money matters than sedentary individuals?

Recent findings indicate that, 'individuals who are more willing to take risks are more likely to migrate' (Jaeger et al., 2010, p. 684). Many migration scholars have emphasized that migrants used family networks to achieve their goals of moving long distances and establishing themselves in new destinations (Baily, 1999; Gabaccia, 1984, 1994; Reeder, 2003; Yans-McLaughlin, 1977). One study illustrates that those who moved first tended to take more money with them than family members who followed (Wegge, 1998). Partly this may have been due to families devising multi-move financing strategies, and partly this may have occurred because migrant 'pioneers' of families were predisposed to making big changes in their lives, despite the risks involved.[10] It is also likely that people with limited resources used family networks more than individuals and families who were financially secure.[11]

Those who remained behind did not move for a number of reasons. Some were too poor to migrate, while others were held back by familial and affective attachments. Others still, lacked the interest or drive. Psychologists Boneva and Frieze, for instance, argue that those who remained behind were more oriented toward family and affiliations, while migrants seemed to be driven by increased work opportunities and better prospects of higher achievement (Boneva & Frieze, 2001), and a greater sense of adventure. Migration is a linking process. Our examination of families who remained behind alongside migrants contributes to a deepening understanding of migration as a linking process in which both migrants and their loved ones who remained in the homeland were affected by migration.

4. The letters: money matters, family relations, and emotions

Long-distance migration often allowed a family member to achieve an improved standard of living, and in most families, others were aware of this. In societies with fewer social safety nets, as was the norm prior to 1930 in most countries, individuals had to request more from their family members than perhaps people in contemporary western economies are used to. Not only were emotional narratives integrated in epistolary exchanges, letters were also commonly associated with intimacy. As William Decker and other historians note, intimacy in letters is attributed to immediacy and to familial ties, which in turn, assumed the existence of a certain confidentiality between family members and other close relations as an enabling process in written correspondence (Decker, 1998, p. 5). Was there an art to asking family members or close relations for money? Here we focus on how migrants and their loved ones communicated with each other about family obligations and money.

A typical item of discussion in the letters between migrants and their families who remained behind was the matter of money mailed or forwarded via a third party – banks, for the most part – across the Atlantic Ocean from the migrant to family members back home. Loved ones who remained behind frequently felt compelled to acknowledge receipt of money and discuss some of the practical bureaucratic issues involved in receiving the money. In most letters the writers thanked the migrant for sending money and in some cases, proceeded to enquire about more money.

In the seven letters held at the Immigration History Research Center written to Alexander Granovsky, siblings Serhii Neprytsky and Lida Neprytsky referred directly to money in five of the letters. They thanked their brother Alexander for sending money, and discussed some of the problems with receiving it (delays) from the local office: 'Thank you for the money. I received the money after Easter in half a month. I had a problem with them for a long time before I received them. The family name was incorrect [and I] had to make corrections' (25 May 1914). They also discussed other expenses related to improving their farm or purchasing clothing and boots. On 25 May 1914, Serhii wrote that he did not have enough money to pay for the burial plot of their mother and had subsequently inquired with others regarding a loan. At Alexander's request, Serhii offered an explanation about their mother's passing. In this letter, we learned of how Serhii himself tried to come to terms with his mother's death, followed by his need to borrow money for her burial:

> Beloved brother you are interested in how mother died. In death there is nothing of interest, only great sorrow. I was present at father's and then mother's deaths. One stands by a living person and in that second they're dead. And even if you wanted to ask something but now you can't … The pulse stopped beating. It was very difficult to look at death. The deed of purchase [burial ground] from Shashkova is in our hands and is laying at Moroziuk's, I haven't paid for it yet. I bought Polkiv's kitchen-garden and the cost of the deed of purchase was 105 rubles. The deed of purchase is at Naha-chevsky's, because I didn't have all of the money. I will return the money to him in the fall and then I'll take the deed of purchase. (25 May 1914)

Serhii reflectively described to his brother in detail his mother's death. This discussion inevitably includes money matters, like the payment for their mother's burial plot and their mother's will. Whether Alexander Granovsky sent money to help his brother Serhii and sister Lida to contribute to the repayment of a debt incurred for their mother's death is unknown. However, a subsequent letter in the collection – written by Serhii, one and a half years later while World War I was in full swing cutting off correspondence between relatives and many families in Ukraine – evokes the need to maintain ties between them and their brother living at the time in Fort Collins, Colorado.

Despite the censorship exercised by the authorities, Serhii managed to provide many details about how difficult life was for him and other family members in the Ukraine:

> Extremely surprised … stopped writing … [what] happened to you, what kind of catastrophic events? It's as if you were dead and no one will give any kind of news. If … Beloved brother maybe you live a better life than us. You probably don't know what happened to our settlement … the entire matter of refugees is directed by the Tatianovsky committee, but such aid only brings them misfortune. There were such people who lived on their farmsteads as lords, and now they've encountered tragedy. We're left without anything. We had a few rubles left from home and now they are gone. How we'll live further I don't know. We're now living in Branlov at Mania's and Halia in Holendura at the factory store. Lidia and I are still at Mania's. I look for employment for myself and Lidia will remain at Mania's … And so please Sasha at least write [us] where and how you live. It will be pleasing to me to know that you are still among the living, otherwise we think that you are dead … What are the wages like in America? What kind of prices on all goods? All work here is standing still and the prices on all goods are … cheaper write, don't forget, that you have, – a brother, and sister. Be healthy, we all kiss you firmly. Your brother Serihiï My address is St. Bratslov' (Pod. Hub.) [Post station Bralov, Podol province] Sender M.M. Borysenko For S. A. Hranovsky Write your exact address. 19 25/XI 15 year. Give us news that you are among the living, I wait impatiently. (25 November 1915)

Letter writing provided opportunities for self-reflection concerning money matters. Some writers, for instance, used letter writing to describe and reflect on their experiences at a specific juncture in their lives, for instance, when they were short of money, when they ventured out of their villages, and when they repeatedly requested news from a loved one. Intimate family ties underscore discourses of affection, resilience, and making do, as we observe in a reading of the Granovsky letters: the war had decimated the settlement in which Serhii lived. Did the family's financial constraints lead Serhii to reestablish ties with his brother Alexander Granovsky in the US? Or was his motivation for writing to his brother based entirely on familial affection? We cannot know for sure.

By contrast, when we consider the Paikens collection – letters originating in Latvia's Aluksne district, exchanged between a mother, her son, and later, her daughter-in-law, other money-related issues emerge in addition to acknowledgements of receipt of money via transfer: 'Hello little son, The money has arrived. The bank statement is dated November 18. I will go and get it on the 26th. When I will get it I will write you back. I heard that your money here is valued very little. When I will get it I'll see it.' (25 November 1956)

Other elements characteristically – like guilt and seeking support – also became part of Anna Paikens's narrative:

> Son, I am happy now that I know about you. Until now I always thought, now it is good that I will be able to work. But, if I will not have strength anymore and won't have anybody to help me, then every time tears are running. Now I know that you will help me if needed. Write me if you are happy in your life, because your happiness is also my happiness. (25 November 1956)

In a later letter, Anna Paikens wrote from Lencini in Latvia to her son and explained the details of her income broken down in money and goods in kind, consisting of rye, wheat, and other grains. In the same letter she discussed the benefits of keeping a pig as well as her concern that the sugar she was expecting from America had not arrived yet:

> Hello dear son, On January 30, I received your letter that you had written on January 6. Thank you. You know well that I am lonely. When I receive your letter it is like the sun after the rain for me. I live and do my job. This year we got paid for 1956, 7 roubles, one kilo and hundred grams

of grain, 600 grams of rye, 500 grams of wheat, and one kilo of fodder. I had 469 working days, I have enough bread for myself but I also have to keep a pig as one cannot go by without a spread. I bought 300 kilos of grain for 800 roubles. It will also be enough for a pig. Pork is expensive. Poor quality pork in stores costs 21 roubles a kilo, good pork 30 roubles and more. The sugar I haven't received. (3 February 1957)[12]

What meaning did these prices have to her son, Edward? Anna Paikens had some financial resources; however, she could not afford to pay customs duties for the gifts her son had sent to her in the mail. She subsequently wrote to Edward: 'If you are sending a package make sure to pay the customs there. Everybody says that nothing has to be paid here. Find out how it is there' (3 February 1957). Did this information lead her son to believe she led a precarious life? Or was it simply a matter of not being able to afford any extras – like customs duties on gifts received – beyond bare necessities?

Most individuals and families back home were aware of the prices of goods relative to wages. This may have been an acute concern for those living on collective farms, which affected, for instance, Anna Paikens's life in Latvia. Some of her statements about pay and prices are confusing, but close readings help us to understand better what she was implying in her letter. Anna Paikens's gratitude to her son for his news and sugar, for instance, continued in subsequent letters, as did her concern about his life and his plans for marriage. On 24 February 1957, she wrote:

> Hello dear son, Heartfelt thanks for the sugar that I received February 22. I don't know how much you had to pay for sending it. It was very cheap for me, 14 roubles. If it is not too expensive then you can send me sugar. Here one cannot get it. One has to wait in line in Riga. And they only give half a kilo. If you can get it from a speculator one has to pay 15 roubles a kilo and the trip also costs 60 roubles and I don't have time to travel, I am at work every day. During daytime I cannot get anywhere to get the sugar. Otherwise all is the same. I am healthy, there is also bread. I bought 800 kilos of grain for 800 roubles, wheat for 3 roubles and 2½ kilos of rye. Why aren't you writing to me about yourself? I am asking you if you are married or just engaged. And if you are satisfied with your life? Son, I am interested in your life. I am happy about your happiness. You have lived there already 6 years. Are you happy in your married life? Write me if Helena also works or just you alone? … I don't know if I will ever see you. Write me if I can hope for seeing you ever again. How much I would want to meet and see you again. Most likely it is just a dream, which cannot be fulfilled.

In this letter, she thanked her son in Minnesota for the sugar he had sent her, and proceeded to discuss the challenges she faced in buying sugar locally as a result of rationing: 'one can purchase it from official stores but one needs to stand in line for a limited amount allowed (half a kilo) or one can travel a long distance to buy it in the black market at a higher, we presume, price.' Anna Paikens seemed to be well versed in what basic necessities cost, what her time was worth and whether it was worthwhile for her to travel. In later letters, loneliness, longing, and curiosity about Edward's new life continued to permeate Anna's letters, as did other financial concerns. On 14 April 1957, she wrote:

> Dear son, do you also have your own house or did Helena have a house or have you taken a loan? You write that your current job is interesting. Write me also what you are doing and how much you earn a month. And how much does butter cost there? We always read that there is hunger, I hope you haven't died from starvation … You got married exactly at the same age as your dad was when he got married. … See, New Years Eve marked 18 years since father was buried. Who knows how long I will live myself. I have big worries. The shepherd's dog died. I don't know how we will manage without him. Sheep are not controllable without a dog … Today is Palm Sunday. Easter is not celebrated, we have to work. When I am at the farm I have my own job. When I have time, I will celebrate. I am also sitting and crying that there is nobody to expect

to arrive for holidays … I am all alone as an old piece of junk. Now I have chattered away too much. Send greetings to Helena and mother. And be greeted yourself. Mother

While we are missing many of the details concerning Anna Paikens and her life as a widow whose son had emigrated to faraway America, we can assume from this excerpt and other letters in the collection that life was both financially and socially hard for her. Still, she seems to fit very well the description by Boneva and Frieze (2001) of family members who remained behind, as being highly oriented towards family.

The letters of Paul Kovac provide a perspective from the other side of the Atlantic, that is, of an American migrant corresponding with his mother who remained in Slovakia. A close reading of the collection provides a lens through which we can observe how bureaucratic procedures and financial security – negotiated transnationally by letter writers – contributed to the mother–son exchanges. From Bridgeport, Connecticut, Paul Kovac wrote to his mother in Hradok, Slovakia on 12 December 1920:

> I'm letting you know that I received your letter and I was in the city hall and I arranged everything for you to be able to get some aid well it was a little bit difficult because you have those belongings so the officials think that you can live off it but I explained that you as my mother are ill and my brothers are not able to work either because they were also unhealthy well they accepted these reasons and now I have to send you this letter sign it where the cross is and a notary should also sign it and put the municipal seal I think that you will be not able to fill it out but go to the next Red Cross they will fill everything out for you but say rightly that you are ill you have a small property off which you can't live properly and get clothed also mention that I had helped you a bit before war but after I had joined the American army where I was two years and where I was maimed now I draw pension from which I can't help you because it is just enough for me well take care of it to arrange everything.

Despite his efforts, described in his letter to his mother, Paul Kovac was unable to successfully secure aid for his family overseas. Frustration, guilt, and disappointment permeate his letter. Still, it seems nothing else could be done, as is evident from a subsequent letter written by Paul:

> Indeed I'd opened enough those offices' doors and written enough letters across America and when it didn't work I wrote you that I hadn't gotten anything for you because the offices thought that you had two sons with healthy hands so these should have provided for you not me with just one hand and a half well what more should I have done. But I know what's going on here You think that I had gotten that money for you and I have kept them But God is my witness that I hadn't gotten even a rusty cent for you and if you don't believe me I will send you that government letter and ask someone to read it because it is in English And as for me I can't help you better because I get a living just for myself You have also written me to send money to one of my brothers and that either could come after me But I don't know what would he do here as many old Americans have nothing to eat here Do you think that he could also draw a pension as I do Or do you think that I'm rich and that I would provide for him and even he could save some money when I can't save anything. (26 July 1922)

In his letters to his mother in Slovakia, Paul was frequently concerned about her well-being and wondered if she had enough to live on. In the above excerpt, Paul explained to his mother the difficulties he experienced in arranging financial aid for her from the US and that it was not a good idea for his brother to join him in the US. It seems fairly certain that Paul could not imagine himself supporting his brother, nor could he imagine his brother not seeking financial security from him.[13] Paul Kovac's financial situation at home, as he implied in subsequent letters, did not improve significantly, and his description of his financial constraints justified his inability to help his mother in Slovakia. As he pointed out, he and his wife had a child. While they were grateful for their good health, he concluded in a last letter written in Hawleyville, Connecticut: 'I have a little bit of job (work) I can make a bit money so we don't live in poverty, So our mommy we have nothing else new to write to you' (5 July 1927).

Family property and the problems associated with family members living thousands of miles away from their property coupled with related issues that emerge as a result of family assets left to the care of other family members prevailed in a number of discussions in the DIL letters. The theme is especially interesting in the Vukasinovich letters, all of which were written by Mike Vukasinovich's mother in Plavnice, a village near Bjelovar in north-west Croatia.[14] In these letters, she discussed how to care for a property both locally and at a distance, and how to best ensure one's legal ownership:

> I am not well and I have not made arrangements for the house for this and next year because I am expecting to hear about whether you are or not [coming back home] and I don't know myself how to set up the agreement if you are not coming in this time of high expenses can't make such a blunder because this year it was set up for a thousand forinti I almost made a mistake not thinking that the taxes will be so high and paid the taxes of 400 forinti so that I don't know if that will be enough or they would ask for more so from that land lease … it was not plentiful all I have done in the hope that you will come home. (Letter 1)

In the Vukasinovich family, assets were threatened first by the difficulty in paying the required tax bills, and secondly by the settlement process of a litigation matter with neighbors who had presumably lent Mike money in previous years. These neighbors had contested for some valuable arable land belonging to the Vukasinovich family as compensation for the money they had loaned Mike. Instead in the settlement agreement, it appears that they received wooded land (arguably less valuable than arable land) as compensation. Mike's mother mentioned that this lawsuit was inevitable since he had refused to sign a power of attorney agreement for the loan to be reimbursed to the neighbors:

> Through the neighbors I lost the wood and I do not need another litigation and I do not wish to have it so that I need to find money to win it and what you write that you sent me money but that was too little … I thought what would be best to do and that is why I sent you a form to transfer the Power of Attorney to sign and you did not want to do that so that I can take from the bank for less interest so that I can rescue myself from these non-neighbors who wished for the few hundred that they lent you for which they wanted to roll over this black land which we could today sell for thousands So that you can return to something … (Letter 4)

The main purpose of the letters was partly to keep her son informed of the details concerning the family property. It was also about explaining to him the hardships she faced in making ends meet now that he was in America. Mike's mother had delayed financial decisions, hoping that her son Mike would return home soon – she told him – and take over the family farm. She had postponed the decision concerning the hay and whether or not to sell some of the family land. She had postponed planting some of the family land and leasing the land, given her uncertainty about whether or not her son Mike would return home to Croatia. Mike's mother seemed relentless about urging her son to come home, writing in Letter 1, 'you won't write though I wishfully expect it to hear whether you had considered and decided to go home or not', in Letter 2, 'I received your letter but in vain because nothing in it makes me happy and in vain when I am calling and you won't come home to be sorry for me as one feels for a mother and returns home', and in Letter 3, 'and you are not deciding when you will come home so that you can work on your own and for me to help you some while I am alive'. In Letter 4 it appears that Mike's mother resorted to guilt, writing first 'heavy is my suffering and I pray to God to help me so that you have something to return to when I know you are mine and that you are of my flesh', and again in Letter 4, 'you have forgotten us and now when you receive this letter from me but you won't because there have been 3 years that I even cannot work and all because of you I am suffering I would turn around my life and all for you I am enduring so that you have something to come back to.' She thus reminded her son of the financial burdens and other predicaments she experienced as a result of his absence. While we can assume that this was possibly a complicated and eventually desperate strategy on the part of Mike's mother to encourage him to return home to Croatia, this excerpt allows us also to underscore the financial constraints that rural-based widowed women faced when they had little familial support around them.

Like Anna Paikens, Mike Vukasinovich's mother was visibly conscious of prices and costs. She described in one letter the high cost of employing workers on the family farm. At some point she relayed to her son that she had sold a calf to pay mowers and other farm workers. She justified her decision by telling her son that because she did not receive his letter on time (presumably with money), she had no choice but to act upon it, writing 'I got the letter and if I had gotten it earlier I would not had sold the calf because it was necessary I needed to pay the mowers and other workers who I need because I cannot work …' (Letter 3). Taxes were very high, which Mike's mother commented on, 'I almost made a mistake not thinking that the taxes will be so high' (Letter 1). The money Mike was sending was seemingly insufficient to pay his pending debts with their neighbors and did not prevent the loss of the wood, with Mike's mother explaining, 'Through the neighbors I lost the wood and I do not need another litigation and I do not wish to have it so that I need to find money to win it and what you write that you sent me money but that was too little' (Letter 4).

While we do not have access to the letters that Mike wrote to his mother, nor do we have more information on the family and its property, we know that Mike died in a St. Paul, Minnesota hospital in 1935 at the age of 54. A permanent return to Croatia appears not to have been possible for him. The fragmentary nature of the collection in the family's history prevents us from reaching any conclusions. We are certain, however, that rural women living alone and subsisting on few resources led a financially stressful life, which in many ways may have underscored their desperate pleas to their sons to return home.

When we consider letter writers with greater economic security, such as Diego Delfino and George Grebenstchikoff and his family, money matters emerge on a less frequent basis.[15] For instance, the discussion of money only came up twice from physician Diego Delfino in Ohio to his daughter living in the convent, Monastero della visitazione di Santa Maria in Reggio Calabria, Italy. On 10 January 1926, for instance, Delfino wrote to his daughter apologizing for being late for the payment of her room and board at the convent. He blamed this delay of payment on the closure of mines in Ohio, which meant that workers had no money to visit his medical practice. While Delfino was not immune to the inherent risks in the local economy where he resided, it stands to reason that he would not discuss financial matters extensively with his young daughter. Still, he insisted on reassuring her that his obligations were not forgotten:

> Until now, it has not been possible for me to send the money for the board, given the dearth of work in this land, as I'm always waiting that the mines reopen, in terms of patients. Here, if the miners don't work, money is short to come by. I'm very sorry that for the first time I have had to forego on my obligations and miss my payments. However, I hope to fulfill my duties more diligently and promptly. Advise the good and generous Mother Superior, that unforeseen and cruel circumstances have forced me to be delinquent against my will. I hope that you are well and

that you enjoy your stay at the convent with your friends. There is no other greater consolation in this world than peace in the family.[16]

While this particular letter expressed some concerns over Delfino's finances, only two letters in the collection mentioned financial issues. Conversely, in the selected Grebenstchikoff family letters – a family of successful writers and artists – concerns over financial matters were rare, if at all, with the exception of discussions over medicines and warm boots, especially because many of these items were hard to find in 1920s Russia.

This analysis of letters of migrants and their families underscores an earlier conclusion that people living in economically challenging conditions wrote a lot more about money and their material needs than individuals and families who did not find themselves facing similar financial constraints. Discussions of this nature took up substantial portions of the letters, with some of the writers' most pressing concerns conveyed through different languages of expression. Did scarcity and economic insecurity pervade the minds and concerns of letter writers and their families? The letters in the Delfino and Grebenstchikoff series, where discussions over money were occasionally juxtaposed by a larger variety of topics addressed in the letters seem to point to some of the marked differences. While part of the reason may be attributed to a greater curiosity about matters outside daily routines, it may also be attributed to the way the writers reflected about their lives. Clearly, in their case, scarcity of money was not a constant concern. Our conclusion in this case appears to be in conversation with the work of Mani, Mullainathan, Shafir, and Zhao who argue that poor people feel greater scarcity: 'Being poor means coping not just with a shortfall of money, but also with a concurrent shortfall of cognitive resources. The poor, in this view, are less capable not because of inherent traits, but because the very context of poverty imposes load …' (Mani, Mullainathan, Shafir, & Zhao, 2013, p. 980; Mullainathan and Shafir, 2013). Poverty and financial stresses thus contribute to preventing migrants and their loved ones in the homeland from fully relating to other important matters in their lives.

5. Concluding remarks

Migrant letters show that family members who faced economic instability frequently discussed money matters using direct or indirect language. The seven collections of letters drawn from the Digitizing Immigrant Letters Project serve to provide a clearer understanding of the numerous discourses and narratives that women, men, mothers, sons, brothers, sisters asked for money and discussed financial issues at home or abroad on an everyday basis. Writing in a context of migration provided individuals the opportunity and motivation to write, reflect, and record their selves as they faced financial difficulties and other restraints as a result of or despite the migration of a family member. For many of our letter writers, communism and war affected their lives. Men and women living in pre-1917 and post-revolution Eastern Europe and Russia were typically poor relative to their family members who had emigrated to the US and had experienced tremendous economic and political turmoil and change in their lives.

Among the three letter writers with the most acute financial constraints, three wrote from the viewpoint of family members who remained behind (Granovsky, Paikens, Vukasinovich), and in these cases, curiosity about prices and wages in the US was prevalent. Many wondered in their letters how their relatives in the US were faring economically.[17] Anna Paikens for instance, wondered how much butter cost in the city where her son lived; she wondered about how much he earned per month. These are good questions. His replies would have helped her understand better what her son's pay was valued at in relative terms (relative to the cost of butter, for instance), and enhanced her knowledge of her son's standard of living in the US. Was it also a strategy to create a polite discussion for more money to be sent? Probably, but we cannot know for sure.

The links between migration, familial relations, and money are numerous and complex. By underscoring dynamics and narratives that relate to all three notions through an interdisciplinary lens, we hope to contribute to a more in-depth understanding of how money mattered to migrants and their families as they lived apart. The DIL collection continues to grow, and we hope that this work will encourage others to compare themes across ethnic and language groups.

Notes

1. See especially Mckay (2007); Singh (2006).
2. See Blegen (1955) and Schapera (1941). A broader literature on letters exists. Letter collections have long been a focus of study for scholars in literature and history. We name just a few examples to underscore some of the variety of reasons for collections of letters. For example, Isak Dinesen's communications from her time in Africa were collected in *Letters from Africa* (Dinesen and Lasson, 1981). Her purpose for writing these letters was manifold: besides the description of life in Africa, she discusses the complicated financial dealings she and her family faced as well as her observations on life in Africa, women, and culture. As an established writer early in her life, the potential audience for her letters went well beyond the letter recipients. In contrast, *Quaker Women* (Holton, 2007) is a very different set of letters: the various authors are from three generations of Quaker women, with the center being Helen Clark, the daughter of the radical Quaker and British politician John Bright; these letters circulated between a set of several families in a mostly Quaker network that spanned both time, across three generations and three centuries, and space, Britain to Pennsylvania. In this community, women were the memory keepers and wrote most of the letters. Among other purposes, the letters served to connect women across a Quaker community spread out over a wide distance.
3. We briefly touch on how economic stress probably affects one's personality and ability to handle financial stress.
4. See the following link, archives.ihrc.umn.edu/dil/index.html
5. For more details, see Cancian and Gabaccia (2013), http://ihrc.umn.edu/research/dil/index.html.
6. The set of rhetorical arguments is also not straightforward and requires a nuanced approach. The DIL letters are between family members, and we see letter writers in the DIL series manifesting feelings of guilt, resilience, making do, desperation, and sometimes plain rudeness. We find that this was fairly common across the different language and ethnic groups we examined.
7. Much data is summarized in Berend (2006): for comparisons of life expectancy between 1900 and 2000, see p. 4; for comparisons of labor productivity see pp. 176–177; for per capita GDP comparisons, see pp. 187–888.
8. See Landes (1998, pp. 240–242, 247, 251–252), and Berend (2006, p. 429).
9. Often migrants received help from family members, in terms of either a gift or a personal loan. Migration historians have direct evidence that over the nineteenth century remittances became a very common way of financing migration to North America.
10. See Wegge (1998, 2008).
11. Wegge (2015) compares Hessians who settled in South America to those who settled in Australia in the 1840s, 1850s and 1860s. Those who settled in South America were the richest and less likely to use family networks over time.
12. It is not clear how working days are counted here, as 469 work days is well above 365. In addition, how she paid 800 roubles for wheat when she earned 7 roubles is not clear.

13. Interestingly, this excerpt also points to the high rate of poverty among elderly people in the US in the years prior to social security being established in 1935.
14. This collection is entirely available online at: http://ihrc.umn.edu/research/dil/Vuk/vuk.htm. Clarification notes added by translator, Marija Dalbello.
15. Both the Delfino and Grebenstchikoff collections can be consulted online at http://ihrc.umn.edu/research/dil/Delfino/delfino.htm and http://ihrc.umn.edu/research/dil/Greben/greb.html, respectively.
16. Money was mentioned only one other time, on 6 October 1926 as a result of a postal delay: 'I don't understand how the bank in this town sent the money order for the payment of your room and board to Reggio Emilia instead of Reggio Calabria. The other day, I received it, and I imagine that the Mother Superior has doubted my sincerity. I mailed it right back and made sure that there would be no mistake this time. It's not my fault, therefore, I'm excused. Your younger brothers are fine. Giovannino and Cosimo assiduously attend school and do well …'.
17. See these letters for questions about prices and wage in North America: Granovsky 25 November 1915; Anna Paikens 14 April 1957.

Acknowledgements

Sonia Cancian and Simone A. Wegge extend sincere thanks to the Immigration History Research Center Archives at the University of Minnesota Libraries. The authors deeply appreciate the efforts of the anonymous referees of this paper, as well as friends and colleagues who have vetted earlier versions of this work, particularly Marcelo Borges, Isabelle Felici, Donna R. Gabaccia, Steven King, Judith Misrahi-Barak, Anne-Marie Motard, Daniel Necas, Linda Reeder, Marlou Schrover, and Elizabeth Zanoni. For many helpful and insightful comments that improved this paper, we thank our discussants at the 2013 German Historical Institute of London conference titled "Writing the Lives of the Poor" in London, U.K., the 2014 Social Science History Association meetings in Toronto, Canada, and at a 2015 research seminar held at the Department of Études Montpelliéraines du Monde Anglophone, Université Paul-Valery Montpellier 3 in Montpellier, France.

Disclosure statement

No potential conflict of interest was reported by the authors.

References

Baily, S. (1999). *Immigrants in the land of promise: Italians in Buenos Aires and New York City, 1870–1914*. Ithaca: Cornell University Press.

Barton, A. (1975). *Letters from the promised land. Swedes in America, 1840-1914*. Minneapolis, MN: University of Minnesota Press.

Berend, I. T. (2006). *An economic history of Twentieth-Century Europe*. Cambridge: Cambridge University Press.

Blegen, T. (1955). *Land of their choice: The immigrants write home*. St Paul, MN: University of Minnesota Press.

Boneva, B. S., & Frieze, I. H. (2001). Toward a concept of a migrant personality. *Journal of Social Issues, 57*, 477–491.

Brettell, C. B., & Hollifield, J. F. (Eds.). (2000). *Migration theory. Talking across disciplines*. New York, NY: Routledge.

Brinks, H. (Ed.). (1995). *Dutch American voices: Letters from the United States, 1850–1930*. Ithaca and London: Cornell University Press.

Cameron, W., Haines, S., & Maude, M. M. (Eds.). (2000). *English immigrant voices: Labourers' letters from Upper Canada in the 1830s*. Montreal and Kingston: McGill-Queen's University Press.

Cancian, S. (2007). Intersecting labour and social networks across cities and borders. *Studi Emigrazione/ Migration Studies*, *166*(April-June), 313–326.

Cancian, S. (2010). *Families, lovers, and their letters: Italian postwar migration to Canada.* Winnipeg: University of Manitoba Press.

Cancian, S. (2012). The language of gender in lovers' correspondence, 1946-1949, Special issue: Gender history across epistemologies. *Gender & History Journal*, *24* (November), 755–765.

Cancian, S., & Gabaccia, D. R. (2013). Migrant Letters Enter the Digital Age: The Digitizing Immigrant Letters Project at the IHRC. Retrieved from http://ihrc.umn.edu/research/dil/index.html

Cancian, S., & Wegge, S. A. (2014). Exploring the digitizing immigrant letters project as a teaching tool. *Journal of American Ethnic History*, *33*, 34–40.

Chiswick, B. R. (2000). Are immigrants favorably self-selected? An economic analysis. In C. B. Brettell & J. F. Hollifield (Eds.), *Migration theory. Talking across disciplines* (pp. 61–76). New York, NY: Routledge.

Cohen, J. H. (2005). Remittance outcomes and migration: Theoretical contests, real opportunities. *Studies in Comparative International Development*, *40*, 88–112.

Conway, A. (Ed.). (1961). *The Welsh in America. Letters from the immigrants.* St. Paul, MN: University of Minnesota Press.

de Haas, H. (2007). Remittances, migration and social development: A conceptual review of the literature. In *Social policy and development programme paper number 34*. Geneva: United Nations Research Institute for Social Development (October), http://www.unrisd.org/80256B3C005BCCF9/ search/8B7D005E37FFC77EC12573A600439846?OpenDocument (accessed March 13, 2016).

Decker, W. (1998). *Epistolary practices: Letter writing in America before telecommunications.* Chapel Hill: University of North Carolina Press.

Digitizing Immigrant Letters Project. 2009. Immigration Research History Center, University of Minnesota, archives.ihrc.umn.edu/dil/index.html

Dinesen, I., & Lasson, F. (1981). *Letters from Africa, 1914–1931.* Chicago, IL: University of Chicago Press.

Erickson, C. (1972). *Invisible immigrants. The adaptation of English and Scottish immigrants in 19th-Century America.* Coral Gables, FL: University of Miami Press.

Fitzpatrick, D. (1994). *Oceans of consolation. Personal accounts of Irish migration to Australia.* Ithaca: Cornell University Press.

Frevert, U. (2011). *Emotions in history – Lost and found.* Budapest and New York: Central European University Press, 2011.

Gabaccia, D. R. (1984). *From Sicily to Elizabeth Street: Housing and social change among Italian immigrants 1880–1930.* Albany, NY: State University of New York Press.

Gabaccia, D. R. (1994). *From the other side: Women, gender, and immigrant life in the U.S. 18820-1990.* Bloomington, IN: Indiana University Press.

Gerber, D. A. (1997). The immigrant letter between positivism and populism: The uses of immigrant personal correspondence in twentieth-century American scholarship. *Journal of American Ethnic History*, *16*, 3–34.

Gerber, D. A. (2004). What is it we seek to find in first-person documents? Documenting society and cultural practices in Irish immigrant writings. *Reviews in American History*, *32*, 305–316.

Gerber, D. A. (2005). Acts of deceiving and withholding in immigrant letters: Personal identity and self-presentation in personal correspondence. *Journal of Social History*, *39* (Winter), 315–330.

Gerber, D. (2006). *Authors of their Lives: The personal correspondence of British immigrants to North America in the 19th century.* New York, NY: New York University Press.

Ghosh, M. (2006). *Migrants' remittances and development: Myths, rhetoric and realities.* Geneva and The Hague: International Organization on Migration and The Hague Process on Refugees and Migration.

Hale, F. (Ed.). (1984). *Danes in North America.* Seattle and London: University of Washington Press.

Harrison, M. (2014). Communism and economic modernization. In S. A. Smith (Ed.), *The Oxford handbook in the history of communism* (pp. 387–406). Oxford: Oxford University Press.

Holton, S. S. (2007). *Quaker women: Personal life, memory and radicalism in the lives of women friends, 1780–1930.* London: Routledge.

Houston, C., & Smyth, W. (1990). *Irish emigration and Canadian settlement: Patterns, links, and letters.* Toronto: University of Toronto Press.

Jaeger, D., Dohmen, T., Falk, A., Huffman, D., Sunde, U., & Bonin, H. (2010). Direct evidence on risk attitudes and migration. *Review of Economics and Statistics, 92*, 684–689.

Kamphoefner, W., Helbich, W., & Sommer, U. (Eds.). (1991). *News from the land of freedom: German immigrants write home.* Ithaca: Cornell University Press.

Landes, D. S. (1998). *The wealth and poverty of nations. Why some are so rich and some so poor.* New York, NY: W. W. Norton & Company.

Liu, H. (2005). *The transnational history of a Chinese family: Immigrant letters, family business, and reverse migration.* New Brunswick, NJ: Rutgers University Press.

Mani, A., Mullainathan, S., Shafir, E., & Zhao, J. (2013). Poverty impedes cognitive function. *Science*, 30 (August), *341*, 976–980.

Martin, P. L. (1993). The migration issue. In R. King (Ed.), *The new geography of European migrations* pp. 1–16. London: Belhaven.

Matt, S. J., & Stearns, P. N., eds. (2014). *Doing emotions history.* Urbana, Chicago, and Springfield: University of Illinois Press, 2014.

Mckay, D. (2007). 'Sending dollars shows feeling' – Emotions and economies in Filipino migration. *Mobilities, 2*, 175–194.

Miller, K. A., Schrier, A., Boling, B. D., & Doyle, D. N. (2003). *Irish immigrants in the land of Canaan: Letters and memoirs from colonial and revolutionary America, 1675–1815.* Oxford and New York: Oxford University Press.

Mullainathan, S., & Shafir, E. (2013). *Scarcity. Why having too little means so much.* New York, NY: Times Books, Henry Holt and Company.

Plamper, J. (2015). *The history of emotions: An introduction.* (K. Tribe, Trans.). Oxford: Oxford University Press.

Reeder, L. (2003). *Widows in white: Migration and the transformation of rural Italian women, Sicily, 1880–1920.* Toronto: University of Toronto Press.

Rosenwein, B. H. (2002). Worrying about emotions in history. *The American Historical Review, 107*, 821–845.

Rumbaut, R. G. (1994). Origins and destinies: Immigration to the United States since World War II. *Sociological Forum, 9*, 583–621.

Schapera, I. (1941). *Married life in an African Tribe.* New York, NY: Sheridan House.

Singh, S. (2006). Towards a sociology of money and family in the Indian diaspora. *Contributions to Indian Sociology, 40*, 375–398.

Sinke, S. (2002). *Dutch immigrant women in the United States, 1880–1920.* Urbana-Champaign, IL: University of Illinois Press.

Thomas, W. I., & Znaniecki, F. (1918–1920). *The Polish peasant in Europe and America.* Boston, MA: Gorham Press.

Wegge, S. A. (1998). Chain migration and information networks: Evidence from nineteenth-century Hesse-Cassel. *The Journal of Economic History, 58*, 957–986.

Wegge, S. A. (2008). Network strategies of nineteenth century Hesse-Cassel emigrants. *The History of the Family, 13*, 296–314.

Wegge, S. A. (2015). Uncommon destinies: 19th century Hessians who emigrated to the Southern Hemisphere. Unpublished working paper. Revised June 2015.

Witold Kula, Nina Assorodobraj-Kula, Marcin Kula. (1986). *Writing home: Immigrants in Brazil and the United States, 1890–1891.* Edited and translated by Josephine Wtulich. New York, NY: Columbia University Press.

Yans-McLaughlin, V. (1977). *Family and Community: Italian immigrants in Buffalo, 1880–1930.* Ithaca, NY: Cornell University Press.

For the good of the family: migratory strategies and affective language in Portuguese migrant letters, 1870s–1920s

Marcelo J. Borges [ID]

ABSTRACT
Labor migration was a common strategy for Portuguese families at the turn of the twentieth century. Correspondence provided a vehicle to keep families connected and a space to sustain and recreate their relationships and emotional bonds. This article analyzes the language of call letters, a particular type of family letter written by migrant men to call their wives and children to join them abroad. In particular, it examines the ways in which migrant husbands and their wives adapted to living in transnational households and to changing roles at home and abroad. It shows how family strategies of migration were discussed within narrative frameworks of family and marital love and duty, by making use of a variety of arguments that combined discourses of both material and emotional well-being. The discussion is based on the narrative patterns, recurrent themes, and argumentative strategies of a corpus of over 2200 letters. Discussions of marital duty, loyalty, and reciprocity contributed to a language of affect built on narratives of responsibility and dependability that reinforced the idea of migration as a family project.

1. Introduction

Migration was a common labor strategy for Portuguese families during the nineteenth century and early twentieth century, making Portugal one of the countries with the highest proportions of emigration according to population size in Europe (Baines, 1995). Emigration was particularly important in the last decade of the nineteenth century and the first three decades of the twentieth century, prompting some demographers to argue its effects were 'restrictive' or 'dissuasive' for population growth in that period (Bandeira, 1996, p. 153; Evangelista, 1971, p. 108).[1] Portuguese migrants participated in long-distance labor circuits that spanned a wide range of destinations, including labor-importing countries in the Americas and Europe as well as Portugal's colonies and other colonial territories in Africa (Morier-Genoud & Cahen, 2012; Newitt, 2015; Serrão, 1982). Brazil attracted the greatest majority of migrants, ranging from more than 90% of departures in the 1890s to close to 70% in the 1920s, followed by other transatlantic destinations like the United States and Argentina, and then by destinations in Europe, such as Spain and France, mostly on a seasonal or temporary basis (Evangelista, 1971). There were, however, important regional variations regarding destinations (see, for example, Baganha, 1990; Borges, 2009; Evangelista, 1971; Miranda, 1999; Vieira, 1990). Socio-occupational backgrounds were also varied, including farmers, commercial clerks, personnel of metropolitan companies, and colonial administrators. There were variations by region, but considering the country as a whole unskilled laborers and farmers constituted the vast majority of migrants (Alves, 1993; Baganha, 2009). Migration was a gendered strategy. The great majority of migrants were men (close to 80% for continental Portugal in the period 1886–1930) (Baganha, 2009). In the case of married migrants, this economic strategy relied on women's central role in the home (Borges, 2009; Brettell, 1986). As migrant men worked abroad, their wives performed numerous economic activities. In rural areas – from which most Portuguese migrants hailed – women took care of the household, worked on the family land, and allocated the money their husbands sent back home. Most male migration was temporary, and it was common for men to migrate several times over the course of their adult lives (Borges, 2009; Brettell, 1979). This practice was rooted in what some scholars have called the 'ideology of return migration' (Brettell, 1979), which fueled large amounts of remittances back home and resulted in high numbers of return, both temporary and permanent (Leite, 2000; Pereira, 1981). When reunification occurred, it was not unusual for migrant families to consider it as a temporary move as well. Not surprisingly, however, temporary reunification often turned into long-term or permanent relocation. As a result of either temporary or long-term separations, migrant husbands and their wives, migrant parents and their children, and migrants and siblings had to adjust to transnational lives with new roles, responsibilities, and expectations.

Correspondence provided a vehicle to keep families connected, in both material and emotional ways. The exchange of letters was the medium through which families separated by migration sustained sentimental relationships and adapted to changing roles at home and abroad. Growing numbers of common Portuguese people confronted the necessity to rely on writing to take care of regular family affairs and express sentiments and ideas about themselves, their families, and the world that was changing around them – in most cases, for the first time in their lives. Despite clear limitations established by high levels of illiteracy (Candeias, 2000), most adapted to their circumstances, relying on rudimentary knowledge of writing and seeking the help of family and acquaintances. As Gibelli (2002) noted, among European popular classes – who provided the majority of people for the two main phenomena of mass population movement at the turn of the twentieth century (emigration and wars) – the border between literacy and illiteracy was flexible and shifting. Lyons' (2013) characterization of the adaptation to writing among migrant families in Spain can be equally applied to the Portuguese case: 'Whatever level of competence ordinary writers enjoyed, writing remained crucial to their lives and identities' (p. 34). Technological changes also helped, making regular communication accessible and more reliable. Portugal established regular transatlantic mail lines in the 1850s, carrying tens of thousands of pieces of mail (Leite, 2000). Postal shipping lines consolidated and mail increased considerably after the 1870s, with the establishment of steam navigation and with Portugal's entry into the Universal Postal Union. By the 1880s, mail exchanges between Portugal and South America had grown to more than 700,000 pieces of mail; and by 1911, they had increased to more than three times that number (Leite, 2000). This increase in postal communication accompanied a remarkable growth in emigration. Migrant departures more than doubled during these decades, from about 132,000 in the 1870s to more than 300,000 in the first decade of the twentieth century (Leite, 1987).

The arrival of letters from abroad in rural towns throughout Portugal played a vital role in communicating and sustaining emotional bonds among migrant families. In rural and small-town Portugal, correspondence was not distributed to individual households, so public distribution of letters became a performative moment with both individual and collective meaning. The scene was so common that it made its way into several works of fiction. One of the earlier descriptions appears in the now classic novel *A morgadinha dos Canaviais*, published in 1868. In a visit from the capital to a rural town in northern Portugal, Henrique, the novel's hero, witnesses the distribution of correspondence and describes it as a momentous occasion in the town's otherwise calm routine. Writer Júlio Dinis (2004 [1868]) depicts the moment evoking its performative nature:

> There are, indeed, few scenes that are so animated as the one created by the arrival of correspondence and the distribution of letters in a small town. As the designated employee reads the names and addresses of the recipients out loud, an observant witness can study the impressions that the reading causes in the faces of those who listen eagerly. He can observe it as if lifting the corner of a curtain that has been drawn to shield us from the scenes of comedy or tragedy of each and every life. (p. 52)[2]

Dinis continues by describing the reactions among the expecting populace as the names of the recipients are read by the local postal distributor:

> What followed was a new and no less interesting spectacle.

> The reading of each name was followed almost always by the sound of a voice, sometimes by a cry; an arm extended above the heads, and we could add even if it was not visible, that a heart became agitated.

> Others, those whose names had not been called yet, look anxiously to the shrinking batch of letters as their looks were getting increasingly somber. (p. 53)

Eighty years later, writer Joaquim Lagoeiro described a similar scene in his novel *Viúvas de vivos* (Widows of the Living), published in 1947. The group in attendance as the distribution of letters unfolded in the local store was composed mostly of women whose husbands were working abroad. Receiving a letter was reassuring at the personal and communal levels; it signaled that women and families had not been forgotten. The gathering of hopeful recipients provided an occasion to exchange information, to learn of stories of success and failure, to hear comforting news and witness distressing silences. Participating in this weekly ritual was an expression of confidence and of lukewarm optimism. As Lagoeiro (1973 [1947]) wrote,

> [the women] knew the origin of the letters by the format of the envelope and the color of the stamp. There were those who, despite their lost men not having written for many years, were still there, without blinking; waiting, always waiting. When with an indifferent motion Zeferino would throw a letter over the counter, all eyes turned to the chosen one who would later exhibit the letter full of vanity. And the distribution went on in silence, only interrupted by some exclamation of surprise or of congratulations. Slow minutes of anxiety and anguish! [...] Scarcely hiding the state of their souls, those who had not been remembered would go near the ones that had received news and, with avid eyes, hoped for some news for themselves under the pretense of learning about the health of the husbands of the other women. (p. 105)

Letters from family members abroad provided a tangible indication of the continuation of family ties. Letters not only served as the medium to exchange news, advice, and information, they also provided spaces for recreating relationships altered by separation and for dealing with tensions and conflicts magnified by absence and long-distance communication. In this sense, migrant letters constituted what David Gerber (2006) has termed a 'singular transnational space' in which these relationships were recreated (p. 92). For families who lived in transnational households as a result of migration, the arrival of letters helped to strengthen the idea of migration as a family strategy that rested on responsibilities for those who left and those who stayed, with regular communication ranking high among them. Silence, on the other hand, bred uncertainty or even worse, fears of abandonment that would signal the end of a common life project.

Through the study of personal letters, this article discusses the ways in which Portuguese migrants and their families evaluated and negotiated their migratory strategies, the opportunities at home and abroad, and the perceptions of a fluid reality created by geographical mobility. I explore how letters were used as vehicles to express, maintain, and sometimes mend affective bonds in transnational contexts. I also show how family strategies of migration were discussed within narrative frameworks of family and marital love and duty, by making use of a variety of arguments that combined discourses of both material and emotional well-being. This analysis is grounded in and contributes to current development in scholarship about migrant letters which considers the ways in which epistolary discourse and writing practices can be used as lenses through which to explore the emotional underpinnings of the migratory project and the negotiating and renegotiating of senses of self and others among individuals and families in contexts of migration (see, for example, Cancian, 2010, 2012; Da Orden, 2010; Elliott, Gerber, & Sinke, 2006; Gerber, 2006; Lyons, 2013).

In particular, this article focuses on the analysis of a variety of migrant correspondence commonly known as call letters (*cartas de chamada*, in Portuguese). These letters were used by Portuguese migrants to ask their families to join them abroad. Portuguese married women and minors were not allowed to emigrate alone without the explicit consent of their husbands or fathers (Ramos, 1913); this requirement was in place until 1969 (Sousa & Perez Dominguez, 1982). Until the 1920s, personal letters were used as proof of authorization when the husband or father was abroad. Somewhere in the text, these letters included a sentence or two which could be interpreted as marital or parental consent (sometimes it was clear and explicit, at other times it was a passing comment about the need or convenience for family reunification). Considered by the government official in charge of granting passports as sufficient proof of the male head of household's authorization, these letters were stamped and included in the passport applications of married women and minors. Portuguese call letters have received limited scholarly attention, mostly circumscribed to one single locality in Portugal or one place of destination; these discussions have presented examples of the variety of topics covered in these letters and have argued for the importance of these sources for a first-person, intimate account of the experience of migration and the migrant's familiar world (for example, Matos, 2013; Rodrigues, 2010; Sarmento, 1999).[3] This article proposes a systematic analysis of Portuguese family letters used as call letters by looking at the country as a whole, including letters from all regions of emigration for which such a source is available and the many destinations to which Portuguese migrants moved. The corpus under analysis here contains over 2200 letters that cover regions with significant migration in northern and central Portugal, Lisbon, the southern region of the Algarve, and the Island of Madeira. The letters span a period of over 50 years (from the 1870s to the 1920s). Most of these letters were written by migrant men to their wives. There was a wide range of call letters used in the passport applications – many were short and to the point, but others were rich in detail about a variety of topics; in the selection for this corpus, I preferred longer letters over short, formulaic ones.[4]

Call letters were part of ongoing epistolary exchanges, but they are unique in that the imminent reunification brings to the fore explicit considerations of family strategies, aspirations, and negotiations between husbands and wives (and other family members), as well as rich information about the journey. There are, of course, some special characteristics of this type of letter as well as limitations. One of them is the blurred boundaries between the private and the public nature of the source, but this is not unusual for family correspondence in general, as letters were commonly read out loud and shared among kin and friends (Lyons, 2013). Call letters add an extra dimension to the private–public continuum because of their use in official business. Some scholars have warned about the possible limitations of this type of private source for public use (see, for example, Stangl, 2010). Indeed many letter writers were aware that their letters would be presented to the authorities, with explicit reminders to the recipient to do so. But even among these writers there was a remarkably candid approach in both style and content, and there is very little evidence of self-imposed censorship. Another obvious caveat is that the predominant voice in these letters is that of male migrants, and particularly husbands. Even through this filter, however, it is possible to uncover glimpses of the perspectives and actions of the women who stayed behind. Finally, unlike other types of migrant letters, call letters are not part of larger family collections. In most cases, there is one letter per family. With these limitations in mind, the letters in this corpus provide a polyphonic perspective of thousands of voices over a vast geographic and temporal space that allows us to identify narrative patterns and recurrent themes without losing sight of unique stories.

2. Love and money: affect and responsibility

The epistolary language used by migrants and their families contributed to building 'transnational affect' (Wise & Velayutham, 2006) by making sense of their separation and connecting members of the family at home and abroad with migration as a family project. How did migrants and their families engage in these exchanges and negotiations of affective bonds? What was the language of affect? What narrative strategies were deployed? What images were conveyed? An initial look at the language of the Portuguese letters under study can give us a general sense. The following words emerge as the top 10 nouns in the complete corpus: letter, money, health, company, family, God, day, mother, children, and house/home. It is true that in part this is because some of these words are common in the openings and closings of letters, but they also represent central concerns of families separated by migration: fluid communication, material well-being, health, family members, and home. The single-most common noun is 'letter' (*carta*), which appears over 4000 times (0.48% of the words in the corpus). The word 'money' is a close second (0.47%); but if in addition to the word *dinheiro* (money), we consider common equivalents (such as diminutives or specific currencies), references to money appear more than 7000 times in the letters (0.78%).[5] In comparison, where is love and affection in the language of these letters? The word *amor* (love in Portuguese) is used 196 times in a corpus of over 900,000 words (0.02%). If we also include the word *amizade* (friendship) which was often used as love or affection (143 times), that brings the total to 339 times (0.03%). Expressions of love and affection appear in these letters, to be sure, including instances of romantic and intimate language which appear sometimes in unexpected and surprising ways for letters that were presented to public authorities as part of the process of emigration. For a true understanding of the language of love, however, one needs to go back to the central concerns listed above for they formed the basis for the language of marital and family affect among migrant families. Letters constituted the vehicle to express them as well as the tangible token of their existence despite the limitations created by time and space.

A closer look at the letters sheds light on the language and the narrative strategies used in the recreation of relationships and emotional bonds. What constituted a loving husband and father among these immigrants was strongly connected to ideas of dependability and responsibility. These ideas were conveyed by references to specific expectations, namely keeping up regular communication, providing for his family back home, protecting them in times of need, and eventually calling them to join him abroad or returning home (in this particular corpus, family reunification abroad was the norm). As the scenes of rural women waiting in vain for letters from their loved ones depicted in the literature illustrate, above all, a loving husband and father did not forget his family. The threat of abandonment permeates these letters. Husbands regularly reassured their wives that, as the mere act of writing indicated, they had not been forgotten. In this view, silence equaled oblivion. Husbands felt the need to explain their reasons for long epistolary delays, and they often did so by using the language of responsibility. For example, António wrote from the Amazonian port of Manaus (Brazil), to his wife Maria, in Tabuaço (Viseu):

> Maria you and all our family must have thought that I had forgotten you and our dear son completely, but you are wrong because you are always in my mind
>
> I have not written to you earlier because of the great misfortune (*infelicidade*) which I have endured so far because of illness and because of the lack of work
>
> But now I am completely recovered and with a boss with whom I earn enough for my expenses and to save some money (*algum vintém*).[6]

In the language of reassurance, migrants wrote more about not having forgotten their families than they wrote about remembering them. Tellingly, the verb *esquecer* (to forget) in all its conjugations appears 769 times in the corpus (0.08%); in contrast, the verb *lembrar* (to remember) in all its conjugations appears only 392 times (0.04%). As the scenes depicted by the novels of Dinis (2004 [1868]) and Lagoeiro (1973 [1947]) illustrate, the arrival of a letter back home in Portugal was the first visible act which expressed to the families left behind that they had not been forgotten and gave them hope they will be cared for.

Writing frequently was a tangible way of proving that immigrants did not forget their families, but sending money along with the letter was an even more substantial fulfillment of their roles of caring husbands and fathers. A migrant from Lousã (Coimbra) expressed this sentiment in no uncertain terms: 'I haven't written to you earlier because a letter without money is worthless paper.'[7] For families separated by migration, remittances were important for subsistence, and crucial for the dream of securing the family's future through savings and investments. In the example above, António restored his epistolary connection with his wife when he recovered from an illness and could save some money. This was a common pattern in these letters. For example, in a letter from Minas Gerais (Brazil), Manuel wrote to his wife Lucinda, in Maia (Porto): 'I beg you that you don't doubt me, because you have as a proof the money that I have already sent you.'[8] Similarly, another migrant from Maia, Manuel, wrote from Rio de Janeiro to his wife Maria: 'I have done my duty because I have sent you everything I have earned, and, mind you, it amounts to a considerable sum.'[9] Finally, in a letter sent from Rio de Janeiro to Porto, Domingos told his wife Maria:

Dear Miquinhas, here I have received two letters already without being able to answer you right away, but it was not because I did not have time, it was only to wait until the end of the month to send you money because I could not do it earlier, and if I would write to you without sending you money I know you would feel very sad.[10]

These are just a few examples of expressions of reassurance by absent husbands in their correspondence to their wives which appear in many letters from this corpus; in them, husbands frequently used remittances as proof that they had not forgotten their families. Albino expressed this sentiment succinctly but clearly, when he sent five pounds sterling from Pará (Brasil) to his wife in Oliveira de Frades (Viseu): 'I am sorry it is little, but it is a little present (*lembrança*) for you to know that I have not lost the love I have for you.'[11] In this case, the connection between money and remembering is further highlighted in the original by the use in Portuguese of *lembrança* (from the verb *lembrar*, to remember) for gift or souvenir. In effect, the money sent by migrant men back home was the most tangible form of expressing their family obligations and the fulfillment of their responsibility as providers – money to help meet their family's needs, to acquire goods for which cash was necessary, to repay debts, to invest in the household and in agriculture or other activities, and in the case of many call letters to facilitate family reunification. Remittances were crucial for the household economies of migrant families and equally important at the macro level, for the Portuguese economy as a whole which relied on and promoted this reliable source of cash from abroad (Baganha, 2009; Chaney, 1986; Pereira, 1981).

Often, reassurances of marital and familial love through remittances were accompanied in the letters by expressions of the sacrifices that senders had to endure to carry out their obligation. In the common narratives of sacrifice, husbands fulfilled their role as providers despite obstacles and by forgoing personal needs. In the example from the letter from Rio de Janeiro above, after explaining the delay in correspondence until he had money to send his wife, Domingos added: 'now I have no money (*fico sem vinténs*) to live during the whole month, and I even had to bother my great friend António.'[12] References to migrants' sacrifices in terms of hard work, frugality, and even privation in order to fulfill the promise of migration and to take care of their families are abundant in the letters. A detailed analysis of the narrative of sacrifice is beyond the scope of this article, but suffice it to say that migrants used a variety of strategic narratives to convey it in their letters, including allusions to long hours of work (after which they still find strength to write), skipping meals, and making shirts and undergarments for themselves out of flour sacks, just to name a few.

3. To love is to provide: language of men as providers

Money sent from abroad was the most tangible way migrants showed commitment to their families and it also provided validation for the migratory strategy that had resulted in their family's transnational existence. Remittances, however, did not operate alone; they were complemented by epistolary language that communicated migrants' responsible behavior as husbands and fathers. This language was equally important to keep men and their families engaged and to give everyone a sense of working for a common goal. The language of marital and parental responsibility also conveyed a sense of presence of the absent men in the affairs of their family back home. It bound couples separated by migration by providing a narrative of common transnational work until the realization of the objective that put the strategy of migration into motion. Migrant men expressed clear ideas of responsibility as

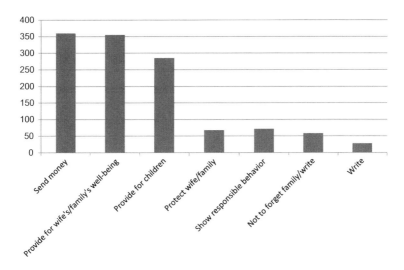

Figure 1. Main themes denoting responsible husbands (by number of letters).

husbands and fathers in their letters home. Figure 1 summarizes the dominant messages communicated in men's references to their fulfillment of family responsibilities; the information is arranged in general thematic clusters identified by my own close reading of the letters, categorization, and coding of passages of text. The most common way in which migrant men conveyed these messages in the letters was by highlighting their role as providers who overcame the limitations of geographical distance and time of separation, and who made sacrifices for their families' well-being.

Images of food insecurity and hunger appear frequently in the letters. Such references served to emphasize the place of migrant men as providers of the most basic of needs among their wives and children. Tellingly, in the majority of instances in which the word 'hunger' (*fome*) appears in the letters, it is used by a male writer to declare that he will not let his family suffer any privation, or to contrast privations at home (sometimes characterized as a *terra de fome* or 'land of hunger') with the possibilities offered by family reunification. As a migrant from Porto put it succinctly in a letter to his wife: 'I still feel strong enough to earn a living so that you will not go hungry.'[13] Migrant letters contain numerous such examples: 'as long as I am alive, you will always have something to eat,' a migrant wrote reassuringly from Rio de Janeiro to his wife in Barcelos (Braga); similarly, another migrant working in Rio de Janeiro wrote to his son in Nelas (Viseu), 'Do not go hungry because as long as I am in good health (*se eu tiver saúde*), I will always send you 500 réis daily so you can eat.'[14] António, a migrant from Famalicão (Braga) working in France during the years of World War I, wrote to his father asking for help in reuniting with his wife and children relying on similar images of migration as an end to hunger: 'Send those poor souls (*Cristianos*) here because I can't forget they are dying of hunger, and I can't be happy until I see them eating by my side.'[15] António's plea was very likely a reaction to privations that were widespread in Portugal during the years of World War I and the interwar years (Medeiros, 1978), but he also was making reference to recognizable language and images used to reinforce the role of husbands and fathers as providers in migrant correspondence.

On the other side of this imagery, letters also include references to being fat as a synonym for being healthy and successful (usually in relationship to the decision of migration and to life in the countries of settlement); this connection becomes apparent in almost every case the word appears in the letters. Writers commonly used it to describe themselves ('I am good and fatter and stronger each day'); other family members ('You know I live with your brother … when I arrived here, I found him well dressed and very fat'); or other migrants ('António is doing well and he is as fat as a turnip, and our father also is very fat').[16] In a 1918 letter from Plymouth, Massachusetts, a migrant from Aveiro summarized this sentiment very vividly: 'I don't remember ever in my life to eat so much like I am eating now, I don't know how I will end up eating so much, and you do the same; I am so fat that when you get here you will not recognize me.'[17] Likewise, migrants often advised their families to take care of themselves and expressed desires for their well-being employing similar images of well-fed and rubicund appearances. 'I want you to do everything possible to eat and to find some distractions so you can arrive here fatter than the way you look in your picture; you look very thin and you can't imagine how my heart suffers with that,' wrote a migrant from Lousã (Coimbra) in a letter from São Paulo.[18] On a more dramatic note, António, a migrant from Penacova (Coimbra) working in Brazil, told his wife Margarida he had received a letter in Santos from a friend expressing concern for Margarida's health. His friend had described Margarida as being 'without color and very thin', which for António was a clear sign of lack of food and attention to her well-being. Reacting to this alarming news, António censured Margarida's behavior and urged her to eat and get well:

> It is not necessary for me to remind you to spare your body (*poupar o corpo*) because I have already told you, and it seems that you are harming your body … What happiness it would be for me if somebody would arrive here and tell me that you are fat and with good color. Instead everybody tells me you are crippled, yellow, and without color … it is not because I have not told you to eat and drink.[19]

As these examples illustrate, the counter-images of food insecurity and well-fed bodies reinforced each other in the language of migrant family letters to talk about need and opportunity – usually located at home and abroad, respectively – and to add force to the role of family men as providers through migration.

Another significant way in which migrant men expressed their position as responsible family providers was in their care for the well-being of children left behind – fulfilling basic needs and caring for their future by securing them access to an occupation, training, and education according to family resources. While women remained in Portugal with their children, letters from their husbands included not only material help in the form of remittances but also frequent advice on children's upbringing and behavior, including attempts to exert paternal authority at a distance over their education, conduct, and even appearance. For example, in an 1898 letter from Rio de Janeiro, José wrote to his wife Maria in Figueira da Foz (Coimbra): 'It is not necessary to recommend you the education of our dear children because they are at a very bad age and without a father to discipline them; I hope they respect you because I was always very respectful of my parents and for that reason I have no problem honoring that debt.'[20] Separation sometimes created tensions about children's upbringing. For instance, a migrant from Viseu in a letter from Rio de Janeiro warned his wife to 'not let our children go around badly dressed because it is shameful for you and for me'; and in a letter from Buenos Aires, a migrant from Faro reproached his wife after he was told by a neighbor that his wife was letting their daughter walk around town without shoes.[21]

In the case of children left in charge of other family members when both parents migrated, letters frequently contained expressions of concern in securing their protection and material needs. The fate of these children created tension when husbands tried to convince their wives to join them abroad alone, leaving children behind in order to save money and increase their earning capabilities. Reassuring their wives of proper care for these children became a regular part of their negotiation of migration strategies. It was common for migrant parents to leave children behind because they were too little and required attention that could be put to use in a more productive way in the countries of immigration, while contributing little or nothing to the family economy. Often children were left in the charge of their grandparents or the siblings of their parents. Letters contained frequent reassurances to be communicated to family members in Portugal that resources to help in the upbringing of these children would be covered regularly with money sent from abroad or with the production of the family land. Also in these cases, their parents' absence sometimes contributed to a sense of diminished parental authority and created tension. This was true not only in monitoring children's behavior, but also in shielding them from abuses from other family members. In a letter to a friend, a migrant from Viseu expressed his concern about his son to be left without parental protection, like a 'bird without a nest'; other writers expressed their worries about their unprotected children in more prosaic terms, expressing their wish to protect them from being 'pushed' or 'kicked' around by anybody.[22] This was the sentiment expressed, for example, by Luiz in a letter he sent to his wife Felismina in 1900. Felismina was considering leaving one of their sons (probably the youngest) with an aunt in Coimbra when joining her husband in the interior of Brazil. But Luiz expressed his concerns in the following terms:

> On the topic of your saying that you think it is a good idea to leave our little Joaquim with our aunt when you come here, I don't think it convenient, and I understand it is better for all of you to come, because that way we can educate them better, and they always know us better and respect us more. We are all mortals; now, let's say that he stays with our aunt and then he is left without her; who would he go to? We have lots of family there, but each one looks for their own interests; then, he would be left to be pushed around by everyone.[23]

Fears sometimes materialized and parents reacted to news of children's misfortune with a sense of helplessness to be remedied only by arranging for their children to join them abroad. In a 1905 letter from a rural town in the interior of São Paulo State, Custódio wrote to his uncle Valentim expressing concern about his daughter Ana, living under the care of another family member (probably an aunt) in Amarante (Porto). The letter conveys a sense of powerlessness created by family separation. Having received news that his daughter was being mistreated, he laments the lack of parental protection resulting from his absence: 'I know well that a child without a father and a mother like she is, that she is likely not well treated, but I think that she did not deserve to be treated the way they are treating her.'[24] The distance between Brazil and Portugal, and the limits to communication created by laconic correspondence accentuated these feelings; in Custódio's words: 'poor he who is a father, because with news like these, which do not explain things well, we are left here in suspense; because based on what he says [in the letter], I think 1000 different things.' Like other migrant parents in similar circumstances, Custódio decided to call for his daughter, asking his uncle to take Maria in and to arrange for her to leave for Brazil accompanied by a fellow migrant who was returning home for a short visit.

Decisions to call for children were more commonly the result of deliberate strategies of family migration than reactions to children's adversities, and these actions were also manifestations of parental responsibility. Men working alone in places of immigration regularly called for their sons after they were considered old enough to be of help (or, at least, not to be a 'burden', as it is expressed in some letters). This was particularly the case among young boys of migrant families for whom migration became a formative step in their path to adulthood. As Domingos explained to his wife Teresa in a letter from Rio de Janeiro, 'it is here that they become men'.[25] Understandings of appropriate working age varied according to the intended occupation and had to take into account periods of apprenticeship and training, especially in artisanal work and commerce. In the case of Salvador, Domingo's and Teresa's son, he migrated when he was 13 years old. Two important considerations were crucial for the family's decision to send Salvador to join his father in Brazil: he had just passed the exam completing his primary education and he had to leave before turning 14 to avoid paying a military deposit before emigrating. This is not an isolated example, but part of a common practice. Pereira (1981) estimates that young boys under 14 constituted at least 20% of legal departures in the late nineteenth century, and that this proportion was probably even larger among undocumented departures. Not surprisingly, education and military service of young boys appear regularly in the discussions about children's future connected to emigration in the letters. Salvador left Guimarães (Braga) for Rio de Janeiro in 1919 to work in commerce. Fulfilling his paternal duty and following well-established practices among Portuguese in Brazil, Domingos had already arranged employment in the commercial establishment of a fellow migrant. This strategy was particularly significant in northwest Portugal where there was a long tradition of commercial employment linked to migration to Brazil (Alves, 1994; Monteiro, 2000). Achieving the necessary skills in writing and arithmetic was important for commercial employment. More than half the references to children's exams in the corpus come from letters from the northwestern districts of Braga, Porto, and Viana do Castelo. But this was a practice exclusive neither to this region nor to commercial employment. There are many more references to the need of sons to learn basic reading and writing skills, as well as to other possibilities to 'make men' out of these young boys in the places of immigration through artisanal work and other activities, in many cases alongside their fathers or family members and migrants from their villages already settled abroad.

There was, of course, no guarantee that migration would secure children's future, especially when family circumstances or the larger context in the places of immigration were less than favorable. When Rafael, the son of a migrant from Esponsende (Braga) who was working in São Paulo, turned 13 and passed his primary education exam, the family had to decide if following the traditional path of his father and two older brothers by migrating to Brazil was the right choice.[26] João, Rafael's father wrote from Brazil expressing some concern about the possibilities for his youngest son, and pondered about the available options in the following terms:

> I see with satisfaction that Rafael passed his exam. Regarding his future, I have thought so much about it but I still don't know how to resolve it. In the meantime, I present you with my ideas, which are the following: first, he could become a teacher, if the educational expenses for that are not too large; second, he could join the Navy voluntarily when he turns 16, which even if it seems like a bad idea and it doesn't make a good impression, military life makes great men!; third, he can come here, even though this is what I like the least because today you need a lot of luck in Brazil. I have used all available means to find suitable jobs for Zacarias and Daniel [presumably, Rafael's older brothers], and I still can't do it. And even I am not doing that well in my job myself because salaries in this place are very small, but even in these circumstances I keep on going because I am afraid that things could turn for the worse.

Despite these doubts, Rafael followed the familiar steps of migration to Brazil before he turned 14 years old, like other young men from his family and from many other families in the district of Braga and northwestern Portugal in general.

Distance could weaken the implementation of parental plans regarding education and desired paths of employment which in turn created conflict. Parents' ideas about the best strategies for their children's future sometimes met with children's resistance or just with unenthusiastic execution. Furthermore, fathers and sons could differ on their ideas about the best way to 'become men' through migration. In a 1919 letter from the United States, João, a migrant from São Brás de Alportel (Faro) expressed his dissatisfaction about some of his young son's choices (abandoning school and becoming an apprentice) and proposed an alternative path through migration to California:

> Since you didn't want to take the second exam, and all because you don't like to study and you say you'd rather go into a trade, then I can see that you are better suited to work; and because I now know that is what you want then I had the idea of calling you to come here, especially because I already have a place where you could finish becoming a man. Because over there, you will always be a nobody (*um desgraçado*), and here if you behave, you can still become a rich man, and well-respected. Because over there, you work for free and here the person who works gets paid … Because here things are better every day to earn money, and there your master will expect you always to work for him for free, but that program is not convenient for me.[27]

Based on these considerations, João asks his son not to delay his departure, as he will turn 15 years old soon and then the family will have to find resources to pay the deposit for military service. The rest of the family was to follow them to California in a few years, before the youngest son also turned 15.

As discussed above, these messages of fulfillment of men's marital and paternal duty were often reinforced by references to migrants' hard work and dedication to the well-being of their families. 'I am always at work, since sunrise to ten at night, sacrificing myself because of you,' wrote a migrant from a town on the hills of Minas Gerais (Brazil) to his wife in Vila Verde (Braga); 'all these sacrifices you can pay me back with very little, with your good behavior and that of our children.'[28] This was certainly an important manifestation of gratitude but as the analysis of the letters in this corpus shows, in recognition for their sacrifices, migrant husbands also expected reciprocity, which manifested itself in myriad other ways, among them protection of family interests, dependability, and especially commitment to migration as a common family project.

4. The loyal wife: manifestations of reciprocity and marital commitment

Correspondence contributed to building a narrative of a common family objective and to keeping it alive during separations that sometimes lasted many years. Waiting and taking care of the family and household were integral parts of the migration strategy, including careful use of resources and investment of remittances when they were available. Characterized by Kwon (2015) as 'unwaged affective labor' (p. 495), this sense of attachment of the spouses left behind was central to the lives of couples separated by migration; as she argues for contemporary Chinese migration to Korea, 'spousal waiting at home forms part of migration' (p. 496) as 'an active attempt to realize a collectively imagined future' (p. 480). The same interdependence between mobility and immobility characterized the experiences of married men and women involved in strategies of male labor migration in turn-of-the-nineteenth-century

Portugal and in comparable transoceanic and long-distance movements (Borges, 2009; Brettell, 1986; Gabaccia, 2001; Reeder, 2003). There are, indeed, many references to the central role played by wives who stayed behind in the running of the household and the protection of the family's interests in these letters which reveal this reality.

The impending departure of their wives and the need to leave their homes in order prompted couples separated by migration to make decisions that could have lasting consequences for their future – such as the advantages of renting or selling their pieces of land; the possibility of using some of the possessions as collateral for travel expenses; whom to leave in charge of their interests; and more fundamentally, whether to keep interests in both their places of origin and destination, or focus fully on a future abroad. Close to a third of the letters in this corpus contain discussions of management of property and other possessions, activities for which wives were responsible while husbands were toiling away far from home; all these cases were discussions of selling (the great majority), renting, or mortgaging. Interestingly, close to 2% of the letters also include discussions of buying property in Portugal, offering a hint of what was surely a common topic in the general correspondence between spouses before reunification abroad became the chosen strategy for the families represented in these letters. Women played an important role in putting these decisions into action. As active participants in household and local economies throughout Portugal (Lamas, 1948; Vaquinhas, 2005), women's position increased even more when men were absent. Many husbands tried to exert control at a distance, but they depended on their wives' willingness to carry their wishes through. A migrant from Olhão (Faro), for example, instructed his wife on the best strategy for a successful sale of their house as follows: 'Do not sell the house for less than 450 milréis, but ask for five hundred and go down little by little; do me the favor of not selling everything for a pittance.'[29] There are even a few revealing examples of disagreement over the best course of action. Such was the case of Manuel, a migrant from Viana do Castelo settled in Brazil who, in 1916, reacted to his wife Beatriz's hesitancy to sell some pieces of land back home with a clear, underlined message: 'It is necessary to sell everything, everything.'[30] Apparently, Beatriz had expressed some reluctance to this idea by telling her husband that it was better to keep their properties because 'nobody can't take the land away'. A reader can also sense that attachment to their land was a manifestation of Beatriz's general lack of enthusiasm for relocating to Brazil with which Manuel vehemently disagreed: 'And do not even dream of returning home when you are old,' he wrote, 'when one goes to Brazil at an age like ours it is more likely that we end our days here than that we go to Portugal to leave our bones.'

Discussions like these offer a glimpse of the types of interaction that occurred in the broader exchange of correspondence between husbands and wives during their separation. Figure 2 summarizes the dominant topics used by husbands to refer to their wives' responsibilities in the letters other than in discussions of selling, renting, or mortgaging lands and possessions. By bringing the possibility of reunification to the fore, the letters in the corpus under analysis shift the discussion to the opportunity of temporary or long-term relocation. Since these letters functioned as call letters, many writers made explicit references to the desire and need for family reunification, and presented both material and emotional arguments for it. For migrant men, their wives' readiness to fulfill their roles became expressions of marital duty, loyalty, and love. It is mainly in these arguments that one can find clues about wives' obligations in Portuguese transnational families in these letters.

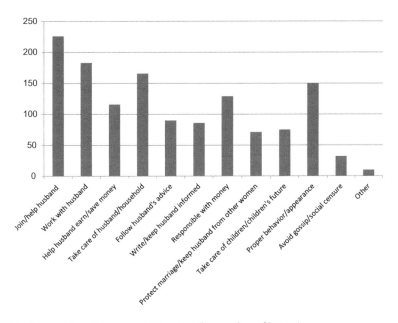

Figure 2. Main themes denoting responsible wives (by number of letters).

Given the nature of the corpus (that is, the letters' function as call letters), it is not surprising that many husbands expected their wives' contribution to manifest itself through shared work in the places of destination. Wives' assistance with their husbands' work and the performance of domestic chores that husbands were unable or unwilling to do alone were the reasons more commonly used in the letters for reunification. These reasons were frequently presented as a fulfillment of wives' obligations as well as a common-sense money-saving strategy. Migrant conditions were as varied as their occupations and personal circumstances, but there are a few recurrent themes in the letters. The need for wives to take care of husbands' domestic necessities is the request cited more often (usually expressed through purported lack of proper meals and clothing). Writers commonly complained about their lack of time for fixing their own meals, the poor and expensive meals available outside the homes, and the state of their clothes in need of washing or fixing, among other needs. Domestic chores required time that migrant men needed to take away from their own jobs or resources to pay somebody else to do it, often not to their liking and always requiring them to spend part of their hard-earned money. The following passages from a 1909 letter from Rio de Janeiro and a 1914 letter from Provincetown, Massachusetts, illustrate these concerns: 'A man alone here cannot save any money, at least if he earns little; because almost everything goes to pay for the eating houses (*casas de pasto*) and for the room and for the washing woman,' wrote Joaquim to his wife Glória; 'I need you here because I cannot continue to pay for everything, for there is not enough honey to satisfy the sweet tooth,' wrote Manuel to his wife Alice.[31] By choice or by necessity, many times migrant men performed all the domestic activities which normally were in the hands of the women of the household. We are 'four men sewing and fixing clothes, you know well how much work that is, and only to see if we can save something, and if you and our daughters were to come, then you could save us from doing that work,' wrote José, who was working in a coffee farm in Brazil with his three sons, to his wife; their son Adolfo confirmed their need for domestic assistance, and added his own request to the letter, 'Mother it would be good if you could do as father asks you, I was not born to be a cook.'[32] Similarly, Augusto, a migrant who hailed from the same rural area outside Coimbra, and who was also established as a coffee farmer in the interior of São Paulo State, expressed his dissatisfaction at living alone, exacerbated by the need to provide for his domestic needs after working all day in the fields. He wrote to his wife:

> Maria, do not make little of my request because here I don't have anybody to do anything for me, not even if I pay for it; there isn't anybody even to wash me a shirt. Maria I am here with a coffee farming contract (empreitada) and I don't have a knack for cooking, as you know. I leave every morning only after having a little coffee and some beans and rice, and I go on like this until the night; when I arrive at home at night you can see how I feel to arrive and to see everything closed, and still to have to cook beans for dinner; then I don't feel like eating anything. Maria, see if you can come, the sooner the better … because I can't be even one more hour without you.[33]

When migrants settled as farmers, shopkeepers, or innkeepers, wives' contributions extended from common domestic needs to shared work in the fields and taking care of workers and customers. In addition to their labor contribution, some husbands emphasized the importance of relying on their own family to protect their economic interests and investment, with the added bonus of reducing the need for hiring strangers. Francisco captured this feeling in a letter in which he asked his wife Ana to join him in Santos (Brazil): 'Nobody works better than the owner of the hound,' he wrote, referencing the common proverb 'Nobody hunts better than the owner of the hound.'[34] Finally, there were also instances in which husbands called their wives to share the burden of gainful work and increase their income, while reducing domestic costs in the places of settlement. Wives' contributions in these cases included working as domestic help (usually in the same homes where their husbands were already employed) as well as engaging in paid work outside the home or, more commonly, in paid labor that could be carried out from the home, such as washing clothes and preparing meals for other workers, and sewing for retailers or manufacturers. Working on their own was not considered appropriate for married women for most Portuguese migrants (Borges, 2009; Matos, 2002; Pascal, 2005).

In most cases, the need for a female presence is expressed in practical terms (to take care of the husband and the household, and to help the husband with his work). Besides addressing the tangible rewards of reunification, however, husbands also discussed it in terms of marital obligations and sentiments. At times, letters included general expressions of a husband's wish to have his wife at his side (for example, using phrases like 'fazes muita falta' – you are very much needed), but more commonly husbands made their case by presenting the fulfillment of this request as an unequivocal manifestation of their wives' duty. António put it very succinctly in a letter sent from Casablanca (Morocco) to his wife Maria Francisca in Loulé (Faro): 'Wherever the husband is, so is the woman'; and a fellow Algarvian migrant echoed this unmistakable message of marital obligation in equally simple words in a letter from Córdoba (Argentina), 'Your duty is to be with your husband.'[35] A frequent approach was for husbands to appeal to a sense of marital love to be demonstrated by their wives by leaving behind their familiar world and joining them abroad. These sentiments are illustrated in these passages from letters sent by migrants from Santos (Brazil) and Rio de Janeiro to their wives in Soure (Coimbra) and Póvoa de Varzim (Porto), respectively: 'If you have affection (amizade) for me and want to live in my company, you will not send any other response [to this letter] than you yourself coming here'; and 'if you have a bit of affection for me and our children, come, and if you want our unhappiness (desgraça), do not come, it is up to you.'[36]

Husbands were aware that the experience of separation might have resulted in their wives developing stronger feelings of attachment to their own families and to their households. Severing those ties by joining their husbands came to be seen by some writers as further evidence of their wives' marital duty and affection. 'I have known for a while that you have not come because you don't want to, because you have more affection (*amizade*) for your land and for what is yours than for me, so in that case do not send me any more laments nor any more pretenses,' bluntly wrote José from Rio de Janeiro to his wife Joana in Porto.[37] Other writers interpreted their wives' hesitancy to leave Portugal in a similar vein; for example, accusing them of having 'more affection for your family than for me' or reminding them that 'a married woman has no business living with her parents but should live with her husband because he is the source of happiness and well-being for his wife', as did two migrants writing from Brazil.[38]

The message of marital duty was clear: loving wives will not hesitate if their husbands require their presence abroad. In a letter sent in 1897 from Santos (Brazil), Francisco conveyed this message to his wife Eduarda in no uncertain terms: 'The woman who has affection (*amizade*) for her husband comes right away even if they tell her she is going to die at sea.'[39] For some writers, wives' attitudes of refusal or hesitancy to leave as well as unexplained delays in their trips put into question their love for their husbands and even raised doubts about the true nature of their marital bond. When José, a migrant from the County of Caminha (Viana do Castelo), realized that not only did his wife Ana show little desire to join him in Rio de Janeiro but she also had plans of working outside the home serving as a domestic, thus showing a spirit of independence and the possibility of securing alternative access to income, he questioned the true nature of her marital love and obligation in these dramatic terms:

> Should I consider myself from now on neither single nor married, not even a widower? How unhappy I am, my God! Why was I even born? Look, you don't want to come here (and you say that you love me – *me tens amor*). Very well, go wherever you desire, but if you don't come here just remember that I am no longer your husband, and that we will be neither single nor married nor widowers.[40]

Other writers opted for more prosaic approaches to request their wives to honor their marital bonds and leave Portugal to join them; common among them were references to the exemplary behavior of other wives who had followed the expected path. Husbands mentioned how ordinary the migration of married women was (for example, 'there are many Portuguese women here, they are arriving in every ship, the men here ask them to come, and you do not disappoint me'[41]) and made regular references to specific fellow migrants whose wives had migrated or who were on their way to join them. These examples of dependability served to reinforce wives' sense of loyalty and marital obligation. As a migrant expressed it in a letter from Buenos Aires, 'those are truly good women who love their husbands well'.[42]

In addition to demands for observance of marital duty, migrant husbands also appealed to family sentiments and to the emotional costs of living apart. References to feelings of weariness and unhappiness caused by separation were common. For some writers, it was in the hands of their wives to put an end to that situation and to make their married lives whole again. 'Enough of living away from each other,' wrote Elias to his wife Maria in a letter from Rio de Janeiro, 'I dreamt that I was not married, that this is no way of living. I ask myself, why is it that I work and sacrifice myself, and I don't have any consolation from anybody.'[43] In these cases too wives were to demonstrate their steadfastness to marital bonds through reunification. Even more, as the letter from the migrant from Caminha cited above illustrates,

103

many husbands sent their wives an unequivocal message that the marriage itself could be in peril if they failed to comply with their husbands' request (the frequency of cases like these appears in Figure 2 under the category 'protect marriage/keep husband from other women'). The ways in which the message was conveyed in the letters varied. Usually, writers made passing mention of the emotional needs as husbands which could only be remedied through reunification. These writers expressed feelings of being 'tired' (aborrecido, cheio) of living alone and separated from their families, and stressed how much happier and worry-free they could be together. A few writers expressed a sense of incompleteness, as did a migrant from Coimbra working in a coffee estate in São Paulo when he wrote to his wife: 'a man alone is nobody'.[44] Some husbands elaborated on these feelings using moving language to describe their condition. Writing from Pernambuco, in northeastern Brazil, in 1918, a migrant from Coimbra also characterized his state as a man without a wife as incomplete: 'Elisa I am nothing without you, I don't even know how I have not gone mad, I have your portrait at my bedside asking God to bring you to me because I cannot be alone.'[45] There are even some instances of exceptional deployment of the emotional language of suffering caused by separation meant to elicit a prompt decision to join their husbands among reluctant wives. António wrote to his wife Encarnação from Boston, in 1917: 'Listen my love, when I go sometimes to the theater at night my heart is sad like the night because I see other men with their wives and I, who have a wife of my own, am here alone; it makes me want to cry when I remember all of that.'[46] In a 1909 letter from Rio de Janeiro, Francisco shared with his wife a similar feeling of sadness for their separation:

> Yesterday … in the morning I was in such a state of sadness that I was about to lose the balance of my life. I found myself so desperate that I even stopped in a solitary place where no one could see me and the only thing I could do was to yearn and cry thinking of my unfortunate destiny. After so much pitying myself God gave me some consolation and I continued working but I did not have the strength to resist my emotions (paixões)![47]

Francisco's lament was cut short by the arrival of a letter from his wife, Emília. After reading it, the desire for reunification only grew stronger, as he explains to his wife: 'Life without you is like a fainted heart, if I continue like this and I don't see you beside me as soon as possible I won't live much longer.'

The repertoire of argumentative strategies used by husbands was varied. Writers conveyed clear ideas of their needs as both husbands and men which went beyond the sentimental. In fact, it was not uncommon for references to needs of a more physical nature to be found alongside a yearning for sentimental fulfillment. 'You know that a man needs a woman, and that is in every sense,' put succinctly but clearly José Maria in a letter sent from São Paulo State to his wife Maria dos Anjos.[48] Likewise, João asked his wife Emília to join him in Rio de Janeiro in order 'to cut the devil's legs' – that is, to avoid temptation; and António stressed the need for his wife Margarida to join him in São Paulo by saying 'before the problem grows, it is better to cut its head'.[49] There are even a few suggestive references to husbands facing an empty bed and expressions of desire to have their wives at their side at the end of the day, among them: 'The only thing missing is you at my side to sleep'; 'I have been cold in bed'; and 'I am going to sleep alone, it is a pity, hopefully it is not for too long.'[50] Few as they are, these references speak louder in these letters which transitioned from their intended private hands to public use, and could illustrate a more prevalent sentiment. In a 1918 letter from Rio de Janeiro, a writer confided to his wife he had dreamt they were sleeping together: 'Last night I dreamt I was in your bed … but I was mistaken and I woke up alone with [word scratched over with a pen] … It was as if I had fallen into your heart.'[51] The intimate nature of this confession is accentuated by the decision to conceal part of the text before the letter was presented to the authorities as part of the passport request (by the writer's wife? we do not know). Other writers conveyed their desires in an equally candid way and their comments were not blotted out by the recipient. Particularly vivid was a 1916 letter written by João, a migrant from Viana do Castelo, who was working in the rural area of Buenos Aires. In what reads as a distressed confession, João revealed to his wife he had been living with another woman and that his attempts to leave her had been unsuccessful. After a frank account of what seems a conflictive passionate relationship, João assured his wife of his true love and begged her to join him. In an interesting twist in his argument which reveals entrenched ideas of marital responsibility, according to João, it was in his wife's hands to save the marriage: 'I only desire for you to come as soon as possible because if you don't it is a destroyed marriage (*um matrimónio desfeito*).'[52] This reference to a relationship with another woman is not unique; there are more than a dozen such cases in the corpus (this may seem like a modest number but one needs to keep in mind that these letters were presented by passport applicants to public authorities, making the inclusion of admissions of unfaithfulness all the more telling).

Allusions to wives' responsibility sometimes included indications of their role in preventing their husbands from acting foolishly or immorally forced by their circumstances of living without female company. A letter sent in 1907 from the interior of the State of Minas Gerais (Brazil) by José to his wife Maria do Rosário, in Penela (Coimbra), included a plea to his son-in-law to convince José's wife to join him in Brazil or to accept the consequences: 'If I were to do something foolish (*uma má cabeçada*), then she'd better not blame me.'[53] Similar sentiments are present in a letter sent in 1917 by Joaquim from São Paulo to his wife Lucinda in the rural parish of Grijó (Porto): 'If you want to save our situation, come here as soon as possible, because if you don't come I will consider myself as if I don't have any family. I don't know if you already heard from somebody what I am doing here, I know it is upsetting (*a desgosto*) for you, but you are the one who gave me reasons for that, if you had done what your (female) neighbors did I would not be making a fool of myself now.'[54] It may be necessary to read in between the lines to fully uncover what Joaquim meant by his upsetting behavior, but there are few doubts that he was holding his wife responsible for his having sought female companionship in São Paulo; and to reinforce the idea of obligation, he mentioned the examples of other women from home who had joined their husbands in Brazil thus preventing any 'foolish' behavior. In all these examples, the message is clear: if the husband seeks the company and help of another woman, the wife's indifference and hesitancy to migrate were to blame.

Fears of infidelity appeared commonly in discussion of wives' migrations, both as a reaction to suspicion of husbands' behavior abroad and as a tool of persuasion used by husbands to convince hesitant wives of the urgency of reunification. This argumentative strategy was effective because separation and lack of companionship bred anxieties about marital fidelity. Falling for other women threatened not only to undermine the emotional foundation of families separated by migration, but also the idea of migration as a common project with mutual obligations. Such behavior had potential moral and material consequences: breaking vows of commitment and also resulting in abandoned wives and children. In some parts of Portugal, migrants who never went back home and did not call their wives were referred to as *os esquecidos* – the forgetful or those who forgot their families (Borges, 2009). They became the counterpart of another popular image in the local culture of regions with heavy migration, the *viúvas de vivos*, or widows of the living (Brettell, 1986), married women whose black clothing underscored their state of unnatural widowhood as they waited for their husbands' return.

5. The threat of abandonment: love and fidelity among migrant couples

Manifestations of love and duty were grounded in general gender and family roles in Portuguese society at the turn of the twentieth century in general (see, for example, Vaquinhas, 2011), but among migrant families they were magnified by separation and by the idea of migration as a family strategy with common goals and shared responsibilities. Distance and time of separation added another layer: the threat of family abandonment and marital infidelity, fueled by the suspicion with which the societies of origin – and particularly women – saw the de facto liberty that their husbands could enjoy abroad while they were separated. This was somewhat limited by the role of gossip as a mechanism of social censure and control, and the role of letters as vehicles through which this mechanism was kept alive across vast distances. Letters include regular references to gossip among family members and fellow villagers, and were often used to dispel, discredit, or confirm such rumors.

Fidelity was discussed by both men and women. Allusions to the temptations of men living alone far from home were also used by wives to call on their husbands' emotional and material obligations. In the letters, husbands sometimes reacted to suspicions of infidelity caused by long silences or conveyed by gossip in letters from other people. Usually men dismissed these rumors as ill-founded products of other peoples' fabrications and envy. Even though there are few examples of letters written by women in this corpus there are enough references and hints in the letters to show that the latent danger of 'forgetful' men was a significant component of the long-distance emotional negotiations that occurred in the epistolary exchange of families separated by migration. The most visible manifestation of this tension appears in the form of husbands' reassurance of fidelity and affection despite their separation. In many cases, these reassurances were a reaction to manifestations of suspicion or outright accusations of unfaithfulness included in letters from their wives. Francisco, a migrant from Estoi (Faro) called his wife Ana when he decided to settle in Buenos Aires, in 1892, after receiving a letter accusing him of living with another woman. Francisco's reaction follows a recognizable form in these epistolary exchanges: assuring his wife of his love, and proving his commitment by reminding her of his sacrifices to fulfill the role of family provider:

> Regarding the letter I received today, the 12th, in which you tell me that I have a woman here, you know well that you offend me with that; me, a husband who as you know adores you and who has always loved you …
>
> …
>
> I have always been dependable (*firme*) and loyal; and with the many sacrifices (*trabalhos*) I have endured in the Matto Grosso and in all of Brazil, exiled in these isles among the blacks … I tolerate (*sofro*) all that you say about me because of the love I have for you; nobody knows the sacrifices I have endured but me.[55]

In these cases, family reunification appeared as the best remedy to discredit the accusation and to put an end to gossip. A migrant from Olhão (Faro) expressed this sentiment in a letter he sent to his wife from Santos (Brazil): 'You wrote that I have a woman here, but I have to tell you that there are many women here but they belong to other men; and even those women are not good enough to kiss the feet of the women back home. To put an end to all of this, see if you can come here as soon as you receive this letter ... come to see the women that I have here, that way you can be satisfied.'[56] Another migrant from Olhão opted for a defiant tone to dismiss his wife's accusations: 'I saw all you wrote in your letter, both lies and truths. Regarding the lover that I have, she is a good girl and I have her always with me; and regarding the whores, I have 25 under my care of the prettiest type.'[57] Here too, reunification was presented as the best way to end rumors, distrust, and marital tension.

Another strategy to deal with accusations in cases like these was to question the sources of information and to condemn the practice of spreading gossip in general. Rumors circulated through other people's correspondence and stories told by returnees; and women with men abroad exchanged information. A migrant from Guimarães (Braga) likened female gossiping in his home town with an informal postal service: 'In that town women only serve as message carriers (*correios*), and you pay them well to have correspondence'; and a migrant from Vouzela (Viseu) characterized his home town as 'the land of gossip (*murmuração*)'.[58] Despite strong censure, however, gossip traveled both ways. As a migrant from Vieira do Minho (Braga) lamented, rumors 'also come in this direction, and it is a pity that the ship that carries them does not sink into the sea so they will not have any possibility of salvation'.[59]

Expectations of fidelity were reciprocal and rumors also contributed to husbands' concern about unsupervised wives. There are, however, few explicit examples of these types of concerns in the letters in the corpus under analysis. After all, mechanisms of social control through gossip were harder to avoid in the small social world of rural towns in Portugal from which most migrants originated; and presumably more effective than in the large cities or scattered rural and mining settlements where most migrants worked. For example, Abílio blamed his wife Maria Francisca's improper behavior for his long epistolary silence. He had received news by other family members of Francisca's talking to a man in their home in Vieira (Braga) on Sundays and also of her frequenting several local fairs. Urging Francisca to change her ways, Abílio reminded her of other women from the village with husbands abroad who have gained a 'bad name' (*fama*).[60]

Thus, suspicions and gossip traveled both ways, and some men denounced what they considered improper behavior among their wives. The stakes, however, were not equally high for men and women. As a migrant in Manaus (Brazil), wrote to his wife in Porto:

> I don't want to believe that you are not my sincere friend and that you are not loyal. However, being as I am so good to you and working with much sacrifice for your well-being, I can't accept any secrets in our home ... .

> ... When a woman marries she must be everything for her husband, because if that is not the case, she is the only one who suffers the consequences ... A man can do some stupid things but he loses nothing for that, which is not the case for a woman, for whom all steps in the wrong direction make her look bad.[61]

Migrant men, on the other hand, sometimes made nonchalant references to living with other women as well as to the sexual needs of men who were far away from their wives for long periods of time. For example, in a 1907 letter from Neves (Brazil), Francisco expressed the need to be reunited with his wife Maria in the following terms:

> I am unhappy in everything, first because I can't live without a woman and if I had a woman with me [other than his wife] it would be shameful and it could end badly, second is that as you know I don't have common sense (*não tenho juízo*) to govern myself, and third that if I were to go with those lost women out there it will damage my health (*estrago a minha saúde*) and I will never be able to save a penny and later I will have nothing for you or for me ...[62]

As in other cases analyzed above, Francisco was using this situation to call on his wife's duty to put an end to this situation of need, both material and sexual, and join him abroad.

Since these letters were put to use as call letters, and in many cases they were the last epistolary contact before the departure of women to join their husbands abroad, concerns about potential threats to female faithfulness during the trip were more common. Once women left their home villages the mechanisms of social control that characterized the confined social lives of rural Portugal diminished but did not necessarily disappear. As many husbands were quick to remind their wives, the censuring power of gossip could indeed reach far – as far as the ships during the ocean crossing. Warnings like that of Júlio to his wife Maria Conceição appear frequently in the letters: 'All respect is not enough; you don't show even your teeth to anyone [on board] … because I don't want anyone to say anything [about you] when you arrive here.'[63] These concerns were part of a larger anxiety among men about the danger of unprotected females and about women's responsibility as faithful wives even far from the vigilant eyes of family and the local community. They are equally connected to ideas of female virtue and male honor. Even though these topics are beyond the coverage of the present article, the importance of these preoccupations with women's behavior in the ships that carried them abroad becomes clear in the thematic clusters about women's responsibilities that appear in Figure 2.

In the majority of instances in which fidelity is discussed in the letters from this corpus, however, it was about the threat of other women to married men living abroad. More often than not, references to the need for female companionship were included by husbands to underscore the sense of urgency in their plea for their wives' migration. In their view, it was in their wives' hands to remedy this situation or else risk their husbands' loyalty or even risk endangering their marriage and losing their husbands altogether. To further underscore the urgency of their plea, some husbands alluded to the possibility of finding another companion if their wives refused or deferred their trip, thus feeding into a frequent anxiety among couples separated by migration (especially among wives left behind).

These sentiments were usually heightened by cultural constructions about the temptation represented by foreign women. In the novel *Viúvas de vivos*, Joaquim Lagoeiro (1973 [1947]) recreates a scene in which the 'widows of the living' who are waiting for the promised, successful return of their husbands put their worries into song while they washed clothes in a stream together. One of them sings the following verses: 'We are not single / nor married / and we have husbands. / Our lost love / belongs to the shameless / foreign women' (pp. 59–60). Similar concerns about the temptations of local women pervaded many marital relationships in transnational couples, and, as the frequency of this argumentative strategy in these letters suggests, were often used by men to persuade their wives of the benefits of family reunification abroad. In their view, if their wives fulfilled their obligation, that danger could be averted. 'Today I need a woman at my side but that is your duty,' wrote Silvestre, a migrant from Viana do Castelo settled with a coffee farm in Brazil, to his wife Maria. Silvestre described in detail the bountiful promise of the land he had recently acquired, but he also told his wife that what he 'liked the most here are the good little black women, big lipped (*beiçudas*) but good for all service', after which observation he went on to describe the attributes of Italian, French, German, Spanish, and Portuguese women present in the multi-ethnic world of coffee towns in southeastern Brazil. At the end of the letter, Silvestre added a final warning: 'Make up your mind (*resolve*) as soon as possible; there is no scarcity of women here.'[64]

As Silvestre's narrative illustrates, for migrant men in Brazil and Portuguese Africa, references to local women also summoned long-established colonial images of non-European women and their sexual power over European men. His use of images of black women evoked a shared imagery rooted in Portugal's long tradition of colonization and settler migration (Castelo, 1998; Gomes, 2011; Matos, 2006). Black and mulatto women, in particular, appeared at the same time as alluring and dangerous to European men; like Silvestre's allusion to their 'big lips', associations to sexual attraction and temptation were common in these images. Tellingly, when an explicit marker of racial or ethnic origin is used to heighten the potential of a female threat to Portuguese migrants in the letters from this corpus, more often than not the comment is about black women (10 out 13 cases). Using a playful tone, José wrote a letter calling his wife Carlota to join him in Rio de Janeiro in which he joked about marrying a 'very black woman' and described Brazilian mulatto women as tricksters that made Portuguese men forget home.

> I don't know if you are aware that I am about to marry a devilish of a black woman who is so black but so black that she is more black than everything that is black. Did you know? And she is as beautiful as she can be! So beautiful that she has hair that grows from her ears to the floor … But don't worry, she is also old, so old that it is not worth it for me to forget you, because I think you are younger and therefore stronger to work. Carlota, I remember that since I am single, as a gentleman I will ask you in marriage. I have been away from you for so long. Can you tell me if I can obtain such a favor? People also say that Brazilian *mulatas* are enticing, that they trick Portuguese men and make them forget about their homeland. But I don't get myself involved in what others say. As you know, I am a very serious young man. It is not just to flatter myself, but I am … or not?[65]

The tone of this passage is certainly playful and idiosyncratic, but the images it invokes would have resonated with the imagery of many readers in Portugal; in a similar way to when another migrant from Porto told his wife that she should accelerate her trip to Rio de Janeiro because the '*mulata* is my perdition, she gives me embraces and many things that I don't tell you'; when a migrant from Guimarães (Braga) reacted to his wife's questioning about his sudden change of address by saying, ironically, 'it was because I had a little *mulata* with me, so beautiful that even you would like her, and I did not want you to see her'; or, more seriously, when a migrant from Cabeceiras de Basto (Braga) warned his wife that if she delayed her trip to Brazil he was going to find himself a black woman with whom to live.[66]

The language of affect among Portuguese couples separated by migration at times resorted to jealousy as part of a broader argumentative strategy that aimed at convincing hesitant wives to join their husbands thus completing the family migratory project. Since in most cases, the initial project was one of male temporary labor migration to return home, this shift to family relocation sometimes met with understandable resistance on the part of migrants' wives. The temptation of foreign women served to stress how much was at stake. Succumbing to these temptations posed a double threat: in the short term, diverting resources from home and resulting in more sporadic communication, thus undermining core principles of marital and family love; in the long term, severing the ties with home and abandoning wife and family to fend for themselves.

6. Conclusion

The call letters analyzed in this article provide a window into the mental and emotional world of late nineteenth- and early twentieth-century Portuguese families living transnational lives as a result of migration. Borrowing the concept from Mark Seymour's analysis of love letters found in Italian judicial records, we can characterize Portuguese call letters as 'normal exceptions' (Seymour, 2010) – exceptional because of their bureaucratic use, 'but very probably quite representative in other respects' (p. 150). The call letters discussed here fit this description. As family letters were put to use as proof of marital and paternal consent for migration, personal and intimate documents found their way into official records. These letters were part of regular epistolary exchanges among migrant families and shared with them form, tone, and preoccupations with families' present and future well-being. At the same time, the imminence of reunification and of relocation to faraway destinations resulted in explicit considerations of the costs and gains of migration as a family strategy, and the roles of husbands and wives in that life project.

Portuguese call letters offer a rare opportunity to explore the dynamic reality of families' adjustment to migration and, in particular, the ways in which migrant couples made sense of their shifting positions and identities as husbands and wives, and of their common transnational enterprise. The language and arguments of common people – the majority of migrants – are hard to come by in the historical record, and call letters offer a glimpse of that perspective – maybe a fragmentary one, but that is true for most historical sources. The discussion that precedes these closing words focused on the ways in which migrant families used letter writing to articulate these ideas and emotions – oftentimes overcoming the limitations of little familiarity with the written word. The argumentative strategies used in letters between migrant husbands and their wives made use of a variety of themes and approaches. Discussions of marital duty, loyalty, and reciprocity contributed to a language of affect built on narratives of responsibility and dependability that reinforced the idea of a common migration project. Letters from migrant husbands to their wives were also attempts to exert authority at a distance in a context of rapid change. Men and women had roles they were expected to fulfill, both materially and emotionally. The transnational lives of migrant households altered traditional gender divisions of authority, gave new meanings to traditional roles, and affected power relations. Distance and length of time of separation often strengthened affective bonds but also put them to the test, sometimes leading to feelings of uncertainty and mistrust. Initial plans often changed and temporary migration turned into long-term or permanent settlement, creating hope but also anxieties. Positive ideas of shared marital responsibility coexisted with fears of infidelity and abandonment. Letters between men and women of Portuguese migrant families helped them make sense of this new reality and work through differences and tensions, keeping anxieties in check and fears at bay. They provided spaces in which relationships altered by migration were recreated in the language of transnational affect, characterized by shared marital duty represented by responsible husbands and loyal wives.

Notes

1. The gross emigration ratio was 0.52 for the years 1890 to 1920; and net emigration ratios were 0.56 for 1900–1911, 0.67 for 1911–1920, and 0.58 for 1920–1930. After 1930, the negative influence of the global economic crisis of 1930 and World War II produced a visible decline in international mobility and net emigration ratios plummeted. High levels of emigration resumed in the postwar period, reaching 0.68 for 1950–1960. This time, destinations in northern Europe, particularly France, attracted the bulk of Portuguese emigrants. See Bandeira (1996, pp. 151–153).
2. All translations are mine.

3. Call letters were also required by some countries of immigration in case of older migrants or when restrictions and quotas were required in the 1920s and 1930s; these letters were intended to show proof of family sponsorship and sometimes employment. In the case of Brazil, call letters of this type are archived in São Paulo's immigrant archive. See Croci (2012) and Matos (2013).

4. The letters come from passport application dossiers in the following Portuguese district/ regional archives: Braga, Castelo Branco, Coimbra, Faro, Leiria, Lisboa, Madeira, Porto, Viseu, and Viana do Castelo. These are all the regional archives in which call letters exist. I have also conducted research in several other archives which did not yield any letters. In some regional archives passport request dossiers have not survived (for example, in Aveiro); or they have survived but without letters (for example, in Angra do Heroísmo, in the Azores); or else the surviving dossiers belong to a period when formal authorizations replaced personal letters as a form of consent – usually after 1922 (for example, in Guarda). Research in these archives extended for many years during which I examined an estimated 100,000 passport dossiers. I wish to express my heartfelt gratitude to the many archivists who facilitated this research. Passport dossiers are organized in different ways in different archives, so selection criteria varied among them (sometimes I looked at complete years, sometimes at complete series of boxes, sometimes at specific ranges of years by smaller administrative divisions, etc.). The objective was to cast a wide net in order to identify dossiers with letters from a variety of years from the 1870s to the 1920s. The breakdown of the letters in the corpus by regional archive is as follows: Braga (294), Castelo Branco (1), Coimbra (475), Faro (408), Leiria (1), Lisboa (89), Madeira (19), Porto (428), Viseu (344), and Viana do Castelo (151); total: 2210. The distribution of letters in the corpus by country or region of origin is as follows (in decreasing order): Brazil (76.6%), Argentina (8.8%), United States (4.8%), Portuguese Africa (3.6%), Gibraltar (2.7%), France (0.6%), Spain (0.5%), and other (2.4%). All selected letters were transcribed and later annotated for content analysis using qualitative data analysis software (MaxQDA). The identifying numbers in the letters correspond to the number in the corpus.

5. Since these letters were used as *cartas de chamada* (call letters) and arrangements for the trip appear very frequently in them, it could be possible that money appears as a more frequent topic than in other letters exchanged by migrant families. The evidence presented by Monteiro (1985) in his analysis of the correspondence of a couple separated by migration, however, suggests otherwise. Money appears as frequently as a topic of discussion, especially in letters sent by the husband (see pp. 150–156).

6. Letter 77, António to his wife Maria Augusta, Manaus, Brazil, 3/3/1898, Arquivo Distrital de Viana do Castelo (hereafter ADVC), Governo Civil, Processos de passaporte [Passport Applications], box 2383 file 23, 30/4/1898. Since all letters come from passport applications handled by the Civil Government, I have omitted this information in the rest of the notes. Variations in archival citation format reflect variations in each archive's classification system at the time of research.

7. Letter 521, José to his wife Maria da Piedade, Campinas, São Paulo, Brazil, 12/2/1910, Arquivo Distrital de Coimbra (hereafter ADC), IID/GC/ILFS/9/1/567, file 1284, 14/6/1910.

8. Letter 1141, Manuel to his wife Lucinda, São António do Monte, Minas Gerais, Brazil, 7/11/1911, Arquivo Distrital do Porto (hereafter ADP), dossier 1747, file 293, 25/01/1912.

9. Letter 832, Manuel to his wife Maria Clara, Rio de Janeiro, Brazil, 5/12/1911, ADP, dossier 1748, file 43, 6/1/1912.

10. Letter 1202, Domingos to his wife Maria Fernanda, Rio de Janeiro, Brazil, 3/12/1907, ADP, dossier 1673, file 598, 15/01/1908.

11. Letter 21, Albino to his wife Maria Joaquina, Pará, Brazil, 25/5/1903, Arquivo Distrital de Viseu (hereafter ADV), box 2044, file 81, 20/7/1903.

12. Letter 1202, Domingos to his wife Maria Fernanda, Rio de Janeiro, Brazil, 3/12/1907, ADP, dossier 1673, file 598, 15/01/1908.

13. Letter 1152, José to his wife Margarida, Rio de Janeiro, Brazil, 27/6/1917, ADP, dossier 1840, file 1091, 11/08/1917.

14. Letter 1701, Júlio to his wife Maria, Rio de Janeiro, Brazil, 20/1/1909, Arquivo Distrital de Braga (hereafter ADB), file 3291, 15/7/1909; Letter 216, Miguel to his son Manuel, Rio de Janeiro, 9/10/1913, ADV, box 2057, file 24, 23/12/1903.

15. Letter 1770, António to his father (name unknown), France, 23/9/1919, ADB, file 25578, 8/10/1919.
16. Letter 223, Anacleto to his wife Julieta, São Paulo, Brazil, 15/2/1919, ADV, box 2430, file 728, 22/5/1919; Letter 447, Augusto to his daughter Elvira, Rio de Janeiro, Brazil, 23/6/1915, ADC, IID/GC/ILFS/9/5/675, file 421, 13/9/1915; Letter 730, Hipólito to his mother (name unknown), São Paulo, Brazil, 30/10/1912, ADC, IID/GC/ILFS/9/4/633, file 5387, 4/12/1912.
17. Letter 2132, António to his wife Amélia, Plymouth, Mass., USA, 22/4/1918, Arquivo Distrital de Lisboa/Arquivo Nacional da Torre do Tombo (hereafter ADL), N.T. 1016, N.R. 1628 A, June 1918.
18. Letter 653, João to his wife Florinda, São Paulo, Brazil, 18/9/1917, ADC, IID/GC/ILFS/10/1/690, file 490, 10/11/1917.
19. Letter 551, António to his wife Margarida, Santos, São Paulo, Brazil, 8/10/1910, ADC, IID/GC/ILFS/9/2/580, file 292, 27/1/1911.
20. Letter 677, José Augusto to his wife Maria, Rio de Janeiro, Brazil, 2/10/1898, ADC, IID/GC/ILFS/8/1/400, file 1832, 10/12/1898.
21. Letter 150, José to his wife Maria do Carmo, Rio de Janeiro, Brazil, 25/9/1916, ADV, box 2440, file 89, 8/11/1916; Letter 1283, José to his wife Maria da Conceição, [Buenos Aires], Argentina, 20/7/1917, Arquivo Distrital de Faro (hereafter ADF), box 631, dossier 1, 9/11/1917.
22. Letter 1061, Bernardino to his cousin (name unknown), São Paulo, Brazil, 15/11/1915, ADP, dossier 1819, file 1143, 28/12/1915.
23. Letter 377, Luiz to his wife Felismina, Coimbra, Minas Gerais, Brazil, 20/7/1900, ADC, IID/GC/ILFS/8/1/418, file 963.
24. Letter 925, Custódio to his uncle Valentim, Espírito Santo do Pinhal, São Paulo, Brazil, 1/8/1905, ADP, dossier 1649, file 310, 29/01/1905.
25. Letter 1942, Domingos to his wife Teresa, Rio de Janeiro, Brazil, 23/3/1919, ADB, file 18560, 9/19/1919.
26. Letter 1727, João to his compadre (name unknown), Juqueri [Franco da Rocha], São Paulo, Brazil, 12/7/1902, ADB, file 12306, 08/28/1903.
27. Letter 1330, João to his son João, Scotia, Cal., USA, 7/8/1919, ADF, box M1040, dossier 1, file 275, 10/10/1919.
28. Letter 1883, João to his wife Maria dos Prazeres, Barbacena, Minas Gerais, Brazil, 10/3/1892, ADB, file 26638, 8/9/1892.
29. Letter 1316, José Joaquim to his wife Maria, Pelotas, Rio Grande do Sul, Brazil, 1/7/1898, ADF, uncatalogued, file 62, 10/9/1898.
30. Letter 2017, Manuel to his wife Beatriz, Rio de Janeiro, Brazil, 18/3/1916, ADVC, file number unknown, 13/06/1916.
31. Letter 1237, Joaquim to his wife Glória, Rio de Janeiro, Brazil, 19/1/1909, ADP, dossier 1695, file 494, 19/02/1909; Letter 1594, Manuel to his wife Alice, Provincetown, Mass., USA, 29/11/1914, ADF, box 604, dossier 1, 17/12/1914.
32. Letter 544, José to his wife Miquelina, Fazenda do Turbo, São Paulo, Brazil, 19/8/1910, ADC, IID/GC/ILFS/9/2/576, file 2767, 26/11/1910.
33. Letter 680, Augusto to his wife Maria da Assunção, [Guariba], São Paulo, Brazil, 1/1/1899, ADC, IID/GC/ILFS/8/1/404, file 521, 11/3/1899.
34. Letter 528, Francisco to his wife Ana, Brazil, date unknown, ADC, IID/GC/ILFS/9/2/571, file 2178, 14/10/1910.
35. Letter 1625, António to his wife Maria Francisca, Casablanca, Morocco, 28/5/1921, ADF, box 613, dossier 1, file 294; Letter 1348, Manuel to his wife Maria Francisca, Córdoba, Argentina, 22/8/1916, ADF, box 169, dossier 1, file number unknown.
36. Letter 642, António to his wife Ana Maria, Santos, Brasil, 22/2/1917, ADC, IID/GC/ILFS/10/1/688, file 194, 7/4/1917; Letter 1203, António to his wife Brígida, Rio de Janeiro, Brazil, 17/11/1916, ADP, dossier 1833, file 1051, 9/01/1917.
37. Letter 893, José to his wife Joana, Rio de Janeiro, Brazil, 23/10/1907, ADP, dossier 1658, file 239 or 241, 10/12/1907.
38. Letter 1670, Albino to his wife Clotilde, Rio de Janeiro, Brazil, 16/2/1914, ADB, file 917, 10/5/1914; Letter 622, Manuel to his wife Maria, Inhangapi, Pará, Brazil, 15/7/1897, ADC, IID/GC/ILFS/7/5/385, file 779, 25/8/1897.

39. Letter 669, Francisco to his wife Eduarda, São Paulo, Brazil, 6/12/1897, ADC, IID/GC/ILFS/7/5/390, file 282, 24/3/1898.
40. Letter 2016, José Maria to his wife Ana Rosa, Rio de Janeiro, Brazil, 27/5/1916, ADVC, file 336, 27/06/1916.
41. Letter 806, António to his wife (name unknown), Brazil, date unknown, ADC, IID/GC/ILFS/7/2/290 file 549, 27/6/1890.
42. Letter 1480, Veríssimo to his wife Mariana, place unknown, Argentina, 13/10/1910, ADF, box 138, 15/12/1910.
43. Letter 876, Elias to his wife Maria, Tijuca, Rio de Janeiro, Brazil, 28/12/1917, ADP, dossier 1846, file 1125, 16/03/1918.
44. Letter 354, José Maria to his wife Emília, [Fazenda dos Carmos, São Paulo], Brazil, 4/12/1899, ADC, IID/GC/ILFS/8/1/412, file 241, 16/3/1900.
45. Letter 753, Alfredo to his wife Elisa, Pernambuco, Brazil, 20/9/1918, ADC, IID/GC/ILFS/10/1/698 file 90, 4/2/1919.
46. Letter 656, António to his wife Encarnação, [Boston, Mass.], USA, 26/11/1917, ADC, IID/GC/ILFS/10/1/692 file 5, 8/1/1918.
47. Letter 1870, Francisco to his wife Emília, Rio de Janeiro, Brazil, 11/4/1909, ADB, file 22634, 4/9/1909.
48. Letter 743, José Maria to his wife Maria dos Anjos, Viradouro, São Paulo, Brazil, 21/12/1893 [?], ADC, IID/GC/ILFS/9/5/661, file 251, 7/2/1914.
49. Letter 868, João to his wife Emília, Rio de Janeiro, Brazil, 25/9/1906, ADP, dossier 1671, file 1119, 16/11/1907; Letter 2, António to his wife Margarida, São Paulo, Brazil, 9/10/1899, ADV, box 2049, file 134, 24/2/1900.
50. Letter 2010, Luís to his wife Maria, Rio de Janeiro, Brazil, 5/10/1890, ADVC, file 670, 10/11/1890; Letter 2094, Manuel to his wife Maria, [Lourenço Marques], Mozambique, date unknown, file 360, 11/09/1902; Letter 555, Sebastião to his wife Maria Augusta, Rio de Janeiro, Brazil, 20/12/1910, ADC, IID/GC/ILFS/9/2/580, file 341, 2/2/1911.
51. Letter 814, Joaquim to his wife Maria Guia, Rio de Janeiro, Brazil, 1/7/1918, ADC, ID/GC/ILFS/10/1/695, file 387, 27/09/1918.
52. Letter 2015, João to his wife Carminda, Ramallo, Buenos Aires, Argentina, 12/4/1916, ADVC, file 322, 30/05/1916.
53. Letter 692, from João to his wife Maria do Rosário, Sabará, Minas Gerais, Brazil, 20/11/1907, ADC, IID/GC/ILFS/8/5/529, file 851, 17/3/1908.
54. Letter 1210, Joaquim to his wife Lucinda, São Paulo, Brazil, 14/1/1917, ADP, dossier, 1835, file 228, 19/03/1917.
55. Letter 1483, Francisco to his wife Ana, Buenos Aires, Argentina, 12/12/1893, ADF, uncatalogued, file 1, 12/1/1893.
56. Letter 1311, Joaquim to his wife Maria Paulina, Espírito Santo do Rio do Peixe, São Paulo, Brasil, 28/5/1895, ADF, uncatalogued, file 9, 12/12/1896.
57. Letter 1313, José to his wife Maria, place unknown, Brazil, 4/6/1907, ADF, uncatalogued, file 3, 4/1/1908.
58. Letter 1930, Eduardo to his wife Rosa, Bagé, Rio Grande do Sul, Brazil, 30/7/1911, ADB, file 17808, 1/9/1911; Letter 199, João to his wife Maria da Conceição, New Bedford, Mass., USA, 5/5/1915, ADV, box 2522, file 46, 3/7/1915.
59. Letter 1877, Manuel to his wife Angelina, Rio de Janeiro, Brazil, 6/8/1913, ADB, file 23049, 29/11/1913.
60. Letter 1873, Abílio to his wife Maria Francisca, Rio de Janeiro, Brazil, 14/11/1911, ADB, file 22835, 12/4/1912.
61. Letter 843, Mário to his wife Margarida, Manaus, Brazil, 22/11/1910, ADP, dossier 1754, file 898, 23/04/1912.
62. Letter 863, Francisco to his wife Maria, Neves, Brazil, 22/8/1907, ADP, dossier 1666, file 362, 11/10/1907.
63. Letter 938, from Júlio to wife Maria Conceição, Manaus, Brazil, 25/1/1910, ADP, dossier 1710, file 252, 23/02/1910.

64. Letter 2093, Silvestre to his wife Maria, Descampado, São Paulo, Brazil, 27/4/1902, ADVC, file 370, 15/09/1902.
65. Letter 886, José to his wife Carlota, Rio de Janeiro, Brazil, 11/1/1909, ADP, dossier 1696, file 893, 8/03/1909.
66. Letter 848, Eduardo to his wife Rosalina, Rio de Janeiro, 12/6/1912, ADP, dossier 1762, file 563, 19/08/1912; Letter 1928, Manuel to his wife Carolina, Niterói, Rio de Janeiro, Brazil, 31/7/1903, ADB, file 17349, 28/8/1903; Letter 1909, Joaquim to his wife Angélica, Silvestre Ferraz [Carmo de Minas], Minas Gerais, Brazil, 6/10/1916, ADB, file 10960, 11/27/1916.

Acknowledgements

Research, analysis, and writing for this article have been generously supported by the following institutions and programs: Dickinson College's Research and Development Committee and the Kalaris Family Fellowship; Central Pennsylvania Consortium–Andrew W. Mellon Foundation Grant; the EURIAS Fellowship Program, co-funded by the EU Marie Curie Actions, under the 7th Framework Programme; and the Netherlands Institute for Advanced Studies in the Humanities and Social Sciences.

Disclosure statement

No potential conflict of interest was reported by the author.

ORCID

Marcelo J. Borges http://orcid.org/0000-0002-0741-5220

Archival sources

Arquivo Distrital de Braga, Universidade do Minho, PortugalGoverno Civil, Processos de Passaporte
Arquivo Distrital de Castelo Branco, PortugalGoverno Civil, Processos de Passaporte
Arquivo Distrital de Coimbra, Universidade de Coimbra, PortugalGoverno Civil, Processos de Passaporte
Arquivo Distrital de Faro, PortugalGoverno Civil, Processos de Passaporte
Arquivo Distrital de Leiria, PortugalGoverno Civil, Processos de Passaporte
Arquivo Distrital de Lisboa, Arquivos Nacionais da Torre do Tombo, PortugalGoverno Civil, Processos de Passaporte
Arquivo Regional da Madeira, PortugalGoverno Civil, Processos de Passaporte
Arquivo Distrital do Porto, PortugalGoverno Civil, Processos de Passaporte
Arquivo Distrital de Viseu, PortugalGoverno Civil, Processos de Passaporte
Arquivo Distrital de Viana do Castelo, PortugalGoverno Civil, Processos de Passaporte

References

Alves, J. F. (1993). Lógicas migratórias no Porto oitocentista. [Migratory logics in nineteenth-century Porto]. In M. N. Silva, M. I. Baganha, M. J. Maranhão, & M. H. Pereira (Eds.), *Emigração/imigração em Portugal* [Emigration/immigration in Portugal] (pp. 78–97). Lisbon: Fragmentos.
Alves, J. F. (1994). *Os Brasileiros: emigração e retorno no Porto oitocentista* [The Brazilians: Emigration and return in nineteenth century Porto]. Porto: Gráficos Reunidos.
Baganha, M. I. (1990). *Portuguese emigration in the United States, 1820–1930*. New York, NY: Garland Publishing.
Baganha, M. I. (2009). Migração transatlântica: Uma síntese histórica [Transatlantic migration: A historical synthesis]. In J. V. Serrão, M. A. Pinheiro, & M. F. Ferreira (Eds.), *Desenvolvimento económico e mudança social: Portugal nos últimos dois séculos, homenagem a Miriam Halpern Pereira* [Economic

development and social change: Portugal during the last two centuries, in honor of Miriam Halpern Pereira] (pp. 405–421). Lisbon: Imprensa de Ciências Sociais.

Baines, D. (1995). *Emigration from Europe, 1815–1930*. Cambridge: Cambridge University Press.

Bandeira, M. L. (1996). *Demografia e modernidade: Família e transição demográfica em Portugal* [Demography and modernity: Family and demographic transition in Portugal]. Lisbon: Imprensa Nacional Casa da Moeda.

Borges, M. (2009). *Chains of gold: Portuguese migration to Argentina in transatlantic perspective*. Leiden: Brill.

Brettell, C. (1979). Emigrar para voltar: A Portuguese ideology of return migration. *Papers in Anthropology, 22*(1), 1–20.

Brettell, C. (1986). *Men who migrate, women who wait: Population and history in a Portuguese parish*. Princeton: Princeton University Press.

Cancian, S. (2010). *Families, lovers, and their letters: Italian postwar migration to Canada*. Winnipeg: University of Mannitoba Press.

Cancian, S. (2012). The language of gender in lovers' correspondence, 1946–1949. *Gender and History, 24*, 755–765.

Candeias, A. (2000). Ritmos e formas de acceso à cultura escrita das populações portuguesas nos séculos XIX e XX: Dados e dúvidas [Rhythms and forms of access to the writing culture in Portuguese populations in the nineteenth and twentieth centuries: Data and doubts]. In M. R. Delgado-Martins, G. Ramalho, & A. Costa (Eds.), *Literacia e sociedade: Contribuções pluridisciplinares* [Literacy and society: Multidisciplinary contributions] (pp. 209–259). Lisbon: Caminho.

Castelo, C. (1998). *"O modo português de estar no mundo": O luso-tropicalismo e a ideologia colonial portuguesa (1933–1960)* ["A Portuguese way of being in the world": Luso-Tropicalism and the Portuguese colonial ideology (1933–1960)]. Porto: Edições Afrontamento.

Chaney, R. (1986). *Regional emigration and remittances in developing countries: The Portuguese experience*. New York, NY: Praeger.

Croci, F. (2012). Imigranti italiani in Brasile: Le lettere di chiamata [Italian immigrant in Brazil: Call letters]. In F. Caffarena & L. Martínez Martín (Eds.). *Scritture migranti: Uno sguardo italo-spagnolo* [Migrant writings: An Italian-Spanish approach] (pp. 125–142). Milan: Franco Angeli.

Da Orden, M. L. (2010). *Una familia y un océano de por medio: La emigración gallega a la Argentina: Una historia a través de la memoria epistolar* [A family and an ocean in between: Galician emigration to Argentina: A history through epistolary memory]. Barcelona: Anthropos.

Dinis, J. (2004 [1868]). *A morgadinha dos Canaviais* [The morgadinha from the Canaviais]. Porto: Porto Editora.

Elliott, B., Gerber, D., & Sinke, S. (Eds.). (2006). *Letters across borders: The epistolary practices of international migrants*. New York, NY: Palgrave Macmillan.

Evangelista, J. (1971). *Um século de população portuguesa, 1864–1960* [A century of Portuguese population, 1864–1960]. Lisbon: Instituto Nacional de Estatística-Centro de Estudos Demográficos.

Gabaccia, D. (2001). When the migrants are men: Italy's women and transnationalism as a working-class way of life. In P. Sharpe (Ed.), *Women, gender, and labour migration: Historical and global perspectives* (pp. 190–208). London: Routledge.

Gerber, D. (2006). *Authors of their lives: The personal correspondence of British immigrants to North America in the nineteenth century*. New York, NY: New York University Press.

Gibelli, A. (2002). Emigrantes y soldados: La escritura popular como práctica de masas en los siglos XIX y XX [Emigrants and soldiers: Popular writing as a practice of the masses in the nineteenth and twentieth centuries]. In A. Castillo Gómez (Ed.), *La conquista del alfabeto: Escritura y clases populares* [The conquest of the alphabet: Writing and popular classes] (pp. 189–223). Gijón: Ediciones Trea.

Gomes, M. S. (2011). *Mulheres brasileiras em Portugal e imaginários sociais: Uma revisão crítica da literatura* [Brazilian women in Portugal and social imaginaries: A critical review of the literature]. (Working Paper No. 106). Retrieved from http://cies.iscte-iul.pt/destaques/documentos/CIES-WP106_Gomes_000.pdf

Kwon, J. H. (2015). The work of waiting: Love and money in Korean Chinese transnational migration. *Cultural Anthropology, 30*, 477–500.

Lagoeiro, J. (1973[1947]). *Viúvas de vivos* [Widows of the living] (3rd ed.). Lisbon: Editorial Minerva.

Lamas, M. (1948). *As mulheres do meu país* [The women of my country]. Lisbon: Actualis.

Leite, J. C. (1987). Emigração portuguesa: A lei e os números (1855–1914) [Portuguese emigration: The law and the numbers (1855–1914)]. *Análise Social, 32*, 463–480.

Leite, J. C. (2000). O Brasil e a emigração portuguesa (1855–1914) [Brazil and Portuguese emigration (1855–1914)]. In B. Fausto (Ed.), *Fazer a América: A imigração em massa para a América Latina* [To make America: Mass migration to Latin America] (2nd ed.). (pp. 177–200). São Paulo: Edusp.

Lyons, M. (2013). *The writing culture of ordinary people in Europe, c. 1860–1920*. New York, NY: Cambridge University Press.

Matos, F. P. (2006). *As côres do império: Representações raciais no império colonial português* [The colors of the empire: Racial representations in the Portuguese colonial empire]. Lisbon: Imprensa de Ciências Sociais.

Matos, M. I. S. (2002). *Cotidiano e cultura: História, cidade e trabalho* [Everyday life and culture: History, city, and labor]. Bauru, São Paulo: Edusc.

Matos, M. I. S. (2013). Na espera da mala postal: Cartas, correspondências e mensagens trocadas entre portugueses (São Paulo-Portugal, 1890–1950) [Waiting for the mail ship: Letters, correspondence, and messages exchanged between Portuguese migrants (São Paulo-Portugal, 1890–1950)]. *Convergência Lusíada, 29*, 7–21.

Medeiros, F. (1978). *A sociedade e a economia portuguesas nas origens do Salazarismo* [Portuguese society and economy at the beginning of Salazarism]. Lisbon: A Regra do Jogo.

Miranda, S. (1999). *A emigração portuguesa e o Atlântico, 1870–1930* [Portuguese emigration and the Atlantic]. Lisbon: Edições Salamandra.

Monteiro, M. (2000). *Migrantes, emigrantes e Brasileiros de Fafe (1834–1926)* [Migrants, emigrants, and Brazilians of Fafe (1834–1926)]. Fafe: Author.

Monteiro, P. (1985). *Terra que já foi terra: Análise sociológica de nove lugares agro-pastoris da Serra da Lousã* [A land which once was home: Sociological analysis of nine agro-pastoral localities in the Serra da Lousã]. Lisbon: Edições Salamandra.

Morier-Genoud, E., & Cahen, M. (Eds.). (2012). *Imperial migrations: Colonial communities and diaspora in the Portuguese world*. New York, NY: Palgrave Macmillan.

Newitt, M. (2015). *Emigration and the sea: An alternative history of Portugal and the Portuguese*. London: Hurst & Company.

Pascal, M. A. M. (2005). *Portugueses em São Paulo: A face feminina da imigração* [Portuguese in São Paulo: The female face of immigration]. São Paulo: Expressão & Arte Editora.

Pereira, M. H. (1981). *A política portuguesa de emigração, 1850–1930* [Portuguese emigration policy, 1850–1930]. Lisbon: A Regra do Jogo.

Ramos, C. V. (1913). *Legislação portuguesa sobre emigração e passaportes* [Portuguese legislation about emigration and passports]. Lisbon: Typographia Adolpho de Mendonça.

Reeder, L. (2003). *Widows in white: Migration and the transformation of rural Italian women, Sicily, 1880–1920*. Toronto: University of Toronto Press.

Rodrigues, H. F. (2010). Imagens da emigração oitocentista na correspondência enviada ao Brasil [Images of nineteenth century emigration in the mail sent to Brazil]. *Cadernos de História, 11*, 94–138. doi:10.5752/P.2237-8871.2010v11n15p94

Sarmento, C. M. (1999). "Minha querida marida": Subsídios para o estudo da família emigrante através das cartas de chamada, 1890–1914 ["My dear wife": Contributions for the study of the emigrant family through call letters]. In P. S. Machado & J. A. M. Marques (Eds.), *Maia, história regional e local: Actas do congresso* [Maia, regional and local history: Conference proceedings] (Vol. 2, pp. 285–296). Maia: Câmara Municipal.

Serrão, J. (1982). *A emigração portuguesa: Sondagem histórica* [Portuguese emigration: A historical survey] (4th ed.). Lisbon: Livros Horizonte.

Seymour, M. (2010). Epistolary emotions: Exploring amorous hinterlands in 1870s southern Italy. *Social History, 35*, 148–164. doi:10.1080/03071021003719139

Sousa, M. S., & Perez Dominguez, M. C. (1982). *Women of Portugal*. (Women of Europe Supplement No. 11). Brussels: EU Commission.

Stangl, W. (2010). Consideraciones metodológicas acerca de las cartas privadas de emigrants españoles desde América, 1492–1824: El caso de las "cartas de llamada" [Methodological considerations about Spanish private letters from the Americas, 1492–1824: The case of "call letters"]. *Jahrbuch für Geschichte Lateinamerikas, 47*, 11–35.

Vaquinhas, I. (2005). *Nem gatas borralheiras, nem bonecas de luxo: As mulheres portuguesas sob o olhar de história (séculos XIX–XX)* [Neither Cinderellas nor luxury dolls: Portuguese women through history (nineteenth–twentieth centuries)]. Lisbon: Livros Horizonte.

Vaquinhas, I. (2011). A família, essa "pátria em miniatura" [The family, a miniature fatherland]. In I. Vaquinhas (Ed.), *História da vida privada em Portugal: a época contemporânea* [History of private life in Portugal: Contemporary period] (pp. 118–151). Lisbon: Círculo de Leitores–Temas e Debates.

Vieira, A. (1990). Migration from the Portuguese Atlantic islands in the second half of the nineteenth century: The case of Madeira. In D. Higgs (Ed.), *Portuguese migration in global perspective* (pp. 42–58). Toronto: The Multicultural History Society of Ontario.

Wise, A., & Velayutham, S. (2006). *Towards a typology of transnational affect* (Working Paper No. 4). Sydney: Centre for Research on Social Inclusion, Macquarie University.

Settler colonialism and migrant letters: the Forbes family and letter-writing in South Africa 1850–1922

Liz Stanley

ABSTRACT

The 'migrant letter' has been proposed as a separate genre of letter-writing around features concerning absence, identity and relationships and location. However, questions arise about this claim, made using largely North American material. Explored in a different context, important complexities and differences come into view. This is discussed regarding the settler colonial context of South Africa using data from the Forbes family collection, containing around 15,000 documents written between 1850 and 1922. The Forbes were Byrne migrants to Natal, then Transvaal. The majority of letters in the collection were written and exchanged within South Africa, with significant numbers from family members remaining in Scotland or who removed elsewhere, and many drafts and copies of letters written by the South African end exist too. The size and composition of contents enable migrant letters to be explored within the greater entirety of the family's letter-writing, conceived as a scriptural economy with characteristic writing practices. This is examined by looking in detail at the writing practices of a range of letter-writers and their correspondences. Important differences concerning how absences, identities and relationships and locations are inscribed in the context of South Africa are explored and traced to features of its settler colonial mode of production.

1. Introduction: the migrant letter in perspective

It is on one level self-evident what a migrant letter is: a letter from someone who has removed 'abroad' to a person remaining 'at home', written in a context of permanent absence, with contents characterized by looking back to shared bonds while valorizing the new circumstances, through this creating a 'third space' of structures supporting letter-exchanges, such letters being more often written by men than women because of literacy differentials. These ideas have been explored in insightful contributions theorizing migrant letter-writing and its role in the migrant experience (Baldasser & Gabaccia, 2010a, 2010b; Cancian, 2010; Chilton, 2007; Elliott, Gerber, & Sinke, 2006; Fitzpatrick, 1994; Fraser, 2000; Gabaccia, 2000; Gerber, 1997, 2000, 2005, 2006; Markelis, 2006; Middleton, 2010; Richards, 2004, 2006; Vargas, 2006).

Relatedly, it has been proposed that these features add up to migrant letters being a separate genre, most influentially by Gerber (2006); see also Elliott et al. (2006). However, questions arise about the general applicability of these ideas, based largely on North American/ northern European data, for there are different migratory origins and points of arrival and settlement and most migrants will have produced many different letters, some to people 'at home', others to connections in the new context. These matters are explored here from the perspective of settler colonial letter-writing in South Africa.

The Forbes brothers were 1850 Byrne migrants to Natal and later lived in the Transvaal. The Forbes collection contains around 15,000 documents written between 1850 and 1922.[1] Letters are a major component, with diaries, accounts, tallies, inventories, ledgers and other papers also present, written by the Forbes family, their kin, friends, neighbors, business associates and officials. The majority of those extant were written and exchanged within South Africa, although significant numbers are from family members who remained in Scotland or removed elsewhere, and there are many drafts and copies of letters written by the South African end as well.[2]

The size and varied composition of collection contents provide the breadth and depth necessary for examining in a methodologically robust way how migrant letters shape up when located within the greater entirety of a family's letter-writing, explored later as a scriptural economy. Doing so enables definitional claims about the migrant letter to be productively considered from a perspective different from the North American and southern European one that has dominated discussion to date. Work on the Forbes collection is part of the Whites Writing Whiteness project (http://www.whiteswritingwhiteness.ed.ac.uk), concerned with letter-writing in South Africa by white settler colonists from the 1770s to the 1970s.[3] Ideas about the migrant letter as a distinct genre are now discussed in more detail, to draw from these some points of comparison in considering what a Forbes and South African settler colonial perspective might add to understanding migrant letter-writing more generally.

The first feature seen to define migrant letter-writing is that it bridges the ontological gap between the migrant in the new settlement, and family connections in the country of origin, through the affirmation received in response to their communications (Gerber, 2006, pp. 2–5, 13–21, 92–94). This is seen to involve interrelated kinds of writing, which are regulative (organizing and maintaining relationships), expressive (representing experience and expressing emotions) and descriptive (writing about quotidian events and routines) in character (Gerber, 2006, pp. 101–131), with emotion and affect viewed as charged aspects of many migrant letter exchanges (Cancian, 2010, pp. 6–7; Cancian & Gabaccia, 2014). However, although such things take particular shape in migrant letter-writing, they are not unique to it, being characteristic of the epistolary genre generally (Decker, 1998; Jolly & Stanley, 2005; Stanley, 2004, 2011, 2012). Letter-writing as a communicative genre is premised on absence and distance between a writer and their addressees; and this is so even if (as with leaving notes for people) the separation is temporary and the distance small. All correspondences over time persist because of continuing bonds. Also, the gap that letter-writing bridges can be (semi-) permanent and involve absence and great distance in more circumstances than migration. The propelling absence, for example, might be a migrant one but with the people concerned 'repeat returning' to the erstwhile homeland (Gabaccia, 2000; Harper, 2005). And regarding South African letters, it could also include (semi-) permanent absences and great distances but with the people concerned living in the same country, and shorter separations between people living on neighboring but still distant farms who rarely saw each other.[4]

Looking back at the shared past, however, is found only rarely in these letters. They are rather descriptive and communicative, inscribing everyday activities, exchanging information, goods and services, and expediting shared activities of different kinds including mutual business matters, and this is as much so for the 'migrant' exchanges as the internal South African ones.

The second feature seen as definitional of the migrant letter is the connection between letter-writing and identity-making, with the person at the migrant end viewed as looking back to use the shared past, and forward to promote the new self (Baldassar & Gabaccia, 2010b ; Elliott et al., 2006; Gerber, 2006, pp. 1–32). Letter-writing here is seen more as a means to identity construction, less as having focused communicative purposes (Gerber, 2006, p. 57). But again, while raising interesting ideas, it is letter-writing generally, not migrant letters especially, that helps maintain networks of communication with identity-making a part of this. This is pertinent regarding war and mass separations (Lyons, 2013) and imprisonment (Maybin, 2006), but occurs too in the most ordinary of letter-writing (Barton & Hall, 1999a, 1999b; Lyons, 2007; Whyman, 2009). However, as discussion later details, in the South African settler context, identity matters in letter-writing take a different form, being characterized by exteriority around sharing everyday detail and joint activities, rather than overt self-fashioning or affect,[5] something also present in letters by other migrant groups where periods of absence and presence alternated and attention was given to practical concerns in the family economy.

The third feature seen to define the migrant letter is the growth of interpersonal and organizational structures around letter-writing and exchanging, drawing on transnationalist thinking about 'third space' (Bhabha, 1990; Davis, 2010; Ikas & Wagener, 2008; Soja, 1996; Vertovec, 2009; and regarding letters, Elliott et al., 2006, p. 12; Gerber, 2006, pp. 92–94; Jones, 2006, p. 190). In relation to letters, this has been seen as 'a unique social space' (Elliott et al., 2006, p. 12), with recent electronic variants such as text and social media seen to have similar features (Haggis & Holmes, 2011).[6] However, migration sociology's emphasis on epistolary and other communications being shaped by local and emergent practices is more helpful in thinking about the coexisting although geographically separate epistolary spaces of letter-writing, for transnationalism covers diasporas experienced very differently by disparate groups and migrations to very different circumstances (Gabaccia, 2000, pp. 81–105; How, 2003).[7] Correspondences are consequently better seen as parallel moments of writing, sending, reading and replying rooted in the material circumstances of both contexts and taking shape around mutual concerns (DeHaan, 2010; Stanley, 2004, 2013b). These heterotopic aspects of epistolary spaces give rise to a shared mode of engagement that distinguishes each correspondence from others, and not surprisingly, the specifics of particular migrations also mark this (Altman, 1982; Decker, 1998; Foucault, 1967; How, 2003).

It may be concluded here that while conceptualizing the migrant letter as a distinct genre has reinvigorated thinking about migrant letter-writing, it has also obscured features shared with letter-writing generally. Wider developments in epistolary scholarship have made little impact in the migrant letters context, although there are some points of crossover, particularly the work of Altman (1982) and Decker (1998). This is to be expected in a still-evolving area of work, and there are now signs, including the existence of this special issue, of more detailed engagements across the boundaries of migration studies, the migrant letter literature, and wider epistolary scholarship.[8] However, the definitional approach to 'the' migrant letter remains problematic, and so the question arises, should these ideas be abandoned? There are two reasons why their development would be more helpful.

First, even if the characteristics noted are not definitional, nonetheless they do characterize *some* migrant letters, primarily those written in the North Americas. These were produced by labor migrants crossing national boundaries and deep cultural divides, and whose mobility challenged notions of national belonging and accompanying cultural mores and practices. However, as the following discussion shows, the Northern European settler colonists migrating to southern Africa did it differently. And while the letters discussed later are no more representative than those of labor migrants to the Americas, they *are* letters by people of different material and ideational circumstances – of the 'middling sort' (Hunt, 1996), who migrated for different reasons – entrepreneurial opportunities, to a very different migratory context – the settler colonies of South Africa. Secondly, what follows is that, if different kinds of migrants and contexts produced different kinds of letter-writing, it is important to detail what these differences are. In this, drawing points from the migrant letters literature – succinctly summarized from the above discussion as absences, identities, relationships, and parallel locations – is helpful in making such comparisons.

Many settler colonists in South Africa amassed large family collections now part of its national archives system, notably those of English-speaking and particularly Scottish backgrounds.[9] The Forbes were Scots from the Perth and Pitlochry area. This collection contains some 15,000 documents written from 1850 and emigration by some family members to Natal and subsequently Transvaal, through to 1922.[10] There are over 4000 letters, with contents also including notes and memos, lists, ledgers and inventories, accounts, diaries, wills and other business and official communications (Stanley, 2015b, 2015d). Family relationships, household, farm, wider economic life, kin relations and entrepreneurial activities were overlaid, encompassing both immediate family and kin, and a range of friends and associates in Natal and the Cape as well as the Transvaal,[11] and internationally, from Scotland and England.[12]

As a result, the range of economic activities the Forbes engaged in cannot be distinguished from their personal and familial relationships, and are both deeply rooted in life in South Africa and encompass equally important connections with people elsewhere. The Forbes were British in origin and also identified as Scots and Transvaalers and had complex allegiances, distinguishing themselves from the way of life of their Boer (later Afrikaner), German and other settler neighbors, while identifying with many aims of the Transvaal's political elite, except with regard to territorial expansion, when British loyalties came into play. Their ideas about belonging were constituted around these multiple identities and allegiances, with their letter-writing both articulating and traversing such distinctions.

Another result is a set of things that are 'the migrant letters' cannot be picked out of these exchanges. Certainly many letters were written and sent, and many were received and read, in circumstances of migration and the new context of settlement. But at the same time, across the generations the Forbes were busy active people, time did not stand still, and they not only established roots but became closely embedded in the developing settler colonial economy in economic ventures that drew in many other people, including locally, in Scotland, elsewhere in South Africa, and Australia. Consequently, 'the migrant letters' thought of in the narrow sense are just letters among the large number of Forbes letter-writings overall and are fully part of the economic and related activities the Forbes were engaged in, not separate from this.

2. Settler colonists: family, household, economy, letter-writing

British migrants to Africa were relatively few compared with numbers migrating to, in ascending order, New Zealand, Australia, Canada and the USA, and also unequally distributed in the different African colonies.[13] Early emigration to South Africa, as distinct from the individualized arrivals of traders and missionaries, took place via emigration companies.[14] Alexander and David Forbes were Byrne 'Emigration and Colonization Company' migrants to Natal in 1850, with younger brother James following in 1859.[15] The interrelated Purcocks, Dingley and McCorkindale families were also Byrne migrants, with Kate Purcocks marrying David Forbes in early 1860.

After arrival in Natal, David Forbes combined hunting and trading with Alexander, and farming cash crops (arrowroot and indigo) for an inter/national market on his own behalf. On one trading trip to south-eastern Transvaal,[16] he was impressed by its rich farmlands and was the source of Alexander McCorkindale negotiating with the Transvaal's President Pretorius to purchase 200 large parcels of land, from which local black peoples had been disappropriated. These were the basis of how McCorkindale attracted people to his Glasgow and South Africa Company migration scheme. While it drew relatively few people direct from Britain, a large number of originally Natal migrants became involved, amounting to a large ox-wagon trek from Natal to McCorkindale's farms. A large number were Scots and the farms were in an area called New Scotland (later New Amsterdam) in the Ermelo district.[17] Soon after the move, with his younger brother James, David combined agri-farming on a large scale with prospecting and mining, first for diamonds at New Rush (Kimberley), later for gold and coal in the Barberton and Swaziland areas.

David Forbes purchased four farms direct from the Transvaal government, then acquired others. Some, centering on the largest, Athole, were farmed by the Forbes; others were leased to tenants, including the Purcocks and Dingleys. After David's death in 1905, two were farmed by Forbes daughters Kitty Rawson and Madge Dunn (later Tonkin). Athole was then run primarily by Kate and their eldest daughter Nellie Forbes until Kate's death in 1922, although with holdings of land and stock retained by Forbes sons David (Dave) junior and his younger brother James (Jim) junior.[18]

The Forbes and other white migrants to South Africa were settler colonists (Elkins & Pedersen, 2005; Veracini, 2010, 2011, 2015; Wolfe, 1999).[19] Over time, these people shifted from being colonists to being the dominant group, in a process which turned indigenous peoples into internal migrants and squatters, and the settlers into land-owners, with key features of settler colonialism not only occupation and possession but also displacement and removal (Bose, 2014; Cavanagh, 2013). The South African case is a variant, with white occupation and its desire for (cheap, black) labor, coexisting with the desire for its displacement (but somewhere conveniently nearby). This characterized the large farming estates of the Transvaal (Krikler, 1993), including those in New Scotland, and produced complicated arrangements for both the availability and removal of black labor.[20]

The settler colonial economies, originally dependent on a metropole, started entering the world market from the 1780s. In South Africa's case, arrowroot, indigo, wool, with lesser successes in coffee and cotton production, were involved from the 1850s on, followed in the 1860s by diamonds and the 1880s by gold, coal and other minerals, and after 1900 by refrigerated and frozen meat, fruit and wine (Denoon, 1983; Feinstein, 2005; Lloyd, Metzer, & Sutch, 2012). The Forbes had stakes in many, starting in the 1860s with arrowroot and indigo, followed by sheep farming for wool, then adding stock-rearing for meat, horse-breeding, coupled with mining ventures in diamonds, gold, and later coal, and dealing in stocks and shares. Farming households of the Transvaal like the Forbes developed around strong ties with others connected by kinship, and also expanded into wider spheres of economic activity as the settler economy grew, substantiating South Africa's settler way of life premised on black labor. The close interrelationship between family, household, kinship, land and production persisted as the settler colonists diversified from their agricultural base and their new economic activities encompassed kin in the original homeland and to an extent other colonies too.[21] These are notable features of the economic lives of the Forbes.

The Forbes came from the 'middling sort'. Adam Forbes and his brother-in-law, Peter Sim, owned a timber-yard in Pitlochry near Perth that exported timber. In 1840, the business failed when their uninsured ship sank. In 1842, Adam's wife Ellen then Adam himself died. Their daughters became upper servants, Lizzie a housekeeper, and Jemima a lady's maid, while their sons Alexander and David did laboring jobs, including in Ireland and Liverpool, then in 1850 became Byrne migrants to Natal, with James following later.[22] The Forbes siblings had little formal education. Lizzie and David became proficient letter-writers, while James's skills improved over time and Jemima's remained elementary.[23] Letters from family and wider kin display varying proficiency in the formalities of letter-writing, but have considerable communicative competence, with the high level of Scottish basic literacy a factor here. Alongside this, there is the monumental fact that the Forbes collection contains over 4000 letters and many other documents. There is little sign the Forbes were readers on any scale, but by any measure they were voluminous writers.

The contents of other South African collections too indicate there was a high degree of literacy among English-speakers and particularly the Scottish migrants there.[24] Many had migrated for opportunity reasons rather than in extremis circumstances. In a large country with great distances between centers of population, white settlers farming outside its towns and villages lived fairly isolated lives: even neighboring farmhouses could be miles apart, for poor-quality land meant large farms. A white household with aspirations could soon find its members living hundreds of miles apart, as children went to school, daughters married out, sons left to establish themselves elsewhere, which resulted in even unpracticed writers frequently putting pen to paper.[25]

The propelling factor in letter-writing is absence and for migrant letters has been seen as permanent absence (Fitzpatrick, 1994; Gerber, 2006; Elliott, Gerber & Sinke, 2006), although actually absence can be of varied kinds and involve different durations and distances. Regarding the Forbes letters, it typically took the form of interrupted presence rather than permanent separation (Stanley, 2015a, pp. 242–244). By 'interrupted presence' is meant that these letter-exchanges concerned shared activities and were conducted with the premise the relationship would resume face-to-face eventually.[26] They concern a flow of activities and are purposive in expediting activity and forwarding plans. For the Forbes, it was not permanent absence and 'back then', but interrupted presence and the activities of 'now', that were central; and this was as much so regarding the letters between correspondents on different continents as those on adjacent farms or temporarily absent.

A particular impetus to Forbes letter-writing came from the economic activities engaged in. Their farming household needed to obtain goods and services from urban centers, maintain contacts with banks and insurance companies, keep records and accounts. Also, the Forbes and their relatives the Purcocks, McCorkindales and Dingleys set up trading stores, sold livestock and arable produce in a market, and bought to lease both farming and urban property. The Forbes themselves diversified into large-scale agri-business, then diamond, gold and coal mining, through which companies were established, stocks and shares bought and sold, with all these undertakings requiring both extensive record-keeping and a continuing flow of correspondence. The Forbes letters are overwhelmingly concerned with these interconnected economic activities, rather than personal life or matters of affect.

There were close links between the household as a focus for production and these wider economic involvements. Athole's homefarm under the aegis of Kate Forbes produced milk, butter and cheese and grew cash crops such as mealies (corn) for a local market; also the related agri-business enterprises engaged in on the homefarm by the six Forbes children as they came to adulthood included sheep and stock farming, horse-breeding, droving and carting.[27] In addition, wider family economic life encompassed the labor and monetary contributions of Alexander senior and James senior, also distance contributions to and by Lizzie Forbes, Jemima Forbes, and after Jemima's marriage her husband David Condie and their children.[28] 'The Forbes', then, was variously a family, a larger household, kin relations, other linked households, and a network of people with shared economic activities.[29] Family, household, kinship and friendship, land and other property, paid occupations, share-holding and share-dealing, and other means of producing income, intersected over the generations and stretched from Natal to the Transvaal, Cape, Swaziland, London, Scotland, and at points Australia too.

While the economic unit underpinning this centered on the Forbes household and Athole Estate, it had generous and permeable boundaries, involving flows of activity, goods, services, money and many movements of people.[30] Because of their shared business ventures, the Forbes and correspondents were necessarily involved in writing and receiving large numbers of letters which rehearsed, expedited and communicated these activities while also keeping in touch and facilitating ongoing relationships. As the discussion following shows, levering apart what was a business/economic letter and what was a private/personal one, and what was a migrant letter and what was not, would miss the point, for the letters concerned made no such distinctions.

3. The Forbes scriptural economy and its writing practices

The Forbes collection consists of a large multi-generational flow of letters over more than 70 years, involving some hundreds of addressees and recipients, with a core group of around 20 letter-writers.[31] It is composed of letters and many other everyday 'documents of life' (Plummer, 2001; Stanley, 2013a). These are components in what Michel de Certeau (1984, pp. 131–164) has termed a 'scriptural economy'. A scriptural economy is organized around epistolary exchanges – letters and correspondences – and related documents. The different forms of writing involved – letters, diaries, inventories, ledgers, etc. – have their own ways of positioning the reader, the writer, and what can appropriately be written in each. Also, Certeau sees each scriptural economy as developing customary practices, which intermesh with and reshape genre conventions, referring to this as an economy because involving flows of writings. These ideas are helpful in thinking about the Forbes letters (and those in other South African collections too).[32]

The Forbes collection as a scriptural economy has a large size and wide temporal span and encompasses the Forbes' many enthusiastic involvements in the settler economy. The people involved wrote, and wrote again.[33] The letters exchanged within South Africa are purposive communications, providing information, making requests and expediting ongoing activity, with the writer and addressee expecting to meet again in the (immediate or further off) future. The letters exchanged with people in the local Ermelo environs, and those in Scotland, are strikingly similar. With the latter, there is sometimes more relaying of news to keep the other person up to date, but these exchanges too are marked by their purposive character and shared activities of a 'will you go to a shareholders meeting' and 'send me your local newspaper' kind.

In the Forbes scriptural economy, the business involved was mainly literally business, with these letters characterized by exteriority (projects, activities) rather than interiority (affect, self-fashioning), purposiveness rather than reflection or retrospection, and communicative focus rather than matters of affect. It is unsurprising that writings such as ledgers, lists, tallies and accounts have these characteristics, but they also mark the many Forbes diaries, which are rarely concerned with anything personal and instead engage with everyday tasks regarding the Athole Estate, and also their letters.

Forbes family letter-writing began around absence: the Forbes sisters in Scotland, and their brothers in Natal. The person who provided the initial momentum was Lizzie Forbes, who ensured her continuing links with her brothers through letter-writing. Through this, a set of practices emerged that were taken up by all the siblings and influenced how the Forbes scriptural economy and its writing practices developed subsequently. The presumption of response is linked to the reciprocity aspect of letter-writing, for a letter's direct address to a named person invites, more strongly implies, an expectation of response (Altman, 1982; Stanley, 2011, 2012). In the 1850s writing to her brothers, Lizzie's letters are directed to one then another in turn, with contents passing on news that each brother had previously told her to the others.[34] At times she played them off against each other, commenting about who had not written and praising who had. Her letters also provided news about people they had known in Scotland, detailing these people's present-time activities and writing that they had requested news from Alexander, David or James. Lizzie also involved her sister in these epistolary practices, chivvying Jemima to write regular detailed letters. What resulted was an interconnected set of exchanges concerned with the unfolding 'now' rather than the past, forming a network involving a number of people, not just one person waiting for letters to be sent to them.

While Jemima at points contemplated joining her brothers in Natal,[35] Lizzie never did, although this was not the finality of permanent absence but by her viewed in interrupted presence terms. Thus in the 1860s she frequently wrote about anticipated reunion with one or more brothers, envisaged as lengthy but temporary Scottish visits following them achieving economic success.[36] The letter-exchanges between the siblings consequently do not look back, but are immersed in a shared 'now' of expanding business concerns. Also Lizzie and Jemima frequently purchased and arranged the shipping of goods to Athole, ranging from clothing to seeds and agricultural tools. Business could concern family matters more directly too, with 'the Forbes' as a collectivity taking responsibility in the 1880s for the Condie children after their parents died, a family trust being established to look after them. Lizzie Forbes oversaw their education and looked after her ailing namesake, Lizzie Condie, until the latter's early death; and she was paid a quarterly sum by the Athole Estate to support her when family responsibilities took precedence over her employment.

Another important characteristic concerns the everyday quotidian of people, places and activities. Lizzie's early letters, for instance, express interest in the minutiae of South African life, asking David to relate what clothes he wore, what lions and other animals looked like, where he lived and so on.[37] After David married, Kate Forbes became the main person corresponding with Lizzie and Jemima in Scotland. Kate too was an inveterate letter-writer, maintaining a range of correspondences including with her sister on the next farm and relations in England and Australia. Her letters prototypically detail the quotidian, as do Lizzie's to her. They shared this focus from their first exchanges in 1860.[38] Their exchanges took parallel form, engaging with what the other had written, describing their own activities, considering shared business and other interests, frequently also sending each other newspapers and magazines. An engagement with the everyday also marks letters between Lizzie, David and James, and later Lizzie's Forbes nieces Nellie, Kitty and Madge too.[39] However, this was not a 'Lizzie thing', for it also characterizes the letters Kate and David sent each other when apart because of his lengthy trading and prospecting trips, the many letters Dave junior wrote to his parents during periods of duty as manager of a coal mine in Swaziland, and the letters Sarah Purcocks (later Straker) wrote to her sister Kate, discussed later.

Forbes letter-writing as a scriptural economy, then, has shared writing practices that can be traced across different correspondences and over a lengthy time period. It involves a network of interrelated epistolary exchanges marked by a focus on 'now' and shared practical activities, the inscription of activity and the quotidian, a surface lack of affect and self-fashioning, and a focused concern with exteriority and practical matters. As later discussion shows, the different letter-writers developed variations and specific content, but within these broad commonalities. This was perhaps because Forbes letters are business-like, in two senses. They are purposeful communications, with matters of affect and relationships typically a matter for sign off only, and a focus on activities and exteriority. They are also concerned with actual business, with this being what is of most interest and concern to the letter-writers involved, something returned to in the concluding discussion.

These observations are now explored in substantive depth. Given the large numbers of letters involved, selections have had to be made and points of focus decided and a methodological strategy for analyzing the workings of the Forbes scriptural economy adopted. Its first aspect has been to explore flows of letters in cross-sections of one randomly selected year per decade of the collection's existence, some 2650 letters, and how they fit together at these temporal junctures (discussed in Stanley, 2015d).[40] Its second aspect, detailed here, focuses on the writing practices of different Forbes letter-writers and their correspondences, involving some 1380 letters. These have been purposively selected as reflecting varied circumstances of absence and distance, with two other themes drawn from the migrant letter literature, concerning how identities and relationships are inscribed, and how the parallel 'here' and 'now' of locations are handled, also discussed. Transcribed extracts from all letters quoted from are provided at http://www.whiteswritingwhiteness.ed.ac.uk/blog/migrant-letter/.

4. The scriptural economy at work

The methodological strategy of examining cross-sections of letters points up the diversity of flows of Forbes letters over time, who was involved in these exchanges, some of the broad changes occurring over this more than 70-year period, and also and importantly how all the letters fit together within this (Stanley, 2015d). In addition, broader aspects bearing on debates concerning the migrant letter are also raised. The ebbs and flows that mark the broad shape of the scriptural economy, for instance, are shown to be located around complex sets of factors, including external events (migrations, wars), life-course and generational matters (relocations, marriage, births, deaths), technological and communication developments, and attrition of different kinds. Within these flows, it also shows that picking out 'types' of letters is analytically problematic, for the letters, all the letters, are closely embedded within the unfolding fabric of activities, relationships and networks involved and there are no separate concerns or ways of writing that can be pulled out and dubbed as 'the migrant letters'.

A cross-sectional analysis necessarily focuses on flows, decennial patterns and broad changes, and what working at this scale does not show is how the writing practices of particular letter-writers developed over time or were modulated regarding the different people they corresponded with.[41] Thus the focus in what follows is particular letter-writers and their writing practices, and within this how absences, identity and relationships, and 'here' and 'now' matters of distance and location, are inscribed. A number of Forbes letter-writers and correspondences have been purposively selected to reflect different kinds and degrees of absence, separation and distance. These range from migratory absence and great distance (Lizzie Forbes), through different kinds of mobilities, including internationally (James Forbes), nationally and internationally (Mary McCorkindale, and in a different way Dave Forbes junior), and nationally (David Forbes), to short separations at local distance (Sarah Purcocks Straker).

4.1. I was right glad to hear: Lizzie Forbes

There are around 370 extant letters by Lizzie Forbes in Scotland, plus drafts of letters sent by her sister-in-law Kate Forbes, additional numbers by Lizzie to other family members in South Africa, also a handful to her from other people she sent on as enclosures.[42] The letters between Lizzie and Kate might be seen as 'classic' migrant ones, except that Kate, who migrated to Natal from England as a child, was later a 'temporary migrant' (six months' sojourn or more) to Britain on three occasions during which letters between her and Lizzie continued with largely unchanged features. Kate's first return was in 1885, with David taking their daughters Nellie, Kitty and Madge to Scotland; during this period, Kate and David were temporary migrants in Britain for over a year and their daughters for nearly four. Kate's second visit, with similar complications for how to perceive letters to Lizzie at the time, was in 1889/1890, accompanying David on a business trip. The third was a farewell visit following David's 1905 death. However, notably there is little significant difference in these letters as compared with those written when Kate was in South Africa and on a different continent; certainly specific local references in their content differ, but otherwise they have similar concerns and structural features.

Lizzie Forbes' letters provide rich detail about her working life, family and kin matters in Scotland, her local church and current affairs, including the American Civil War, bank crashes and other public matters.[43] A letter of 2 August 1862 to Kate is prototypical.[44] It provides a strong indication of 'here', with Lizzie and Jemima in Edinburgh anxiously awaiting a letter, then details Lizzie's conversation with a family connection, Mrs McTear. It engages with 'there', regarding a trading trip by her brothers, Cape news, the migration of a cousin (another Alexander known as Alick Forbes) to Natal, and reading in a newspaper Kate had sent about a photographic studio opening in Durban. Family networks are an important aspect, with

Alexander, James, Jemima, the Natal Alick Forbes, the McTears, and Kate's children Nellie and Ackie (Alexander junior), all mentioned. 'I' is present in relation to other people, while 'you' is a strong presence regarding 'your letter', 'none of you writing' and so on. The letter conveys Lizzie's emphasis on the practical aspects of family bonds, with the undemonstrative way this is expressed and the rather formal signing off to her letters a Forbes convention which is not to be read just on the surface, for the correspondence and the relationship were lifelong and clearly important on both sides.[45]

Two of Lizzie's letters to Kate, one undated although from 1890,[46] the other dated 1 September 1899, provide interesting departures from the typical.[47] Her long 1890 letter is mainly about James,[48] who first returned to Britain in 1888 and left finally for South Africa in 1893.[49] His health problems (an ulcer or the onset of stomach cancer) are mentioned, but the letter is mainly concerned with what Lizzie saw as James's incomprehensible behavior regarding business matters. There is much detail on the Forbes Henderson mining company James and David had started, its directors and share prices. Indeed, the letter is actually all about business, with James's conduct a topic because of possible economic consequences for his family. While David was the person with most direct interest in this, the letter is to Kate, who had independent investments in the company.

Lizzie's letter of 1 September 1899 is particularly concerned with her niece Lizzie Condie's death the previous Saturday.[50] This is written about largely in terms of practicalities – interrupted prayers, Lizzie Forbes telling Susie and Nellie Condie about their sister's death, them fetching her possessions, arranging the funeral. There is little about emotional aspects, apart from 'poor Nellie' being told about her sister's death and having to work her nursing shift with 'breaking heart'. And while Lizzie does comment about being 'torn with anxiety', this is connected with the start of the South African War, not personal matters.[51]

Lizzie's letters generally have such 'here and there' and 'I and you' aspects and emphasize everyday detail and business matters. However, her letters to different people are modulated, shown by comparing ones to her middle Forbes niece Kitty on 9 September 1904, and the eldest, Nellie, on 14 July 1904. Her letter to Kitty, then 29, is friendly and describes people and activities. That to Nellie, then 44 and a friend as well as niece, is fuller and more concerned with 'here and I' aspects because relating information about Edinburgh people Nellie had known while living there as a young adult.[52]

Clearly the letters between Lizzie and Kate Forbes were predicated upon absence, which lasted for lengthy time-periods and was both at great distance and a shorter one when Kate too was in Britain. But putting on one side details of specific content, the 'migrant' and 'non-migrant' letters here share structural features such as few overt signs of interiority and identity-making, a focus on business interests connected with the family economy, shared detail on the everyday quotidian, and regular exchanges which included goods and services as well as letters. And while Lizzie's letters were modulated for different correspondents, this occurred within this broad framework.

4.2. Send also the dynamite: James Forbes senior

There are more than 100 letters by and to James Forbes senior, with his main correspondents his brother David and nephew Dave junior, with many partially dated or undated. Typically they have a brevity and focus which bring them closer to notes than letters. The first is dated September 1857 and the last February 1895.[53] James migrated to Natal in 1859, later spending two 'temporary migrant' periods in Scotland and London in the late 1880s and early 1890s, returning to South Africa in 1893. His letters encompass circumstances of being a migrant, a temporary migrant, and interrupted presence during frequent periods when he lived in different places while on trading and prospecting trips although with Athole as his base.

From being a young man on, James was seen as deficient about keeping in touch, with many laments about this in his sisters' letters. He was not 'a letter-writer' in the strong sense, unlike David and Lizzie, also Kate and later Dave junior, with his letters usually short and activity-focused, and when longer focusing on prospecting, mining and business matters. A letter of 5 December 1882 to David at Athole while James was away prospecting, for example, is typical in its immersion in activities ('I heard..., got..., started a cradle..., load up your things..., sent the cart...'), with 'here' entirely implicit, for it remains unclear where James was except that he would 'start working again tomorrow'.[54] 'I' is certainly present as agentic, but there is nothing about self or other people beyond activities engaged in.

James's letter of 14 June 1888 was written in London, to David in South Africa.[55] 'Here' is again implicit, embedded in reporting conversations with Farrant and Faviell, rival members of a consortium that had bought out the Forbes Henderson Company. The letter's specific concern is share prices and cartage costs, both significant for the Forbes family business. Activity and the agentic 'I' who expedites action appear throughout. There is little of 'you' present – David is merely recipient of such activities, apart from being invoked as a source of authority to co-director and rival Farrant. The same emphasis on activities connected with business interests occurs across James's letters, regardless of where they were written. A letter of 29 December 1890 to Dave junior, written at great distance while James was in Edinburgh, and that of 12 January 1895 written from Darkton just 50 miles away, for instance, have similar focus and emphasis on activities.[56]

The few extant letters by James to his Forbes nieces provide interesting comparison. A 26 February 1892 letter to Nellie Forbes, written while he was in London, is similar to those discussed above in its immersion in activities around family business interests.[57] However, it differs in its expression of affection and family bonds. Usually it is only in signing off that James acknowledges (and then just in passing) such bonds. In contrast, this letter provides information about Edinburgh people Nellie knew and shows they were James's friends too; and expresses affection for Nellie and her sister Madge, wishing for their company and letters from them. In this respect, Kate Forbes' letter to James of 26 February 1896, sent when he became ill, is relevant.[58] It is affable, writing that 'we are all very sorry' and he should 'come home' (that is, to Athole), but also restrained and measured, offering practical help with little emotional expression.

Apart from the few to Nellie and Maggie, James's letters are often more like notes. They lack full dates and addresses, have considerable brevity, and are focused on expediting activity. It is activity and purposiveness that shape James's letters across the different kinds and extents of distance and absence they were written in, characterizing things he wrote to people just a few miles away as much as those that traversed continents. Most of his extant letters are to David and Dave junior, part of their shared involvements in prospecting and mining; and while Kate Forbes, like them, was also a keeper of letters, there are few from James to her and vice versa. This and the affectionately demonstrative letters to his two nieces indicate less a gendered dimension, more that his letter-writing was marked by closeness (of interests, of affection) to others or its lack.

4.3. Your affecte aunt: Mary McCorkindale

Mary McCorkindale (1807–1879), a Dingley by birth, was maternal aunt to Kate Forbes and Kate's sister Sarah Purcocks, whose mother was her younger sister Anne Purcocks. Married to the entrepreneur and founder of the 'Glasgow and South African Emigration Company', Alexander McCorkindale, Mary was educated while Anne was functionally literate only; Mary also lived a geographically and socially more mobile life than most of her family. Over 100 of her letters are in the collection, predominantly to Kate and, like those of James and Dave junior, they straddle varied circumstances of absence, interrupted presence and distance.[59] Mary and Alexander McCorkindale lived initially at Sinquassi Manor in Natal, about 10 miles from Doorn Kloof farm, where David and Kate moved after marrying, although only a short 'running over' distance from the Purcocks in Sinquassi.[60] When the Forbes and other Natalians moved to New Scotland, the McCorkindales moved near them, to Lake Banagher. However, following Alexander's sudden death from malaria in 1871, Mary lived at further remove, in Pretoria, then Britain, then Natal, then Pretoria again. During her sojourn in Britain, Mary McCorkindale's letters were 'temporary migrant' ones, and she spent long periods of varying distances from her family although still in South Africa. In all, her letters have similar concerns and emphases, with those to Kate, the family member she was closest to, helpful in exploring this.

The earliest extant letter from Mary McCorkindale to Kate Forbes is dated 14 March 1860, a few weeks after Kate's marriage, with the last in 1879 just before Mary died.[61] The purpose of the first is firm advice about how Kate should comport herself. Kate is told about proper conduct regarding her handwriting, not washing things when servants could do this, and keeping up her appearance, while there is little sense of 'here' or 'there' apart from brief news about family connections.[62] She wrote a similarly instructional letter later to Kate's sister Sarah Purcocks, dated 25 October 1869 and sent from London, where the McCorkindales had gone on business.[63] It emphasizes that Sarah, then 19, was not to think of marriage until her aunt's return. The context was Anne Purcocks' uncertain health and that her daughters looked to their aunt for guidance.[64] Both letters, the first from a seven-mile distance and the other from several thousand miles away, should be seen in quasi-parental terms. Directly instructional letters ceased when her nieces reached maturity, although focused activity remains evident across Mary McCorkindale's letters. For instance, a letter to Kate on 24 December 1868 concerns how to handle a 'difficult' servant and business matters regarding her husband Alexander's land schemes.[65] Letters to Kate on 8 August 1875 and David on 10 August 1877, both from Pretoria, focus on legal issues occurring in the wake of Alexander McCorkindale's death and the Transvaal Raad (parliament) enforcing an interdict until these were decided.[66]

Mary McCorkindale's letters are primarily concerned with activities and business matters, with just a handful about everyday matters.[67] In this they are more like, for instance, the letters of James than those of Lizzie Forbes or Kate Forbes. While kindly, her letters are undemonstrative, with statements of affection and relational bonds confined to signing off, again similar to James Forbes. They were written in varied circumstances of interrupted presence and absence. This is however difficult to discern apart from addresses at their head, for focused purposiveness is their main characteristic, with absence and distance rarely mentioned. They are also marked by differences in age and authority between her and her correspondents, with this coming across clearly in letters to David Forbes as well as nieces Kate and Sarah and sister Anne Purcocks. There is also a gender dimension here, with her letters' purposive contents often enlisting male members of her extended family for practical help, for example marshaling David, Joshua Straker (married to Sarah), and nephews Vincent Purcocks and James Dingley in reclaiming farms when the McCorkindale case was settled in 1877.

4.4. Your letter with enclosed letters: Dave Forbes junior

There are over 380 letters by David Forbes junior (1863–1941), known as Dave. From a young age, he was an inveterate writer of letters, notes, lists, inventories and later a memoir (Forbes, 1938). From early adulthood, he worked for lengthy periods in a different country, Swaziland, although regularly returning on furlough to Athole, 60 miles away. His letters were written in South Africa or just over its borders in changing circumstances of absence and interrupted presence, although differently configured ones from those experienced by Mary McCorkindale and James Forbes. His first extant letter is dated 1874 and the last 1921.[68]

Kate and David Forbes' eldest son, Alexander Forbes junior (1862–1885, known as Alex), died of malaria during his parents' 1885 absence in Britain. Dave junior and Jim junior remained in South Africa, supervised by Sarah Purcocks, with Dave becoming responsible under her aegis for the stock and carting components of the Forbes agri-businesses as well as for Jim junior. The Forbes' three sons and three daughters had been given land in Athole's environs, keeping horses and stock as well as growing crops on this, with Dave and Jim then branching out into carting and sheep droving at significant levels. By the time his parents spent a second sojourn in Britain in 1889/1890, Dave junior had become involved in mining, initially with the Forbes Henderson Company, later the Swazi coal mine.[69] From the early 1890s to 1916 he was its manager, also purchasing a nearby farm although maintaining close economic and other involvements with the Athole Estate and spending extended furloughs there.

Dave junior's letters share the customary Forbes focus on activity and business, with 'here and there' implied through activities rather than explicitly invoked, and with affect and interiority largely absent. His letters of 25 June 1888 to his father at Athole, and of 19 September 1890 when David was in Britain, show the complications that arose regarding management of 'the Forbes' as an economic enterprise as the Forbes children came to maturity.[70] In particular these letters signal the changing terms of the relationship between the two Davids, with his father still largely in control, but challenges from Dave junior. Dave's 25 June 1888 letter is a careful mixture of 'we' and 'I' inscribed with an implied instructional aspect. This is closely linked to his father as its addressee. It refers to a letter Dave was sent by David about Athole farming matters, writing that while business instructions received had not been carried out, he had found third parties to encourage his father to sell family shares in the Forbes Henderson Company. While Dave's reasons were economically correct,[71] the sense of a new guard straining to take over comes across, with this stronger in his 19 September 1890 letter.[72] This too is a response to a letter from his father, and again Dave's own agenda is pursued in pushing a point his father's letter had made in passing, not to buy more shares in the mining company. Dave writes here in an instructional way about things his father should and should not do: he should not put more money into the reef, should put more stock on the farm, should make excuses to the Company's Board, should get rid of the coal concession.

It is not possible to tell from content, however, that David was in South Africa when Dave junior's 26 June 1888 letter was written, and on a different continent when that of 19 September 1890 was sent. His father is the object of the contents, although there is nothing that indicates where David was and what he might be doing. But that Dave junior wrote these letters while he was in different places *is* apparent, in the June 1888 one because concerning people and activities in Barberton, a mining area; and in the September 1890 one because the Swazi reef and its mine are mentioned. It is Dave junior's activities concerning money, shares, the company, reef and farm stock, drilling and mining, that are the focus of both letters, as key strands of Forbes business ventures that Dave was wanting to shape. Two more letters of Dave's are worth noting here.

The first is to his youngest sister Madge dated 22 July 1896, one of a number concerned with training her to manage property interests (Dave's, also the Forbes' generally), in drawing up leases, sending accounts, ensuring lettings were made and negotiating payments.[73] It is not instructional in tone, however, but matter-of-fact about Madge acting as Dave's agent in these dealings, perhaps because no re-negotiation of their relationship was needed for him to exert authority, unlike with his father. The second is from Dave to his mother, dated 10 February 1912.[74] Their spheres of economic activity were fairly separate, with Kate as book-keeper and accountant, a very hands-on manager of the homefarm, and in control for her lifetime of the Athole Estate, although she had partially divided some farms between herself and her children following David's death in November 1905, with considerable protections for her position of control.[75] For some years thereafter, letters between Dave and his mother convey no sense of change to Kate's authority.[76] However, his 10 February 1912 letter is different.[77] Albeit with gestures towards tentativeness ('with your approval', 'Jim also to get permission'), it announces a conclusion, implied as Jim's initiative but patently coming from Dave himself. This was to reduce the Athole Estate to the homefarm, sell off Tolderia (which Jim farmed), money going to Kate and the sisters, and the brothers changing their focus to horse-breeding and stock-raising.

For more than 30 years, Dave junior cyclically split his time and economic activities between the mine and farm in Swaziland, and the Athole Estate. While absent from Athole, its life went on, activities were engaged in, decisions made, and a large number of workers managed by his mother and siblings. Dave was alternately distant, excepting his frequent letters, and present, a difficult balancing act. It is likely his instructional letters to David and Kate were a product, writing rather starkly things that would probably have been expressed differently face to face.

Dave junior's letters are very activity-focused and absence is of an interrupted presence kind, with content routinely anticipating the face-to-face meeting about to occur.[78] Dave was to inherit the main part of Athole, and although the Estate was reorganized so all the siblings received portions of similar value, his letters are marked by his status as eldest son and Athole owner-to-be, as well as by worldly concerns that make them overtly gendered. One aspect has already been noted, him squaring up to his father about the direction of family business involvements. Another is implicit, that Dave was involved throughout his working life in the heavily masculine and racially hierarchical activities of prospecting and mining. This had ramifications for his management of relationships with others and how he wrote about them, particularly noticeable in routine use of pejorative racial terms in his letters (Stanley, 2015b).

4.5. Do all your business: David Forbes senior

David Forbes was a focal point for many letters, including from Lizzie, James senior, Dave junior, the Condie children and others, also for official letters in the collection.[79] He is not quite its major letter-writer in terms of numbers of letters extant, although if more of his letter-books had survived he certainly would have been.[80] The scale of his letter-writing is shown once the facts that some of his main correspondents, particularly siblings Lizzie and James, did not keep letters to them, and that he was ordinarily at home and did not regularly write to Kate, who *did* preserve letters, are taken into account.[81] The first letter extant by David is dated 12 April 1860 and the last, 2 September 1903, with around 350 in total.[82] A significant proportion of his 'actual' letters (as distinct from the many copies and drafts) were written to Kate while he was on trips away.[83] They were a recurrent feature because concerning important ventures in building up capital so as to finance other family economic activities.

Two letters from David to Kate of 16 December and 26 December 1866 were sent during the lengthy trek of some 30 ox-wagons and over 200 people travelling from Natal to begin the New Scotland farms that McCorkindale had purchased then sold on or leased.[84] Although the letters were addressed by place (e.g. Ladysmith), these were just brief halting-points to re-provision and rest. David was away for over six months, during which he was neither at home nor abroad nor a temporary migrant. Letter-collection and delivery were very uncertain because of the remoteness of places passed through, and there was clearly distance and separation, while the absence his letters inscribe is of an interrupted presence and future-oriented kind.

In both letters, 'here' is primarily the ox-wagon David traveled in with his brother-in-law, with 'we' being both them and the convoy. Related comments include whether the route being traveled was good or bad, events en route, and activities at halting-places. In his 16 December letter, this concerns David hearing a bishop preach[85] and visiting his brother Alexander's grave;[86] and more schematically in the 26 December one, waiting for other wagons, having a 'very poor X mass', and worrying because letters for him had not arrived. 'There' inheres in Kate and their children and David's anxieties about Kate's pregnancy and childbirth. It also arises around Kate acting legally in selling land formerly belonging to Alexander (who had died the previous year).

Matters of affect are raised by both letters, and also one David received from Kate dated 21 December 1866.[87] All three have an affectionate sign off and express loving concern for each other. Thus on 16 December, David wrote, 'I am always thinking of you' and 'about little Georgie … you must not fret too much'.[88] In her letter of 21 December Kate wrote, 'You must be careful of yourself' and 'I am so dreadfully nervous about you'. And on 26 December, David wrote, 'the post is in and no letter for me my dear Kitty I hope there is nothing the matter with you'. Such comments appear before or after detail on more mundane matters and are contained by these. This is particularly notable regarding David's 16 December rather sententious comment that Kate should not 'fret' about the then-recent death of Georgie, their infant son, which is preceded by comments about a sick horse, and followed by briskly describing his brother Alexander's grave. Kate's 21 December letter relates her post-partum ill-health and while protesting 'I do not grieve', a sad sentence about Georgie's 'winning ways' suggests otherwise. However, this too is preceded by quotidian detail, about one of David's letters having been opened en route, David being careful, and their daughter Nellie making herself sick eating bananas, and followed by further everyday matters.

The letters convey a life shared which they express and further the purposes of through David's trip. There is a low-key loving kindness in how these and other letters during his time away are written, with matters of affect contained and in their proper place as part of the shared life. Examples are 'I often regret coming away but it was for the best' in David's 7 June 1871 letter,[89] and stress on judiciousness about grief in the 16 December 1866 one. And while Kate departed from this in grieving for Georgie, she repeatedly stressed that David should complete the purposes of his trip before thinking of returning, for these were to further their shared future.

While away, David was unsurprisingly more concerned with worldly matters outside their farm than Kate. However, there is still a strong sense of mutual business in which Kate was a full part, including her concluding land sales, having David's general power of attorney and making all decisions while he was away,[90] as well as having her own responsibilities for the household and homefarm at Athole. Their letters also show the importance of interconnected networks in facilitating Kate's activities, combining family, business, and neighborly links she was part of and that appear across their letters.[91]

Their letter-writing during David's trips away related 'now' and its daily events through epistolary practices that helped maintain the enduring bonds of their relationship, enabling them to meet after a long separation having shared at least a small part of each other's lives while apart. These 'now' aspects of their letter-writing also reference the future, the greater prosperity that was to come, which David's trips were bringing about. His absences were of long duration and involved much hardship, during which he was in an ever-changing elsewhere with no fixed reference points other than his ox-wagon and companion and his home. Fears and worries were for him, in literally unknown territory, while it was specifically around the dangers of childbirth that there were concerns for Kate, not that she was left in charge of a large farm and managing its many workers, which their letters represent as order and safety. Loving affection is certainly a dimension, expressed in measured ways as part of the entirety of their life together. There is also a gendered division of labor represented in their letters, David abroad trading and prospecting, Kate at home and experiencing difficult pregnancies. However, this should not be seen in binary terms, for during this trip Kate managed the large farm-estate with around 100 workers and had a complete power of attorney to make all legal and financial decisions, while David was a home- and child-centered man, in love with his wife and missing his home and family. On the next long trip, the whole family trekked to New Rush/Kimberley, to pursue the economic possibilities of diamond-mining together.

4.6. All the news: Sarah Purcocks Straker

Squaring the circle of kinds and degrees of absence and separation in Forbes letter-writing, there are some 80 letters by Sarah Purcocks (1850–1911), written in circumstances of a different kind of interrupted presence from that just discussed.[92] From the move to New Scotland on, Sarah ran the Purcocks' Westoe farm, seven miles from Athole, including after marrying Joshua Straker in 1880.[93] The majority of extant letters are to her sister Kate Forbes, with some written as amanuensis for their mother Anne, functionally literate only. These are the remaining part of a constant stream of notes, invoices, goods, services and labor as well as letters that flowed between the sisters from Kate's marriage until Sarah's death.[94]

A 23 April 1866 letter, written before the Forbes and Purcocks trekked to the New Scotland farms, was sent from Sinquassi in Natal to Kate at Doorn Kloof, 10 miles away.[95]

At the time, this was an insuperable distance for casual visiting, although letters, goods and services were exchanged, sent via African farm employees to expedite the many economic concerns shared between these households. This letter details people and everyday activities, with Sarah writing 'I have told you all the news', although reticent about her own activities as mainstay of the Purcocks household. A year later, her letter of 29 May 1867 provides more information about her doings.[96] In the intervening period, the Purcocks parents had lost the Sinquassi farm through non-payment of lease money and fallen on difficult times, with Sarah trying to ameliorate the problems, and David later giving or leasing Westoe to them.

Twenty years later, a letter of 1 August 1886 from Sarah to Kate, then in Britain, is also filled with everyday detail, but with Sarah's driving involvements having become her interconnected business activities.[97] One element was as manager of a pig farming business shared with Dave junior and Jim junior. As they were too squeamish, she and a farm-worker, Bismark, did the slaughtering before selling the carcasses to a butchery. In this letter, 'business' also includes Sarah taking responsibility for Athole while the Forbes parents were away, superintending building work there, keeping a close eye on her nephews, dealing with a farm sale, a mining concession being assayed, the continuing fallout of McCorkindale Estate matters, and running Westoe.[98] Sarah's letters of 16 July 1889 and 4 May 1890 were written while Kate was in Britain again, and have similar concerns.[99] Her business as a farmer is embedded in comments such as, in the July 1889 letter, regarding farm workers, a visit from her nephew Jim junior from the Tolderia farm, putting up fence-posts, pig-killing at Westoe and at Dave's Swazi reef; and in her May 1890 letter, regarding wool sales and her investments in stocks and shares.

In Sarah's letters to Kate, degrees and kinds of absence do not make a significant difference. What *do* make a difference are Sarah's responsibilities at the time of writing. As a young woman in April 1866 she was involved in managing family troubles, while as an older one in August 1886 she had major farming and business involvements, with these material circumstances dominating letter-content. Although Kate was just a few miles away and Sarah would see her soon after the 1866 letter was sent, and some thousands of miles away long-term in Britain when her 1886 one was, the two are structured similarly in combining local news with shared business matters and anticipating face-to-face meetings.

Sarah Purcocks Straker's letter-writing activities occurred in varied but local circumstances of separation, distance and interruptions of presence. As a girl and young woman, the geographical distance from her key correspondent was not large but Kate's move to Doorn Kloof prevented easy face-to-face meetings and required written means of communicating, as did the distance later between Westoe and Athole. There was a gender dimension here, for although as an adult woman Sarah eventually commandeered a saddle, bought a horse and rode between the farms, earlier she had been as protected as the Forbes daughters were a generation later, until they too struck out for freedom of movement, while their brothers experienced no such restriction. However, there were also new technologies that helped reshape Sarah's experience of absence and separation, in particular her early embrace of both the telephone and the motorcar. These restored elements of the swift voice-to-voice and face-to-face family communications of her youth, and it is notable that her Forbes nieces enthusiastically embraced them too.

5. Settler colonialism and migrant letters: concluding thoughts

The Forbes letters show that the South African settler context and the character of its migrant population made a difference. These letters are unlike 'the migrant letter' as largely considered to date and discussed earlier. In the South African colonial context, settlers of the middling sort with some literacy skills migrated for opportunity reasons and produced letter-writing with characteristics different from those discussed in the migrant letter literature. Trying to isolate migrant or other types of letters among them is problematic, for these were 'just letters' and integral to this settler colonial family's letter-writing in total. When its shape, flows and dynamics are explored over an extensive time-period, as here, while attributes assigned to 'the migrant letter' can be found, this is because these are aspects of letter-writing as such and also they feature in very different ways. The differentiating factor here is the Forbes scriptural economy and the ways in which its writing practices were used, developed and modulated by the different letter-writers concerned. There are a number of these customary practices involved that bear on absences and distance, identities and relationships, and locations, as raised at the start of this discussion.

Absence as the basis of letter-writing is often treated as unitary, but once people's practical living and writing circumstances are considered, then greater complications are seen. The premise of Forbes letter-writing was that relationships between correspondents would continue in a face-to-face way at some point, perhaps in a few days, perhaps at longer intervals. Rather than absence as unitary and permanent, these letters are marked by and help bridge different kinds and durations of interrupted presence, with the writing practices involved modulated by the different letter-writers. Accompanying this, other shared features include using letters in purposive ways, a concern with everyday business matters, an emphasis on 'now' and its activities rather than looking back, and focusing on exteriority and measured restraint rather than interiority, introspection or affect.

It should not be thought from this that the Forbes or their correspondents lacked emotion or did not prize their bonds with others. Emotion is at points quite apparent. But this is seen to have a proper place, both in life and as expressed within the regulated spaces of letter-writing (How, 2003; Milne, 2010). Examples include David's comments about Kate's grief over the death of Georgie, and Lizzie Forbes writing about someone else's breaking heart and not her own when Lizzie Condie died. The convention marking the Forbes writing practices here was measure and restraint. Affect was indeed indicated through such idioms themselves, which formed a taken-for-granted bedrock with people assumed to know the emotions underlying restrained turns of phrase and a shift from a charged topic to one less so.[100]

This also points to customary ways in which self-fashioning occurred. The self in this scriptural economy was importantly shaped around letter-writing itself, in writing regularly, seeking opportunities for dispatching letters, which were of fitting length, with content deemed proper, and containing appropriate mixtures of the communicative and purposive. As represented across the letters, this self focused on shared business and other interests, attended to obligations and responsibilities, provided judicious information about people known in common, and signaled but contained affect. The foundation was sharing an ongoing relationship with their addressees, with epistolary exchanges a necessary adjunct when separations of time and distance existed.

Gender, age and generation are discernible although complicated factors in the Forbes scriptural economy, and also point up some changes over time. There is no indication of binary spheres around gender in either epistolary exchanges or many business and other interests. Letter-writing is equally a female and male activity with no evidence of different levels of literacy,[101] while letter-content is similarly diverse, although there are some activities – in particular childcare and household responsibilities, and hunting and mining – that mark women's letters but not men's and vice versa. But alongside this, Lizzie, Jemima, Kate, Sarah and also Anne Purcocks and Mary McCorkindale all had independent as well as family economic involvements.[102] Sarah Purcocks Straker was a major farmer with a range of business interests, and both Kitty and Madge Forbes in the next generation followed a similar path after their marriages and became leading farming presences in the Ermelo area. Sarah's letters were to keep in touch and expedite activity, and early mentions of the telephone and motorcar appear. Relatedly, just handfuls of Kitty's and Madge's letters and only a few more of Nellie's survive, with the indications being that few were written, for unlike their brother Dave they were not 'letter-writers' and favored alternative communicative means.

This brings to attention changes over the generations connected with technology and communications. The early installation of the telephone at Athole, Westoe and other family households, and equally early embrace of motorized transport, made important differences to letter-writing in the scriptural economy, reducing letter flows except on occasions such as birthdays and festivals (although other components, such as accounts and diaries, were unaffected), and increasing the amount of routine visiting. Other developments, especially the move from sail to steam then the introduction of fast steamers with a significant reduction in passage costs, further changed generational patterns. This included an impact on the character of migration itself. For the first generation, while some particularly entrepreneurial migrants like the Forbes might 'return', for most migration was seen as a permanent move, and thus Lizzie's decision to stay and Jemima's hesitation about leaving Britain. For Jemima's daughter Susie Condie, however, it was different; Susie visited South Africa on two occasions, first as a 'temporary migrant', then as a wartime nurse, but on both occasions eventually decided to return.[103]

Letter-writing for the Forbes adds up to a scriptural economy in which the extended networks of the Forbes and their connections engaged through its customary writing practices. Its migrant letters, conceived narrowly, cannot be sensibly separated from Forbes letter-writing generally, for these writing practices were utilized across the range of different circumstances its letters were written in. The letters are points of exchange in continuing flows, linking differently located people in varied circumstances, and doing so across different kinds and degrees of absence and separation. The concept of a scriptural economy gives shape to such complexities, which add up to what is precisely an economy, a diverse set of flows of epistolary products with changing exchange values. Conceiving this as a scriptural economy is apposite too because letter-writing was completely integral to, indeed constitutive of, Forbes business activities, not separate from these.

Taking into account settler colonial letter-writing has import for how migrant letter-writing should be seen. It has been through taking into account an entire large collection of settler colonial letters, the Forbes papers, rather than focusing on smaller groups of letters identified as migrant ones, that has uncovered such differences and how they play out in the writing practices of this scriptural economy. Working in this inclusive fashion may be the state of the art, but it has been done only rarely to date in considering migrant letters, perhaps because many migrant groups do not 'settle' in the colonialist way that people did in South Africa, nor take with them established cultural practices concerning both writing and also preserving letters in the way the Forbes – and also the Pringles, Findlays, Schreiner-Hemmings and others in the South African context – did.

From this the question arises, are the Forbes letters exceptional, rather than having more general import? The collection involves letters from and to many people who are not Forbes in any direct sense, not only Kate Forbes née Purcocks, Mary McCorkindale née Dingley and Sarah Purcocks, but the hundreds of other people whose letters it contains. Also, there are other family collections in South Africa with similar characteristics. The core letter-writers in these, as with the Forbes, were English-speakers, with the Pringles, Findlays and Forbes also Scottish by background, and so a related question is whether there might an English-speaking, British or Scottish aspect here. The different educational and aspirational background of English-speaking migrants in South Africa generally and Scots particularly was noted earlier. However, the same background existed for the North American/English-speaking migrants whose very different letter-writings have been discussed by Gerber and others. One possibility is that there could be a Presbyterian or Calvinist aspect here, although many letter-writers in the South African collections were neither Scottish nor had Presbyterian connections but still wrote letters with similar characteristics. This brings the South African context of arrival and settlement into center-frame, and particularly some connected features of its mode of production.

The Forbes scriptural economy was the product of a large network focused around expediting the economic and business interests of those concerned. Its customary writing practices were primarily about 'the business' and resulted in letter-writing with a particular organization and shape, around focused purposive concerns, shared economic activity, and contained affect. It was propelled by the Forbes' multi-focal entrepreneurial involvements in the wider settler economy. The writing practices involved were not personal preferences, but resulted from shared matters in hand, particularly concerning the family/household as a wide-ranging economic and business entity in which the scriptural economy was central, not an optional extra.

South Africa's particular settler economy and its mode of production helped shape this, through institutionalizing the provision of cheap labor, advantageously positioning settler farming households in relation to inter/national markets, and enabling entrepreneurial activities to develop largely unfettered, with the flows of letter-writing essential and not adjunct to the activities involved. The specific settler colonial context made a significant difference, and from this it can be concluded that exploring letters (and recent variants) sent from and to a range of (historical and contemporary) migratory contexts is a central task for epistolary scholarship.

Archival sources

All letters referred to and referenced in full in the Endnotes are part of the Forbes Collection, National Archives Repository, Pretoria, South Africa.

Notes

1. Different temporal ends to the collection can be posited. The family figuration of letter-writing largely concludes in 1922, when Kate Forbes died. However, between then and 1930 there are some additional letters, although concerning more distant family members. Between

1930 and 1938, there are handfuls of letters but with the writers and recipients not traced to the Forbes family figuration, although almost certainly connected in some way. The very last document is dated 1938, when the collection was donated to the National Archives Repository of South Africa. Consequently 1922 has been used as the cut-off date for the analysis here.

2. The various archiving activities of Kate, Dave junior and a succession of estate managers were involved. The collection is organized in a confusing and at times muddled way, with some boxes covering periods of years and then writers within this, but in a higgledy-piggledy fashion with regard to specific date order; other boxes contain bundles of letters by particular writers with no date order; some have wide mixtures of dated letters and writers but in no order at all; yet others contain partially or entirely undated letters placed in no order. Systematic work on the collection could not occur until all items were entered into a database then on to the VRE (Virtual Research Environment) that manages Whites Writing Whiteness project (http://www. whiteswritingwhiteness@ed.ac.uk) data. The extant letters it seems have been structured by various 'local' factors rather than any deliberate destructions. The main keepers of letters were Kate and David Forbes senior and their son Dave junior when at home at Athole. The main gaps are (i) the 'actual' letters sent to Lizzie Forbes, Jemima Condie and Jemima's children in Scotland, although many drafts especially of the former survive; (ii) letters to James senior and Jim junior, who both lived in a mobile peripatetic way because of their economic and business involvements and did not keep their letters; (iii) similarly Dave junior when on duty as the manager of the Swazi coal mine; (iv) letters to Lizzie Forbes after 1903; (v) letters by Sarah Purcocks Straker after 1899; (vi) all letters during the South African War (1899–1902); (vii) most letters around the decline and death of David senior in 1905; (viii) letters following Kate Forbes' last illness then death in 1922.

3. See http://www.whiteswritingwhiteness.ed.ac.uk. This research includes a number of large family and organizational collections, as well as case studies of particular networks. Family collections researched thus far are those of the Findlays, Forbes, Pringles, Schreiner-Hemmings, Whites and Godlontons, with combined contents of around 23,000 letters, plus many other documents. Other family collections are being added. The organizational collections are the South African part of London Missionary Society papers, and the papers of the Cecil Rhodes-controlled group of businesses. There are also case studies focused on particular letter-writers or topics.

4. Something that occurred regarding settlers in North America and also Australia and New Zealand too.

5. On affect, see Cancian (2010); Gerber (2006); for a view similar to that discussed here, see Fitzpatrick (1994).

6. For a counter-view, see Stanley (2015a).

7. For interesting discussions using a Bourdieusian framework, see Davis (2010); Erel (2010, 2012); Noble (2013); Nowicka (2013); Plüss (2013); Pöllman (2013).

8. See Davis (2010); DeHaan (2010); Middleton (2010).

9. The literature indicates these migrants included a higher proportion of people of an educated 'respectable' and 'middling sort', with a higher than usual literacy level, although not necessarily much formal schooling.

10. See note 1 concerning the end-date of the collection. All letters discussed are from the Forbes Collection, National Archives Repository, Pretoria, South Africa.

11. South Africa was not a unified political entity until 1910. Before then, there were four settler colonies: the two Boer Republics of the Transvaal and Orange Free State, and two British colonies, Natal and the Cape.

12. And at times also South Australia, where other kin had migrated.

13. The most substantial African settlements were in the South African settler colonies of the Cape and Natal, recognizing that Britons were a minority of white migrants apart from in Natal, and also there were more black migrants from elsewhere in southern Africa than those from white European backgrounds. See Conway and Leonard (2014); Family and Colonialism Network (2014); Harper and Constantine (2010, pp. 111–147); Murdock (2004); Richards (2004).

14. The best-known are Benjamin Moodie's 1817 emigration scheme, taking around 200 Scottish indentured laborers to the Western Cape; the well-known '1820 Settlers' of some 4000 government-sponsored British migrants to the Eastern Cape; Edward Brenton's schemes for child emigration between 1832 and 1841; and Joseph Byrne's 'Emigration and Colonisation' venture that took around 2500 British migrants to Natal between 1849 and the early 1850s; with a late-1850s smaller initiative by Alexander McCorkindale through his (variously named) Glasgow and South African Company also taking migrants to Natal (Harper, 2003; MacKenzie, 2007, pp. 157–161).

15. The first generation of Forbes siblings were Alexander (1825–1866), David (1829–1905), Lizzie (1831–1916), James (1835–1896) and Jemima (1837–1889). The Forbes men have appeared in a number of published accounts, although the family tradition of recycling personal names across generations and different parts of the family has led to sometimes inaccurate attributions. For the most interesting, see Bonner (1982); Crush (1987); MacKenzie (2007, pp. 146–149).

16. Now Mpumalanga.

17. For detailed discussion of the factors underpinning the scale and structure of Scottish migrations, see especially Harper (2003); also Brock (1999).

18. The children of Kate and David senior who survived to adulthood were, in birth order, Nellie, Alexander junior (Alex), David junior (Dave), James junior (Jim), Catherine (Kitty) and Madge. Alex junior died of malaria in 1885. The Forbes daughters had equal shares in the economic and finance aspects with their brothers, although for them this resided mainly in land and crops rather than stock until after their father's death in 1905, when they became important farmers.

19. Settler colonialism involves domination over an indigenous people, with settler colonists founding a social and political order, rather than joining a pre-existing one, as most migrants do (Lambert & Lester, 2006; Lester, 2001; Stanley, 2015b).

20. This eventuated from the earlier period when both white and black engaged in peasant farming of a pastoral or small-holding kind, via the rapid creation by white settlers of cheap black labor as the equivalent of new technology. See Bundy (1988); Stanley (2015b).

21. See Cavanagh (2013); Markelis (2006); Mosley (1983); Versteegh (2000); and on the Forbes, Stanley (2015b). This has been described as proto-capitalism (Krikler, 1993, pp. 128–131). However, it is more accurately seen as thoroughly if not entirely imbued with capitalist forms of production (Denoon, 1983, 1995), with black labor being both the 'engine' and also the recurrent 'technology' that enabled many such farms to only partially mechanize production methods (Stanley, 2015b).

22. See here note 15. Natal was chosen because David was a good shot, and hunting and trading among the Zulu were envisaged as providing better economic opportunities than elsewhere.

23. Few letters to or by Alexander Forbes senior are extant and only a small number of Jemima's.

24. The dearth of archival collections suggests this was less so regarding migrant groups from elsewhere in Europe and Russia, and less so again respecting the longer-term resident Boer farmer population of mixed Dutch and other origins.

25. There are, for example, many letters to and from children at school in the Findlay collection and significant numbers in the Forbes collection, and also from marriages in and out in the Pringle and Schreiner-Hemming collections.

26. Rather than absence as a permanency, 'interruption of presence' signifies that letter-writing occurs with the expectation of future meetings. This is a general characteristic of letter-writing, not just of the Forbes or other South African letter-writers.

27. In birth order, Nellie, Alex, Dave, Jim, Kitty and Madge.

28. In birth order, Nellie, Susie, Lizzie and John Condie.

29. There is no easy means of referring to this complex entity, for none of the available conceptual categories such as family, household, domus and so on stretch far enough. In relation to the wider Whites Writing Whiteness project and its analytical purposes, it is most usefully thought about in Norbert Elias' terms as a figuration. See Elias (1994); Ladurie (1980 [1978]); http://www.whiteswritingwhiteness.ed.ac.uk/forbes-domus-figurations/.

30. Stanley (2015b); see also http://www.whiteswritingwhiteness.ed.ac.uk/action-research/the-scriptural-economy/.

31. See Stanley (2015c) on methodological aspects of working with very large letter collections, using the Findlay Papers as an exemplar. See also Cochran and Hsieh's (2013) work on the letters of the (partly migratory) Liu family of Shanghai, Rothschild's (2011) epistolary history of the Scottish Johnstone family living in different areas of the British Empire, and Hougaz's (2015) work on the stories of multi-generational Italian-Australian business dynasties.

32. Discussion of materials concerning the Forbes, Findlay, Pringle and Schreiner-Hemming collections will be found at http://www.whiteswritingwhiteness.ed.ac.uk/.

33. They included Forbes siblings, partners, offspring, uncles, aunts, cousins, nephews, nieces, friends, employees, neighbors, business connections, shop owners, merchants, tax inspectors, vets, bank managers, magistrates and others. A central sub-set was David Forbes senior, his sisters Lizzie Forbes and Jemima Condie and brothers Alexander senior and James senior; David's wife Kate, their children Alex junior, Dave junior, Jim junior, Nellie, Kitty and Madge; Kate's parents David and Anne Purcocks, her sister Sarah and brothers George, Vincent and David; and Kate and Sarah's maternal aunt Mary McCorkindale and her husband Alexander. The women involved wrote as much as, and when the full range of Forbes documents of life are considered more than, the men, contra the contention otherwise in the migrant letter literature.

34. They were not together. Jim was still in Europe at this time, and while Alexander and David sometimes worked together, they also at times engaged in different economic pursuits in different areas.

35. In part, Jemima's indecisiveness was because she worried about leaving Lizzie with no immediate family in Scotland; see National Archives Repository South Africa, Forbes Collection 7/6, Jemima Forbes to David Forbes senior, 3 October 1859.

36. Just before Alexander's early death from an abscess on the liver, following a grueling trading trip, Lizzie had been anticipating his return, with this a likely reality rather than fantasy as shown by later extended returns by both David and James. These visits included Kate Forbes on three occasions, and the three or four year residency in Scotland of David and Kate's daughters Nellie, Kitty and Maggie Forbes while at school. There were also later lengthy visits to South Africa by two of Jemima's children, Susie Condie (who contemplated migration) and John Condie (who did migrate, to Cape Town).

37. When the letters commenced in 1850, there was very little visual imagery available to guide the imagination, as even engravings of 'ordinary' South Africa were then rare.

38. They included Lizzie relaying to Kate the events of her working life and friendships, business matters, reports of fashion and later, after Kate's first 'return' visit to Britain, news of people known in common, with Kate reciprocating similarly.

39. Although they made at least one lengthy trip to Britain and Lizzie met them, there are very few letters to her Forbes nephews Dave junior and Jim junior extant.

40. See Stanley (2015d); the randomly selected years are 1854, 1866, 1876, 1885, 1893, 1908, 1917 and 1921.

41. There would also be issues in confining analysis to temporal considerations and general flows. First, there are over 400 partially or wholly undated letters that cannot be included in such an exercise. As many are by James senior and Dave junior, a temporal approach underestimates their presence and significance in the collection as a whole. Secondly, there are distributional skews resulting from who was a keeper of letters and who was not, and a cross-sectional analysis can compound the effects because the absences that propel letter-writing tend to be bunched in particular time-periods rather than evenly distributed across years. An example here is that David senior was on a lengthy prospecting trip during 1887 and his letters to Kate (a letter-keeper) survive, but not any to James senior (who was not), although James was his major collaborator in such ventures and the indications are that David wrote frequently to him. Thirdly and as noted above, letters are written by individuals, and a temporal approach on its own conveys little of the specific writing practices and variant usages of the different letter-writers. Relatedly, correspondences are part of a relationship between a letter-writer

and their addressee, something also difficult to convey in a temporal examination of so many letters as exist in the Forbes collection. Thus the two-part strategy adopted.

42. After the death of David Forbes in 1905, relatively few letters by Lizzie are extant. However, mentions in letters by others indicate that the flow continued, so these seem to have been mislaid or lost.

43. Lizzie Forbes' letters pass on information about events in southern Africa that her family there might not have heard about. And after the establishment of the Forbes Henderson mining company, they comment on share prices and fluctuations, particularly regarding family investments and shareholder meetings Lizzie or family friends attended. Kate Forbes' letters survive mainly as drafts, while their contents can also be gauged through Lizzie's often quite detailed responses. Over time, Kate became the record-keeper and accountant of the farming side of the Forbes' economic undertakings and in this capacity produced lists, inventories, accounts of financial incomings and outgoings documenting the economic fabric of the Athole Estate, as well as drafting important letters for others and making handwritten copies of key incoming communications. Although there are fewer letters by her in the collection than by, for example, her son Dave junior, overall the majority of Forbes documents are in her hand. Kate's last letter to Lizzie in 1916 was returned with news of her death.

44. See National Archives Repository South Africa, Forbes Collection 7/51, Lizzie Forbes to Kate Forbes, 2 August 1862. Verbatim extracts of all Lizzie Forbes letters quoted from or referenced will be found at Whites Writing Whiteness/In Progress/Migrant Letter (http://www.whiteswritingwhiteness.ed.ac.uk/blog/migrant-letter/). The transcription conventions followed are that: nd shows that no date was provided for a letter by the author nor can it be surmised from a post-mark, a question-mark in front of a ?word indicates a doubtful reading, while ^insertion^ marks text inserted by the writer and deletions are also by them, with … indicating a researcher-omission of text, and comments [in square brackets] being researcher-provided elucidations.

45. It also comments about her brothers' trading trip, whether it had produced 'good returns' and that improved trade would make 'money easier got'. This reflects Lizzie's wish that they should buy farms because she considered (correctly) that hunting and trading entailed considerable danger.

46. Extracts from these and other Lizzie/Kate letters discussed will be found at Whites Writing Whiteness/In Progress/Migrant Letter (http://www.whiteswritingwhiteness.ed.ac.uk/blog/migrant-letter/). All transcriptions are verbatim.

47. National Archives Repository South Africa, Forbes Collection 11/245, Lizzie Forbes to Kate Forbes, no date but ?1890; and National Archives Repository South Africa, Forbes Collection 9/290, Lizzie Forbes to Kate Forbes, 1 September 1899.

48. The backcloth was that James senior had always been 'unsteady', not settling, fathering a number of illegitimate children (financially supported by Lizzie on behalf of 'the Estate'), liking the good life and drinking too much.

49. While there, James senior lived in Edinburgh, London and the Highlands; he seems also to have made a return trip to South Africa and back, around his mining interests.

50. Lizzie Condie had spent most of her short life being ill and looked after by her aunt; she had at this point recently been committed to an asylum, but probably had a brain tumor.

51. This was between Britain and the Boer Republics of the Transvaal and Orange Free State and began on 1 October 1899. During the War, the Forbes were evacuated from Athole. They returned in mid-1902 to find Athole largely destroyed.

52. 'There' aspects are still present although background, concerning the death of Paul Kruger (ex-President of the Transvaal), linked with Sir Alfred Milner 'putting right' Swaziland land concessions for mining rights, something all the Forbes had financial stakes in.

53. Extracts from all James Forbes senior letters discussed will be found at Whites Writing Whiteness / In Progress / Migrant Letter (http://www.whiteswritingwhiteness.ed.ac.uk/blog/migrant-letter/). A high proportion of his extant letters are undated or minimally dated with just a day and the addresses they were sent from are usually perfunctorily indicated.

54. National Archives Repository South Africa, Forbes Collection 11/29, James Forbes senior to David Forbes senior, 5 December 1882.

55. National Archives Repository South Africa, Forbes Collection 7/252, James Forbes senior to David Forbes senior, 14 June 1888.

56. National Archives Repository South Africa, Forbes Collection 8/141, James Forbes senior to DF junior 29 December 1890; and National Archives Repository South Africa, Forbes Collection 8/261, James Forbes senior to DF senior, 12 January 1895.

57. National Archives Repository South Africa, Forbes Collection 8/171, James Forbes senior to Nellie Forbes, 26 February 1892. Its detailed comments also confirm that Nellie was fully knowledgeable about these business matters.

58. National Archives Repository South Africa, Forbes Collection 9/11, Kate Forbes to James Forbes senior, 26 February 1896. Initially it was supposed James had typhoid, but this was instead the final stages of stomach cancer exacerbated by liver failure from his alcoholism. James died in early March 1896. David senior traveled to Johannesburg and looked after him during his last few days.

59. Mary McCorkindale's key correspondents in the collection were Kate Forbes, Sarah Purcocks, David Forbes senior and Joshua Straker (who married Sarah in 1880). Most are to Kate, who carefully kept them as a group separate from her other letters.

60. Now Zinkwazi.

61. Extracts from this and other Mary McCorkindale letters will be found at Whites Writing Whiteness/In Progress/Migrant Letter (http://www.whiteswritingwhiteness.ed.ac.uk/blog/migrant-letter/).

62. National Archives Repository South Africa, Forbes Collection Annex 7/261, Mary McCorkindale to Kate Forbes, 14 March 1860.

63. National Archives Repository South Africa, Forbes Collection Annex 7/278, Mary McCorkindale to Sarah Purcocks, 25 October 1869.

64. After Kate's marriage in 1860, the 10-year-old Sarah kept the accounts and did other business tasks for her mother, wrote letters for her parents, then as a 13-year-old sorted out her parents' housing problems; later, she also ran what was in name her father's farm at Westoe.

65. National Archives Repository South Africa, Forbes Collection 7/107, Mary McCorkindale to Kate Forbes, 24 December 1868.

66. National Archives Repository South Africa, Forbes Collection Annex 7/295, Mary McCorkindale to Kate Forbes, 8 August 1875; and National Archives Repository South Africa, Forbes Collection Annex 7/315, Mary McCorkindale to David Forbes senior, 10 August 1877.

67. One of the few is to Anne Purcocks in 1865, detailing a sea-voyage and visit to Cape Town. See National Archives Repository South Africa, Forbes Collection 7/161, Mary McCorkindale to Anne Purcocks, 12 March 1865.

68. Extracts from Dave Forbes junior letters will be found at Whites Writing Whiteness/In Progress/Migrant Letter (http://www.whiteswritingwhiteness.ed.ac.uk/blog/migrant-letter/). His first letter was written when he was 13, when with his brother Alex junior he had been commandeered for commando duty.

69. Dave junior had obtained a concession for this, then sold it, although retaining its wood and water rights.

70. National Archives Repository South Africa, Forbes Collection 7/252, Dave Forbes junior to David Forbes senior, 25 June 1888; and National Archives Repository South Africa, Forbes Collection 8/1, Dave Forbes junior to David Forbes senior, 19 September 1890.

71. His father David senior agreed, but also thought that selling out because of his insider knowledge before a price collapse occurred would be unethical.

72. National Archives Repository South Africa, Forbes Collection 8/1, Dave Forbes junior to David Forbes senior, 19 September 1890.

73. National Archives Repository South Africa, Forbes Collection 9/46, Dave Forbes junior to Madge Forbes, 22 July 1896.

74. National Archives Repository South Africa, Forbes Collection 10/176, Dave Forbes junior to Kate Forbes, 10 February 1912.

75. National Archives Repository South Africa, Forbes Collection 15/147, Kate Forbes to J. Macintosh, 17 January 1910.
76. Dave junior's letter to Kate of 22 July 1908 is indicative in its to-ing and fro-ing of business and farming matters. National Archives Repository South Africa, Forbes Collection 10/143, Dave Forbes junior to Kate Forbes, 22 July 1908.
77. National Archives Repository South Africa, Forbes Collection 10/176, Dave Forbes junior to Kate Forbes, 10 February 1912.
78. There are relatively few letters by Jim junior and fewer still from Nellie, Kitty and Madge Forbes, probably mainly because Jim farmed at nearby Tolderia and the sisters were 'at home'; those that do exist have the characteristic writing practices noted.
79. After David senior's death, official communications were sent to Kate and Dave junior because the two were executors of the David Forbes Estate.
80. Containing bound duplicates made by a 'manifold writer' carbon device.
81. Kate Forbes and Dave junior were the family archivists. They were also major letter-writers and also wrote other kinds of documents of life, including in Kate's case a farming diary, and in Dave's a memoir. Dave also ensured the preservation of the family papers as a collection.
82. Extracts from these and other David Forbes senior letters will be found at Whites Writing Whiteness/In Progress/Migrant Letter (http://www.whiteswritingwhiteness.ed.ac.uk/blog/migrant-letter/). David senior wrote many letters before 1860, but the recipients by and large did not keep them; the earliest extant is to Kate, written a short time after their marriage.
83. In broad chronological order, these were for trading and hunting, land surveying, trekking, diamonds digging, gold prospecting, and business trips including but not only to Britain.
84. National Archives Repository South Africa, Forbes Collection 7/82, David Forbes senior to Kate Forbes, 16 December 1866; and National Archives Repository South Africa, Forbes Collection 7/81, David Forbes senior to Kate Forbes, 26 December 1866.
85. This was Bishop John Colenso, both a travel writer and in 1861 author of a controversial commentary on the *Epistle to the Romans*. This rejected the idea of external punishment, a foretaste of even more controversial religious pronouncements from him later.
86. Kate and David had nursed the dying Alexander.
87. None would have arrived with their respective addressees until probably February.
88. Georgie was one of a number of Forbes children who died very young.
89. National Archives Repository South Africa, Forbes Collection 7/127, David Forbes senior to Kate Forbes, 7 June 1871.
90. As in a 13 July 1871 letter commenting that 'I am doing it without consulting you'; National Archives Repository South Africa, Forbes Collection 7/129, Kate Forbes to David Forbes senior, 13 July 1871.
91. A focus on the correspondence between David senior and James senior and to a lesser extent him and Dave junior shows the existence of family economy networks that David was part of but Kate was not, specifically regarding prospecting and mining.
92. Extracts from all Sarah Purcocks Straker letters referenced or quoted will be found at Whites Writing Whiteness/In Progress/Migrant Letter (http://www.whiteswritingwhiteness.ed.ac.uk/blog/migrant-letter/).
93. Sarah was widowed in 1883, when Joshua Straker died from heart disease. Westoe was given by or leased from David Forbes senior. Nominally, until his death in 1899, her father David Purcocks senior ran it, but in practice this had been Sarah from when she was a young woman.
94. From the recurrence of breast cancer, following earlier medical treatment.
95. National Archives Repository South Africa, Forbes Collection 7/75, Sarah Purcocks to Kate Forbes, 23 April 1866.
96. National Archives Repository South Africa, Forbes Collection 7/94, Sarah Purcocks to Kate Forbes, 29 May 1867.
97. National Archives Repository South Africa, Forbes Collection 7/230, Sarah Purcocks to Kate Forbes, 1 August 1886.
98. Sarah had financial interests in the trusts established under the wills of Mary McCorkindale, David Purcocks senior, and also David Forbes senior.

99. National Archives Repository South Africa, Forbes Collection 8/115, Sarah Purcocks Straker to Kate Forbes, 16 July 1889; and National Archives Repository South Africa, Forbes Collection 8/35, Sarah Purcocks Straker to Kate Forbes, 4 May 1890.
100. Letters by Bella Pryde, an acquaintance of Nellie, Kitty and Madge Forbes employed locally as a governess, are very demonstrative. This was disapproved of, with comments made about its inappropriateness.
101. For instance, Anne Purcocks was functionally literate, her husband David was not literate at all, and the three Purcocks sons varied.
102. For instance, Anne Purcocks was a lodging-house keeper in Zinkwazi, and Mary McCorkindale had her own investments and later took over the McCorkindale Estate.
103. Susie Condie became a specialist nurse, and better professional training opportunities in Europe seem to have been involved in her decision. Her brother John Condie went to Cape Town for a trial period and decided to stay.

Acknowledgements

Whites Writing Whiteness research is supported by the UK's Economic and Social Research Council (ESRC) as a Professorial Research Fellowship (ES J022977/1). The ESRC's support is gratefully acknowledged. No financial interest or benefit has arisen from this research.

Disclosure statement

No potential conflict of interest was reported by the author.

References

Altman, J. G. (1982). *Epistolarity: Approaches to a form*. Ohio: Ohio State University Press.

Baldasser, L., & Gabaccia, D. (Eds.). (2010a). *Intimacy and Italian migration: Gender and domestic lives in a mobile world*. New York, NY: Fordham University Press.

Baldassar, L., & Gabaccia, D. (2010b). Home, family and the Italian nation in a mobile world. In L. Baldassar & D. Gabaccia (Eds.), *Intimacy and Italian migration: Gender and domestic lives in a mobile world* (1–23). New York, NY: Fordham University Press.

Barton, D., & Hall, N. (Eds.). (1999a). *Letter writing as a social practice*. Amsterdam: John Benjamins.

Barton, D., & Hall, N. (1999b). Introduction. In D. Barton & N. Hall (Eds.), *Letter writing as a social practice* (1–14). Amsterdam: John Benjamins.

Bhabha, H. (1990). Third space. In J. Rutherford (Ed.), *Identity: Community, culture, difference* (72–94). London: Lawrence and Wishart.

Bonner, P. (1982). *Kings, commoners and concessionaires: The evolution and dissolution of the nineteenth century Swazi state*. Cambridge: Cambridge University Press.

Bose, N. (2014). New settler colonial histories at the edges of empire: "Asiatics", settlers and law in colonial South Africa. *Journal of Colonialism and Colonial History, 15*, 1, Retrieved November 9, 2015, from http://muse.jhu.edu/login?auth=0&type=summary&url=/journals/journal_of_colonialism_and_colonial_history/v015/15.1.bose.html

Brock, J. (1999). *The mobile scot: A study of emigration and migration 1861–1911*. Edinburgh: John Donald Publishers.

Bundy, C. (1988). *The rise and fall of the South African peasantry*. London: James Currey.

Cancian, S. (2010). *Families, lovers and their letters: Italian post-war emigration to Canada*. Winnipeg: University of Manitoba Press.

Cancian, S., & Gabaccia, G. (2014). *Digitizing immigrant letters' immigration history. research center*. University of Minnesota. Retrieved November 9, 2015, from http://ihrc.umn.edu/research/dil/

Cavanagh, E. (2013). *Settler colonialism and land rights in South Africa*. Basingstoke: Palgrave Macmillan.

de Certeau, M. (1984). *The practice of everyday life*. Berkeley: University of California Press.

Chilton, L. (2007). *Agents of empire: British female migration*. Toronto: University of Toronto Press.

Cochran, S., & Hsieh, A. (2013). *The lius of shanghai*. Cambridge, Mass: Harvard University Press.

Conway, D., & Leonard, P. (2014). *Migration, space and transnational identities*. Basingstoke: Palgrave Macmillan.

Crush, J. (1987). *The struggle for Swazi labour 1890–1920*. Kingston and Montreal: McGill-Queen's University Press.

Davis, D. (2010). Third spaces or heterotopias? recreating and negotiating migrant identity using online spaces. *Sociology, 44*, 661–677.

Decker, W. D. (1998). *Epistolary practices: Letter-writing in America before telecommunications*. Chapel Hill: University of North Carolina Press.

DeHaan, K. (2010). Negotiating the transnational moment: immigrant letters as performance of a diasporic identity. *National Identities, 12*, 107–131.

Denoon, D. (1983). *Settler capitalism: The dynamics of dependent development in the southern hemisphere*. Oxford: Oxford University Press.

Denoon, D. (1995). Settling settler capitalism. *New Zealand Journal of History, 29*, 129–141.

Elias, N. (1994). / 2000 edition. *The civilizing process*. Oxford: Blackwell.

Elkins, E., & Pedersen, S. (Eds.). (2005). *Settler colonialism in the twentieth century*. London: Routledge.

Elliott, B., Gerber, D., & Sinke, S. (Eds.). (2006). *Letters across borders: The epistolary practices of international migrants*. Basingstoke: Palgrave Macmillan.

Elliott, B., Gerber, D., & Sinke, S. (2006). Introduction. In B. Elliott, D. Gerber, & S. Sinke (Eds.), *Letters across Borders* (1–25). Basingstoke: Palgrave Macmillan.

Erel, U. (2010). Migrating cultural capital. *Sociology, 44*, 642–660.

Erel, U. (2012). Engendering transnational space. *European Journal of Women's Studies, 19*, 460–474.

Family and Colonialism Network. (2014). Migration to the colonies (Part V): South Africa. Retrieved November 9, 2015, from https://colonialfamilies.wordpress.com/2014/05/16/migration-to-the-colonies-part-v-south-africa/

Feinstein, C. (2005). *An economic history of South Africa*. Cambridge: Cambridge University Press.

Fitzpatrick, D. (1994). *Oceans of consolation: Personal accounts of Irish migration to America*. Ithaca: Cornell University Press.

Forbes, D. (1938). *My life in South Africa*. London: Witherby Ltd.

Foucault, M. (1967). Of other spaces / heterotopias. Retrieved November 9, 2015, from http://www.foucault.info/documents/heteroTopia/foucault.heteroTopia.en.html

Fraser, L. (2000). *A distant shore: Irish migration and New Zealand settlement*. Dunedin: Otago University Press.

Gabaccia, D. (2000). *Italy's many diasporas*. London: Routledge.

Gerber, D. (1997). The immigrant letter between positivism and populism. *Journal of American Ethnic History, 16*, 3–34.

Gerber, D. (2000). Epistolary ethics: Personal correspondence and the culture of emigration in the nineteenth century. *Journal of American Ethnic History, 19*, 3–23.

Gerber, D. (2005). Acts of deceiving and withholding in immigration letters. *Journal of Social History, 39*, 315–330.

Gerber, D. (2006). *Authors of their lives: The personal correspondence of British migrants to North America in the nineteenth century*. New York, NY: New York University Press.

Haggis, J., & Holmes, M. (2011). Epistles to emails. *Life Writing, 8*, 169–185.

Harper, M. (2003). *Adventurers and exiles: The great Scottish exodus*. London: Profile Books.

Harper, M. (Ed.). (2005). *Emigrant homecomings: The return movement of migrants 1600–2000*. Manchester, NH: Manchester University Press.

Harper, M., & Constantine, S. (2010). *Migration and empire*. Oxford: Oxford University Press.

Hougaz, L. (2015). *Entrepreneurship in family business dynasties: Stories of Italian-Australian family businesses over 100 years*. Dordrecht, The Netherlands: Springer.

How, J. (2003). *Epistolary spaces*. Farnham: Ashgate.

Hunt, M. (1996). *The middling sort: Commerce, gender and the family*. Berkeley: University of California Press.

Ikas, K., & Wagener, G. (Eds.). (2008). *Communicating in the third space*. New York, NY: Routledge.

Jolly, M., & Stanley, L. (2005). Letters as/not a genre. *Life Writing, 2*, 91–118.

Jones, W. D. (2006). Going into print: Published immigrant letters, webs of personal relations and the emergence of the Welsh public sphere. In B. Elliott, D. Gerber, & S. Sinke (Eds.), *Letters across borders: The epistolary practices of international migrants* (175–199). Basingstoke: Palgrave Macmillan.

Krikler, J. (1993). *Revolution from above, rebellion from below*. Oxford: Clarendon Press.

Ladurie, E. L. (1980 [1978]). *Montaillou*. Harmondsworth: Penguin.

Lambert, D., & Lester, A. (Eds.). (2006). *Colonial lives across the British empire: Imperial careering in the long nineteenth century*. Cambridge: Cambridge University Press.

Lester, A. (2001). *Imperial networks: Creating identities in nineteenth-century South Africa and Britain*. London: Routledge.

Lloyd, C., Metzer, J., & Sutch, R. (Eds.). (2012). *Settler economies in world history*. Leiden: Brill Publishers.

Lyon, M. (Ed.). (2007). *Ordinary writings, personal narratives*. Oxford: Peter Lang.

Lyons, M. (2013). *The writing culture of ordinary people in Europe 1860–1920*. Cambridge: Cambridge University Press.

MacKenzie, J. (2007). *The Scots in South Africa: Ethnicity, identity, gender and race 1772–1914*. Manchester, NH: Manchester University Press.

Markelis, D. (2006). "Every person like a letter": The importance of correspondence in Lithuanian immigrant life. In B. Elliott, D. Gerber, & S. Sinke (Eds.), *Letters across borders: The epistolary practices of international migrants* (107–123). Basingstoke: Palgrave Macmillan.

Maybin, J. (2006). Death row penfriends: Configuring time, space, and selves. *a/b: Auto/Biographical Studies, 21*, 58–69.

Middleton, S. (2010). Labourers' letters from wellington to surrey, 1840–1845: Lefebvre, Bernstein and pedagogies of appropriation. *History of Education, 39*, 459–479.

Milne, E. (2010). *Letters, postcards, email: Technologies of presence*. London: Routledge.

Mosley, P. (1983). *The settler economies*. Cambridge: Cambridge University Press.

Murdock, A. (2004). *British Emigration, 1603-1914*. Basingstoke: Palgrave Macmillan.

Noble, G. (2013). 'It is home, but it is not home': habitus, field and the migrant. *Journal of Sociology, 49*, 341–356.

Nowicka, M. (2013). Positioning strategies of polish entrepreneurs in Germany. *International Sociology, 28*, 29–47.

Plummer, K. (2001). *Documents of life 2*. London: Sage.

Plüss, C. (2013). Migrants' social positioning and inequalities: The intersections of capital, locations, and aspirations. *International Sociology, 28*, 4–11.

Pöllman, A. (2013). Intercultural capital: towards the conceptualization, operationalization, and empirical investigation of sociocultural distinction. *Sage Open, 3*, 2. doi:10.1177/2158244013486117

Richards, E. (2004). *Britannia's children: Emigration from England, Scotland, Wales and Ireland since 1600*. London: Continuum.

Richards, E. (2006). The limits of the Australian emigrant letter. In B. Elliott, D. Gerber, & S. Sinke (Eds.), *Letters across borders: The epistolary practices of international migrants* (56–74). Basingstoke: Palgrave Macmillan.

Rothschild, E. (2011). *The inner life of empires: An eighteenth century history*. Princeton: Princeton University Press.

Soja, E. (1996). *Third space: Journeys to Los Angeles and other real and imagined spaces*. Cambridge, MA: Blackwell.

Stanley, L. (2004). The epistolarium: On theorising letters and correspondences. *Auto/Biography, 12*, 216–250.

Stanley, L. (2011). The epistolary gift: The editorial third party, counter-epistolaria: rethinking the epistolarium. *Life Writing, 8*, 137–154.

Stanley, L. (2012). The epistolary pact, letterness, and the schreiner epistolarium. *a/b: Auto/Biography Studies, 27*, 262–293.

Stanley, L. (Ed.). (2013a). *Documents of life revisited*. Farnham: Ashgate.

Stanley, L. (2013b). Whites writing: Letters and documents of life in a QLR project. In L. Stanley (Ed.), *Documents of life revisited* (59–73). Farnham: Ashgate.

Stanley, L. (2015a). The death of the letter: Epistolary intent, letterness and the many ends of the letter. *Cultural Sociology, 9*, 240–255.

Stanley, L. (2015b). The scriptural economy, the Forbes figuration and the racial order: Everyday life in South Africa 1850-1938. *Sociology, 49*, 837–852.

Stanley, L. (2015c). Operationalising a QLR project on social change and whiteness in South Africa, 1770s–1970s. *International Journal of Social Research Methodology, 18*, 251–265.

Stanley, L. (2015d). *Forbes letters, decade by decade*. Edinburgh. Whites Writing Whiteness Working Paper. http://www.whiteswritingwhiteness.ed.ac.uk/publications/working-papers/Forbes-By-Decade

Vargas, M. A. (2006). Epistolary communication between migrant workers and their families. In B. Elliott, D. Gerber, & S. Sinke (Eds.), *Letters across borders: The epistolary practices of international migrants* (124–138). Basingstoke: Palgrave Macmillan.

Veracini, L. (2010). *Settler colonialism*. Basingstoke: Palgrave Macmillan.

Veracini, L. (2011). Introducing settler colonial studies. *Settler Colonial Studies, 1*, 1–12.

Veracini, L. (2015). *The settler colonial present*. London: Palgrave Macmillan.

Versteegh, P. (2000). "The ties that bind" The role of family and ethnic networks in the settlement of polish migrants in Pennsylvania 1890–1940. *The History of the Family, 5*, 111–148.

Vertovec, S. (2009). *Transnationalism*. London: Routledge.

Whyman, S. (2009). *The pen and the people*. Oxford: Oxford University Press.

Wolfe, P. (1999). *Settler colonialism and the transformation of anthropology*. London: Cassell.

Shared letters: writing and reading practices in the correspondence of migrant families in northern Spain

Laura Martínez Martín

ABSTRACT

Letters generated in the emigration context are produced in a family environment and designed to circulate within it. This correspondence had great symbolic value: it represented those who were absent, and it was vital to ensuring family support. To explore these family documents, it is necessary to devote some time to the situations in which the texts were generated and the contexts in which they were received. Approaches to epistolary testimony such as this usually take as reference the sender and recipient of the letter, and consider the exchange as something that took place between two individuals who based their relationship on paper. But behind this sender and this receiver, there was often a whole community of scribes and readers. When we study these writings, we notice the polyphonic nature of these letters. When a family member emigrated, it was not only the nuclear family that was broken up; there was a multiplication of voices interested in getting noticed through paper and pen, and they did so by delegating the act of writing and by including their own notes in the writings of others. In this sense, the letters allow us to glimpse different voices, and follow numerous individuals in their exchange of letters. This shared form of writing is the focus of analysis in this article. Here, I draw my analysis from a series of correspondence exchanged by emigrants and their families from the region of Asturias (in northern Spain) who immigrated to different parts of America from the 1850s to the 1930s. These letters offer rich historical testimonies of immigrants and their loved ones who stayed in touch over large distances.

1. Emigration, a family question

The histories of families whose children, parents or siblings had departed from various points of Europe en route to the Americas were largely sustained for decades through personal letters. These writings offer a glimpse (sometimes the only one we have available) into the relationships of otherwise anonymous families separated by distance, who would have found the situation difficult to bear without such support. This correspondence between emigrants and their families, which went on for decades in some cases, allowed people to feel close to their loved ones, maintain affective bonds and help the absent member to feel part of the family group despite the marching of time.

This research focuses on the missives that traveled between the region of Asturias in northern Spain and various parts of the American continent from the middle of the nineteenth century until the 1930s, letters written by emigrants and their relatives and friends that are archived in the Museo del Pueblo de Asturias (in Gijón).[1] This center has for some years led initiatives to recover and preserve letters. It presently holds around 5000 letters connected to the world of emigration. This analysis is part of a larger study of 305 letters written by Asturian migrants and their families between 1856 and 1936. This time span encompasses the origin of the phenomenon of emigration from Asturias, its visible growth in the 1880s, and the changes in the years leading to the outbreak of the Spanish Civil War. The second half of the nineteenth century corresponds to fewer cases, in part because of a lower volume of letters, and also because a small number of letters have survived. An initial research in the available collections at the Museo del Pueblo de Asturias resulted in 735 letters, reduced in a subsequent selection to a total of 305 letters. These letters belong to 25 different family collections, with varying numbers of letters for each. Regarding the place of production of these letters, around 70% were sent from different locations in the Americas, 22% were sent from Asturias, and the rest from other locations. The composition of writers by gender confirms the characterization of a male-dominated transatlantic flow; 63% of the letters from the Americas were written by male writers. In contrast, letters sent from Asturias were written in equal proportions by male and female writers.

The considerable interest in Asturias in the phenomenon of emigration and all related aspects reflects the range of influence that migration has had in the region. Asturias has a long migratory tradition that dates to the eighteenth century. Initial moves were of short distance. This was especially the case for seasonal migration of shepherds, shoemakers, boilermakers, stone masons, tile makers, and general laborers to Castile. Over time, these early flows of migrant labor reached other Spanish regions and, in the nineteenth century, the Americas became a preferred destination for many Asturian migrants. Figures available for the period between 1884 and 1930, when the flow had become a mass population movement, indicate that more than 330,000 Asturians left for the Americas, making this the second largest Spanish emigrant community after Galicia (Anes y Álvarez de Castrillón, 2012, p. 27). The majority of Asturian migrants left for Cuba, Argentina, and Mexico. At the turn of the twentieth century, Uruguay and Chile also became important destinations.

Many of the factors influencing Asturian emigration were common to other emigration regions in Spain. This included the influence of a culture of migration and the experience of previous migrants who 'made it in America' and facilitated the migration of other family members and friends. Once they became regions of emigration, Asturias and other regions maintained high levels of departures for a long time (Sánchez Alonso, 1995, p. 205). Among the reasons for emigration, first we need to mention the crises of subsistence that characterized the 1850s. As a result of better diets, increased productivity of the land, and high birth rates, there was a marked growth in population which was not accompanied by an increased availability of resources. In addition, changes in traditional agrarian structures resulted in loss of opportunities for work. This was compounded by a low level of profitability of the land. The local economy's dearth of opportunities available to a higher proportion of the population created incentives for people to leave.

Another key factor that influenced emigration was the desire to escape military service among young men, specifically men between the ages of 19 and 20 years. Military service was fully in place from 1876, but until 1912, young men could avoid it through payment or

Table 1. Illiteracy in Spain and Asturias (1887–1930).

	Illiteracy rates in Spain			Illiteracy rates in Asturias		
	Total	Men	Women	Total	Men	Women
1887	65	52	77	59	35	77
1900	59	47	69	50	30	67
1910	52	42	61	33	20	43
1920	44	36	52	32	24	40
1930	32	24	40	15	8	21

Note: Vilanova Ribas and Moreno Juliá (1992, pp. 166–194).

by finding a substitute to serve for them. For poor families, sending a son to military service translated into an enormous loss because during his absence (a period of up to four years in the period under analysis here), he could not contribute to the family economy (Molina Luque, 1998, p. 42). The possibility of avoiding or reducing the time of military service for families with economic means contributed to a general feeling of injustice and resulted in an army largely composed of sons of the lower classes whose families could not afford to avoid it. Beginning in 1878, the price for exemption from service was set at 2000 Pesetas – that is, 10 times the cost of a third-class ticket to the Americas. This helps to explain why emigration appeared as a more sensible option for so many young men (Gómez Gómez, 2000, p. 110).

Thirdly, the attraction of potential destinations also intervened in prospective migrants' decision to leave. Preferred destinations were countries that were expanding with large investments in railroad building, and with a growing foreign trade. These countries needed labor and, in some cases, new inhabitants. Some created incentives for the arrival of migrants and advertised them through migration agents or offices. For example, after the abolition of slavery, Brazil promoted the arrival of foreign workers to replace former slaves; and in Argentina, beginning with the Constitution of 1853 a pro-immigration sentiment took hold illustrated by the phrase 'to govern is to populate' (García Sánchez, 2002, p. 41).

In order to fully understand the importance of the letters analyzed here, it is necessary to look into the state of literacy among the Spanish and Asturian population at that time. As Table 1 illustrates, Asturias held literacy rates that were above the national average. However, within the larger European context, Spain lagged behind other countries. In 1887, 65% of the Spanish population and 59% of the Asturian population were considered illiterate. By comparison, by the second half of the nineteenth century, illiteracy had already reached minimum levels in the populations of Scandinavia, Switzerland, England, Scotland, and Germany; it was 16% in Austria and Ireland; and around 10% in Belgium (Kaelble, 1994, pp. 115–116).

Limitations to literacy aside, the case of Asturias shows that emigration and the opportunities that emigration created increased the importance of written culture and promoted literacy among larger sectors of the population. Some authors claim a strong relationship between higher levels of literacy and emigration in Asturias (Núñez, 1993a, p. 231), and the same connection has been made for other cases such as Great Britain and Australia in the nineteenth century (Richards, 2006, p. 65). Literate individuals presented a greater degree of geographic mobility as they were better prepared to perform new tasks. This connection between literacy and migration is apparent when looking at the levels of literacy among migrants. Several scholars have shown how migrants had high levels of literacy. For example, Fe Iglesias found that almost 80% of Spanish immigrants in Cuba in the nineteenth century were literate; and Clara Eugenia Núñez's study shows that in Argentina literacy levels among recently arrived migrants in 1895 were 65%, compared to 46.3% among the local populations; and in Chile, 46.3% of immigrants were literate in 1854, compared to only 13.3% of the total local population (Iglesias García, 1988, p. 286; Núñez, 1993b, pp. 370–371). In fact, when we can reconstruct the personal history of some migrants, we find examples of learning and improvement in handwriting and an increasing of the epistolary form, as a result of a deep desire to prosper (Martínez Martín, 2010b, 2012).

There is another connection between written culture and emigration in Asturias. At the turn of the twentieth century, this region had the highest number of students beyond the age of mandatory schooling in all of Spain. The students' (and parents') desire for a more solid preparation for a future of emigration helps to explain this practice (Mato Díaz, 2012, p. 72). Finally, it is necessary to remember that men were more numerous than women among the emigrant population. As a result of this, it is expected that literacy levels were higher in male-dominated migratory flows. In addition, the arrival in America allowed many emigrants to learn to read and write rapidly, for both personal and professional reasons. As Antonio Gibelli and Fabio Caffarena points out, some of them acquired an 'emergency literacy' which involves a poor graphic level, based on an imitative learning and a weak internalization of norms of written language (Gibelli & Caffarena, 2001, p. 569).

In short, emigration promoted the qualifications of those who left and, at the same time, gave more value to reading and writing among those who stayed behind for whom the written word became a way to maintain the contact with absent family and friends. The moment of separation brought to the fore the limitations that many had to carry on an exchange of correspondence as well as the heavy burden of the lack of schooling for personal advancement.

The deeply familiar nature of the migratory experience was reinforced by the constant exchange during the separation of pictures, gifts, food, press, remittances and, obviously, letters. On the economic level, an unequivocal sign of the solidarity that developed among loved ones was the sending of remittances. Small amounts were regularly sent from America to the family in Asturias with great influence in domestic and local economies and in the growth of the Spanish financial system. When migrants were adapted to the new country, they used to help their families by sending these small amounts to compensate the financial support that they had received to leave. But it was not just a way to return the money they had received; there was also a strong emotional component that pushed migrants not to neglect their commitment to the family. Through this regular entry of money it was possible to pay off debts, buy properties and cattle, improve housing, arrange exemption from military service for a family member or pay passages of other relatives (García López, 1992).

On the emotional level, privileged partners of the letters were pictures. These representations of absents were the best way to remain in the memory of others, hence they had a privileged place in homes[2]: 'You tell me that you put my portrait on Antroyo Day [Carnival] on the table and you remembered me dearly; I also remembered you.'[3] Thanks to the photographs they could know new family members or confirm what was narrated in the letters, for example, about work, parties, friends or homes. Thus was configured both individual and familiar identity, using the family albums as proof of the existence and cohesion of a group of people who, although they were separated by a large distance, were recognized and acted as one (Slater, 1997, pp. 173, 178). These pictures broke the 'fossilization of memory' because they made it possible to update the memory of landscapes, places and people left behind. In consequence, the images were a way of sharing the experiences of loved ones, capturing time, registering pieces of reality that could be transmitted in space (Croci & Caffarena, 2009, p. 4).

The letters are undoubtedly one of the most striking exponents of the important role played by the family structures that sustained and nurtured emigration. The main function of these correspondences was to communicate. Such communication allowed these pluri-located families to remain connected, bear the distance and maintain an emotional and economic structure that the distance could have destroyed. In this context, the family group should be understood as a core with three faces: first, affective, with reciprocity in feelings and emotions; secondly, solidarity, since different members provide mutual support; finally, economic, where monetary elements delimit the relations of power and dependency developed inside, because 'it is unquestionable that families were units of decision-making and that conceived strategies to protect their members and ensure maximum benefit for themselves' (Reher, 1996, p. 20). Therefore, logically, these family letters were witness of all these characteristic aspects of a family and of the vital milestones of these people: the arrival at the new destination, the settlement, job search and the labor market situation, relevant events (births, deaths or marriages), important news about other friends and family, sentimental and daily information, concerns and fears, disagreements and conflicts, the desire to meet again, that is, all the issues that could have been addressed if they had stayed together.

A large group of fundamental information that could support, put out or reactivated the migratory networks depending on needs of each situation, and that helped migrants to increase safety when they arrived in America. Thanks to these informal structures they had the invaluable help of solidarity networks to choose safe destinations, process the arrival, find a job or get out of difficulties if necessary. The important role of these correspondences in the migration microcosm is reflected, for example, in the ability which they had, more than once, the same as returned emigrants, to stop or to promote departures of friends and family: 'Letters from abroad and specially the advice of returned immigrants provided valuable information on every phase of the experience for those contemplating the trip. Veterans who had made the journey before regularly served as guides for the first-timers' (Baily, 1999, p. 48). When news from America was good and promising opportunities and prosperity, departures to America were increased. Other times, if the news talked about awful working conditions, inclement weather, natural disasters, conflicts or epidemics, it could dissuade loved ones (Martínez Martín, 2014; Ramella, 1995; Vázquez González, 1992).

The emigrants themselves became bridges that connected two realities that were at disparate moments in history, a connection supported by correspondences that were used to put two different worldviews together. The letters, transformed into transnational narratives, helped to transcend the physical borders and put down on paper the two stable contexts where emigrants felt rooted: on the one hand, the new destination where they had settled and built another life; on the other, the past for them, but present for their families, their birthplaces. Therefore, the memory of emigration has been suitably defined as a 'memory between two seashores', product of an identity characterized by an almost pathological provisional nature, because in this relationship there is a 'mourning' produced by the separation of the community of origin that is difficult, if not impossible, to comprehend (Croci & Caffarena, 2009, p. 11).

This new spatial, cultural and social construction remains in the letters, for example, the adaptation of emigrants to an urban environment, the transformation of values, the adoption of new behaviors or new points of view, prejudices, different existential patterns, and the variation of mentalities. The letters were not only the instrument to bear the absences, but also were used for individuals separated from the larger group to keep linked to the original community identity, remaining rooted somehow in its past.

Traveling back and forth between Asturias and the Americas, they cemented relationships that would otherwise have been difficult to maintain, while they themselves constituted material evidence of a powerful sense of interconnectedness that the interlocutors clearly felt with regard to their lives and writings. Epistolary exchanges are commonly understood as experiences shared by two or more people, but in a social context in which family and community were strong these social structures also interacted with the practices of letter writing and letter reading. The analysis we propose in this article shows how the social group was always present in the process of letter production and reception. In this way, the limits of individual intimacy were crossed in favor of the collective message. This practice resulted in the formation of communities of writers and readers who not only shared information and news, but also shared the act of writing and reading. Letters traveled along family circuits which, for people who were not as competent in writing and even for people who were illiterate, opened up possibilities of joining the writing community. This writing cooperation was only possible in a context of trust and support which was common among Asturian families during the period under analysis. The collective nature of many letters sometimes led to demands for privacy or secrecy among writers who wanted to avoid their letters reaching people who had not been invited to participate in the epistolary ritual.

2. Delegated writing: writing with other hands

The phenomenon of delegated writing is not unusual in epistolary exchange. Over the centuries it has been a fundamental means by which the illiterate and semi-literate would make use of writing in its most varied forms (Kalman, 2003; Lyons, 2014; Petrucci, 1999, pp. 105–116). Many people resorted to the services of writing delegates because they could not write themselves or had insufficient mastery of the skill. These mediators could just as easily be close friends and relatives of the sender, as was usual in the nineteenth and twentieth centuries (Sierra Blas, 2008a, p. 449) as writing professionals. The practice was common among emigrants and their families because people felt impelled by distance to write in order to stay in touch with their loved ones. However, not everyone was able to keep in touch at the moment when a family was separated. The migratory context therefore offered distinct examples of the process of writing using someone else's hands. For example, in her study of Lithuanian emigrants in the United States during the period of mass emigration between 1880 and 1920, Daiva Markelis showed that it was usual to get help in writing and reading letters from more literate friends and neighbors. This occurred as an extension to the concept of *talka*, the Lithuanian tradition of collective assistance at the moment of writing and reading letters (Markelis, 2006, p. 108). This practice can be documented in the letters of Asturian emigrants too, although it should be noted that its presence is limited. There were some people who approached others (usually friends or relatives) to help them put their thoughts on paper.

Writing delegation encompasses various possible levels of interaction and dependence. As Antonio Castillo has pointed out, there were different situations in which intermediation was used: first, in cases of actual illiteracy (that is to say, absolute graphic incompetence on the part of the author of the text); secondly, in cases of potential illiteracy, in which the hand that writes is not that of the author of the letter although there is no explicit indication of that author's illiteracy; and the third, which is circumstantial, occurred when these practices resulted not from authorial incapacity, but instead from other factors, personal or physical, that prevented the sender from using their writing capacity. These diverse circumstances are proof that the writing delegation did not always take place because the authors were illiterate (Castillo Gómez, 1997, pp. 314–317). In a context characterized by high levels of illiteracy or partial literacy, the family offered, as Armando Petrucci has pointed out, an ideal place for the practice of writing delegation conducted by those family members with a higher level of writing and reading competence (Petrucci, 1999, p. 51). The hands of a brother, a son or a friend were the first option in these cases, as they were close, they could be trusted, and they did not cost any money.

In the corpus of Asturian migrant family letters under analysis there are no examples of a totally illiterate person resorting to the services of a writing delegate, although of course this does not mean that it did not happen. All the cases dealt with here are thus examples of circumstantial writing delegation, which occurred for very different reasons.

In the first place, there were people who were not very agile with the pen, though they could just about write for themselves. This is the situation that we have with Dionisio Menéndez from whom we have a total of seven letters produced between 1909 and 1922. Four were written by his daughter Marcelina and addressed to his son Santos, who had emigrated to the Americas (Puerto Rico, Cuba and the United States), while for another two he resorted to delegates that we cannot identify. All those written by others were signed by him in his hand, and there is one letter that we suspect he may have written himself (Figure 3).[4] He may have made the effort to put pen to paper on that one occasion because he needed urgently to make contact with a friend of the family, Marcelino Argüelles, who was with his son Santos Menéndez. Dionisio had been trying to get the young man off military service, but he had not sent the necessary documentation or got into contact with him. However, he had certain difficulties with writing, as he had not properly mastered the rules of page layout and word segmentation, and frequently confused spelling rules. This meant that his texts were not very easy to read.

Figure 1. Marcelina Menéndez Selgas (1908, March 15, Loro, Pravia, Asturias) [Letter to her brother Santos Menéndez Selgas (Cuba or Puerto Rico)].

Between 1909 and 1911, Dionisio sent four letters to his son Santos, written by his daughter Marcelina, who acted as her father's scribe during those years. We know for sure that it was Marcelina writing these letters for two reasons. First, in one of them, she tells her brother Santos that she is hurt and has had to have an operation on her right hand ('I tell you that this letter I'm writing needs a great deal of effort, too much, because I have hurt my right hand which is the one is not doing well';[5]) this clearly identifies her as the writer, allowing us to identify her handwriting. Secondly, Marcelina later migrated to Cuba, and from the moment she left, Dionisio's letters disappeared, perhaps because he had no one else in his close circle that he could trust with the information that he wanted put into writing. It is obvious from the letters that Marcelina was not a professional scribe, nor indeed particularly skilled at writing, but this did not seem to hinder her own correspondence (there are 15 letters written and signed by her) or prevent her from serving as a scribe for her father.

We have sources that allow us to compare the letters signed by Marcelina and by Dionisio at around the same time (Figures 1 and 2). There are several features that seem to confirm that the same person is writing in both cases. One characteristic is undoubtedly the way of forming the capital letters, particularly the final broad stroke of the 'D' or the 'S'. In the same way, it is possible to identify the same use of a double 'r' at the beginning of the word, as occurs in 'rrecibo' (received) or 'rregular' (regular); the confusion is repeated in the use of the 'h', and some small letters have a particularly recognizable shape, such as 'f', 'g' and 'h', and the number '1'. On another level, the segmentation is completely random, and, on some occasions, she uses identical formulaic expressions (such as 'having received these short letters, I hope that you are fully enjoying good health just as you wish this for me'), which enabled us to carry out a word-by-word comparison of the handwriting and allowed us to affirm that Marcelina must indeed have acted as a writing delegate for her father Dionisio.

Later, in 1922, after Marcelina herself had emigrated and could no longer write letters for her father, Dionisio had on two occasions to make use of other people that could write better than him. On the first occasion, on 24 July (Figure 4), he had news to convey that was

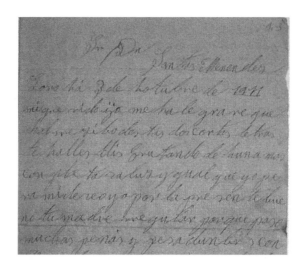

Figure 2. Dionisio Menéndez Díaz (1911, October 3, Loro, Pravia, Asturias) [Letter to his son Santos Menéndez Selgas (Cuba or Puerto Rico)].

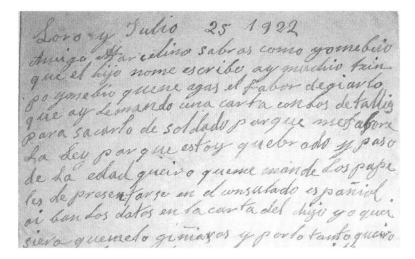

Figure 3. Dionisio Menéndez Díaz (1922, July 25, Loro, Pravia, Asturias). [Letter to his friend Marcelino Argüelles (Tampa, Florida, USA?)].

particularly important and consequential, as the situation regarding his son's military service had not yet been cleared. For a number of years he had been trying various ways to ensure that Santos was not declared a draft dodger. The indications that he gave in his letter were very important and needed to be clearly communicated. Santos had migrated before he was of military age and, therefore, he faced the possibility of being considered a fugitive under Spanish law. If he had returned to Spain, he would have been detained and condemned for not meeting his military service obligation; additional reprisals could have been in store for his family. Perhaps for this reason, Dionisio decided to ask another person to write the letter for him (we do not know if this person was a professional scribe or an individual who acted as one). We know that Dionisio had no physical impediment of any other kind at that time because we have another letter written by him to his friend Marcelino Argüelles, who had also emigrated, explaining that he had written to his son on the same date (Figure 3).

Dionisio resorted to another writing delegate some months later, on 17 October 1922. The hand that wrote this letter (Figure 5) differs from the other letter written by a delegate (Figure 4); this hand wrote the whole text, including the signature. The writing style employed by the second intermediary suggests it was someone from his close circle. It does not seem like that of a professional scribe because the writing has a limited capacity for expression, it demonstrates insecurity and lack of agility. Moreover, it includes several orthographic doubts, and grammatically inaccurate word segmentation – all of these features are common in people who did not write often. The letter deals with topics such as Santos' military service, his mother's health problems, and a small family conflict. They are all personal matters that Dionisio wanted his son to know of quickly.

If we compare these samples of writing defined as delegated (those written between 24 July and 17 October 1922, Figures 4 and 5) with the one that we have attributed to Dionisio himself (Figure 3), we can observe that the general outline of the letters, the uniformity of the module and the calligraphy are different (note the inclination of the text). In the case of the two delegates, we find ourselves faced with two hands that are well versed in the art of writing. Not only are the textual appearance and layout different, there are also specific

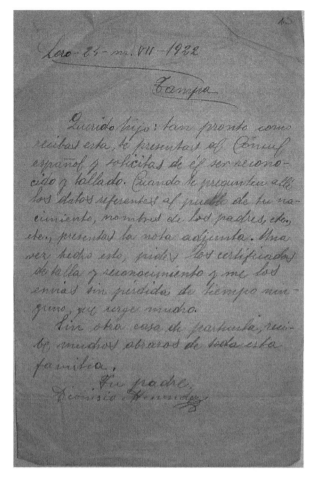

Figure 4. Delegated writing of Dionisio Menéndez. Dionisio Menéndez Díaz (1922, July 24, Loro, Pravia, Asturias) [Letter to his son Santos Menéndez Selgas (Tampa, Florida, USA)].

details that accentuate the differences. In the case of the capital letters, for example, they are executed differently in three cases. The writing of the second delegate also exhibits some difficulties with spelling and word segmentation, while the text of the first delegate in general follows accepted grammatical standards.

We do not know why he resorted to a graphic delegate on this last occasion, as there is no explicit mention of the situation that motivated the mediation. However, in other cases, the reason is made explicit. For example, in the letters that were written by Obdulia González on behalf of her grandmother to her cousin, Manuel Suárez, who had emigrated to Havana, we are told explicitly in some of the letters that her grandmother was unable to read and write because she could not see well, probably due to her advanced age, and she had to ask her granddaughter to keep up the correspondence for her: 'Without anything of yours to refer to, I tell you that I am answering the letter you wrote on Grandma's behalf because, as you will understand, the "poor" can't see well enough to write';[6] 'As I told you in the previous letter, I am writing on Grandma's behalf and so that you can see I am not lazy, I am writing back the moment we received your letter'.[7]

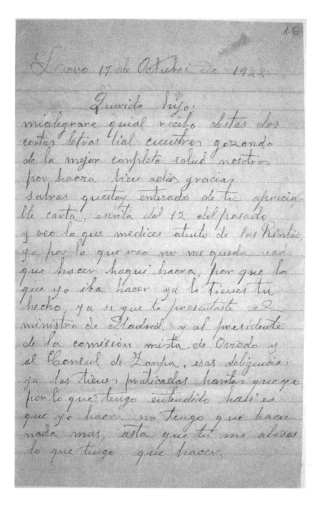

Figure 5. Delegated writing of Dionisio Menéndez. Dionisio Menéndez Díaz (1922, October 17, Loro, Pravia, Asturias) [Letter to his son Santos Menéndez Selgas (Tampa, Florida, USA)].

However it was not only the elderly that had problems dealing with correspondence themselves. There are also cases in which an occasional disability lay behind the use of a writing intermediary. The fact of not wanting to delay too long in replying so as not to worry the family was one of the reasons why friends were often asked to put down the words that the author wanted to transmit:

> [...] can't tell you any more because the person that is writing these four letters is a friend of mine. I can't write because a nail got stuck in my right hand and for 4 months has left my arm useless [...].[8]

Another interesting form of writing delegation involved children of emigrants who wrote on behalf of their parents. It was usual for children to be asked to write a few lines to their relatives in Asturias, especially to grandparents. The reason given was frequently that the parents' numerous occupations prevented them from writing themselves, but it is equally likely that, on these occasions, they asked the children to write for them in order to reinforce the affective bonds between them and their grandparents, often nurtured only through letters and photographs. In this regard, the words of nine-year-old María Luisa Albuerne are significant in the missive that she sent in 1892 to her grandfather Francisco Albuerne. María Luisa acted as family intermediary, excusing her father who could not write because of his many obligations, and her mother who at the moment of writing was unwell. María Luisa conveys messages from her parents and concludes the letter by apologizing for her bad handwriting, attributing it to her young age:

> I decided to send you this because papa is very busy and also so that you can see that you have in this country a little granddaughter that loves you very much and that would give anything to see you. Grandpa, as soon as he can, Dad will have a picture of Mom and Constantino and Alicia, my younger brother and sister taken so that you can have the pleasure of seeing us all in a portrait as the distance prevents it from being any other way. Grandpa, Dad has asked me to tell you that his friend Agustín received what he requested, and sends many thanks, and that if he can, he will send you for Christmas Eve some chorizos made by his sisters, my Aunties Maria and Quirina and my uncle Albaro.

> Dear Grandpa, Mom has asked me to say, because she is indisposed that she cannot write but never mind because she thinks it will come out well and then will write to you with the letter from Dad […].

> I hope you will forgive my bad handwriting and the lack of harmony of my words but as you will understand they are due to my few years, as you know I am only nine. With time I believe it will get better […].[9]

In short, the examples from the corpus show the existence of collaborative letter writing in the context of Asturian migration. The fact that there is no example of a completely illiterate person who sought the aid of a graphic mediator is not necessarily representative of the general Asturian context. Similarly to other cases of family letters, one can observe the presence of different individuals who in some circumstances sought the help of other hands to put ideas and emotions on paper. Reasons to rely on a graphic mediator varied – Dionisio Menéndez asked for assistance because he did not have a solid command of writing practices; Obdulia helped her grandmother who, given her advanced age, could not read and write on her own; in other cases, busy parents needed to delegate letter writing to their children who communicated with their distant grandparents. Since this process took place primarily with the assistance of other family members, it meant the loss of intimacy usually reserved to the singular writer and reader which is characteristic of the epistolary genre. On the other hand, this practice served to reinforce the bonds and obligations of the family, and made visible the importance of solidarity and assistance among loved ones. It resulted in a transformation of a practice that originally had an individual character into one of collective writing. It was also a process mediated by orality which constituted a central mechanism in the decision of what to write on paper.

3. Sharing pen and paper: writing in the family

The marked familial nature of these letters is shown by the way they were produced and received, indicating the communal function that they often performed.[10] In this context, we should not underestimate the enormous symbolic value that this correspondence had on both sides of the ocean. The letters concentrated into a few lines fragments of the lives of loved ones and the voices of those who were far away, making them into memory objects, containers of other people's recollections and an important vehicle for the configuration of identity (Mandingorra Llavata, 2000, p. 8). The fact that they were designed to move within a family circle means that they corresponded to specific contexts of production and reception, and this also largely determined their content, which reflected also a larger communal reality, with a strong presence of families and social networks that came into being in the world of emigration. Hence, it is necessary to focus on the situations in which these texts were generated and received.

When analyzing epistolary sources, it is common to consider the sender and receiver as if it were an exchange between two individuals who continue their relationship on paper. But behind the author and the addressee, there was often a whole community of writers or readers (Sierra Blas, 2008b). As we go deeper into the analysis of the letters, we begin to notice the polyphonic character of some of them. Occasionally, the distinct voices that wished to intervene in the letter have done so through a single writing hand. This hand might also have been the one that signed the letter. Despite this limitation, traces were left in the texts showing that this person was often acting as the representative of the whole family group. In this sense, the letters allow us to glimpse distinct marks by which we can follow the various individuals who intervened in an epistolary exchange. Particularly common are the references to another person that was at the writer's side and dictated some of the words inserted into the text in the form of a direct quotation. This was underscored also in the use of plurals in the letters indicating that various people were collaborating in the preparation of the letter. Evidence that points to multiple participants in the writing of a text is not exclusive to this type of letter or this context. Other scholars have also noted it, pointing out that in many cases the person who was thought to have the best spelling was given the responsibility of putting down words on paper (Cameron, Haines, & McDougall Maude, 2000; Sierra Blas, 2008a, pp. 470–490). We see this phenomenon occurring, for example, in a letter addressed to Jesús Valdés, who had emigrated to Camagüey (Cuba). This letter was written by his sister Mercedes Valdés, despite the fact that their other sister Antonia also appears in the salutation and final signatures.[11]

Undoubtedly, the clearest example of multiple writing is where we find more than one hand at work in the same letter, a practice that appears in a number of correspondence collections, and that was particularly common among Asturian migrants and their families. The writing space became a collective domain that included comments, opinions, advice and expressions of affection from various individuals who took advantage of this outlet to include their own words. In this way, the letter serves as a single vehicle for multiple messages.

The most obvious case of this practice of multiple writing in our corpus is found in the letters of the González Mana family, whose young family member, José Ramón González emigrated to Cuba. The family members who stayed behind in Spain wrote long letters to their relative in Cuba (in total, there are 94 missives belonging to the González Mana Family collection). In this selection, Castora González and Vicente González, José Ramón's sister and father respectively, stand out as the persons responsible for the largest number of letters. They wrote separately and jointly, and sometimes they invited other members of the family, such as José Rodríguez, Castora's husband; her children Antonio and Rita Rodríguez, and her aunt Carmen López. There are 43 letters in which Vicente or Castora intervene individually or together, and in the latter situation (which occurs in 20 letters), the usual practice entailed both senders writing on the same day, with the exception of a few cases in which there is a day's difference between the writing of one and the other. Thus, the most common pattern

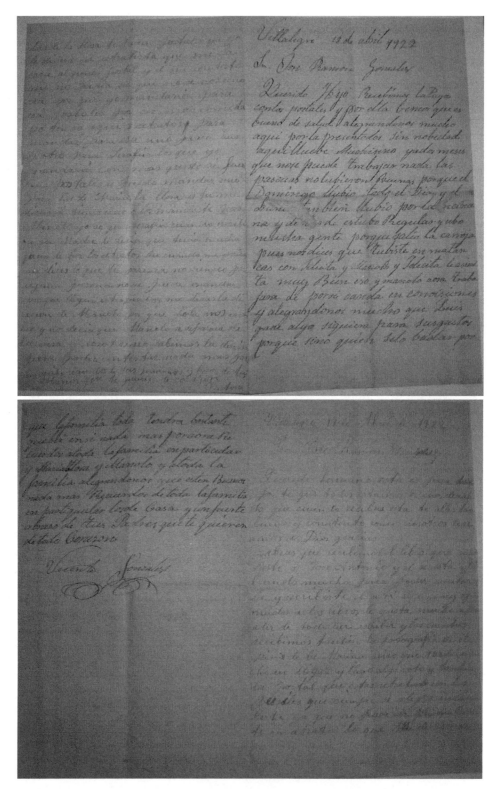

Figure 6. Vicente González and Castora González López (1922, April 18 and 19, Villalegre, Avilés, Asturias) [Letter to his son and brother José Ramón González López (Havana, Cuba)].

was for each of them to pen their own texts independently, as if they were autonomous missives sharing the same medium.

The letter that Vicente and his daughter Castora wrote from Villalegre (Avilés, Asturias) to José Ramón (Havana, Cuba) on 18 and 19 April 1922 (Figure 6) shows how they typically structured their letters: the person that began the letter would occupy the front and back of the first page, while the second writer did the same with the next page. The members of this family would compose a choral letter, which integrated the personal narrations of each writer in a single graphic space without renouncing the individuality of each writer. This system allowed them to write independent missives in which the writer's personal voice was differentiated. A further distinction was accentuated visibly by the different styles of handwriting (Vicente's more hesitant and cursive, compared to Castora's rounder style) as well as by differences in the writing implement or ink used and in the pressure with which writing was executed (which causes Vicente's text to be more intensely imprinted on the paper than Castora's, which is lighter).

The González Mana family's custom of sharing the graphic space led them to occasionally invite the youngsters to participate in the epistolary ritual. Castora and Vicente let their children and grandchildren address a few lines to their uncle José Ramón who was far away, as observed in the letter that they sent on 27 November 1929. In addition to texts written by Vicente and Castora, this letter contains a small fragment by Rita. The little girl's lines are integrated into her mother's text, and although they do not carry much information, they bear witness to the participation of the most inexperienced writers in the epistolary ritual that this family maintained for years in order to keep alive the contact with the loved one that was far away.[12]

In the case of the González Mana, the writers individualized their texts, drawing up their independent missives while sharing the same medium. However, there are a few examples of another form of collaboration, a mode of cooperative writing used by married couples, a phenomenon that other authors have also identified in other migration contexts (Gerber, 2009, pp. 11–12).[13] This practice can be seen in the letter that José Moldes (Castropol, Asturias) sent in 1903 to his brother Florentino, who was in Iquique (Chile). In this letter, it is José that begins to write the first pages and informs his brother of the irreparable loss that they had just suffered, for their mother had just died. After providing many details about that event, José leaves the letter incomplete. It is continued by his wife, Lucila, who takes up the thread of his narrative and completes the letter, because, as she explains at the beginning of her section, José had to leave to do some errands in Oviedo.

As can be seen in the fragment that follows, the texts of two different people function autonomously. Here, there are two differentiated but connected voices because Lucila, who writes after her husband, can read what he has written, thus breaking the confidentiality of the letter which was originally between the two brothers. In this way, Lucila takes advantage of writing after her husband to include her own opinion which is in disagreement with her husband's.

> Poor Dad is undoubtedly the one that has felt this terrible loss most keenly. He hasn't slept these last three nights, and it was he who put her in the box himself, fulfilling her last wishes. He behaved like a hero, and now that I have seen so much self-sacrifice and suffering, I love him even more because, despite his advanced years, he has given us lessons that we should imitate. The crisis has now passed and he'll recover little by little, which will be a blessing because the poor man has worn himself down so much that I feared we will also lose him.

Needless to say, José Antonio behaved very well, doing everything he could.

To follow social custom, I had to wear mourning clothes made for the whole family. But if I were you, I wouldn't spend a cent on this because true mourning takes place hidden in the heart, not in full sight of everyone, as if I had just one regret for him.

Dear Florentino

Pepe has gone to Oviedo with Leopoldo to buy furniture and has left me to finish this letter. Unlike him, I think you should put on deep mourning. I think that everyone thinks badly of people that don't wear mourning for their parents, if they are able to: society makes many demands, and whether or not they're right, anyone that wants to get on with other people has to accept them.[14]

Just as in the writing phase, the reception of these letters often was also an event that transcended the individual experience. Some missives had multiple addressees, as can be seen in the salutations, or in the names of addressees mentioned throughout the text. One of the most clear-cut examples in this corpus is by a young man, Francisco Fernández, an emigrant to the United States, who on one occasion used the same letter to address his three sisters:

Miss Josefa

Dear Sister: I have in my possession [your letter], which makes me very happy. I'm very pleased that you like them. Josefa, I want to go there in order to rest a while. I have only 6 hours to sleep, 8 hours for work, the rest at school, I don't have even 1 hour free to wander about. I arrive home from work, sleep as usual, I catch the *streetcar*[15] to school and then go from school to work. As soon as it is time, I think it is time to rest …

For some time, I've been healing my eyes, and I want to heal them enough to not have to use lenses, your *brother*[16] Frank

Miss Asunción

Dear Sister: I am very pleased that you have received the jackets. What others talk about do not worry, nor anyone's life, what others say you laugh. Tell me if you are with the Milagros, give her greetings from my father … Tell me if you do not hear from my old girlfriend and our aunt … You have the esteem of your brother that has never forgotten you, Frank.

I received the medal which I like and tell me that who sent me the list of bells, and what came inside who sent it? tell me that as you don't tell me anything and my father who doesn't write to me, what's wrong?

Greetings, I am fine [illegible] g. r. l.[?]

Canton, 4-1-1924[17]

Senders also used more indirect strategies to involve more people in the epistolary exchange. One of the sections of the letters that provides most information is the salutation, which was often collective. Similarly, letter closings containing good wishes and goodbyes were not restricted to the addressee of the letter, but also included a few words for different relatives and friends in the hope that the sender be kept alive in the memory of those mentioned. As Martyn Lyons points out: 'Emigrants' letters performed a collective ritual. Their elaborate theatre of formal greeting and farewell re-located the absent author within the social group which had given his life a context and a meaning' (Lyons, 2013, p. 201). Those in Spain wanted to know what had happened to those who had left and, as it was not possible for migrants to write to everyone they had left behind, the only way to remain in contact with many people was to mention them in their letters, something that could be done with a mere 'Dear friends'. In these circumstances, even when the letter was not shared in its totality with others, its content could be known by other people beyond the senders. In this case, this information could become the subject of rumors and hearsay within the communities

(Gerber, 2006, p. 108). The end of the letters could therefore offer an opportunity to expand the circle of people involved, including the greetings to and from loved ones, as well as sending kisses to others, transforming the letter into a collective scenario in which many were invited to engage (Blazquez, Bruneton-Governatori, & Papy, 2002, p. 215; Bruneton-Governatori & Soust, 1997, p. 472):

> Regards to aunt Amparo, Palmira and Domitila and Luis, aunt Sofia, Adolfo, Gustabo, a Higida, a Olbido, a Carmina and Antonio and all the rest of the family, and Pacita, Concha and father, Felicidad, Soledad, and Abelín, and Berginia, to all your friends tell Pilar to write to me, that I don't forget that that wasn't what she wanted for me and Maria that they are not so lazy, so many wishes I have to know about you all. Goodbye, till yours.[18]

Greetings and messages to multiple individuals were often channeled orally through the practice of reading aloud, which was common among migrants and their families, as other studies have shown (Bruneton-Governatori & Soust, 1997, p. 478; Fitzpatrick, 2006, p. 105; Kula, 1993; Soutelo Vázquez, 2012, pp. 101–124). When a letter arrived from the Americas, a community of readers would often get together around the piece of paper that brought news of a loved one. It is possible that not everyone present will have been directly invited to participate in the reading event, but as soon as the letter was in the hands of the addressee, the sender had no real control over who would participate in his words. David Gerber has shown this situation with regard to the correspondence of emigrants who arrived in Sweden and Norway, which was read out in public and circulated widely, although this was not always the purpose of the person who had written the letter (Gerber, 2006, p. 76). Sometimes, writers themselves mentioned the audience to which letters were specifically addressed: '[…] and Pepe and Milio how are they, do they remember me? and don't be offended because I don't write to them, I write for everyone, and father, I know he doesn't write because he doesn't know how to').[19] The existence of this larger community of letter writers and readers made it possible to include everyone in the epistolary exchange, both the literate and the illiterate, that is people who would not otherwise have been able to keep in contact with those who were thousands of kilometers away. The following fragment, extracted from a late nineteenth-century short story published in a journal, shows how the written word was transformed into the verbalized word:

> The postman brings the letter from Miguel.
>
> The envelope is wrinkled, dirty, greasy, ripped, as if the paper had spent a lot of time in a pocket.
>
> – Letter from Miguel, grandma! shouts Antonia. Stop spinning and gather round to hear […] (Sepúlveda, 1896, p. 9).

Letter carriers were not only bearers of messages from other lands; on occasions, they also became delegated readers. In other cases, they might have been expressly asked to deliver the letters to the right people so that letters would not be seen by indiscreet eyes, as we know from the comment that Anita García included in one of her letters: '[I ask that] the postman doesn't give the letters to anyone [else]',[20] which leads us to suspect that the letter's addressee may not always have been the first person to know its content. They also should be careful when letters circulated out of the postal system. Even though over the years the postal operation between America and Spain was improving and times were reduced considerably, it was common for migrants and their families to take advantage of the relatives' and friends' trips to carry letters to loved ones. This also multiplied the possibilities that some people not invited to the epistolary exchange had access to the content of the letters, violating the essential privacy of the same.

The fact that these letters had multiple readers is shown first and foremost by the multiple repeated remarks about exercising caution. Both senders and recipients were conscious that other people could intervene at any moment in an epistolary exchange. As there were few topics that were not dealt with in letters, warnings to hide the letters from third parties were sometimes included. Of course, the need to safeguard information was not as pressing in family letters as in other types of correspondence, but there were cases in which other family members were not invited to the reading of letters because of family disputes, economic conflicts or simply to protect sentimental confidences. That was the case of Marcelina Menéndez, who in her August 1923 letter from Havana, Cuba requested her brother Santos, in Tampa, Florida to be prudent about what he told his father in his letters back home to Spain, as other people could have access to them as well: 'don't tell our father that you send me money, in case by chance the Clabeles get hold of the letters'.[21]

Not only did the content of the letters invite confidentiality, but the materiality of the letters (what types of envelopes or paper were used) also manifested the desire to preserve the news they bore. This is clearly shown in the long letter that the school mistress Ana María Cruz sent to her fiancé, José Manuel Rodríguez, both Asturian migrants in Mexico. The letter is a long reproach, as Ana María considers that he did not pay her enough attention and was worried that he was no longer in love. At the end of the letter, Ana included a sheet on which she wrote only three lines. This is enough to warn José Manuel that this is to protect the intimacy of the content, as the quality of the envelope was not very good and the letter could be seen through it. The extra sheet served to safeguard the missive from possible prying eyes: 'As your envelope was flimsy and you can read everything from the outside, I am covering well mine, for both of us' (Sierra Blas & Martínez Martín, 2010).[22]

As many of these examples from Asturian migrant correspondence show, migrant letters brought together people who were not necessarily circumscribed to the family circle, but might also include friends, more distant relatives or neighbors. In some cases, words were also included for them or information given about them: 'I haven't seen the Pravians except for Vicentín and Manolo, the husband of Perfecta; you wouldn't recognize Vicentín because he's so grown up, Manolo seems thinner, he asks me to give you all his regards'.[23] This was the kind of information that was often transmitted to the relatives of those mentioned, who were often eager to receive information about their loved ones. Hence, the reception of these letters from America became an event for the whole of the emigrant's community.

The disadvantage of this extensive circulation of letters was that news was not always positive and that sometimes migrants wanted to make matters known only at a particular moment. There are several cases in which the missives announced matters that were relevant to other people's lives. Some information coming from the Americas referred to problems experienced by other countrymen, topics that the families of those affected would have likely preferred to keep confidential, and restricted to a private circle of people. But in some cases this information was about matters that could hardly escape the commentary of outsiders and that circulated with fluidity in migrant letters, thus generating a community of reception which was kept promptly informed of the news of migrants and their families. This was the case of the news of the suicide of Vicente, a young man who was the acquaintance of the

Solares Rivas family because he had been employed in the store of a family's relative. Deeply affected by the horrific news, Alonso Solares, a friend of the young man who lived in Buenos Aires, wrote on the same day to his father recounting the details of the event. After a heated discussion with his boss, Vicente had been fired from his job, and when he was on his way to change his clothes before leaving,

> he fired a shot to his cranium, or better to his head, thinking he was going to die fast, but it was not like that, because he shot himself at 1:20 a.m., or better, in the afternoon, and he died this morning at 1:30, I mean at one thirty, you could imagine how much the poor thing suffered.[24]

Even if Vicente's family in Asturias would have liked to 'silence' the story of his death, the communication among friends and acquaintances would have made any attempt to lie about it or to cover it up impossible. Even more, people affected by rumors were aware that despite the thousands of kilometers of separation, anything that happened abroad was rapidly known by families in Asturias and could have immediate consequences. This situation is illustrated by Policarpo de Prada in one of his letters to his father, in which he mentioned the other people with whom he moved from Havana to Cárdenas, Cuba: 'Dear father: I believe you already know about my move to Havana because although I didn't write in the last post, certainly some friend will already have announced it [...]'.[25] In this particular case, Policarpo's tone is somewhat ironic because his behavior as a migrant had been questioned repeatedly by his parents, and he was well aware that the source of the complaints was the prompt reports about Policarpo's comings and goings sent to his father by other relatives who had also migrated from Asturias to Cuba.

A final practice that was common in these letters and which clearly shows the communal concept that the emigrants and their families had of the letters and their circulation is the chain or successive circulation of them. In this way, it was not only the addressee that was invited to know the content but also others who had access to them, reinforcing thus the letters' collective character.

The most palpable evidence of this phenomenon in our corpus can be observed in the letters of Luis Carrera Sordo, sent in the last decades of the nineteenth century from various points of Mexico (Silao and Guadalupe Hidalgo). During the years in which we have news of his stay there, Luis sent various missives to Asturias, addressed to his parents Manuel Carrera and Florentina Sordo. Although we might have expected the two addressees to have received and read the correspondence at the same time, the letters themselves show that this was not the case. Throughout the year, the parents were separated for a time, with Florentina remaining in Posada, where the family home was, while Manuel was displaced to San Claudio, for apparent work reasons. Luis' letters mostly arrived at Posada, although they were sometimes sent to San Claudio. Instead of writing new letters in which they extracted what had been recounted by their son and adding to them the information that they considered pertinent, the addressees forwarded the letter that had arrived from America on to the other correspondent. They took advantage of blank space, normally at the end of the letter, to write their own comments. These additional comments sometimes acted as independent texts dealing with completely different matters, while others served as complementary notes to the news contained in Luis' original letter:

> And I send you the letter from Luis. If you receive one from him, send it to me. Everyone continues without news. [You must tell] Antonio to send me the sample of the pens because I have lost the one he sent me. Look after yourself.

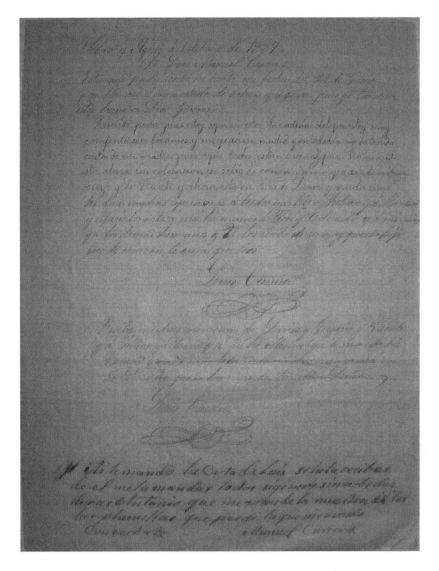

Figure 7. Luis Carrera Sordo (1887, August 1, Silao, Mexico) [Letter to his father Manuel Carrera (San Claudio, Asturias)].

This annotation in the lower margin of the sheet (Figure 7) stood out visually as it was written in a darker ink than the rest of the letter.

The annotations in these letters were not limited to occasional observations. Sometimes Manuel and Florentina took advantage of their son's letter to write new letters to each other. For example, Luis' brief letter from Guadalupe Hidalgo (Figure 8) only occupied the first sheet of paper and so it left enough space for his mother Florentina to include a new letter in the remaining space, as she forwarded it to her husband. This new text reads like a totally independent letter, in terms of both material and content.

Figure 8. Luis Carrera Sordo (1893, May 26, Guadalupe Hidalgo, Mexico) [Letter to his father Manuel Carrera (Posada, Llanes, Asturias)].

4. Conclusion

Asturian migrant correspondence offers us a privileged view of the historical experience of migrant families. Separated by migration, countless men and women were obliged to use pen and pencil to keep affective and even economic ties alive. Letters constituted a concrete result of the experience of separation. They were a vital source that allowed individuals to reconstruct events and relationships that sustained separation. Migration was a family affair and so was migrant correspondence. As the above discussion shows, family letters extended their original intimate person-to-person character by including other people and by being considered by writers and readers as documents that were almost semi-public. The sheets of paper traveling to and from Asturias and the Americas acquired a communal nature. Those who left and those who stayed behind found ways to share ideas, news, and sentiments. The examples presented in this analysis illustrate the different strategies deployed in a process of collectivization of the written word used by migrants and their families in both the production and the reception of the letters.

The existence of different forms of graphic delegation in the examples analyzed here indicates a practice that was common to other family correspondence. This strategy was particularly valuable in contexts of high levels of illiteracy or semi-literacy, and in situations in which there were other obstacles for individuals to write their own letters. With the assistance of other hands, even those individuals who were not fully familiar with writing could participate in the exchange of news and information. This phenomenon was reinforced by the common practice of reading letters aloud which, in turn, transformed the practice of reading into a collective experience. These strategies allowed family members to surpass any limitation which they might have had or felt, and maintain written contact with their loved ones, while reinforcing bonds and obligations built through family networks.

The cooperative nature of letter writing had also other manifestations. On the side of production, we have seen cases of writing by several people on the same paper and the consequent renunciation of any form intimacy by these writers. On the side of reception, we have seen examples of constant – and sometimes undesired – circulation of news received in letters to a wider circle of people, which led some senders to take measures to avoid writing about their secrets. Also, by combining both sides (sender and receiver), we have identified the existence of the chain circulation of letters that allowed for writing and reading texts in two phases. All of this reflects the complex nature of these written documents which were created with the assumption that news would be circulated widely. The wide diffusion of the content of letters visible among Asturian migrants and their families gave the letters a double function: on the one hand, they were domestic texts for family use; on the other, they were public texts, first-hand sources of information that were trusted in a way that official statistics and emigration agents tended not to be (Croci & Caffarena, 2009, pp. 3–4).

At a time and place when letters had an enormous symbolic value, migrant letters acted as repositories for memory and affect. They often went beyond the sphere of the individual and contributed to the maintenance and evolution of family ties. As was the case with Asturian migration as a whole, migrant letters became familiar and cooperative spaces that involved communities. As a result of their chance survival, these letters are witnesses of the multiple voices involved in their writing, reading, and diffusion.

These families and the written products that they generated function as an exceptional viewpoint from which to carry out the analysis of a case that can be extrapolated to other circles. The study of family correspondence has allowed us, through a particular and circumscribed example, to go in depth into the large and complex emigrant universe; it is due to these families that we can observe on a micro scale what the emigrant society reproduced on a macro scale: values, habits, customs, solidarity, control mechanisms, affections, emotions … So it is shown that family letters share functions, models and practices, beyond the issues narrated in them. Inquiry into their process of production, circulation and reception gives us the keys to better understand the role of writing and reading in the emigrant society. Thus, in addition, we can advance knowledge of other spheres of migration to improve the overall vision of this important historical phenomenon listening to the voices of the real anonymous protagonists.

Notes

1. Some of the letters preserved in this museum were published in Martínez Martín (2010a). All these correspondences, preserved in the 'Museo del Pueblo de Asturias Archive', are classified according to the family to which they belong and after depending on their authors chronologically.
2. The deep relationship between correspondence and photography can be seen in Gibelli (2005, pp. 131–147). See also *Asturianos en América (1840-1940) Asturians in America (1840-1940)* (2000).
3. Braulio Rodríguez (1908, March 22, Havana, Cuba) [Letter to his father (unknown name) (Inclán, Pravia, Asturias)].
4. Dionisio Menéndez Díaz (1909, April 4, Loro, Pravia, Asturias) [Letter to his son Santos Menéndez Selgas (Cuba or Puerto Rico)]; Dionisio Menéndez Díaz (1910, March 8, Loro, Pravia, Asturias) [Letter to his son Santos Menéndez Selgas (Cuba or Puerto Rico)]; Dionisio Menéndez Díaz (1911, October 3, Loro, Pravia, Asturias) [Letter to his son Santos Menéndez Selgas (Cuba or Puerto Rico)]; Dionisio Menéndez Díaz (1911, December 10, Loro, Pravia, Asturias) [Letter to his son Santos Menéndez Selgas (Cuba or Puerto Rico)]; Dionisio Menéndez Díaz (1922, July 24, Loro, Pravia, Asturias) [Letter to his son Santos Menéndez Selgas (Tampa, Florida, USA)]; Dionisio Menéndez Díaz (1922, July 25, Loro, Pravia, Asturias) [Letter to his friend Marcelino Argüelles (Tampa, Florida, USA?)]; Dionisio Menéndez Díaz (1922, October 17, Loro, Pravia, Asturias) [Letter to his son Santos Menéndez Selgas (Tampa, Florida, USA)].
5. Marcelina Menéndez Selgas (1923, June 16, Havana, Cuba) [Letter to her brother Santos Menéndez Selgas (Tampa, Florida, USA?)].
6. González (1921, March 20, Nubledo, Corvera de Asturias, Asturias) [Letter to her cousin Manuel Suárez Roza (Havana, Cuba)].
7. Obdulia González (1921, May 30, Nubledo, Corvera de Asturias, Asturias) [Letter to her cousin Manuel Suárez Roza (Havana, Cuba)].
8. Celestino Fernández (1910, November 2, Havana, Cuba) [Letter to his parents Cosme Fernández and (unknown name) (Naveces, Castrillón, Asturias)].
9. María Luisa Albuerne (1892, November 9, Cuevitas, USA?) [Letter to her grandfather Francisco Albuerne (Cudillero, Asturias)].
10. The familiar character of these correspondences, both positive and negative aspects, is studied in Martínez Martín (2014).
11. Mercedes and Antonia Valdés Bango (1909, November 2, Pravia, Asturias) [Letter to her brother Jesús Valdés Bango (Camagüey, Cuba)].
12. Vicente González, Castora González López and Rita Rodríguez González (1929, November 27, Villalegre, Avilés, Asturias) [Letter to his son, brother and uncle José Ramón González López (Havana, Cuba)].
13. There is, for example, the case documented by David Gerber of Joseph and Rebecca Hartley, who married in 1861, after which they jointly wrote a good number of letters. Joseph had more difficulties writing, but so as not to break his promise, Rebecca took charge of the task for the most part. Joseph's voice is produced regularly enough for us to know that it is present. On one occasion, we are allowed to witness an argument that they were having as they wrote the letter, as she wanted to describe what she was preparing for supper while he thought that trivial information that was of no interest.
14. The moment when Lucila takes over the writing is marked by bold. José Moldes Barreras and Lucila Gallego (1903, September, Castropol, Asturias) [Letter to his brother and brother-in-law Florentino Moldes Barreras (Iquique, Chile)].
15. 'extricar' in the original.

16. 'brohter' in the original.
17. Francisco Fernández (1924, January 4, Canton, Ohio, USA) [Letter to his sisters Gertrudis, Josefa and Asunción Fernández (Naveces, Castrillón, Asturias)].
18. Esperanza Menéndez and her husband Gerardo (1924, April 27, Havana, Cuba) [Letter to Esperanza´s grandmother, Carolina Quintero (Inclán, Pravia, Asturias)].
19. Anita García González (1931, December 8, Santiago de Cuba, Cuba) [Letter to her sister Luisa García González (San Cristóbal, Avilés, Asturias)].
20. Anita García González (1935, July 17, Santiago de Cuba, Cuba) [Letter to her parents Aurelia González and Emilio García (San Cristóbal, Avilés, Asturias)].
21. Marcelina Menéndez Selgas (1923, August 6, Havana, Cuba) [Letter to her brother Santos Menéndez Selgas (Tampa, Florida, USA?)].
22. Ana María Cruz (c. 1932, Peñasco, Cuba) [Letter to her boyfriend José Manuel Rodríguez (no place)].
23. Policarpo de Prada (1862, January 4, Havana, Cuba) [Letter to his parents Andrés de Prada and Esperanza Valdés Bango (Pravia, Asturias)].
24. Alonso Solares (1919, September 9, Buenos Aires, Argentina) [Letter to his father Vicente Solares Rivas (La Llera, Colunga, Asturias)].
25. Policarpo de Prada (1866, February 27, Cárdenas, Cuba) [Letter to his father Andrés de Prada (Pravia, Asturias)].

Disclosure statement

No potential conflict of interest was reported by the author.

Funding

This work was supported by the European Research Council under Grant 'Post Scriptum: A Digital Archive of Ordinary Writings (Early Modern Portugal and Spain)' [7FP/ERC Advanced Grant – GA295562], directed by Rita Marquilhas; and by the project 'Cultura Escrita y Memoria Popular: Tipologías, funciones y políticas de conservación (siglos XVI a XX)' (Ministerio de Economía y Competitividad [HAR2011-25944]), directed by Antonio Castillo Gómez.

References

Alonso Solares (1919, September 9, Buenos Aires, Argentina) [Letter to his father Vicente Solares Rivas (La Llera, Colunga, Asturias)].
Ana María Cruz (c. 1932, Peñasco, Cuba) [Letter to her boyfriend José Manuel Rodríguez (no place)].
Anita García González (1931, December 8, Santiago de Cuba, Cuba) [Letter to her sister Luisa García González (San Cristóbal, Avilés, Asturias)].
Anita García González (1935, July 17, Santiago de Cuba, Cuba) [Letter to her parents Aurelia González and Emilio García (San Cristóbal, Avilés, Asturias)].
Braulio Rodríguez (1908, March 22, Havana, Cuba) [Letter to his father (unknown name) (Inclán, Pravia, Asturias)].
Celestino Fernández (1910, November 2, Havana, Cuba) [Letter to his parents Cosme Fernández and (unknown name) (Naveces, Castrillón, Asturias)].
Dionisio Menéndez Díaz (1909, April 4, Loro, Pravia, Asturias) [Letter to his son Santos Menéndez Selgas (Cuba or Puerto Rico)].
Dionisio Menéndez Díaz (1910, March 8, Loro, Pravia, Asturias) [Letter to his son Santos Menéndez Selgas (Cuba or Puerto Rico)].
Dionisio Menéndez Díaz (1911, October 3, Loro, Pravia, Asturias) [Letter to his son Santos Menéndez Selgas (Cuba or Puerto Rico)].

Dionisio Menéndez Díaz (1911, December 10, Loro, Pravia, Asturias) [Letter to his son Santos Menéndez Selgas (Cuba or Puerto Rico)].

Dionisio Menéndez Díaz (1922, July 24, Loro, Pravia, Asturias) [Letter to his son Santos Menéndez Selgas (Tampa, Florida, USA)].

Dionisio Menéndez Díaz (1922, July 25, Loro, Pravia, Asturias) [Letter to his friend Marcelino Argüelles (Tampa, Florida, USA?)].

Dionisio Menéndez Díaz (1922, October 17, Loro, Pravia, Asturias) [Letter to his son Santos Menéndez Selgas (Tampa, Florida, USA)].

Esperanza Menéndez and her husband Gerardo (1924, April 27, Havana, Cuba) [Letter to Esperanza´s grandmother, Carolina Quintero (Inclán, Pravia, Asturias)].

Francisco Fernández (1924, January 4, Canton, Ohio, USA) [Letter to his sisters Gertrudis, Josefa and Asunción Fernández (Naveces, Castrillón, Asturias)].

José Moldes Barreras and Lucila Gallego (1903, September, Castropol, Asturias) [Letter to his brother and brother-in-law Florentino Moldes Barreras (Iquique, Chile)].

Luis Carrera Sordo (1887, August 1, Silao, Mexico) [Letter to his father Manuel Carrera (San Claudio, Asturias)].

Luis Carrera Sordo (1893, May 26, Guadalupe Hidalgo, Mexico) [Letter to his father Manuel Carrera (Posada, Llanes, Asturias)].

Marcelina Menéndez Selgas (1908, March 15, Loro, Pravia, Asturias) [Letter to her brother Santos Menéndez Selgas (Cuba or Puerto Rico)].

Marcelina Menéndez Selgas (1923, June 16, Havana, Cuba) [Letter to her brother Santos Menéndez Selgas (Tampa, Florida, USA?)].

Marcelina Menéndez Selgas (1923, August 6, Havana, Cuba) [Letter to her brother Santos Menéndez Selgas (Tampa, Florida, USA?)].

María Luisa Albuerne (1892, November 9, Cuevitas, USA?) [Letter to her grandfather Francisco Albuerne (Cudillero, Asturias)].

Mercedes and Antonia Valdés Bango (1909, November 2, Pravia, Asturias) [Letter to her brother Jesús Valdés Bango (Camagüey, Cuba)].

Obdulia González (1921, March 20, Nubledo, Corvera de Asturias, Asturias) [Letter to her cousin Manuel Suárez Roza (Havana, Cuba)].

Obdulia González (1921, May 30, Nubledo, Corvera de Asturias, Asturias) [Letter to her cousin Manuel Suárez Roza (Havana, Cuba)].

Policarpo de Prada (1862, January 4, Havana, Cuba) [Letter to his parents Andrés de Prada and Esperanza Valdés Bango (Pravia, Asturias)].

Policarpo de Prada (1866, February 27, Cárdenas, Cuba) [Letter to his father Andrés de Prada (Pravia, Asturias)].

Vicente González and Castora González López (1922, April 18 and 19, Villalegre, Avilés, Asturias) [Letter to his son and brother José Ramón González López (Havana, Cuba)].

Vicente González, Castora González López and Rita Rodríguez González (1929, November 27, Villalegre, Avilés, Asturias) [Letter to his son, brother and uncle José Ramón González López (Havana, Cuba)].

References

Anes y Álvarez de Castrillón, R. (2012). Emigrantes del Norte de España a América [Emigrants from Northern Spain to America]. In M. Llordén Miñambres & J. M. Prieto Fernández del Viso (Coords.), *El asociacionismo y la promoción escolar de los emigrantes del Norte Peninsular a América* [Associationism and the promotion of schooling amongst the emigrants from Northern Iberia to America] (pp. 15–33). Boal: Ayuntamiento de Boal.

Asturianos en América (1840–1940) Asturians in America (1840–1940). (2000). *Fotografía y Emigración* [Photography and Emigration] . Gijón: Fundación Municipal de Cultura, Educación y Universidad Popular; Ayuntamiento de Gijón.

Baily, S. L. (1999). *Immigrants in the lands of promise. Italians in buenos aires and new york city, 1870–1914*. New York, NY: Cornell University.

Blazquez, A., Bruneton-Governatori, A. & Papy, M. (2002). La documentación privada y la emigración: la correspondencia de emigrantes bearneses hacia América [Private documentation and emigration: the correspondence of Bearnese emigrants to America]. In Ó. Álvarez Gila & A. Angulo Morales (Eds.), *Las migraciones vascas en perspectiva histórica* (siglos XVI-XX) [Basque migrations in historical perspective] (pp. 209-233). Bilbao: University of País Vasco.

Bruneton-Governatori, A., & Soust, J. (1997). Pourquoi écrire? Question posée à un corpus de lettres d'émigrés béarnais aux Amériques (1850-1950) [Why write? A query to a corpus of letters from Bearnese emigrants to America (1850-1950)]. In P. Albert (Dir.), *Correspondre jadis et naguère* [Corresponding in the distant and recent past] (pp. 467-480). Paris: CTHS.

Cameron, W., Haines, S. & McDougall Maude, M. (Eds.). (2000). *English immigrants voices: Labourers' letters from upper Canada in the 1830s*. Montreal, Kingston: University McGill-Queen's.

Castillo Gómez, A. (1997). *Escrituras y escribientes: prácticas de la cultura escrita en una ciudad del Renacimiento* [Writing and writers: practices of written culture in a Renaissance city]. Las Palmas de Gran Canaria: Gobierno de Canarias, Fundación de Enseñanza Superior a Distancia.

Croci, F., & Caffarena, F. (2009). Parole migranti. Il ruolo della lettera nell'emigrazione [Migrant words: the role of the letter in emigration]. In T. Grassi, C. Monacelli, & G. Chiarilli (Dirs.), *Segni e sogni dell'emigrazione. L'Italia dall'emigrazione all'immigrazione* [Signs and dreams of emigration. Italy from emigration to immigration] (pp. 1-11). Roma: Ministero degli Esteri, Museo dell'Emigrazione "Pietro Conti", Università La Sapienza, Eurispes, Edizioni Eurilink.

Fitzpatrick, D. (2006). Irish emigration and the art of letter-writing. In B. Elliot, D. Gerber, & S. Sinke (Eds.), *Letters across Borders. The epistolary practices of international migrants* (pp. 97-106). New York, NY: Palgrave Macmillan.

García López, J. R. (1992). *Las remesas de los emigrantes españoles en América. Siglos XIX y XX* [Remittances of Spanish emigrants in America. 19th and 20th centuries]. Gijón: Ediciones Júcar; Archivo de Indianos.

García Sánchez, A. (2002). *La Rioja y los riojanos en Chile (1818-1970)* [La Rioja and the Riojans in Chile (1818-1970)]. Logroño: Instituto de Estudios Riojanos.

Gerber, D. (2006). *Authors of their lives. The personal correspondence of British immigrants to North America in the nineteenth century*. New York: University of New York.

Gerber, D. (2009). "Yankeys now": Joseph and Rebecca Hartley's circuitous path to American identity - A case study in the use of immigrant letters as social documentation. *Journal of American Ethnic history, 3-28*, 7-33.

Gibelli, A. (2005). "Fatemi unpo sapere"… Scrittura e fotografia nella corrispondenza degli emigranti liguri ["Let me know". Writing and photography in the correspondence of Ligurian emigrants]. *Esuli pensieri. Scritture migranti*. Special issue *Storia e problemi contemporanei, 38*, 131-147.

Gibelli, A. & Caffarena, F. (2001). Le lettere degli emigranti [Emigrants' letters]. In P. Bevilacqua; A. de Clementi & E. Franzina, *Storia dell´emigrazione italiana* [History of Italian emigration] (Vol. I, pp. 563-574). Roma: Donzelli Editore.

Gómez Gómez, P. (2000). *La emigración a América y otras emigraciones (Llanes 1830-1950)* [Emigration to America and other migrations (Llanes 1830-1950)]. Llanes: El Oriente de Asturias.

Iglesias García, F. (1988). Características de la inmigración española en Cuba, 1904-1930 [Characteristics of Spanish immigration in Cuba, 1904-1930]. In N. Sánchez-Albornoz (Comp.), *Españoles hacia América. La emigración en masa, 1880-1930* [Spaniards to America. Mass emigration, 1880-1930] (pp. 270-295). Madrid: Alianza Editorial.

Kaelble, H. (1994). *Desigualdad y movilidad social en los siglos XIX y XX* [Inequality and social mobility in the XIXth and XXth centuries]. Madrid: Ministerio de Trabajo y Seguridad Social.

Kalman, J. (2003). *Escribir en la plaza* [Writing on the Plaza]. México: Fondo de Cultura Económica.

Kula, W. (1993). Lettres d'Amérique (1890-1891): l'émigration des paysans polonais vue par eux-mêmes [Letters from America (1890-1891): the emigration of Polish peasants seen by themselves]. *Revue de la Bibliothèque Nationale, 50*, 48-57.

Lyons, M. (2013). *The writing culture of ordinary people in Europe, c. 1860-1920*. Cambridge: Cambridge University Press.

Lyons, M. (2014). The power of the scribe: Delegated writing in modern Europe. *European History Quaterly, 44-2*, 244-262.

Mandingorra Llavata M. L. (2000). *Conservar las escrituras privadas, configurar las identidades* [Preserving private writings, configuring identities]. Valencia: Seminari internacional d'Estudis sobre la Cultura Escrita (Arché, 7).

Markelis, D. (2006). "Every person like a letter": The importance of correspondence in Lithuanian immigrant life. In B. Elliot, D. Gerber, & S. Sinke (Eds.), *Letters across Borders. The epistolary practices of international migrants* (pp. 107–123). New York, NY: Palgrave Macmillan.

Martínez Martín, L. (2010a). *"Asturias que perdimos, no nos pierdas". Cartas de emigrantes asturianos en América, 1863–1936* ["Asturias we lost, do not lose us". Letters of Asturian Emigrants in America, 1863–1936]. Gijón: Museo del Pueblo de Asturias.

Martínez Martín, L. (2010b). The correspondence of asturian emigrants at the turn of the century: The case of José Moldes (c. 1860–1921). *The European Legacy, 15–6*, 735–750.

Martínez Martín, L. (2012). "Querido Floro": Gestos, ritos y emociones en la correspondencia de un emigrante asturiano ["Dear Floro": Gestures, rituals and emotions in an Asturian emigrant correspondence]. In F. Caffarena & L. Martínez Martín (Dirs.), *Scritture Migranti: uno sguardo italo-spagnolo / Escrituras migrantes: una mirada ítalo-española* [Migrant Writings: an Italian-Spanish look] (pp. 23–42). Milan: FrancoAngeli.

Martínez Martín, L. (2014). Escribir en cadena. Solidaridad y control en las cartas de los emigrantes [Writing chain. Solidarity and control in the letters of emigrants]. In A. Castillo Gómez & V. Sierra Blas (Dirs.), *Cartas - Lettres - Lettere. Discursos, prácticas y representaciones epistolares (siglos XIV-XX)* [Cartas - Lettres - Lettere. Epistolary discourses, practices and representations (XIV-XX centuries)] (pp. 445–464). Alcalá de Henares: Universidad de Alcalá.

Mato Díaz, A. (2012). Las escuelas de indianos en Asturias [Indianos schools in Asturias]. In M. Llordén Miñambres & J. M. Prieto Fernández del Viso (Coords.), *El asociacionismo y la promoción escolar de los emigrantes del Norte Peninsular a América* [Associationism and school promotion of Northern Peninsular emigrants to America] (pp. 71–90). Boal: Ayuntamiento de Boal.

Molina Luque, J. F. (1998). *Quintas y servicio militar: Aspectos sociológicos y antropológicos de la conscripción (Lleida, 1878–1960)* [Draft and military service: sociological and anthropological aspects of conscription (Lleida, 1878–1960)]. Lleida: Servei de Publicacions de la Universitat de Lleida.

Núñez, C. E. (1993a). Alfabetización y desarrollo económico en España: una visión a largo plazo [Literacy and economic development in Spain: A long-term vision]. In C. E. Núñez & G. Tortella (Eds.), *La maldición divina. Ignorancia y atraso económico en perspectiva histórica* [Divine curse. Ignorance and economic backwardness in historical perspective] (pp. 223–236). Madrid: Alianza Editorial.

Núñez, C. E. (1993b). Educación y desarrollo económico en el continente americano [Education and Economic Development in the Americas]. In C. E. Núñez & G. Tortella (Eds.), *La maldición divina. Ignorancia y atraso económico en perspectiva histórica* [Divine curse. Ignorance and economic backwardness in historical perspective] (pp. 359–380). Madrid: Alianza Editorial.

Petrucci, A. (1999). *Alfabetismo, Escritura, Sociedad* [Literacy, Writing, Society]. Barcelona: Gedisa.

Ramella, F. (1995). Por un uso fuerte del concepto de red en los estudios migratorios [For a strong use of the concept of network on migration studies]. In M. Bjerg & H. Otero (Comps.), *Inmigración y redes sociales en la Argentina moderna* [Immigration and social networks in modern Argentina] (pp. 9–22). Tandil: CEMLA-IEHS.

Reher, D. S. (1996). *La familia en España. Pasado y presente* [The family in Spain. Past and present]. Madrid: Alianza Editorial.

Richards, E. (2006). The limits of the Australian emigrant letter. In B. Elliot, D. Gerber & S. Sinke (Eds.), *Letters across Borders. The epistolary practices of international migrants* (pp. 56–74). New York, NY: Palgrave Macmillan.

Sánchez Alonso, B. (1995). Los determinantes de la emigración: análisis provincial [The determinants of migration: provincial analysis]. In B. Sánchez (Ed.), *Alonso, Las causas de la emigración española 1880–1930* [The causes of Spanish emigration 1880–1930] (pp. 203–270). Madrid: Alianza Universidad.

Sepúlveda, E. (1896, March 14). El escapulario (Cuento de la guerra) [The escapular (a war tale)]. *Blanco y Negro*, 9.

Sierra Blas, V. (2008a). *Letras huérfanas. Cultura escrita y exilio infantil en la Guerra Civil española* [Orphan letters: Written culture and child exile in the Spanish civil war] (Doctoral thesis). University of Alcala,

Alcalá de Henares [Published in 2009 as Palabras huérfanas. Los niños y la Guerra Civil [Orphan words. Children ans rhe Civil War. Madrid: Taurus].

Sierra Blas, V. (2008b). "Con el corazón en la mano". Cultura escrita, exilio y vida cotidiana en las cartas de los padres de los Niños de Morelia ["With your heart in your hand". Written culture, exile and daily life in the letters of the parents of the Morelia children]. In A. Castillo Gómez (Dir.) & V. Sierra Blas (Ed.), *Mis primeros pasos. Alfabetización, escuela y usos cotidianos de la escritura (siglos XIX y XX)* [My first steps. Literacy, school and everyday uses of writing (19 and 20 centuries)] (pp. 411–454). Gijón: Trea.

Sierra Blas, V. & Martínez Martín, L. (2010). "Guardar Silencio…" El secreto en la epistolografía de la emigración ["Don't tell…" Secrets in emigration epistolography]. In M. Casado Arboniés, A. Diez Torres, P. Numhauser, & E. Sola (Eds.), *Escrituras silenciadas: historia, memoria y procesos culturales. Homenaje a José Francisco de la Peña* [Silenced writings: history, memory and cultural processes. Homage to José Francisco de la Peña] (pp. 734–758). Alcalá de Henares: Servicio de Publicaciones de la Universidad.

Slater, D. (1997). La fotografía doméstica y la cultura digital [Domestic photography and digital culture]. In M. Lister (Comp.), *La imagen fotográfica en la cultura digital* [The photographic image in digital culture] (pp. 175–195). Barcelona: Paidós.

Soutelo Vázquez, R. (2012). Correspondencias familiares y emigración en Galicia: vías de recuperación y utilidad didáctica e investigadora [Family correspondence and emigration in Galicia: recovery routes and educational and research use]. In F. Caffarena & L. Martínez Martín (Dirs.), *Scritture Migranti. Uno sguardo italo-spagnolo / Escrituras migrantes: una mirada ítalo-española* [Migrant writing: an Italo-Spanish view] (pp. 101–124). Milan: FrancoAngeli.

Vázquez González, A. (1992). Las dimensiones microsociales de la emigración gallega a América: la función de las redes sociales informales [The microsocial dimensions of the Galician emigration to America: the role of informal social networks]. *Estudios migratorios latinoamericanos, 7–22*, 497–533.

Vilanova Ribas, M., & Moreno Juliá, X. (1992). *Atlas de la evolución del analfabetismo en España de 1887 a 1981* [Atlas of evolution of illiteracy in Spain from 1887 to 1981], Madrid: Centro de Publicaciones del Ministerio de Educación y Ciencia, (C.I.D.E.).

The transnational life and letters of the Venegas family, 1920s to 1950s

Romeo Guzmán

ABSTRACT

Married in 1919, Miguel and Dolores migrated from Zapotlanejo, Jalisco to Los Angeles, California in 1927, where they raised 10 children: nine boys and one girl. Like Mexican migrant families throughout the US Southwest they experienced leaving Mexico and making a new home, endured the Great Depression, and in many cases, sent their children off to fight in World War II. Throughout this time period, they corresponded with their relatives in Mexico, providing historians with a rare collection of Mexican migrant personal correspondences. By conceptualizing correspondence as a migrant strategy and using these sources as a window into the transnational practices, I make two arguments about the Venegas family. First, I argue that through letter writing the Venegas formed a transnational family. I demonstrate that members of this family replicated their roles despite the distance between them. In the process, they created a transnational space in both Los Angeles and Guadalajara. Second, family members in both Mexico and the United States practiced a form of 'cultural citizenship': migrant-defined ideas of belonging and rights that transcend the formal boundaries of both nation-states. The family provided a set of strategies to navigate the Great Depression and World War II. This article contributes to a growing literature on Mexican migration, transnationalism, the 'Mexican American' generation, and Mexican migrant letter writing.

When Dolores Venegas passed away in March of 1991, her husband Miguel was left with a series of mundane and sacred tasks, among them reflecting on their life together. Married in 1919, Miguel and Dolores migrated to the United States in 1927, where they raised 10 children: nine boys and one girl. Looking back at her life and their life together, Miguel reached into the bedroom closet and pulled out a neatly bundled collection of letters. After opening and reading each letter, he carefully laid them out on the carpet. His daughter, María Teresa, entered the room and immediately recognized the importance of the history that lay between her and her 94-year-old father. With the help of her brother Carlos, she began organizing and transcribing the letters and eventually donated the material to Loyola Marymount University's Department of Archives and Special Collections (personal communication with Carlos and María Teresa Venegas, 26 January 2015; Venegas, 2012).[1]

If the Venegas family were Irish, Italian, English, or German their archive would be no more than a ripple in the ocean of European migrant personal correspondence and its related literature. European migrant letters were central to the development of immigration scholarship in the early twentieth century (Elliott, Gerber, & Sinke, 2006, p. 4). George Stephenson, Marcus Lee Hansen, and Theodore Blegen, who began their careers in the 1920s and 1930s, are often described as the first social historians of immigration history. Each the child of European migrants, they used personal correspondences to put a face and a voice to the migrant experience. In the introduction to *Grassroots History*, Blegen (1969) lauded the field's effort: 'We have pushed behind the barricade of statistics to learn that the American immigrant was not a line in a graph, a statistic, or merely a problem, but a human being' (p. 7). Characterized by David Gerber (1997) as 'populist', these historians were joined by scholars working in a more deductive manner, or to borrow from Gerber's terminology: 'positivists'. If this first camp was interested in reproducing the migrant voice, the latter used migrant letters to further their theoretical goals and arguments. William I. Thomas and Florian Znaniecki's (1927) *The Polish Peasant in Europe and America* and Oscar Handlin's *The Uprooted* – the most popular and influential book on European immigration to the United States – are good examples of the positivist tradition. Scholars continue to use migrants' personal correspondences in a deductive manner and organize them into collections in a populist vein, yet these two camps can no longer represent all the possible uses of migrant letters. New theoretical frameworks and methodologies, particularly those associated with the cultural turn, allow historians to pay closer attention to migrant agency and subjectivity. Yet, despite the more than 100-year history of migration from the United States' southern neighbor, there is a dearth of scholarship based on Mexican migrant letters.[2]

The absence of scholarly literature might lead one to believe that Mexicans did not write, but this is not the case. Throughout the first decades of the twentieth century, as I document in my dissertation, migrants in the United States wrote to Mexican consular offices, to the Secretary of Foreign Relations, to the Secretary of Public Education, and to Mexican presidents (Guzmán, 2016). Migrants' countless handwritten, and in some cases typed, letters asked the state to address problems in their place of settlement, which included the repatriation of families and small groups of migrants and the establishment of schools in the United States for migrant children. Family members of migrants who remained in Mexico were just as likely to write to their government and often asked for help in locating their loved ones and, in the unfortunate event of death, for help in processing insurance claims. These letters, while rich, only document specific grievances and rarely involved more than a few letters between the migrants and representatives of the Mexican state. They do, however, unequivocally demonstrate that Mexican migrants and their families were capable of and invested in writing and reading letters.

The lack of secondary literature on Mexican letter writing and archival collections dedicated to Mexican correspondence is a product of American immigration history and not a reflection of Mexican migrant practices. As the historian George Sanchez (1999) and others have argued, the field of US immigration history developed around European migration. The exclusion of Mexicans as subjects of historical research was coupled with the discourse of the 'immigrant paradigm', which posited that the United States was a nation of immigrants and that their incorporation into the nation 'symbolizes the promise and accomplishment of American democracy' (Gabaccia, 1999, p. 1115).[3] In the absence of pioneers and the creation of Mexican historical societies, the collecting and archiving of migrant correspondence has been neglected and relegated to individuals, often the children of Mexican migrants and first generation scholars, like María Teresa Venegas, Ana Rosas, and Miroslava Chávez-García.[4]

Opened to the public in 2012, the Venegas Family Papers document the arrival, settlement, and transnational lives of Dolores, Miguel, and their children. The Venegas family was part of one of the most important demographic changes of the first half of the twentieth century. Spurred by the Mexican Revolution and World War I, Mexicans migrated to the southwestern states of California, Texas, and Arizona in unprecedented numbers. As Mexican nationals, migrants gave birth to and raised children in the United States. While the Venegas family fled for political reasons and had access to capital, they joined Mexican migrant families throughout the US Southwest in leaving Mexico and making a new home, enduring the Great Depression, and in many cases, sending their children off to fight in World War II.

Scholarship on migrant families and children of immigrants, referred to as the 'Mexican American' generation, is too often framed within the US nation (García, 1991; Sanchez, 1993; Ybarra, 1983).[5] Historians tend to adopt linear narratives and emphasize arrival, settlement, and incorporation. The Venegas Family Papers provide us with a unique opportunity to situate one of these families transnationally, in Mexico and the United States. Letters, to borrow from one scholar, exist in 'a unique social space that exists neither in the homeland nor the land of resettlement, but in a third space that is, in effect, in both simultaneously' (Elliott et al., 2006, p. 12). By conceptualizing correspondence as a migrant strategy and as a window into transnational strategies, I argue that letter writing enabled the Venegas to form a transnational family and that the family practices a form of 'cultural citizenship': migrant-defined ideas of belonging and rights that transcended the formal boundaries of both nation-states (Flores & Benmayor, 1997; Camacho, 2008). I demonstrate that letters and photographs enabled the Venegas family to replicate the roles of its individual members despite the distance between them. Through photographs and letters, relatives in Guadalajara and Los Angeles maintained and formed emotional bonds. This was particularly important as the family grew and included new individuals. As a historical source, this body of letters provides a window into the transnational lives of the Venegas family. It sheds light on the identity formation of the Venegas children and strategies to navigate the Great Depression and World War II, which included youth labor, consulting with family in Mexico, the separation of the family, and transnational living. This family portrait contributes to a growing body of literature that uses race, religion, identity, the border, citizenship, labor and the family, and Mexican nation-state formation, among others, as categories of analysis to transnationalize the history of Mexican migration (Arredondo, 2008; Fitzgerald, 2009; Hernández, 2010; Rosas, 2014; Weise, 2008, 2015; Young, 2012, 2015).

1. Family cohesion across the US–Mexico border

Dolores and Miguel were born in Zapotlanejo, a small town located in Los Altos de Jalisco. This predominately agricultural region was made up of mestizos and became known as a migrant-sending region by the mid-twentieth century (Fitzgerald, 2009). They wed in 1919 and the following year had their first boy, whom they named José Miguel. On 22 February 1921 Dolores gave birth to Ricardo, their second son. One year later Miguel, Dolores and their two children moved into their new home. Here, they welcomed Guillermo on 9 April 1924 and Eduardo on 10 May 1926. The family enjoyed a comfortable existence. Miguel operated a profitable store in the town, both his and Dolores' parents and siblings lived nearby, and they all frequented the town's church on Sundays. This would all quickly change.

President Plutarco Elías Calles' efforts to enforce the anti-clerical Articles of the Mexican Constitution of 1917 led to the Cristero Rebellion (1926–1929), an armed conflict between church and state. The Articles sought to ban religious primary schools, prohibit the church from owning property, and to subordinate the church and clergy to the Mexican state. Devout Catholics, and those against the encroachment of a liberal state, in the western states of Mexico organized, protested, and eventually formed armed militias (Butler, 1999, 2004; Purnell, 1999; Young, 2012, 2015). As a member of *Union Popular* – a civic and religious organization based in Guadalajara that was connected to the National League for the Defense of Religious Liberty – and a resident of the small town of Zapotlanejo, Miguel Venegas was quickly engulfed in this conflict. He attended meetings, distributed propaganda at his general grocery store, and for a short period formed part of the armed insurgents. In an interview with María Teresa, Miguel narrated his growing involvement:

> The day before January six [1927], I went to meeting in Guadalajara and was told by Gomez Loza that I would not be returning home because he wanted me to lead them to Los Altos since I knew the area well … So we traveled that night and went as far as Paredones where we spend the cold night with nothing to protect us from the cold except what we had on. The next morning we went as far as el Cerro Gordo where we met the rest of the insurgents. (Venegas, 2012, p. 12)

There, in the hills of Los Altos, Miguel was charged with leading a group of armed followers, 'Well, each one carried his small pistol, his small knife, and rode his small horse. To defend religion, you know? … except that we never had an exchange of fire' (quoted in Venegas, 2012, p. 13). Back in Zapotlanejo, the local government closed down his general store, and froze his assets. To make matters worse, the Mexican state found a fervent supporter in Rosario Orozco, the local *cacique*. As the conflict intensified, Miguel had two viable options: wait and engage the state in armed conflict or migrate to the United States. While Miguel was a devout Catholic throughout his life, he did not want to be responsible for taking another human's life (Venegas, 2012).[6] Like most Catholics during this time period, he probably would have desired to defy the state through everyday actions instead of armed rebellion (Butler, 1999). The local context, however, forced Miguel into a much more staunch position. From camp, he sent word to Dolores and she and their four boys joined him. Together, they journeyed north to Aguascalientes where they decided that Dolores and the children would take a train to Guadalajara and Miguel would continue north, to the United States (Venegas, 2012, p. 8).

Miguel crossed through the port of El Paso, Texas on 17 May 1927 and proceeded west, to Los Angeles, California, where he waited for his family.[7] One month after his entrance into the United States, Dolores and their four boys visited a photography studio to attain passport photos and a family portrait. José Miguel, Ricardo, Guillermo, and Eduardo, who at the time were just seven, five, three, and one, dressed up for the occasion, with the two oldest boys wearing ties.[8] It was likely mailed to Miguel, the only absent member. The following September, Dolores, their four children, and Dolores' father Silviano journeyed north and joined Miguel in Los Angeles.

While Dolores and the four boys were reunited with Miguel, the Venegas family was separated from their kin: parents/grandparents, brothers/uncles, sisters/aunts, and nephews/cousins. Correspondences, handwritten letters and photographs, became their only way to maintain communication. While scholars working on European migration argue that men wrote more than women, writing for them and their children, this was not the case with the Venegas family. Dolores wrote regularly, and the children put pen to paper, but less frequently. Miguel mainly wrote to his father Juan Venegas and brother Francisco, while Dolores corresponded most frequently with her *comadre* Lupe and also wrote to her parents, Miguel's parents, and her brother-in-law Francisco.

The content of the letters reflects and carried out the gendered division of labor common among Mexican migrant families (Griswold del Castillo, 1984; Hondagneu-Sotelo, 1994). Correspondence, as I illustrate below, enabled this family to replicate the roles of each family member across the US–Mexico border. Male relatives in Mexico followed and provided feedback on the economic decisions of the Venegas family, while the women of the families tended to communicate about the household and children. Collectively, however, all family members in Mexico experienced migrant realities and longing and the growth of the children. The Venegas family, in turn, learned about the economic and political realities of their hometown and the health of those in Zapotlanejo. Gendered and semi-public, correspondence involved the labor of many of its members and was intended for the entire family.

The most common topics in Miguel's letters were related to the 'male sphere': labor, the economy, and politics. In October of 1927, just a few months after his arrival in Los Angeles, Miguel informed his father that he was considering purchasing a store for 1000 dollars.[9] He was motivated to start his own business by the lack of jobs and low wages.[10] Miguel had some reservations, mainly because of his inability to speak English, but someone assured him that speaking English was not necessary.[11] Since the father's response did not make it into the archive, it is not clear if he supported this decision. Miguel moved forward with this venture and bought the store on 26 November. Writing to his father, Miguel noted that on 22 December of that year he sold 40 dollars' worth of goods and on less fortunate days 18 or 20 dollars' worth. While Miguel operated the store, Dolores stayed at home.[12] According to Miguel, Dolores did not help in the store for a number of reasons: it was not attached to the house, as was the custom in many places in Mexico, she did not speak English, and needed to watch the '*muchachos*'.[13] However, Dolores was versed in the economic affairs of the family and in the winter of 1931, described the economic activities of the family store to her father-in-law, with a good degree of detail.[14] In a letter the following month, Juan Venegas, in turn, wrote to Dolores about his own business affairs.[15] Based on the family correspondence, however, Miguel made most of the business decisions.[16]

Miguel's letters also document the emotional and philosophical concerns of recent migrants. In the summer of 1928, he informed his brother that they were physically well, but that they 'dream every night of being over there'.[17] For Miguel and other migrants missing Mexico went hand in hand with comparing Mexico to the United States, which scholars like José Limón (1998) argue could produce a migrant nationalism outside both US and Mexican nationalism and what David Gerber (2006) refers to as 'existential accounting': weighing the costs and benefits of migration. Writing to Francisco, Miguel described this process: 'Little by little, one begins to compare things here and there, and without noticing it, to notice the differences that exist among other things, with respect to personal security and public services'.[18] According to Miguel, the major obstacle in the United States was to earn a living. Once this was taken care of it was not too difficult to provide for other necessities. Parents, Miguel argued, could select their children's education freely and live with a degree of comfort. Despite these benefits, Miguel poetically mused, 'you don't hear anyone say they are ok with leaving their bones here'.[19]

By the summer of 1929, the decision to return was now measured against the decision to stay, despite political changes in his hometown. Miguel expressed optimism in Mexico's future: 'ever since the situation began to change, those of us that are over here and have not forgotten about our patria, have been very happy'.[20] Weary of continued political instability he asked his father to tell him 'everything'.[21] As the fall arrived, Miguel's stance became more balanced and he expressed a degree of skepticism. Miguel's rhetorical question to his brother, 'Can I return soon to my country?' was followed by

> For my part I am seeing that it is not so easy to return after what we all know has happened, a lot of time needs to pass for so much hatred to disappear and for so many things to be forgotten.[22]

This sentence contains silences about the past and provides an ambiguous reason for the prolonged or indefinite return to Mexico: the time necessary for hatred to dissolve.

As the anniversary of his departure approached (4 January), Miguel continued to reflect on his motivation for migrating. 'Time has passed' he wrote to his father, 'and yet the reasons that many Mexicans abandoned our respective places have not.' 'Time,' Miguel noted, 'does not stop and as you say we have to look forward.' One of the last sentences in this letter eloquently combined Miguel's longing for Mexico and the possibility of never returning,

> May God grant us the opportunity to see each other, even if it is before death. And if not, let us plead to God that we may be reunited in Heaven, even if it is in a hidden corner, which I desire for everyone.[23]

Sharing these thoughts allowed the family in Mexico to understand and take part in this emotionally challenging and existential conversation. From Guadalajara, Juan Venegas and Francisco, like Miguel, could explore the advantages of staying in Los Angeles. In short, the process of migrating to the United States involved more than just those who were physically absent (McKeown, 1999).

Dolores also contemplated the family's return, but her letters are devoid of the soul-wrenching statements found in Miguel's letters. In their fieldwork and ethnography, Luin Goldring (1996) and Pierrette Hondagneu-Sotelo (1994) found that both nostalgia and the desire to return are gendered, with males consistently looking more favorably upon the latter. While it is difficult to deploy their analysis to Dolores and Miguel's view of settlement and return, it is clear that Dolores' correspondence lacks comparisons between Mexico and the United States, or discussions of Mexican politics. 'We are always with the desire to go to visit but the day does not arrive,' she wrote to Juan Venegas in February of 1932.[24] Yet, instead of relating this to a larger context, she followed this sentiment with the sentence: 'God only knows how long he will have us here.'[25] In a letter earlier that year, Dolores deployed a similar structure. After she wrote, 'last night I dreamt that I was over there' she asked, 'what do you say, will my dream come true?'[26] Instead of politics and the economy, Dolores' letters focused on daily routine, children, and health – things she, and women of her generation, were charged with upholding. This gendered division of labor in writing, a reflection of daily life in both Mexico and the United States, provided relatives in Mexico with a portrait of family life (Figure 1).

Though Dolores wrote more frequently about their children, both her and Miguel's letters allowed the extended family in Guadalajara to follow and experience the growth of José Miguel, Ricardo, Guillermo, Eduardo, and welcome new children, such as Juan in the summer of 1928 and María Teresa in November of 1930. In one letter, Dolores informed her father-in-law that Guillermo got eyeglasses because his 'vision was very weak' and he was unable

Figure 1. José Miguel (top left) Ricardo (top right) Guillermo (bottom left) and Eduardo (center), 1927. Venegas Family Papers, Collection 099, Department of Archives and Special Collections, William H. Hannon Library, Loyola Marymount University.

to 'focus his sight'.[27] These mundane details, of interest only to family members, were accompanied by more urgent news. In January of 1928, 'Miguelito' was hit by a car and dragged underneath it. Nothing was broken and it appears that it was no more than a '*bump*', but the image of their eight-year-old grandson and nephew being struck by a car was enough to rattle their nerves. 'My dad', Anita wrote to Dolores, 'cried.' For Anita this was the first and only time she saw her father shed tears. She joined him, moved by 'just thinking about the mortification that you went through'.[28] Together, in Mexico and Los Angeles, the family shared similar emotions and in doing so, provided support.

Dolores' letters also provided the extended kin with a glimpse into the personalities of the younger Venegas children. 'The one who I cannot keep up with', Dolores wrote to Julia Venegas 'is Juanito'. Since he was the fifth child, the uncles, aunts, and grandparents did not get a chance to witness Juanito walk or speak or interact with his siblings. He was not 'stubborn', but he was definitely a 'troublemaker'. On one occasion, Dolores narrated, he picked up a chair, took it to the stove, and with a knife took out a bean from a pot of cooking beans. The beans, Dolores wrote, 'did not even have salt', implying that they were not ready. The older boys, it appears, dealt with the brunt of their little brother's mischief. For example, when Juanito went after Eduardo with scissors, Eduardo's only defense was to say, 'No Juanito, no'. For further proof of their grandchild's playful nature, Dolores asked her relatives in Mexico to 'look closely [at the photo], his face says what he is'.[29] As the family grew, Dolores and Miguel introduced the family in Mexico to the new kin. The birth of María Teresa, in 1930, provides a good example. Writing to Juan Venegas, Dolores described their first girl as 'chubby', 'rosy-cheeked', and very 'cute'. She promised to send a photograph in the next few days. The images of Juanito and María Teresa were meant to affirm Dolores' description of them as a playful troublemaker and a gracious, adorable girl (Figure 2).

Dolores' description of her children points to the centrality of photographs in the family's correspondence. They were mailed along with letters and less frequently, but we should not conceptualize the visual as an additional or secondary element. Like handwritten letters, they were objects to be shared, held, and cherished (Campt, 2012).[30] If the text narrated the author's voice for the reader, the image provided the gift of sight, and together they aroused affect. Studio portraits, snapshots of the family in their front yards, family outings, which included visits to parks, a seminary in Compton, and even the beach, traveled south. These photographs reflect choices and, to quote Tina Campt (2012), 'express how ordinary individuals envisioned their sense of self, their subjectivity, and their social status; and as objects that capture and preserve those articulations in the present as well as for the future' (p. 7). In one of these images from 1928, for example, the parents, four boys and the new baby pose in their Sunday best. Dressed in a suit, tie, and wearing a hat, Miguel holds his fourth boy. To his right, in a dress with a coat, Dolores holds baby María Teresa. Addressed to Anita, the text on the back of the photograph reads, 'When you see this think that your brothers and nephews will never forget you.'[31] This photograph, as well as others, articulated migrant success and well-being in Los Angeles, but it also affirmed the family's desire to remain connected and committed to relatives in Mexico. For the Venegas family, economic success did not signal separation from their family in Mexico.

Photographs of Dolores, Miguel, and their children continued to flow south throughout the 1930s and 1940s. This included portraits of the boys as US servicemen, now young adults leaving their Los Angeles home to fight abroad. The family in Guadalajara was able to literally see the Venegas children become adolescents and young adults. In doing so, they likely spotted a familiar nose, eyes, and other facial features. The backdrop of these images allowed uncles, aunts, and grandparents to become familiar with parks, streets, and public spaces of Los Angeles.

Images created a transnational space in the various households of relatives in Mexico as well as the Venegas home in Los Angeles. Photographs of Miguel and Dolores' parents,

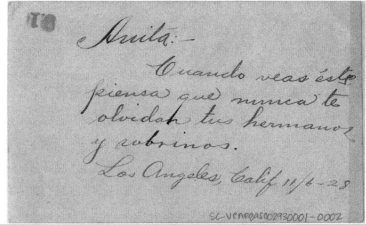

Figure 2. Venegas family at a park in Los Angeles, California, 1928. Venegas Family Papers, Collection 099, Department of Archives and Special Collections, William H. Hannon Library, Loyola Marymount University.

siblings and nephews were likely stored in photo albums and maybe even framed and hung around the house. While we have to conjecture about how the photographs were received and experienced in Mexico, the Venegas collection illustrates the role that visual images and the home played in the identity formation of the Venegas children. A portrait of Juan Venegas was particularly moving. '*Los muchachos*', according to Miguel, were happy to see this image and responded by remembering their time in Mexico. True to form, Dolores' writing expanded on the children's reaction: '[they] began to remember their time in Mexico and when they played with the *muchachos*. They remembered when we would visit the ranch and asked if the donkey and dog are still there.'[32] Dolores noted in jest that even Eduardo, who was only one year old when they left, recalled his time in Mexico (Figure 3).

A series of postcards added to the children's visual vocabulary of Zapotlanejo. Taken inside the church, one postcard captured the interior. On the bottom right and left of the image, two men pray, while in the center and foreground resides a painting of La Virgen de Guadalupe, a flag of Mexico to her right and left, and directly below her, two women praying.

Figure 3. Postcard of Zapotlanejo, Jalisco, Mexico. Venegas Family Papers, Collection 099, Department of Archives and Special Collections, William H. Hannon Library, Loyola Marymount University.

The composition guides the viewer through the image, moving one from the Virgin to her devotees. This pious image was accompanied by one image of the façade of the church and a street view.[33] Postcards of the Plaza de Zapotlanejo and of a street, dated 1934 and 1936 respectively, added to the children's knowledge of their parents' hometown.[34] Dolores and Miguel might have used these postcards to narrate stories about the family's departures, about their kin, and about daily life in their hometown.

As the years passed, photographs of weddings, new family members, and postcards continued to arrive. Far from Mexico, these images helped the Venegas children sustain visual images of home, to recall specific places, and of course, to learn about new places and their family members. Like their relatives in Mexico, they were able to see their cousins and uncles and aunts age.

The Venegas children participated in family correspondences in one additional manner: as authors and recipients. References to the children in the letters of Dolores and Miguel indicate that the children wrote to their family in Mexico throughout the 1930s and even into the 1940s. In a letter from 1937, Lupe asked Dolores to tell 'Richi' (short for Ricardo) that she was not able to write on his saint's day, but that she would write soon.[35] Two years later, Francisco asked Miguel to apologize to Ricardo and José Miguel for not writing.[36] The only letters from the children to their family in Mexico that survived are a set of correspondence that involved José Miguel from January 1928 to August 1931. While it is difficult to make claims about letter writing for all the Venegas children, José Miguel's correspondence further illustrates the relationship between extended kin and the formation of a transnational family. The oldest of the siblings, José Miguel left Mexico when he was approximately six or seven, old enough to have memories of his relatives and of Los Altos de Jalisco.

Almost all of José Miguel's letters expressed a desire to be with his extended family. In a letter from 1928 he noted how he missed his grandfather making toys for the boys.[37] While we do not have many of the responses from his uncles/aunts and grandparents, a letter dated 4 June 1931 from his uncle Francisco illustrates long-distance rearing. In this letter

Francisco asked José Miguel to view his various tasks as a grace from God and not as a burden. This labor, according to his uncle, would impart to José Miguel, at a very young age, a strong and serious character, 'clear conscience' and a noble and generous heart. These virtues, according to Francisco, would enable him to triumph over life's challenges. The uncle also told José Miguel to deposit in the 'tender hearts' of his siblings 'the fear of God' and to make them understand the 'sacred obligation' that they have to their parents. To make his point clear, he told José Miguel to think of the love that a mother has for her children, a love comparable to the love of Jesus Christ. According to his uncle, Jesus Christ died on the cross as mothers die for their children.[38]

2. Returning to Mexico

Letter writing was fundamental to the formation of a transnational family and was a strategy used to weather the Great Depression. Through correspondence family members in Mexico described the political and economic climate and gave Miguel advice. For historians, these letters also demonstrate the multiple ways in which the Venegas deployed their resources in Mexico and in the United States, which included the labor of the Venegas children.

In the late 1920s and 1930s, the Great Depression provoked the repatriation of Mexicans throughout the United States. While there were a few efforts by US officials to deport Mexicans, repatriation was mainly a mixture of voluntary and coerced return, with US and Mexican government collaboration and the support of Mexican mutual aid organizations. US-based scholars working on repatriation emphasize the state's desire to deport and return Mexican migrant families to Mexico, and the hardship that these families experienced (Balderrama & Rodríguez, 2006; Guerin-Gonzales, 1994; Hoffman, 1974). This civil rights framework, according to Benny J. Andrés Jr, has 'straitjacketed American scholars', and in the process overlooked migrant desires and agency (Andrés, 2011). Scholars working in Mexico focus on the Mexican state's discourse and policy (Alanís Enciso, 2005, 2007; Carreras de Velasco, 1974.) Both US and Mexican historians of repatriation note the prominence of families during repatriation, but do not use the family or transnationalism as categories of analysis. Migrant correspondences demonstrate that the nuclear and extended family provided key resources for weathering this challenging time. Below, I highlight the role of letter writing, the agency of the Venegas children, lending of financial resources by extended family in Guadalajara, the labor of the oldest boys, and temporary separation.

By March of 1930, the Venegas family felt the effects of the depression. Miguel noted that there was very little work, which had a direct impact on the sales of the store. Since many transactions were done through credit, clients were unable to settle their accounts.[39] According to Miguel, work was scarce even for the 'sons of this country'.[40] Indeed, when he went downtown Americans asked him for money. In February of the following year, he noted that he received a bad check for the amount of 60 dollars, a significant amount of money at the time.[41] To make matters worse, the general hostility towards Mexicans added to the lack of employment opportunities. In the same month, Miguel informed his father that detectives searched for illegal Mexicans to deport. This produced fear among the entire Mexican population, including those with visas, like the Venegas family. While we know from the secondary literature that this effort was short lived, it clearly had its intended effect.

Throughout the Great Depression Miguel Venegas kept his father abreast of the crisis and more importantly asked him for advice. Like migration to the United States, transnational ties supported movement to Mexico. Before migrating, north or south, individuals consulted with those they knew. This was the case with Miguel and his father. At the outset of 1931, Miguel heard of an opportunity to acquire land in newly irrigated lands in Baja California. He was under the impression that this was a public venture by the Mexican government and at the time he considered agriculture a safe bet.[42] A month later, he told his father that the venture was private and not public and that representatives of the project had yet to come to Los Angeles. These new developments did not discourage Miguel. Indeed, Miguel suggested to his father that, if he deemed the project serious, they could meet in Tijuana and travel together to look at the land. Miguel also invited his father to spend a few days in Los Angeles.[43] We do not know the father's response, but this proposition's absence from letters written shortly after indicates that Miguel decided against the idea, likely in accord with his father's advice.

As the summer arrived, another transnational possibility presented itself. Trino Alvarez, a Los Angeles resident and godson of Juan Venegas, offered to trade properties. In exchange for two homes, Miguel would give Trino a *terreno*, a plot of rural agricultural land in Mexico. Since the Alvarez family was familiar with this terreno and Miguel was in Los Angeles, both parties would have known the properties under consideration. Moreover, Trino's brother wanted to return to Mexico and Trino himself would return if he ran out of work.[44] Ultimately, Miguel told his father that he decided not to trade the properties. Trino owed too much on each house and Miguel feared that with so many Mexicans returning to Mexico it would have been difficult to rent the homes.[45] Miguel also considered opening up a bakery in Mexico, but this appeared in Dolores' and not Miguel's letter.[46] While Dolores' correspondences do not propose transnational land ventures, they nevertheless served a similar function. In a letter to her father-in-law, she noted that their *compadre* José and his entire family left for the capital of Mexico. José informed Miguel and Dolores that every day things were getting worse and that they should not return to Mexico.

Even though it is doubtful that the children of migrants had an active role in the decision-making process, they nonetheless played a prominent role during the Great Depression.[47] In 1931, José Miguel, at the time 11 years old, and Ricardo, the second oldest, opened a savings account and accumulated 32 dollars and five cents and 20 dollars and five cents respectively. They earned this money by helping their father around the house. The savings, José Miguel told one of his uncles, would be used to buy a Ford coach car or to purchase tickets on the Pullman train.[48] As 1931 progressed José Miguel's efforts to save his allowance did not suffice. While teaching their son the value of money remained important, they needed extra income. By selling newspapers he was able to add three dollars and 50 cents to the family's weekly income.[49] This quotidian labor reflected a larger, more significant contribution: a positive disposition towards returning to Mexico. This was no small feat. Writing during this time period, Manuel Gamio and Emory Bogardus found that children of migrants did not wish to return to their parents' ancestral lands (cited in Hondagneu-Sotelo, 1994, p. 215).

In the spring of 1932, Miguel took a quick trip to Zapotlanejo to evaluate local conditions.[50] He decided that they should remain in Los Angeles, but the family did move back to Mexico from 1940 to 1942. This time, José Miguel, Ricardo, and Guillermo, along with the family in Mexico, played a prominent role. Before their departure, Miguel corresponded with Francisco and Agustin Venegas, who were both businessmen. In the summer of 1939, Francisco informed his brother that a bus company with service from Guadalajara to Morelia, Michoacán was looking for investors. But, he wrote, 'if you want to give commerce a shot, when you arrive we can see what would be advantageous. You know you can count on us.'[51] A year after this correspondence, Miguel, Dolores, Eduardo, Juan José, María Teresa, Alfonso, and a one-year-old Enrique, left for Mexico. José Miguel, Ricardo, and Guillermo, the three oldest brothers, stayed in Los Angeles to run the store. Youth labor, Vicki Ruiz demonstrates, contributed to the income of migrant families in mid-twentieth-century Los Angeles (Ruiz, 1987). With the Venegas family, the family income took on a transnational dimension. With help from Francisco, Miguel opened and operated a *cristalería* (glassware shop) in Guadalajara (personal communication with Carlos and María Teresa Venegas, 26 January 2015).

With two incomes and two homes, the Venegas family began their effort at transnational living. In Guadalajara, the children attended school and Dolores ran the household and watched Eduardo. On 4 October 1940, nine-year-old María Teresa briefly narrated her time in Mexico to her older brother Ricardo,

> I could not write because I did not know how to in Spanish, but now I can because I am going to Catholic school and I am studying Spanish. I know how to read and write. I think we are going to stay in Mexico and I am very eager to see you guys.[52]

Writing to his older brother Guillermo, Juan expressed excitement over the 16th of September, which 'is like the 4th of July over there', and the family's trip to Morelia.[53] While the children adjusted well to life in Mexico, both of the businesses struggled. The glassworks store in Guadalajara was not profitable and the boys mismanaged the store in Los Angeles. Miguel headed back to Los Angeles, followed by the rest of the family in the summer of 1942 (personal communication with Carlos and María Teresa Venegas, 26 January 2015).

3. The Venegas children and Mexico

In his letters, Miguel expressed a desire to send his children south.[54] Miguel, like many of the migrants interviewed by Manuel Gamio in the late 1920s, wanted his children to know and visit Mexico. In one correspondence, he invited his father to come to Los Angeles and insisted that upon his return to Zapotlanejo one of the boys could accompany him and that he could either send him back or have him stay and receive an education in Mexico. For Miguel, both of these options could serve to encourage the Venegas boys and the entire Venegas family to return to Mexico. He wanted his children, especially those born in the United States, to receive an education 'a la Mexicana'.[55] A similar sentiment is found in José Miguel's letters. For example, when the family considered returning to Mexico in the early 1930s José Miguel expressed frustration with what he believed was his parents' indecision: he told his uncle that his parents only talked of going back to Mexico and that time passed like 'water'.[56] He also noted that he would like to attend a seminary, either in the US or in Mexico.[57]

The Venegas children, especially the younger ones, learned about Mexico and their uncles, aunts, and grandparents, through photographs and letters. While some of the family lived in Mexico during the Great Depression, José Miguel, Enrique, Eduardo, and María Teresa spent additional time in Mexico and under drastically different circumstances. As children of Mexican migrants who came of age in the early-to-mid twentieth century, the Venegas children formed part of the 'Mexican American generation'. Because this cohort was composed predominately of United States citizens, Chicano/a scholars have emphasized their commitment to US civil rights and first class citizenship. 'Mexican Americans', claims Mario García, 'expected more from American life than immigrants. For "Mexican Americans", there was no going back to Mexico' (García, 1991, p. 15).[58] Whether it was a trip to explore moving to Mexico, a temporary stay, absconding from World War II, or doctoral research, visiting and living in Mexico was an important experience for the Venegas children. Their relationship with and sentiment towards Mexico challenge linear interpretations of 'Mexican American' identity.

In July of 1938, José Miguel traveled south to consider joining the seminary. He stayed at his grandparents' house in Zapotlanejo, and visited his uncles and aunts in the city of Guadalajara. In early September, he headed to Mexico City to participate in 'El Grito de Independencia' and a religious procession to the 'Basilica'. According to José Miguel, the parade included about 3000 people chanting 'viva a la virgen morenita' and 'viva a cristo rey', albeit in an orderly fashion. The parade left a particularly strong impression on him. In a letter to his father, he wrote: 'If you would have seen all the enthusiasm that was manifested in all the acts of the gathering, there were times of immense happiness and at the same time sentiments that almost made me cry.' On their journey back to Guadalajara, they stopped at la Isla de Janitzio del Lago de Patzcuaro in Michoacán to see the recently erected monument for Independence leader José María Morelos.[59] The adventure continued upon his arrival. He jokingly informed his father that he was not drinking a lot of water and that surely he was exempt from the negative effects of drinking alcohol.[60] Through these correspondences we also learn that he had a girlfriend, which, according to a young and boastful José Miguel, was unavoidable.

During his five-month visit, José Miguel contemplated staying in Guadalajara. 'Oh mom,' he wrote, 'if you could see how happy I am! So much that I do not have any desire to return: but I do want to see all of you.' Relatives and friends frequently suggested that he make Mexico his permanent home and asked him if the entire Venegas family planned to return to 'their patria'. In a letter to his father, he provided his answer to friends and relatives: 'It was not for lack of desire and if it was not for many reasons they would already be here among our family.'[61] While he was tempted to stay, he felt his place was in Los Angeles.

As the probing questions about staying implied, traveling and remaining in Mexico involved more than just the Venegas children and their parents. Enrique's time in Mexico in the summer of 1943 and a letter from Lupe to Dolores in December of the same year, in anticipation of Miguel's visit, demonstrate the role of these trips in sustaining emotional ties across the US–Mexico border as well as desire and longing for reunification. Most importantly, Lupe's words and emotions served to communicate an open invitation.

In the summer of 1943, a four-year-old Enrique spent some time alone with his aunt Lupe and uncle Francisco in Guadalajara. During his visit, as we might expect, Francisco wrote to Miguel while Lupe corresponded with Dolores. These sets of correspondences, especially Lupe's letters, demonstrate the importance of these visits for family in Mexico. As other letters, they are filled with mundane details, which would be of interest to any parent, but not necessarily to most historians. Enrique, we learn, enjoyed drinking coconut water and Coca-Cola and insisted on wearing clean clothes for fear of 'what the people might say'.[62] He fell ill, but proved to be a good patient as he 'graciously' asked his aunt Lupe to 'cure him so his mucus will come out'.[63] 'El gordo', as Lupe affectionately referred to him, insisted on drinking Coca-Cola at 'room temperature or hot' and told the doctor that he should be given, 'refried beans with panela and tortilla'.[64] The doctor, Lupe wrote to Dolores, laughed, most likely as a result of Enrique's pronunciation: beans is spelled 'filos' instead of 'frijoles'. To accompany these updates, Francisco mailed, as was customary, photos of Enrique.[65]

These details added up to a valuable and emotional experience for Lupe and Francisco. 'If we loved him a lot before,' Francisco began, 'now that we have shared time with him, it is as if he is our own.'[66] Contemplating Enrique's return, Francisco anticipated that they would 'suffer a lot.'[67] Enrique's presence created place-specific memories throughout their household, which in his absence were deeply felt: 'sometimes we don't want to be here because everything reminds us of him'.[68] This trip and 'el gordo's' antics would likely be retold throughout the years and form part of the family's folklore.

A few months later, Lupe began writing a letter to Dolores, her 'comadrita'. Written over three sessions, which included 16 December 1943, 3 January and 3 February of the following year, Lupe wrote, according to her husband, like a 'machine'. The lack of commas and periods might be distracting for contemporary readers. However, this punctuation approximated her speech patterns. In describing the anticipation experienced by the expected arrival of Miguel, her words provide a visual portrait of longing,

> when we hear the trains we want them to be from Nogales [,] the cars that arrive here we think they are coming on the highway [,] when the plane passes we think that any moment he will arrive and nothing.[69]

Every mode of transportation was imagined as a possible means of arrival until the family received confirmation from Trino that Miguel would arrive on a particular night and by train. Lupe and Francisco planned to eat dinner, watch a movie, and then head to the train station, until they heard it would arrive the following morning. Disheartened, they skipped the film and opted to head home, drink milk with coffee and go to sleep. The following morning they headed out to the train station one more time. As the passengers exited, they spotted a waving arm attached to a green-bluish sleeve like that of Miguel's suit only to be disappointed. As they waited, Lupe even imagined that her 'dear gordo' would arrive. This frustration was tinted with a bit of despair and playful drama, 'Why did you have children and why did I meet you [,] better if I had never met you.'[70] This letter assured the family that the doors of their house would also be wide open (Figure 4).

The possibility of one of the Venegas boys living with Lupe and Francisco became a reality with the United States' entry into World War II. José Miguel, Ricardo, and Guillermo formed part of the 15,000 Mexican nationals and 380,000 Latinos/as that joined the war effort (Zamora, 2009).[71] Through an agreement between the US and Mexican governments, signed

Figure 4. Pictured from left to right, Ricardo, José Miguel, and Guillermo. Venegas Family Papers, Collection 099, Department of Archives and Special Collections, William H. Hannon Library, Loyola Marymount University.

on 22 January 1943, the United States granted citizenship to Mexican nationals who served in the armed forces. Working with a sample of surveys conducted by the Mexican government, Emilio Zamora provides a portrait of Mexican nationals from Texas: the majority (58.8%) migrated between 1916 and 1926 and arrived in the United States as young children (the average age was 3.9). He postulates that they were 'more socially and culturally similar to US born Mexicans' and most importantly that they might have been motivated by the possibility of gaining US citizenship (Zamora, 2009, p. 99). José Miguel, Ricardo, and Guillermo fit this general description. The two oldest brothers enlisted in December of 1942 and Ricardo petitioned for US citizenship in Tampa, Florida, on 12 March 1943 just seven weeks after the US–Mexico agreement.[72] Family correspondence, however, adds an important transnational dimension to historical narratives of World War II veterans, Mexican migrant families, and citizenship.

'God' Lupe wrote to Dolores when the two oldest boys joined, 'will take care of them … don't stop asking the Virgen de Guadalupe to take care of them and tell Alicia [José Miguel's new wife] to ask the dark skinned [Virgen] from Tepeyac to bring her husband back safe and sound.'[73] In Mexico, Lupe noted, the extended family was saddened by the subsequent departure of a third member of the Venegas household. Again, Lupe hoped that the 'Virgin de Guadalupe would bring him back to us healthy and soon.'[74] Through letter writing the entire kin followed the Venegas boys into World War II. The three boys wrote to each other, to Dolores and Miguel, to their aunt Lupe and uncle Francisco, and to their grandfather Juan Venegas. Unfortunately, of all the letters from the boys, only one survived. Addressed to 'Querida Mami', and dated 9 December 1943, Ricardo notified her that he received her letter and one from 'mi papi'. 'Do you know him?' Ricardo playfully asked his mother. 'Yesterday,' he wrote, 'I received a letter from Miguel.' In this letter, Miguel informed Ricardo that he was now in Washington and would be in Utah in a few days. He promised to send a photograph of his son, 'Ricardito', whom he described as 'very curious'. 'Here,' Ricardo wrote to his mother, 'it is getting really cold, it always snows. Mom, have a good night, with this cold, it makes me want to go "mimi" very early.'[75] Letter writing would prove to provide more than news and updates.

As Eduardo's eighteenth birthday (10 May 1944) approached, the family was confronted with the possibility of sending a fourth family member into the service. 'The uncles [Lupe and Francisco] in Mexico', María Teresa recalled in a recent interview, 'wanted him badly. They don't have children … they said they would educate him and on and on' (personal communication with Carlos and María Teresa Venegas, 26 January 2015).[76] Miguel, Dolores and Eduardo, likely in consultation with Lupe and Francisco, decided that he should go to familiar instead of foreign lands. Born in Mexico, but raised in the United States, Eduardo was as 'Mexican American' and 'Mexican' as his three older brothers. Leaving for Mexico was based not on his location on a spectrum of 'Americanness' but on the particular context of one family. Joined by his father and José Miguel's wife, Eduardo arrived in Guadalajara in early May.[77] While Lupe wrote that he was 'very happy', Eduardo tried to re-enter the United States on 5 October 1945, just one month after the official end of World War II. He was denied entry on the ground of 'evasion' and returned to Guadalajara.[78]

While not many of his letters survived, the two letters that did along with the numerous letters from Lupe to Dolores allow us to reconstruct his adjustment to life in Mexico. In 1948, four years after his arrival, Lupe enthusiastically reported that he was recovering from his operation and sickness. His 'color' and his appetite returned. 'But', she warned Dolores,

Eduardo was 'in love' and 'without a cure'.[79] On 4 April 1948, the same year, Eduardo was married to María Refugio Partida in Guadalajara in the presence of their kin and even his parents.[80] Their first boy, whom they named Eduardo, was born in the summer of 1949. Writing to Miguel, Juan Venegas described the boy as 'healthy and very fat' and noted that he looked 'nothing like the Venegas'.[81] The family of three expanded to four in the spring of 1950 with the birth of Dolores. Unlike the boy, this 'little niñita … looks like the Venegas family'.[82] She was small, 'bonita', and 'light-skinned like Lalo'.[83] Eduardo and María had three more children in Guadalajara, Francisco Javier (named after uncle Francisco) in 1951, María Refugio in 1952, and an additional María, María Guadalupe, in 1954 (Figure 5).

Eduardo supported his growing family by deploying business skills he acquired in the family store and linguistic knowledge learned in US schools. The family-run Venegas store exposed him to the buying and selling of goods, which required careful observation of the market, book-keeping, and developing strong relationships with clients. All of these things proved instrumental to running the shoe section of his uncle Francisco's department store. Mirroring his father's initiative, he looked into additional money-making ventures. In August of 1949, he took courses at the American Consulate in Guadalajara to teach English language courses. Teachers, Eduardo informed his father, earned 10 dollars per hour. Raised in Los Angeles, Eduardo was likely more proficient in English than most Guadalajara residents. He planned to work half a day as a teacher and the other half doing wholesale. 'I want to do both in case one fails', he wrote to Miguel.[84] Just a few months after Eduardo wrote to his father the prospect of failure was on the horizon. 'Here,' Eduardo informed his father,

> things have gotten a little ugly, well since about three months, the question of the shoe has been a bit difficult … it's hard to find leather, because a Mr Pasque is exporting all of it to the United States and the little that remains here is very bad and expensive.[85]

Figure 5. Eduardo sitting at his desk. Date unknown, likely mid-1940s. Venegas Family Papers, Collection 099, Department of Archives and Special Collections, William H. Hannon Library, Loyola Marymount University.

Eduardo was unable to meet his customers' demands and his sales were cut in half. Fortunately, he was earning approximately 325.00 dollars a month from teaching English classes. While Eduardo anticipated that things would improve in two to three months, his English language skills were key to his family's sustenance.

After living in Mexico for a decade, Eduardo and his five Mexican-born children and wife attempted to return to Los Angeles. They relied, as we might expect, on their family. His five children and wife crossed first and arrived at Miguel and Dolores' house, while Eduardo relocated to Tijuana. The most important source of support came from the three oldest Venegas children. Armed with US citizenship and the pride and entitlement that came from fighting overseas, Mexicans fought for first class citizenship (Rivas-Rodriguez & Olguín, 2014).[86] In Texas, the Mexican government and organizations and individuals on both sides of the US–Mexico border sought to secure the passage of civil rights legislation in 1941, 1943, and 1945 (Guglielmo, 2006). And, with varying results, Mexican veterans sought to take advantage of the various privileges granted through the GI Bill (Rosales, 2011; Rodríguez, Heilig, & Prochnow, 2014). For the Venegas brothers, first class citizenship encompassed the inclusion of their younger brother into the US nation. They embodied, to quote Ramón Saldívar, a 'transcultural Mexican American social imaginary' (Saldívar, 2006, p. 37). Reflecting on Eduardo's time in Guadalajara, María Teresa Venegas recounted how the three World War II veterans, now citizens, interceded on Eduardo's behalf and successfully secured his re-entry (personal communication with Carlos and María Teresa Venegas, 26 January 2015).[87] The family was at the center of Eduardo's departure to and settlement in Mexico and eventual return to the United States: neither evading the draft nor returning to the US would have been possible without his family.[88]

During the 1950s, 1960s, and 1970s, the Venegas children became established in their respective professional paths and had children of their own. For Dolores and Miguel, this created an incentive to stay in the United States as well as the freedom to travel more frequently to Mexico. Returning to Mexico of course is a gendered process, with males looking favorably upon return and mothers desiring to stay for a number of reasons including proximity to their children, more egalitarian gender relations, and the availability of time-saving technology (Goldring, 1996; Hondagneu-Sotelo, 1994). There is some evidence that Dolores played a role in this decision. First, they did not move back permanently, but split their time between Los Angeles and Zapotlanejo. Based on recent studies, this arrangement reflects the desires of both male and female migrants. Second, their new home in Zapotlanejo was an old colonial building inherited by Dolores.

Always the savvy businessman, Miguel converted part of the colonial house into a three-story complex. The first level housed stores, the second functioned as an apartment, and the third level housed the Venegas couple. On the roof, they created a self-contained studio, which included its own shower. For three months in 1973, it was the home of a 42-year-old María Teresa, then a PhD Candidate at UCLA. She conducted interviews with the town's residents and made its folklore the subject of her dissertation, 'Local Legends in a Changing Society' (1975). This was a powerful experience for the child of Mexican migrants and the first doctor in her family. 'I am standing up at the top,' she fondly remembered during our conversation, 'and here I am, a PhD Candidate, standing and looking down and saying, "had mom and dad not left this town, who would I be today?"' (personal communication with Carlos and María Teresa Venegas, 26 January 2015). Her time in Zapotlanejo was paved as much by her parents' migration north as by the movement of letters, photographs, and

Venegas family members to Mexico over a 40-year period. If the Venegas family had not formed a transnational family, María Teresa might not have studied Zapotlanejo or preserved and archived her family's correspondence.

4. Conclusion

The Venegas Family Papers provide us with a unique opportunity to situate the first Mexican migrant families of the twentieth century within a transnational framework. By using correspondence to replicate familial roles, the Venegas formed a transnational family. Miguel corresponded most with his brother and father and focused on business decisions, the economy and politics of Mexico, and staying or returning to Mexico. Dolores, on the other hand, wrote most about the daily routine and the Venegas children. Through this labor, they remained connected and committed to their family in Mexico. While the children did not write as often, they were the subject and objects of many letters. For example, the letters and photographs that flowed north from Jalisco, Mexico allowed the children to learn about their uncles, aunts, grandparents, and their parents' hometown. For José Miguel, correspondence served an additional purpose. Francisco imparted to his young nephew advice on how to become a good son and older brother. Letters and photographs that traveled south allowed relatives in Mexico to experience the Venegas children growing and to learn about new family members. In short, correspondence helped bind family members across the US–Mexico border.

   This collection of letters also allows us to reconstruct the Venegas' transnational strategies to navigate the Great Depression and World War II. The family, I demonstrate, played a central role in navigating these two watershed moments. In both instances, the formation of a transnational family proved to be instrumental. During the economic crisis, Juan and Francisco provided Miguel and Dolores with advice and most importantly the financial resources for the Venegas family to return to Mexico in 1940. The close connection between the Venegas children and relatives in Mexico also enabled the family to send Eduardo to Mexico in order to avoid joining the armed services. The Venegas children were active and contributing members at both of these moments. José Miguel and Ricardo contributed funds to the family's income in the early 1930s and from 1940 to 1942, they, along with Guillermo, took care of the family home and business in Los Angeles. In the 1950s, as veterans of World War II, the Venegas children aided their younger brother Eduardo and his new family in their return to the United States.

   The Venegas children's experiences and identities challenge Chicano/a historians' view of the 'Mexican American' generation. By situating them transnationally, it becomes clear that growing up in the United States to migrant parents connected them to both Mexico and the United States. The Venegas children could become Mexican in the United States and 'Mexican American' in Mexico, and both in the spaces in between (Alamillo, 2010). All of the children spent some time in Mexico. José Miguel considered joining the seminary, while Eduardo moved back to Mexico and formed a family. While in Mexico, Eduardo used skills that he learned in the United States, including mastery of the English language, to provide for his wife and Mexican-born children. For María Teresa, her family's history inspired her doctoral research and led to the preservation of her family's letters and photographs, among other items. Rather than seeming a foreign country, Mexico was an important place for these children, even if they all ended up living in the United States.

This portrait of a migrant family pushes against scholarship that posits a linear narrative of migration, settlement, and incorporation. Indeed, this form of transnationalism resonates with scholarship by sociologists, anthropologists, and political scientists on contemporary migrants. Flexible families, transnational parenting, identity formation among the second generation, the agency of children and youth, transnational living, and financial remittances are all well documented. Ethnography and participant observation in the sending and receiving country allow these scholars to literally follow their subjects across borders. Migrant correspondences cannot replicate these methodologies, but they provide historians with sources to construct migrant strategies, sentiments, and daily life. They also allow scholars to follow migrants as they move between Mexico and the United States, to include family members that did not migrate, and to situate families in their homes, wherever they may be.

Archival sources

Department of Archives and Special Collections, William H. Hannon Library, Loyola Marymount University, Venegas Family Papers, Collection 099.

Online database

www.ancestry.com

Notes

1. Letters cited were translated by the author and are from the Venegas Family Papers, Collection 099, Department of Archives and Special Collections, William H. Hannon Library, Loyola Marymount University. Hereafter cited as VFP. This article also relies on the unpublished book by María Teresa Venegas and personal communication with the Venegas family.
2. Scholars of European migration often grapple with the representative nature of migrant correspondences and reference the lack of research on the founding of collections and archives, but only as it relates to Europeans. For a study on donors of migrant letters in Germany see Helbich and Kamphoefner (2006). There is only one edited collection of Mexican and Central American letters. See Siems (1992).
3. Donna R. Gabaccia notes that immigration historians criticized this paradigm (Gabaccia, 1999). Nonetheless, it was the rise of ethnic studies that resulted in the study of Mexican and Asian migrants, particularly the intersections of race, citizenship, nation, and empire. For more on the immigrant paradigm and immigration see also Gabaccia (1998). In a recent article, Adam Goodman proposes that scholars frame United States history around a 'migration' instead of 'immigration' paradigm, in order to include the histories of non-European groups as well as African-Americans and Native Americans (Goodman, 2015).
4. This collection, Ana Rosas' recent monograph (2014), Vargas' ethnography (2006), and Miroslava Chávez-García's current research project 'Migrant Longing and Letter Writing across the Borderlands', based on her family's letters from the 1960s, are a reminder to historians of Mexican migration of the thousands of personal archives stored in homes in Mexico and the United States.
5. While early works on the 'Mexican American' generation situate this cohort within the US nation, there is a growing body of work that seeks to place this generation in a transnational content. See José M. Alamillo (2010), Ramón Saldívar (2006), Edward Telles and Vilma Ortiz (Telles & Ortiz, 2008), Jessica M. Vasquez (2001). The first wave of scholarship about Mexican migrant families during the 1940s to the 1960s evaluated migrant families by their distance from the Anglo

family models. This simple and subjective view of the family, especially the characterization of machismo and patriarchy, was criticized sharply by Chicano/a academics in the following decades. See Ybarra (1983). In his early work on migrant families, Richard Griswold del Castillo traces family relations and patterns, gender roles and labor across the twentieth century, but continued to examine migrant families within a US framework (Griswold del Castillo, 1984).

6. This sentiment is expressed in his conversation with José Jauregui, 'But the idea of killing, no! Organizers, yes …' (Venegas, 2012, p. 13).
7. VFP. Box 6. Miguel Venegas Head Tax.
8. VFP. Box 14. Note made by María Teresa Venegas.
9. VFP. Box 1. Miguel (3 October 1927). [Letter to Juan Venegas].
10. VFP. Box 1. Miguel (25 November 1927). [Letter to Juan Venegas].
11. VFP. Box 1. Miguel (3 October 1927). [Letter to Juan Venegas].
12. VFP. Box 1. Miguel (22 December 1927). [Letter to Juan Venegas].
13. VFP. Box 1. Miguel (22 December 1927). [Letter to Juan Venegas].
14. Moreover, in later years she did help in the store. VFP. Box 1. Dolores (22 December 1931). [Letter to Juan Venegas].
15. VFP. Box 1. Juan (28 January 1932). [Letter to Dolores Venegas].
16. VFP. Box 1. Dolores (11 February 1932). [Letter to Juan Venegas].
17. VFP. Box 1. Miguel (12 June 1928). [Letter to Francisco Venegas].
18. VFP. Box 1. Miguel to (12 June 1928). [Letter to Francisco Venegas].
19. Adrián Félix's work on the 'political life cycle' of contemporary Mexican migrants documents the practice of postmortem repatriation (Félix, 2011).
20. VFP. Box 1. Miguel (17 July 1929). [Letter to Juan Venegas].
21. VFP. Box 1. Miguel (17 July 1929). [Letter to Juan Venegas].
22. VFP. Box 1. Miguel (31 October 1929). [Letter to Francisco Venegas].
23. VFP. Box 1. Miguel (1 January 1930). [Letter to Juan Venegas].
24. VFP. Box 1. Dolores (11 February 1932). [Letter to Juan Venegas].
25. VFP. Box 1. Dolores (11 February 1932). [Letter to Juan Venegas].
26. VFP. Box 1. Dolores (1 January 1932). [Letter to Juan Venegas].
27. VFP. Box 1. Dolores (22 December 1931). [Letter to Juan Venegas].
28. VFP. Box 2. Anita (3 March 1928). [Letter to Dolores Venegas].
29. VFP. Box 1. Dolores (13 April 1930). [Letter to Julia Venegas].
30. These photographs, like the content of the letters, were intended for the entire family. For example, in 1929 Francisco mailed a portrait and addressed it 'to my beloved brothers and nephews'.
31. VFP. Box 10.
32. VFP. Box 1. Dolores (22 December 1931). [Letter to Juan Venegas].
33. VFP. Box 10.
34. VFP. Box 10.
35. VFP. Box 2. Lupe (February 1937. Day not specified). [Letter to Dolores].
36. VFP. Box 2. Francisco (29 August 1939). [Letter to Miguel].
37. VFP. Box 2. José Miguel (26 January 1928). [Letter to Julia Venegas].
38. VFP. Box 2. Francisco (4 June 1931). [Letter to José Miguel].
39. VFP. Miguel (6 March 1930). [Letter to Juan Venegas].
40. VFP. Miguel (29 January 1931). [Letter to Juan Venegas].
41. VFP. Box 1. Miguel (14 March 1931). [Letter to Juan Venegas].
42. VFP. Box 1. Miguel (17 February 1931). [Letter to Juan Venegas].
43. VFP. Box 1. Miguel (10 April 1931). [Letter to Juan Venegas].
44. VFP. Box 1. Miguel (24 June 1931). [Letter to Juan Venegas].
45. VFP. Box 1. Miguel (21 September 1931). [Letter to Juan Venegas].
46. VFP. Box 1. Miguel (11 February 1932). [Letter to Juan Venegas].
47. Scholars working on more contemporary migrant families emphasize the agency of migrant children and youth. Marjorie Faulstich Orellana, for example, examines their role as linguistic and cultural brokers (Orellana, 2009).

48. VFP. Box 2. José Miguel (23 March 1931). [Letter to Ignacio Venegas].
49. VFP. Box 2. José Miguel (23 March 1931). [Letter to Ignacio Venegas].
50. VFP. Box 1. Miguel (22 April 1932). [Letter to Juan Venegas].
51. VFP. Box 2. Francisco (29 August 1939). [Letter to Miguel].
52. VFP. Box 16. María Teresa (4 October 1940). [Letter to Ricardo Venegas].
53. VFP. Box 2. Juan (4 October 1940). [Letter to Guillermo Venegas].
54. For example, in a letter to his father, Miguel wrote about a prank they played on Guillermo. After they told Guillermo they were going to send him to Mexico, he got dressed and packed his bags, only to be disappointed when his parents informed him it was not true. VFP. Box 1. Miguel (1 January 1930). [Letter to Juan Venegas].
55. VFP. Box 1. Miguel (10 April 1931). [Letter to Juan Venegas].
56. VFP. Box 2. José Miguel (24 March 1931). [Letter to Francisco Venegas].
57. VFP. Box 2. José Miguel (1 August 1931). [Letter to Guadalupe Venegas].
58. See Alamillo (2010).
59. VFP. Box 1. José Miguel (22 September 1938). [Letter to Miguel Venegas].
60. VFP. Box 1. José Miguel (4 November 1938). [Letter to Miguel Venegas].
61. VFP. Box 1. José Miguel (17 August 1938). [Letter to Miguel Venegas]. As we might expect, the letters between José Miguel and his siblings and parents were filled with request for photographs: José Miguel wanted to see his siblings, especially the younger ones, and of course his relatives in Mexico wanted to see all of the Venegas children. The photographs and content of the letters were likely shared with all of the Venegas children.
62. VFP. Box 2. Francisco (2 June 1943). [Letter to Miguel Venegas]; VFP. Box 2. Lupe (17 September 1943). [Letter to Dolores Venegas].
63. VFP. Box 2. Lupe (17 September 1943). [Letter to Dolores Venegas].
64. VFP. Box 2. Lupe (16 December 1943). [Letter to Dolores Venegas].
65. VFP. Box 2. Francisco (2 June 1943 and 12 July 1943). [Letter to Miguel Venegas].
66. VFP. Box 2. Francisco (12 July 1943). [Letter to Miguel Venegas].
67. VFP. Box 2. Francisco (12 July 1943). [Letter to Miguel Venegas].
68. VFP. Box 2. Lupe (17 September 1943). [Letter to Dolores Venegas].
69. VFP. Box 2. Lupe (16 December 1943). [Letter to Dolores Venegas].
70. VFP. Box 2. Lupe (16 December 1943). [Letter to Dolores].
71. For a discussion on the challenge of tabulating the participation of Latinas and Latinos in World War II see Rivas-Rodriguez and Olguín (2014).
72. Enlistment record for José Miguel and Ricardo's petition for naturalization, retrieved 10 February 2015, from Ancestry.com. Original documents from Records of the National Archives and Records Administration Record Group 84, World War II Army Enlistment Records and Florida, Naturalization Records, 1847–1995.
73. VFP. Box 2. Lupe (17 September 1943). [Letter to Dolores].
74. VFP. Box 2. Lupe (3 January 1944). [Letter to Dolores].
75. VFP. Box 2. Ricardo (9 December 1943). [Letter to Dolores Venegas].
76. This could be read as an effort by María Teresa Venegas to place the agency on her uncle and aunt. However, this statement reflects sentiments expressed by Francisco and Lupe.
77. In a letter to Dolores, Lupe notes Miguel and Alicia's return to Los Angeles. VFP. Box 2. Lupe (11 May 1944). [Letter to Dolores].
78. Border crossing card, retrieved 10 February 2015, from Ancestry.com.
79. VFP. Box 2. Lupe (16 January 1948). [Letter to Dolores Venegas].
80. VFP. Box 2. Efrain and Josefina (4 May 1948). [Letter to Miguel Venegas and Dolores]; VFP. Box 2. Francisco (11 February 1948). [Letter to Miguel].
81. VFP. Box 2. Juan (August 1949). [Letter to Miguel Venegas].
82. VFP. Box 2. Lupe (29 March 1950). [Letter to Dolores Venegas].
83. VFP. Box 2. Lupe (29 March 1950). [Letter to Dolores Venegas].
84. VFP. Box 2. Eduardo (11 August 1949). [Letter to Miguel Venegas].
85. VFP. Box 2. Eduardo (6 February 1950). [Letter to Miguel Venegas].

86. The Voces Oral History Project, founded in 1999 at the University of Texas, Austin (originally titled 'U.S. Latino & Latina World War II Oral History Project'), has stimulated the production of approximately 1000 oral histories with veterans and four edited volumes. Luis Alvarez's contribution in the most recent volume demonstrates the richness of this growing field. Focusing on Latina/os fight for first class citizenship during the war Alvarez argues that 'Latino soldiering encompassed a range of multiracial and transnational experiences that foreshadowed the diverse theories of Latinidad in more recent decades' (Alvarez, 2014, p. 76).
87. Based on the birth of his sixth child in Los Angeles, he likely returned in 1954 or 1955.
88. In 1987 Eduardo and Maria filed naturalization papers, likely in response to the Immigration Reform and Control Act of 1986. Retrieved 10 February 2015, from Ancestry.com. See California, Naturalization Records, 1940 to 1991, Petition Number 00681230, 31 March 1987.

Acknowledgements

I thank the participants of the Columbia Latin American History Workshop, Carribean Fragoza, Eric Frith, Fredy González, Adam Goodman, Nara Milanich, Israel Pastrana, Clay Stalls, an anonymous reviewer, and the editors of the special issue for feedback on earlier drafts. Special thanks to María Teresa Venegas and Carlos Venegas for archiving this collection and taking time to talk with me about their family's history.

Disclosure statement

No potential conflict of interest was reported by the author.

Funding

Research for this article was conducted with funding from Columbia University's Graduate School of Arts and Sciences. A substantial portion of the writing was done while in residence at the National American History Museum as a Smithsonian Latino Research Fellow.

References

Alamillo, M. J. (2010). Playing across borders: Transnational sport and identities in Southern California and Mexico, 1930–1945. *Pacific Historical Review, 79*, 360–392.
Alanís Enciso, S. F. (2005). Regreso a casa: la repatriación de mexicanos en Estados Unidos durante la gran depresión el caso de San Luis Potosí, 1929–1934 [Return home: The repatriation of Mexicans in the United States during the great depression, the case of San Luis Potosí, 1929–1934]. In M. Terrazas, Basante, & A. Ávila (Eds.), *Estudios de Historia Moderna y Contemporánea de México* (vol. 29, pp. 119–148). México: Universidad Nacional Autónoma de México, Instituto de Inestigaciones Históricas.
Alanís Enciso, S. F. (2007). *Que se Queden Allá: El gobierno de México y la repatriación de mexicanos en Estados Unidos (1934–1940)* [Have them stay over there: The Mexican government and Mexican repatriaiton from the United States, 1934–1940]. Tijuana: El Colegio de la Frontera Norte/El Colegio de San Luis 2007.
Alvarez, L. (2014). Transnational latino soldiering: Military service and ethnic politics during world war II. In M. Rivas-Rodriguez & V. B. Olguín (Eds.), *Latina/OS and world war II: Mobility, agency, and ideology* (pp. 75–94). Austin: University of Texas Press.
Andrés, J. B. (2011). Invisible borders: Repatriation and colonization of Mexican migrant workers along the California borderlands during the 1930s. *California History, 88*, 63–65.
Arredondo, F. G. (2008). *Mexican Chicago: race, identity, and nation, 1916–39*. Urbana and Chicago: University of Illinois.

Balderrama, E. F., & Rodríguez, R. (2006). *Decade of betrayal: Mexican repatriation in the 1930s* (2nd ed.). Albuquerque, NM: University of New Mexico Press.

Blegen, C. T. (1969) *Grassroots history*. Port Washington, New York, and London, Kennikat Press.

Butler, M. (1999). The 'liberal' cristero: Ladislao molina and the cristero rebellion in michoacan, 1927–9. *Journal of Latin American Studies, 31*, 645–671.

Butler, M. (2004). *Popular piety and political identity in Mexico's cristero rebellion: Michoacán, 1927–9*. Oxford: Oxford Press.

Camacho, S. A. (2008). *Migrant imaginaries: Latino cultural politics in the U.S.-Mexico borderlands*. New York, NY: NYU Press

Campt, M. T. (2012). *Image matters: Archive, photography, and the African diaspora in Europe*. North Carolina: Duke University Press.

Carreras de Velasco, M. (1974). *Los Mexicanos Que Devolvio La Crisis: 1929–1932*. [The Mexicans who were returned by the crisis, 1929–1932]. Tlatelolco, México: Secretaría de Relaciones Exteriores.

Edward, T., & Ortiz, V. (2008). *Generations of exclusion: Mexican Americans, assimilation, and race*. New York, NY: Russell Sage Foundation.

Elliott, S. B., Gerber, A. D., & Sinke, M. S. (2006). Introduction. In S. B. Elliott, D. E. Gerber, & M. S. Sinke (Eds.), *Letters across borders: The epistolary practices of international migrants* (pp. 1–25). New York, NY: Palgrave MacMillan, published in association with the Carleton Center for the History of Migration.

Félix, A. (2011). Posthumous transnationalism: Postmortem repatriation from the United States to México. *Latin American Research Review, 46*, 157–179.

Fitzgerald, D. (2009). *A nation of emigrants: How Mexico manages its migration Berkeley*. Los Angeles, London: University of California Press.

Flores, W., & Benmayor, R. (Eds.). (1997). *Latino cultural citizenship: Claiming identity, space, and rights*. Boston, MA: Beacon Press.

Gabaccia, R. D. (1998). Do we still need immigration history? *Polish American Studies, 55*, 45–68.

Gabaccia, R. D. (1999). Is everywhere nowhere? Nomads, nations, and the immigrant paradigm of United States history. *The Nation and Beyond: Transnational Perspectives on United States History: A Special Issue, The Journal of American History, 86*, 1115–1134.

García, T. M. (1991). *Mexican Americans: Leadership, Ideology, and Identity, 1930–1960*. New Haven, CT: Yale University Press.

Gerber, A. D. (1997). The immigrant letter between positivism and populism: The uses of immigrant personal correspondence in twentieth-century American scholarship. *Journal of American Ethnic History, 16*, 3–34.

Gerber, A. D. (2006). *Author of their lives: The personal correspondence of British immigrants to North America in the nineteenth century*. New York and London: New York University Press.

Goldring, L. (1996). Gendered memory: Constructions of rurality among Mexican transnational migrants. In M. E. Dupuis & P. Vendergeest (Eds.), *Creating the countryside: The politics of rural and environmental discourse* (pp. 303–329). Philadelphia, PA: Temple University Press.

Goodman, A. (2015). Nation of migrants, historians of migration. *Journal of American Ethnic History, 34*, 7–16.

Griswold del Castillo, R. (1984). *La familia: Chicano families in the Urban Southwest, 1848 to the present*. Notre Dame, Indiana: University of Notre Dame.

Guerin-Gonzales, C. (1994). *Mexican workers and American dreams: Immigration, repatriation, and California farm labor, 1900–1939*. New Brunswick, New Jersey: Rutgers University Press.

Guglielmo, A. T. (2006). Fighting for caucasian rights: Mexicans, Mexican Americans, and the transnational struggle for civil rights in world war II Texas. *The Journal of American History, 92*, 1212–1237.

Guzmán, R. (2016). *Negotiated citizenship: Mexican migrant families, youth, and citizenship, 1920s to 1940s* (in preparation). New York, NY: Columbia University.

Helbich, W., & Kamphoefner, D. W. (2006). How representative are Emigrant letters? An exploration of the German case. In S. B. Elliott, D. E. Gerber, & M. S. Sinke (Eds.), *Letters across borders: the epistolary practices of international migrants* (pp. 29–55). New York, NY: Palgrave MacMillan, Published in association with the Carleton Center for the History of Migration.

Hernández, L. K. (2010) *Migra!: A history of the U.S. border patrol*. Berkeley, Los Angeles, London: University of California Press.

Hoffman, A. (1974). *Unwanted Mexican Americans in the great depression: Repatriation pressures, 1929–1939*. Tucson, AZ: The University of Arizona Press.

Hondagneu-Sotelo, P. (1994). *Gendered transitions: Mexican experiences of immigration*. Berkeley, Los Angeles, London: University of California Press.

Limón, E. J. (1998). *American encounters: Greater Mexico, the United States, and the erotics of culture*. Boston, MA: Beacon Press.

McKeown, A. (1999). Conceptualizing Chinese diasporas, 1842 to 1949. *Journal of Asian Studies, 58*, 306–337.

Orellana, F. M. (2009). *Translating childhoods: Immigrant youth, language, and culture*. New Brunswick, NJ: Rutgers University Press.

Purnell, J. (1999). *Popular movements and state formation in revolutionary Mexico: The agraristas and Cristeros of Michoacán*. Durham, N.C.: Duke University Press.

Rivas-Rodrigues, M., & Olguín, B. V. (Eds.). (2014). *Latina/os and World War II: Mobility, agency, and ideology*. Austin, TX: University of Texas Press.

Rodríguez, A. A., Heilig, V. J., & Prochnow, A. A. (2014). Higher education, the GI Bill, and the postwar lives of Latino veterans and their families. In M. Rivas-Rodrigues & B. V. Olguín (Eds.), *Latina/os and Wolrd War II* (pp. 59–74). Austin: University of Texas Press.

Rosales, S. (2011). Fighting the peace at home: Mexican american veterans and the 1944 Gi Bill of rights. *Pacific Historical Review, 80*, 597–627.

Rosas, A. (2014). *Abrazando el Espiritu: Bracero families confront the US-Mexico border* [Embracing the spirit: Bracero families confront the US-Mexico border]. Oakland, California: University of California Press.

Ruiz, V. (1987). *Cannery women, cannery lives: Mexican women, unionization, and the California processing industry, 1930–1950*. Albuquerque, NM: University of New Mexico Press.

Saldívar, R. (2006). *The borderlands of culture: Américo paredes and the transnational imaginary*. Durham, NC: Duke University Press.

Sanchez, J. G. (1993). *Becoming Mexican American: Ethnicity, culture, and identity in Chicano Los Angeles, 1900–1945*. New York and Oxford: Oxford University Press.

Sanchez, J. G. (1999). Race, nation, and culture in recent immigration studies. *Journal of American Ethnic History, 18*, 66–84.

Siems, L. (Ed.). (1992). *Between the lines: Letters between undocumented Mexican and central American immigrants and their families and friends*. Tucson and London: University of Arizona Press.

Telles, E., & Ortiz, V. (2008). *Generations of exclusion: Mexican Americans, assimilation, and race*. New York, NY: Russell Sage Foundation.

Thomas, I. W., & Znaniecki, F. (1927). *The polish peasant in Europe and America*. New York, NY: Alfred A. Knopf.

Vargas, A. M. (2006). Epistolary communication between migrant workers and their families. In S. B. Elliott, D. E. Gerber, & M. S. Sinke (Eds.), *Letters across borders: The epistolary practices of international migrants* (pp. 124–138). New York, NY: Palgrave MacMillan, Published in association with the Carleton Center for the History of Migration.

Vasquez, M. J. (2001). *Mexican Americans across generations: Immigrant families, racial realities*. New York and London: New York University.

Venegas, M. T. (2012). *Letters home: Mexican exile correspondence from Los Angeles, 1927–1932*. Los Angeles, CA: Self Published.

Weise, M. J. (2008). Mexican nationalisms, Southern racisms: Mexican and Mexican Americans in the U.S. south, 1908–1939. *American Quarterly, 60*, 749–777.

Weise, M. J. (2015). *Corazón de Dixie: Mexicanos in the U.S. South since 1910*. Chapel Hill, NC: The University of North Carolina Press.

Ybarra, L. (1983) Empirical and theoretical developments in the study of Chicano families. In A. Valdez, A. Camarillo, & T. Almaguer (Eds.), *State of Chicano research on family, labor, and migration: Proceedings of the first stanford symposium on Chicano research and public policy* (pp. 91–110). Stanford: Stanford Center for Chicano Research.

Young, G. J. (2012). Cristero diaspora: Mexican immigrants, the U.S. Catholic Church, and Mexico's cristero war, 1926–29. *The Catholic Historical Review, 98*, 271–300.

Young, G. J. (2015). *Mexican exodus: Emigrants, exiles, and refugees of the cristero war*. England, New York: Oxford University Press.

Zamora, E. (2009). Mexican nationals in the U.S. military: Diplomacy and battlefield sacrifice. In M. Rivas-Rodriguez & E. Zamora (Eds.), *Beyond the latino world war II hero: The social and political legacy of a generation* (pp. 90–109). Austin: University of Texas Press.

Index